Contribution of Minor Cereals to Sustainable Diets and Agro-Food Biodiversity

Contribution of Minor Cereals to Sustainable Diets and Agro-Food Biodiversity

Editors

Laura Gazza
Francesca Nocente

MDPI

Basel • Beijing • Wuhan • Barcelona • Belgrade • Novi Sad • Cluj • Manchester

Editors
Laura Gazza
CREA - Research Centre for Engineering and Agro-Food Processing
Rome
Italy

Francesca Nocente
CREA - Research Centre for Engineering and Agro-Food Processing
Rome
Italy

Editorial Office
MDPI
St. Alban-Anlage 66
4052 Basel, Switzerland

This is a reprint of articles from the Special Issue published online in the open access journal *Foods* (ISSN 2304-8158) (available at: https://www.mdpi.com/journal/foods/special_issues/minor_cereals_sustainable_biodiversity).

For citation purposes, cite each article independently as indicated on the article page online and as indicated below:

Lastname, A.A.; Lastname, B.B. Article Title. *Journal Name* **Year**, *Volume Number*, Page Range.

ISBN 978-3-7258-0507-5 (Hbk)
ISBN 978-3-7258-0508-2 (PDF)
doi.org/10.3390/books978-3-7258-0508-2

Contents

About the Editors

Laura Gazza

Laura Gazza is a senior researcher at CREA Research Centre for Engineering and Agro-Food Processing in Rome, Italy, with a Master degree in Biological Sciences and a PhD in Plant Biotechnology. For more than 20 years she has been carrying out research activities in the context of national, regional and international projects in collaboration with Universities, research centers and SMEs in the sectors of molecular genetics, biochemistry and technology of cereals (wheat, einkorn, oats and other minor cereals with a reduced or no gluten index such as tritordeum, triticale, sorghum and teff), mainly interested in genes coding for storage proteins, genes and proteins involved in determining the texture of the kernel, genes and proteins involved in celiac disease and gluten intolerances and wheat allergies. She studies and applies innovative processing technologies in pilot plants aimed at obtaining transformed products, mainly pasta, with increased nutritional and health potential. She published more than 60 peer-reviewed scientific papers (HI=23). She is member of the Editorial Board of the Open Access Journals 'Foods'. She is member of the executive board of 'Associazione Italiana di Scienza e Tecnologia dei Cereali' (AISTEC), and she is the Italian National Delegate for ICC.

Francesca Nocente

Francesca Nocente is a researcher at CREA Research Centre for Engineering and Agro-Food Processing in Rome, Italy. She got a Degree in Biological Sciences at University "La Sapienza" of Rome and a Ph.D. in Biochemistry and Technology applied to Food and Nutrition at Campus Bio-Medico University of Rome. She is involved in research activities on cereals within national and international projects. Experienced in wheat diseases and breeding for disease resistance by classical and marker-assisted selection methods. For more than 15 years she has been studying and applying innovative cereal processing technologies useful for obtaining products, mainly pasta, with improved nutritional and healthy properties, also through the reuse of by-products deriving from agro-food processes. The research activity also concerns studies on malting process of major and minor cereals. She has skills on nutritional and technological quality evaluation of the raw materials and of the processed products. Research activity is documented from more than 60 national and international scientific papers. She is a reviewer of many scientific journals. Since 2014 to 2021, she was tutor of Food technology within the degree course in Food Sciences and Human Nutrition at the Campus Bio-Medico University of Rome, and since 2022 she is Professor of Food technology.

foods

Editorial

The Contribution of Minor Cereals to Sustainable Diets and Agro-Food Biodiversity

Laura Gazza * and Francesca Nocente

CREA–Research Centre for Engineering and Agro-Food Processing, Via Manziana, 30-00189 Rome, Italy; francesca.nocente@crea.gov.it
* Correspondence: laura.gazza@crea.gov.it; Tel.: +39-063295705

Since the second half of the 20th century, the intensification of agriculture by increasing external inputs (fertilizers, pesticides), cropland expansion, and the cultivation of only a few selected cereal species or varieties have caused the loss of biodiversity and ecosystem services on farmland. As a result, at present, only three major cereals—wheat, rice, and corn—dominate agriculture and human sources of nutrition on a global scale, whilst many traditional cereal species, varieties, and landraces have gradually disappeared from fields, or their cultivation is limited to a small scale. However, the need for sustainable agriculture in the context of climate change has sparked interest in 'minor or underutilized' cereals that can be utilized on a global level. These cereals, some of which still represent the main staple food at the national or regional level, include einkorn, emmer, millet, oats, rye, spelt, sorghum, teff, triticale, and tritordeum. Indeed, despite their low yield, minor cereals have proven to be inherently resilient and rustic and are therefore able to withstand adverse climatic conditions and are well suited to grow under low-input cultivation management on marginal lands; thus, they have less negative impacts on the environment. Due to the increased demand for healthy, nutritious, non-conventional, and sustainably produced food, minor cereals have re-gained the attention of researchers, farmers, producers, and consumers. Indeed, as a source of carbohydrates, proteins, vitamins, minerals, fiber, and antioxidant compounds, their inclusion into daily diets can reduce the risk of chronic diseases such as cancers, type II diabetes, obesity, and cardiovascular diseases. To ensure their sustainable production on a large scale in the future, it is absolutely essential to strengthen research to ascertain the genetic variability of minor cereals and select genotypes with promising traits for yield, disease resistance, climate resilience, and nutritional quality. Research should also be directed toward optimizing agronomic practices and developing technological processes able to produce innovative foods, preserve nutrients and bioactives, and meet consumer expectations. In this Special Issue, twelve papers (including ten original research articles and two reviews) address the topic of 'Sustainable Diets and Agro-Food Biodiversity', investigating the possible contribution of minor cereals to tackle the future demand for healthy and sustainable food. Among minor cereals, sorghum was the most investigated, probably due to its ability to grow in semi-arid climates, its nutritional characteristics, as well as its being a gluten-free cereal. Robles-Plata et al. [1] analyzed the biophysical, nutraceutical, and techno-functional properties of pigmented sorghum (red and yellow) and popcorn (blue, purple, red, black, and yellow). Besides differences in biophysical and proximate composition among species and varieties, sorghum exhibited higher total phenolic content, whereas higher total anthocyanin content was found in the purple, blue, and black popcorn, as well as in red sorghum.

In a study by Renzetti et al. [2], the physical and sensory properties and consumers' perceptions of bread obtained from a flour blend of sorghum, cassava, and cowpea were assessed. The overall results suggest these African resilient crops have potential as an alternative to wheat in bread-type products, especially in Sub-Saharan Africa.

Sorghum was also investigated in a research article by Mawouma et al. [3], which analyzed the nutritional and phytochemical profiles and antioxidant activity of sorghum and

Citation: Gazza, L.; Nocente, F. The Contribution of Minor Cereals to Sustainable Diets and Agro-Food Biodiversity. *Foods* **2023**, *12*, 3500. https://doi.org/10.3390/foods12183500

Received: 7 September 2023
Accepted: 19 September 2023
Published: 20 September 2023

pearl millet local varieties that are regularly produced and consumed in Cameroon. Thus, the most promising cultivars of sorghum and pearl millet to tackle nutrient deficiencies and non-communicable diseases were identified.

Banu and Aprodu [4] performed a comparative study of the physicochemical and functional properties of seven gluten-free flours obtained from cereals (sorghum, rice, oat, and foxtail millet) and pseudocereals (amaranth, quinoa, and buckwheat), as well as the thermo-mechanical properties of their dough.

Pontieri et al. [5] compared both the chemical composition and the content of fatty acids and minerals of three sorghum varieties that differed in pericarp color (white, red, or black) grown in the Mediterranean basin. Results indicated that grain pericarp color is associated with unique nutritional profiles and that the sorghum varieties developed for commercial production in the USA were also suitable to be grown in the Mediterranean environment.

Another example of using minor cereals for functional food is reported in a paper by Živkovic et al. [6] that explored the effect of germination on the secondary metabolite composition in spelt grains. According to the results, germinated kernels showed a significant increase in the total phenolic content of several secondary metabolites, as well as antioxidant activity, especially after 96 h of germination, indicating this biotechnology could be used in a strategy to enhance cereal health-promoting effects.

In a study by Gazza et al. [7], the flours of two einkorn varieties, obtained by an ultra-fine milling process, were used to produce wholewheat dry pasta. The technological, nutritional, and sensorial characteristics of einkorn spaghetti were assessed, and results indicated that, despite the very weak gluten network, einkorn proved to be a viable alternative cereal to durum wheat to produce dry pasta.

In a research article by Nocente et al. [8], two ancient Caucasian hulled wheats grown in Italy, Triticum timopheevii and Triticum zhukovskyi, were analyzed for physical, nutritional, and technological characteristics. Both Caucasian species had high protein content and antioxidant activity and good technological and rheological performances, suggesting these wheats can serve as a promising raw material for the formulation of flatbreads, biscuits, and pasta.

The article by Onyango et al. [9] compared the impact of native, steamed, or malted finger millet and amaranth seeds on the rheological properties of dough and the physicochemical quality of composite breads. As per their findings, malting and steaming appear to be promising approaches for amaranth to improve composite bread quality, whereas, with respect to finger millet, the treatments were not suitable to improve its breadmaking potential.

Spaggiari et al. [10] characterized three common wheat evolutionary populations (EP), a cultivation technique characterized by mixing and sowing many wheat genotypes together to allow the crop to adapt genetically over several years in relation to specific pedoclimatic conditions. The nutritional, chemical, and sensory qualities of three different breads obtained using organic EP flours that were produced following a traditional sourdough process were investigated. Although the technological quality of EP flours seemed unsuitable for bread-making, sourdough baking allowed excellent workability of the EP doughs and good structure of the loaves.

The topic of the role of minor cereals in achieving the goal of food sustainability and diversity was also addressed in a comprehensive review by Majzoobi et al. [11]. In their review, the authors report previous knowledge published on ancient cereals and pseudocereals in terms of physicochemical properties, nutritional profile, and food industry applications and the comparison with modern crop counterparts. The review also discusses the opportunities and challenges of ancient cereals as useful crops to address Goal 2: Zero Hunger—United Nations Sustainable Development Program, as well as the issue of malnutrition globally, providing a guide for decision-makers and policies to face these threats.

In a more targeted way, the review of Gowda et al. [12] focuses on millet, one of the major underutilized, highly nutritive food crops. The review provides an overview of original research articles and reviews that highlight the nutritional characteristics of Indian millets (foxtail, kodo, proso, little, and pearl millets) and the effects of primary (dehulling, soaking, germination, drying, polishing, and milling) and secondary (fermentation, germination, extrusion, cooking, puffing, popping, malting, baking, flaking, and extrusion) processing techniques on the nutritional features of this cereal. Germination and fermentation improve the overall nutritional characteristics of millets, whereas excessive dehulling, polishing, and milling reduce dietary fiber and micronutrients. This overview on millet can help encourage farmers, the food industry, researchers, and consumers in millet utilization and in selecting suitable processing techniques to optimize nutrient value, increase the bioavailability of nutrients, and help combat food and nutrition security.

In conclusions, this Special Issue provides a fundamental understanding of the current strategies for the revitalization of underutilized cereals, which represent a reservoir of biodiversity that is useful to ensure sustainable production and food security in the context of climate change.

Author Contributions: Conceptualization, L.G. and F.N.; methodology, L.G. and F.N.; writing—original draft preparation, L.G. and F.N.; writing—review and editing, L.G. and F.N. All authors have read and agreed to the published version of the manuscript.

Funding: This research received no external funding.

Conflicts of Interest: The authors declare no conflict of interest.

References

1. Robles-Plata, V.T.; Serna Saldivar, S.; de Dios Figueroa-Cárdenas, J.; Rooney, W.L.; Dávila-Vega, J.P.; Chuck-Hernández, C.; Escalante-Aburto, A. Biophysical, Nutraceutical, and Technofunctional Features of Specialty Cereals: Pigmented Popcorn and Sorghum. *Foods* **2023**, *12*, 2301. [CrossRef] [PubMed]
2. Renzetti, S.; Aisala, H.; Ngadze, R.T.; Linnemann, A.R.; Noort, M.W. Bread Products from Blends of African Climate Resilient Crops: Baking Quality, Sensory Profile and Consumers' Perception. *Foods* **2023**, *12*, 689. [CrossRef] [PubMed]
3. Mawouma, S.; Condurache, N.N.; Turturică, M.; Constantin, O.E.; Croitoru, C.; Rapeanu, G. Chemical Composition and Antioxidant Profile of Sorghum (*Sorghum bicolor* (L.) Moench) and Pearl Millet (*Pennisetum glaucum* (L.) R.Br.) Grains Cultivated in the Far-North Region of Cameroon. *Foods* **2022**, *11*, 2026. [CrossRef] [PubMed]
4. Banu, I.; Aprodu, I. Investigations on Functional and Thermo-Mechanical Properties of Gluten Free Cereal and Pseudocereal Flours. *Foods* **2022**, *11*, 1857. [CrossRef] [PubMed]
5. Pontieri, P.; Troisi, J.; Calcagnile, M.; Bean, S.R.; Tilley, M.; Aramouni, F.; Boffa, A.; Pepe, G.; Campiglia, P.; Del Giudice, F.; et al. Chemical Composition, Fatty Acid and Mineral Content of Food-Grade White, Red and Black Sorghum Varieties Grown in the Mediterranean Environment. *Foods* **2022**, *11*, 436. [CrossRef] [PubMed]
6. Živković, A.; Godevac, D.; Cigić, B.; Polak, T.; Požrl, T. Identification and Quantification of Selected Benzoxazinoids and Phenolics in Germinated Spelt (*Triticum spelta*). *Foods* **2023**, *12*, 1769. [CrossRef] [PubMed]
7. Gazza, L.; Galassi, E.; Nocente, F.; Natale, C.; Taddei, F. Cooking Quality and Chemical and Technological Characteristics of Wholegrain Einkorn Pasta Obtained from Micronized Flour. *Foods* **2022**, *11*, 2905. [CrossRef] [PubMed]
8. Nocente, F.; Galassi, E.; Taddei, F.; Natale, C.; Gazza, L. Ancient Caucasian Wheats: A Contribution for Sustainable Diets and Food Diversity. *Foods* **2022**, *11*, 1209. [CrossRef] [PubMed]
9. Onyango, C.; Luvitaa, S.K.; Lagat, K.; Hüsken, A.; Smit, I.; Schmidt, M. Utilisation of Amaranth and Finger Millet as Ingredients in Wheat Dough and Bread for Increased Agro-Food Biodiversity. *Foods* **2022**, *11*, 911. [CrossRef] [PubMed]
10. Spaggiari, M.; Marchini, M.; Calani, L.; Dodi, R.; Di Pede, G.; Dall'Asta, M.; Scazzina, F.; Barbieri, A.; Righetti, L.; Folloni, S.; et al. Evolutionary Wheat Populations in High-Quality Breadmaking as a Tool to Preserve Agri-Food Biodiversity. *Foods* **2022**, *11*, 495. [CrossRef] [PubMed]
11. Majzoobi, M.; Jafarzadeh, S.; Teimouri, S.; Ghasemlou, M.; Hadidi, M.; Brennan, C.S. The Role of Ancient Grains in Alleviating Hunger and Malnutrition. *Foods* **2023**, *12*, 2213. [CrossRef] [PubMed]
12. Gowda, N.A.N.; Siliveru, K.; Prasad, P.V.V.; Bhatt, Y.; Netravati, B.P.; Gurikar, C. Modern Processing of Indian Millets: A Perspective on Changes in Nutritional Properties. *Foods* **2022**, *11*, 499. [CrossRef] [PubMed]

foods

MDPI

Article

Biophysical, Nutraceutical, and Technofunctional Features of Specialty Cereals: Pigmented Popcorn and Sorghum

Valery Tixian Robles-Plata [1], Sergio Serna Saldivar [2,*], Juan de Dios Figueroa-Cárdenas [3], William L. Rooney [4], Juan Pablo Dávila-Vega [2], Cristina Chuck-Hernández [5] and Anayansi Escalante-Aburto [5,*]

1 Escuela de Ingeniera y Ciencias, Tecnologico de Monterrey, Monterrey 64849, Mexico; a01746831@tec.mx
2 Tecnologico de Monterrey, Centro de Investigación y Desarrollo de Protenas (CIDPRO), Monterrey 64849, Mexico; jpdavila@tec.mx
3 Centro de Investigación y Estudios Avanzados (CINVESTAV), Unidad Querétaro, Querétaro 76230, Mexico; jfigueroa@cinvestav.mx
4 Department of Soil and Crop Sciences, Texas A&M University, College Station, TX 77843, USA; wlr@tamu.edu
5 Tecnologico de Monterrey, The Institute for Obesity Research, Monterrey 64849, Mexico; cristina.chuck@tec.mx
* Correspondence: sserna@tec.mx (S.S.S.); anayansi.escalante@tec.mx (A.E.-A.)

Citation: Robles-Plata, V.T.; Serna Saldivar, S.; de Dios Figueroa-Cárdenas, J.; Rooney, W.L.; Dávila-Vega, J.P.; Chuck-Hernández, C.; Escalante-Aburto, A. Biophysical, Nutraceutical, and Technofunctional Features of Specialty Cereals: Pigmented Popcorn and Sorghum. *Foods* **2023**, *12*, 2301. https://doi.org/10.3390/foods12122301

Academic Editors: Laura Gazza and Francesca Nocente

Received: 25 April 2023
Revised: 29 May 2023
Accepted: 4 June 2023
Published: 7 June 2023

Abstract: Different pigmented corn and sorghum types were evaluated to characterize their biophysical, nutraceutical, and technofunctional properties for the first time. Commercially pigmented (blue, purple, red, black, and yellow) popcorn (*Zea mays* var. *everta*) and sorghum (*Sorghum bicolor* L.) of yellow and red colors were analyzed. Biophysical and proximal analyses were performed using official methods. The nutraceutical profile included the total phenolic and anthocyanin content. In addition, rheological, structural, and morphological studies were conducted. The results demonstrated significant differences between the popcorn samples and grain types, especially in terms of their biophysical and proximate features. The nutraceutical profile revealed that these specialty grains contained higher concentrations of antioxidant compounds (up to 3-fold when compared with the other grains). The rheological analysis demonstrated that sorghum grains developed higher peak viscosities than popcorn. According to the structural assessments, the type A pattern displayed peaks at the interplanar spaces corresponding to the crystalline and amorphous regions in all the samples. The data obtained in this study provides a base to further investigate the products obtained using these biomaterials.

Keywords: popcorn; pigmented maize; sorghum; rheological properties; nutraceuticals; cereals

1. Introduction

Producing and consuming nonconventional cereals is considered essential to ensure availability for future inhabitants [1]. Maize (*Zea mays* L.) is one of the most versatile crops worldwide. In recent decades, pigmented varieties from *Cacahuacintle* and popcorn (*Z. mays* var. *everta*) races have been investigated because of their nutritional and antioxidant properties [2,3]. Maize is pigmented mainly due to the presence of a substantial number of secondary metabolites, such as phenolic acids, carotenoids, and anthocyanins, that are chiefly responsible for producing different pigments and can serve as beneficial dietary elements because of their antioxidative properties and potential anti-inflammatory effects. Pigments are primarily concentrated on the thick pericarp or aleurone layers of kernels and corn cobs. Physical qualities, such as grain size, density, hardness, and chemical composition, contribute to the variation in different pigmented corn types; therefore, each variety has a specific observable property [4].

Moreover, after wheat, rice, maize, and barley, sorghum (*Sorghum bicolor* L.) is the most produced cereal worldwide. Because of its outstanding production and tolerance to heat, drought, and pests, this crop is replacing corn in some areas [5]. Sorghum contains high levels of polyphenols, such as phenolic acids, flavonoids, and anthocyanins, that offer various health benefits. In sorghum grains, polyphenols are mainly located in the layers of the pericarp, testa, and aleurone [6]. Moreover, numerous studies have reported that some compounds in sorghum exhibit beneficial effects against the most prevalent human illnesses, such as diabetes, obesity, metabolic disorders, and inflammation [7].

Popcorn and sorghum can be used to obtain second-generation snacks as their grains can be directly expanded by applying heat [8]. The pop-ability of popcorn and other related cereals, such as sorghum, is strongly associated with the physical properties of kernels, especially pericarp thickness and the structure of vitreous endosperm cells [9]. Furthermore, information regarding the biophysical, morphological, and nutraceutical traits of grains is essential for selecting high-yield seeds, which is also associated with economic issues [10]. This is the first study to evaluate the biophysical, nutraceutical, and technofunctional properties of five popcorn and two sorghum varieties. This characterization helps in evaluating future applications to produce functional foods with added value.

2. Materials and Methods

2.1. Biological Materials

Six commercial types of pigmented popcorn maize (*Z. mays* var. *everta*; blue, purple, red, black, and yellow), purchased from a local market, and two cultivars of yellow and red sorghum (*Sorghum bicolor* L.) were used. The yellow sorghum variety was developed in the experimental fields of Texas A&M and the red sorghum variety was obtained from a local supplier in Queretaro, México. All the samples were purchased in 2022. The grains were cleaned using a 149-µm US sieve No. 100 in order to remove foreign material. The biophysical properties were evaluated using cleaned whole kernels. Grains processed in a grinder with a stainless steel blade (Krups®, model F203, Port Orchard, WA, USA) were used for other determinations. Popcorn, sorghum grains, and flours were stored at 5 °C in sealed polyethylene bags until use.

2.2. Biophysical Properties

In total, 1000 grains were weighed (g) on an analytical balance (Sartorius, model MCE, Aubagne, France) in triplicate. In addition, the length, width, and thickness (mm) of 30 grains randomly obtained for each type of corn and sorghum were measured using a digital vernier (Leidsany, Britt Technology Inc., Louisville, KY, USA) [11].

2.3. Proximal Analysis

The proximal analysis was performed in triplicate according to the following official methods of AOAC. The protein analysis was conducted using the official method 978.02 with a 6.25 conversion factor, the moisture analysis was performed using the gravimetric method 925.10, the ash content was determined using the 923.03 procedure, and the crude fiber content was measured using the 962.09 method [12]. The crude fat content was determined using the AACC method 30–20.01 protocol [13]. The content of the nitrogen-free extract (NFE %) was calculated by difference [14] as follows:

$$NFE\ (\%) = 100 - \%Protein - \%Moisture - \%Ash - \%Crude\ fiber - \%Crude\ fat \quad (1)$$

2.4. Nutraceutical Properties

2.4.1. Quantification of Total Phenolic Compounds

The Folin–Ciocalteu (FC) test [15] was used to determine the total phenolic content of each extract using methanol as the solvent. The sample extract was obtained by weighing 500 mg of the sample and adding 5 mL of anhydrous methanol (Sigma-Aldrich®, 99.8% purity, Burlington, MA, USA). This mixture was vigorously vortexed. Then, the samples were placed in a sonicator (Brandson 5510, Danbury, CT, USA) at 40 kHz for 30 min and centrifuged at 4000 rpm for 30 min. A 100 L aliquot of the sample was placed in a 2 mL microtube. Then, 200 µL of FC reagent at 10% (v/v) (Phenol Reagent of Folin–Ciocalteu,

Sigma-Aldrich®, Burlington, MA, USA) was added to the sample and was rigorously vortexed. The mixture was left for 2 min. Then, 800 L of 700 mM Na_2CO_3 (Sigma-Aldrich®, 99% purity, Burlington, MA, USA) was added to the mixture and incubated for 2 h at room temperature. The total phenolic content was determined at an absorbance of 765 nm using a spectrophotometer (Thermo Scientific, Model Evolution 300, Austin, TX, USA). Gallic acid (Sigma-Aldrich, 98% purity) was used for the calibration curve (0–0.05 mg mL^{-1}), and the total phenolic content was calculated and expressed as milligrams of gallic acid equivalents per gram of sample dry weight (mg GAE g^{-1}).

2.4.2. Quantification of Total Anthocyanins

Total anthocyanins were examined using a previous method [16] with some modifications. First, 600 mg of the sample was weighed and 4.8 mL of acidified ethanol (AZ®, 96%) (ethanol + 1 N HCl, 85:15 v/v) was added (36.55–38% HCl, J.T. Baker™, Mexico City, Mexico). The mixture was vortexed for 30 min. The tubes were centrifuged at 3000 rpm for 10 min, and the supernatant was obtained. Absorbance was measured at 520 nm using the UV-Vis spectrophotometer (Thermo Scientific, Model Evolution 300, Fitchburg, WI, USA). Cyanidin-3-glucoside (kuromanin chloride analytical standard, ≥98% purity, Merk®, Darmstadt, Germany) was used as a standard pigment. A series of standard solutions of cyanidin-3-glucoside was prepared at 0–0.02 mmol (0–27 μg/mL). Data were expressed as milligrams of cyanidin-3-glycoside equivalents per kilogram of dry weight (mg C3G kg^{-1}).

2.5. Rheological Assessment

Rheological analyses were performed using 4 g of each sample. The sample was conditioned to a moisture content of 14% and weighed in an aluminum can. Then, 24 mL of distilled water was added. The dispersed solution was stirred with a plastic paddle, and a heating cycle was started at a controlled rate (50° C–90 °C–50 °C). The maximum viscosity, final viscosity, retention force, breakdown, and setback in cP were analyzed, and the rheological behavior was analyzed using a Rapid Visco Analyser (model RVA-3D, Newport Scientific, Warriewood, Australia) [17].

2.6. Structural Properties (X-ray Diffraction)

The milled grain samples were adjusted to a moisture content of 7% according to Escalante-Aburto et al.'s procedure [17]. A structural property analysis was conducted using an X-ray diffractometer (DMAX-2100, Rigaku, Tokyo, Japan), which was operated under the following conditions: 30 kV and 16 mA with CuKa radiation of $\lambda = 1.5405$. The flour samples were scanned from 5° to 50° on the 2θ scale. The Bragg equation was used to calculate the interplanar spacing (d) of the peaks.

2.7. Morphological Assessments

Grain morphology was examined using a scanning electron microscope (Phillips model XL30) at an accelerating 20 kV (50 mA) voltage. The grains were segmented longitudinally using a razor blade and were fixed over an aluminum base. Images were captured at 500×, 1500×, and 5000× magnification from the hard, intermediate, and soft endosperm and the protein bodies within the matrix.

2.8. Design of Experiments and Statistical Analysis

A completely randomized design of experiments was used. All the determinations were performed in triplicates, and the means and standard deviations (SDs) were reported. A one-factor ANOVA and a mean comparison analysis (Tukey test) were performed with 95% confidence. Both analyses considered $p < 0.05$ to be of statistical significance. Minitab® LLC (State College, PA, USA), statistical analysis software version 21.4.0.0 was used.

3. Results and Discussion

3.1. Biophysical Properties

Tables 1 and 2 present the biophysical parameters of the popcorn and sorghum cultivars. As expected, significant differences were observed between the popcorn and sorghum cultivars because of their botanical and agronomic origins.

Table 1. Biophysical properties of different popcorn grains.

Sample	1000 Grains Weight (g)	Length (mm)	Width (mm)	Thickness (mm)
Blue	163.757 ±1.43 [a]	8.66 ± 0.41 [ab]	5.46 ± 0.36 [b]	4.34 ± 0.46 [a]
Purple	136.16 ± 2.32 [c]	8.79 ± 0.61 [a]	5.41 ± 0.57 [b]	4.21 ± 0.43 [ab]
Black	95.77 ± 1.82 [e]	8.07 ± 0.61 [c]	4.86 ± 0.42 [d]	3.96 ± 0.53 [bc]
Red 1	124.33± 3.14 [d]	8.40 ± 0.58 [bc]	5.20 ± 0.44 [bc]	3.65 ± 0.36 [c]
Red 2	123.84 ± 0.71 [d]	8.25 ± 0.40 [c]	5.00 ± 0.41 [cd]	3.67 ± 0.37 [c]
Yellow	158.16 ± 1.06 [b]	8.71 ± 0.49 [ab]	5.89 ± 0.49 [a]	3.95 ± 0.44 [bc]

Average values ± SD. Different letters in the same column are significantly different at $p < 0.05$.

Table 2. Biophysical properties of the sorghum grain types.

Sample	1000 Grains Weight (g)	Length (mm)	Width (mm)	Thickness (mm)
Red	25.18 ± 0.31 [a]	4.12 ± 0.37 [a]	3.53 ± 0.22 [a]	2.55 ± 0.21 [a]
Yellow	25.52 ± 0.21 [a]	4.11 ± 0.22 [a]	3.40 ± 0.24 [b]	2.53 ± 0.21 [a]

Average values ± SD. Different letters in the same column are significantly different at $p < 0.05$.

Among the popcorn varieties, the blue grains presented with the highest 1000-grain weight value. All the other corn samples exhibited significantly lower values, but the black grains had the lowest values. Both sorghum samples exhibited significantly lower 1000-grain weight values than the popcorn samples. Yellow and red sorghum had the same 1000-grain weight, and no significant differences were noted (Table 2).

The values for the geometrical measurements were similar among the popcorn samples. Nevertheless, significant differences were observed in length, where blue, purple, and yellow popcorn exhibited the highest values of length. The yellow popcorn exhibited the highest width. The blue and purple samples presented the highest values of thickness. Tian et al. [18] evaluated three popcorn varieties of yellow commercial grains and found that the size of the kernel was highly associated with their densities and expansion volume.

No statistical differences were observed in the geometrical features of the sorghum varieties. However, the physical features of the grains also account for their engineering properties, and the information they provide is essential for designing specialized equipment and for determining their behavior during handling and processing. Surpam et al. [19] evaluated the engineering properties of sorghum (Rabi Jowar) and reported average values of 4.3, 4.2, and 2.6 mm for length, width, and thickness, respectively, which are similar to the values reported for our samples.

3.2. Proximal Analysis

Tables 3 and 4 present the results of the proximal assessments of popcorn and sorghum cultivars. The moisture content of black popcorn was the lowest compared with those of other popcorn grains and was similar to those of sorghum grains. No significant differences in moisture content were observed between the samples. All the grain samples were stored at adequate relative moisture conditions in order to avoid microbial spoilage [20]. The average protein content of the popcorn samples was 11.90%, and no significant differences were reported in protein content. These protein content values are similar to those reported by Farahnaky et al. [21] for two popcorn genotypes (hybrid KSC 600PC and another from a local market). They reported protein contents of 12.4% and 11.4%, respectively. Yellow sorghum grains exhibited protein content levels similar to those of the popcorn varieties; red sorghum exhibited the lowest protein content (almost 45% less protein). In fact, the protein content of both sorghum types was significantly lower than that of four African samples (white, yellow pale, yellow, and red), accounting for an average protein content of 22.53% in dry weight [22].

Table 3. Physicochemical properties of different pigmented popcorn grains.

Sample	Moisture	Protein	Crude fat	Ash	Crude Fiber	NFE
			% (Dry Basis)			
Blue	12.69 ± 0.30 abc	11.08 ± 0.28 a	3.00 ± 0.59 bc	1.60 ± 0.26 a	4.51 ± 0.21 ab	67.08 ± 0.79 bc
Purple	13.06 ± 0.12 ab	11.25 ± 0.15 a	3.79 ± 0.12 ab	1.46 ± 0.23 a	3.98 ± 0.55 abc	66.44 ± 0.15 bc
Black	11.67 ± 0.21 cd	11.91 ± 0.34 a	2.96 ± 0.65 bc	1.53 ± 0.23 a	3.88 ± 0.24 abc	68.02 ± 1.17 b
Red 1	13.76 ± 0.31 a	13.12 ± 0.33 a	3.79 ± 0.13 ab	1.83 ± 0.25 a	2.16 ± 0.11 e	65.29 ± 0.71 bc
Red 2	13.16 ± 0.92 ab	12.94 ± 0.20 a	4.11 ± 0.21 a	1.66 ± 0.30 a	3.48 ± 0.35 cd	64.68 ± 1.23 c
Yellow	12.55 ± 0.01 bc	11.15 ± 2.24 a	3.87 ± 0.48 ab	1.73 ± 0.05 a	3.59 ± 0.23 bc	67.08 ± 1.83 bc

Average values ± SD. Different letters in the same column are statistically different at $p < 0.05$. Abbreviation: NFE, nitrogen-free extract.

Table 4. Physicochemical properties of the two types of sorghum grains.

Sample	Moisture	Protein	Crude Fat	Ash	Crude Fiber	NFE
			% (Dry Basis)			
Red	11.11 ± 0.38 a	7.93 ± 0.24 b	2.57 ± 0.11 b	1.53 ± 0.05 a	2.61 ± 0.48 b	74.21 ± 0.85 a
Yellow	11.22 ±0.03 a	10.95 ± 0.11 a	3.34 ± 0.22 a	1.53 ± 0.05 a	4.80 ± 0.22 a	68.12 ± 0.19 b

Average values ± SD. Different letters in the same column are statistically different at $p < 0.05$. Abbreviation: NFE, nitrogen-free extract.

Nevertheless, the moisture content of the sorghum samples used in this study was significantly higher than that of an Indian variety (9.25%) [19]. The lipid content ranged from 2.96% to 4.11% for the popcorn samples and 2.57% to 3.34% for the sorghum grains. The fat content of our samples was significantly higher than those reported by Palavecino et al. [23] in commercial samples from Central Argentina. They reported fat concentrations of up to 5.73% in hybrid sorghum cultivated in Argentina (Pioneer-80T25).

No significant differences in ash content were observed among the grain types and cultivars. The blue, purple, and black popcorn exhibited the highest crude fiber content, but the yellow sorghum variety significantly differed from the red variety in crude fiber content. The sorghum varieties presented the highest NFE values (71.16%) compared with all the popcorn samples, which had NFE values ranging from 64.68% to 68.02%.

The crude fat and ash contents of the sorghum grains were in the same magnitude as those of a white sorghum *Paloma* variety reported by Hernández-Becerra et al. [24]. They reported crude fat and ash contents of 2.7% and 1.3%, respectively. According to Khalid et al. [7], the total carbohydrate content of sorghum is between 57% and 80.6%, and this result is similar to our findings.

3.3. Nutraceutical Characteristics

The nutraceutical properties evaluated in the specialty grains are shown in Figure 1.

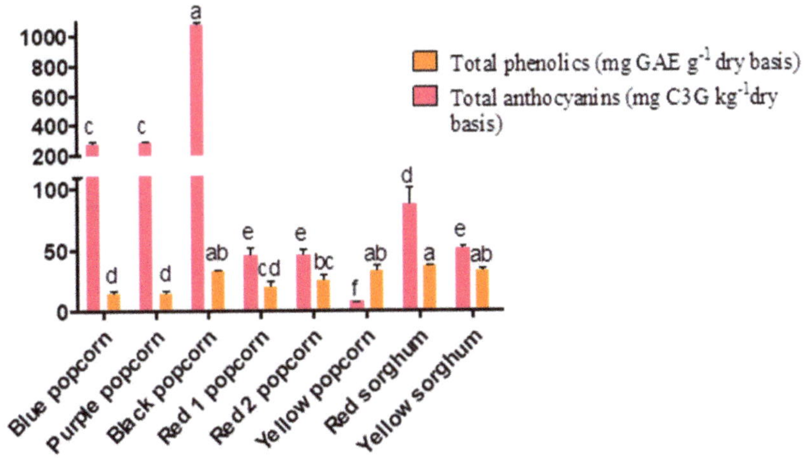

Figure 1. Functional properties of popcorn and sorghum grains: phenolic and anthocyanin content. Different letters represent statistical differences at $p < 0.05$. The bars indicate the SD.

The anthocyanin content of all the popcorn samples ranged from 6.9 to 1073.5 mg C3G kg^{-1}, and black popcorn presented the highest concentration of this antioxidant molecule. The average anthocyanin content of popcorn and sorghum was 287.41 and 69.03 mg C3G kg^{-1}, respectively. Among all the samples, red sorghum had the highest anthocyanin content. However, this value was lower than that reported by Xu et al. [25] for red pericarp sorghums (2660–8930 mg C3G kg^{-1}). On the other hand, the highest total phenolic content was observed in the black and yellow popcorn samples. The total phenolic contents of the blue, purple, and red 1 popcorn samples were lower. The total phenolic contents varied from 32.34 to 13.80 mg GAE g^{-1} for the popcorn samples. Our popcorn samples exhibited a higher total phenolic content than Iranian popcorn (*Z. mays* var. *everta*) grains (0.13 mg GAE g^{-1}) [26]. These assessments in raw popcorn samples are crucial because some studies have suggested that the total phenolic content and antioxidant capacity (evaluated by FRAP) of pigmented raw and popped kernels do not differ significantly [27].

Both sorghum varieties exhibited the same total phenolic content; the average total phenolic content was 34.27 mg GAE g^{-1}. However, the red sorghum grains exhibited a higher concentration of total phenolics than the yellow sorghum grains. The total phenolic content of our sorghum samples was higher than those reported by Bhukya et al. [28] in 60-grain sorghum genotypes, including white, red, and brown pericarps. They reported a total phenolic content of 0.05–4.23 GAE g^{-1}. The total phenolic content in our samples was up to 3-fold higher than that reported in six sorghum varieties of brown, red, and white pericarps (11.50–0.24 mg GAE g^{-1}) [29]. Similarly, the total polyphenol content of red sorghum purchased from Maroua, Cameroon (82.2 mg GAE g^{-1}) [22] was higher than that of our study samples. In addition to the agronomical, harvesting, and storage conditions of the samples, extraction procedures (refluxing, maceration, milling, and solvent types) commonly influence the total phenolic and anthocyanin content in these grains. Regarding the milling factor, Rumler et al. [30] evaluated dried and dehusked red sorghum (variety *Armorik*, obtained in Austria) and reported total phenolic contents of 152.2, 237.2, and 155.5 mg FAE 100 g^{-1} in whole sorghum flours obtained using a dry-flake squeezer, a pilot-scale stone mill, and an industry-scale roller mill, respectively. The particle size and milling process remarkably affects the extraction rate of these compounds. Furthermore, during extraction, some pericarp remains intact in the flour. Thus, additional studies must be conducted to avoid underestimation when quantifying these compounds.

3.4. Rheological Behavior

Figure 2 presents the rheological behavior of raw grains from the popcorn and sorghum varieties. The sorghums presented higher viscosity than all the popcorn samples. The yellow sample exhibited the highest peak viscosity among all the popcorn samples. Both sorghum varieties exhibited higher values than the popcorn lines for all the parameters evaluated in the viscoamylographic analysis, except for the breakdown parameter (Table 3).

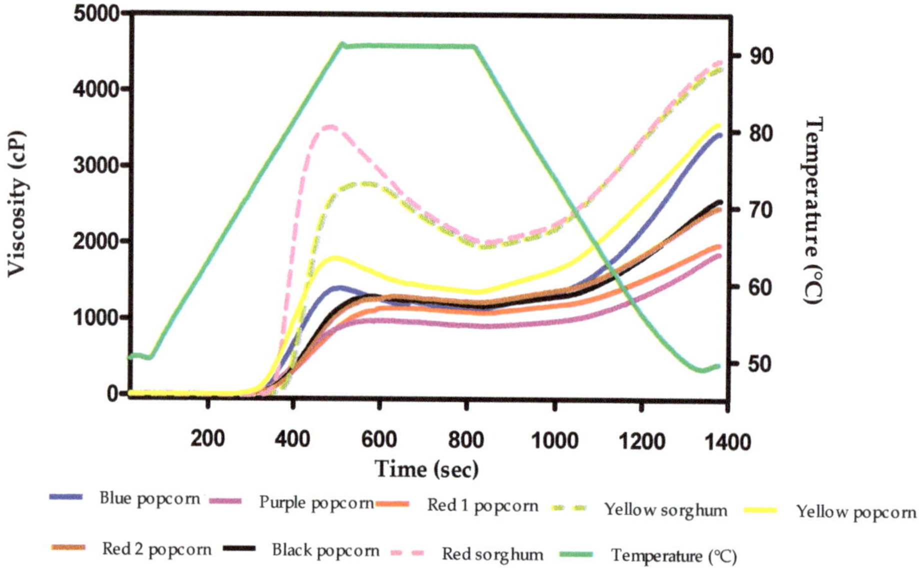

Figure 2. Rheological behavior of the evaluated popcorn and sorghum grains.

Tables 5 and 6 list the specific parameters of rheological behavior (RVA profile). The sorghum lines exhibited higher peak viscosities than the popcorn varieties, which was expected because, at this stage of the RVA analysis, the hydration of starch molecules occurred. According to the proximal analysis results, the sorghum grains contain more starch than the popcorn samples (Table 6). The peak viscosity values increased due to increased interactions between water molecules and starch granules during gelatinization. In this context, the peak viscosities of both sorghum varieties differed from those reported by Sang et al. [31]. They reported peak viscosities of 2750, 1750, and 1250 cP for evaluated waxy, heterowaxy, and normal sorghum hybrids, respectively. This indicated that the varieties used in the present study had some characteristics of waxy endosperm; hence, they contained less amylose content. Consequently, the breakdown values of the sorghum samples were considerably higher than those of all the popcorn samples. Breakdown is related to the differences in the type of starch and its structure, such as granule rigidity and crystallinity, as well as the amylose and lipid content [32]. The lower breakdown values of popcorn samples could also be attributed to increased interactions between starch and protein. These interactions make the starch granules rigid and reduce the susceptibility of grains to breakage during heating and shearing cycles [33]. Consequently, the breakdown values of the popcorn samples used in the present study differed from those of the yellow popcorn samples analyzed by Paraginski et al. [33]. They reported breakdown values between 421.5 and 91 cP.

Table 5. Rheological parameters (RVA analysis) of different popcorn grains.

Sample	Peak Viscosity	Breakdown	Holding Strength	Setback Region	Total Setback	Final Viscosity
			cP			
Blue	1445 ± 7 [b]	184 ± 6 [b]	1261 ± 13 [b]	2929 ± 87 [a]	3113 ± 93 [a]	4374 ± 82 [a]
Purple	965 ± 12 [f]	55 ± 12 [c]	909 ± 6 [e]	969 ± 15 [e]	1024 ± 9 [e]	1933 ± 4 [d]
Black	1261 ± 10 [d]	58 ± 8 [c]	1203 ± 3 [c]	2287 ± 96 [b]	2345 ± 91 [b]	3548 ± 88 [b]
Red 1	1135 ± 8 [e]	47 ± 8 [c]	1088 ± 1 [d]	867 ± 16 [e]	914 ± 92 [e]	2002 ± 9 [d]
Red 2	1304 ± 1 [c]	68 ± 7 [c]	1236 ± 6 [b]	1551 ± 15 [d]	1618 ± 14 [d]	2855 ± 14 [c]
Yellow	1834 ± 12 [a]	431 ± 31 [a]	1404 ± 23 [a]	1738 ± 54 [c]	2168 ± 22 [c]	3572 ± 45 [b]

Average values ± SD. Different letters in the same column are statistically different at $p < 0.05$.

Table 6. Rheological parameters (RVA analysis) of two types of sorghum grains.

Sample	Peak Viscosity	Breakdown	Holding Strength	Setback Region	Total Setback	Final Viscosity
			cP			
Red sorghum	3564 ± 12 [a]	1502 ± 3 [a]	2061 ± 12 [a]	833 ± 25 [b]	2335 ± 23 [a]	4397 ± 30 [a]
Yellow sorghum	2750 ± 9 [b]	778 ± 11 [b]	1972 ± 4 [b]	1551 ± 6 [a]	2329 ± 50 [a]	4301 ± 4 [b]

Average values ± SD. Different letters in the same column are statistically different at $p < 0.05$.

Melting of the crystalline regions increases the movement of water molecules inside the starch granules. This represents holding strength. Holding strength is the lowest viscosity value measured at the end of the heating cycle (holding stage) [32]. The blue and yellow popcorn grains exhibited the highest breakdown values. These popcorn grains likely have a larger proportion of vitreous endosperm cells, which increases the breakdown values (184 and 431 cP, respectively). This can be attributed to the compactness of the endosperm, which prevents all the water molecules from gelatinizing all the starch granules. The sorghum samples exhibited significantly higher holding strength values. The holding strength values of our samples were lower than those of 13-grain sorghum varieties cultivated in New South Wales (mean: 2969 cP). Nevertheless, some varieties exhibited similar holding strength results, which could be related to chemical interactions between kafirin and phenolic contents with starch. These interactions require further investigation in future studies [34].

Concerning the setback (SB) region, the blue and black popcorn grains presented significantly higher values. This parameter represents the increase in viscosity when the cooling stage ends and starch retrogradation occurs. The leached amylose and amylopectin chains form a new crystalline structure through realignment [32]. Thus, these popcorn grains could have more intergranular interactions in the suspension, such as entanglement between the surface particles of the adjacent starch granules, thereby increasing the viscosity values [35]. The sorghum grains presented lower SB values than those reported by Truong et al. [34]. They also found a significant relationship between SB and the ferulic acid content in sorghum kernels. The final viscosities in the red and yellow sorghum samples were not of the same magnitude as those reported in 20 high-yield sorghum hybrids harvested in South America. These sorghum hybrids had white, red, and brown pericarps, and their final viscosities ranged between 3030 and 4402 mPa s [23].

3.5. Structural Properties (X-ray Diffraction)

Figure 3 depicts the diffractograms obtained from the specialty cereals of popcorn and sorghum. The typical structure of X-ray diffraction patterns for the popcorn lines and sorghum varieties was type A, which corresponds to native starches found in cereals [36].

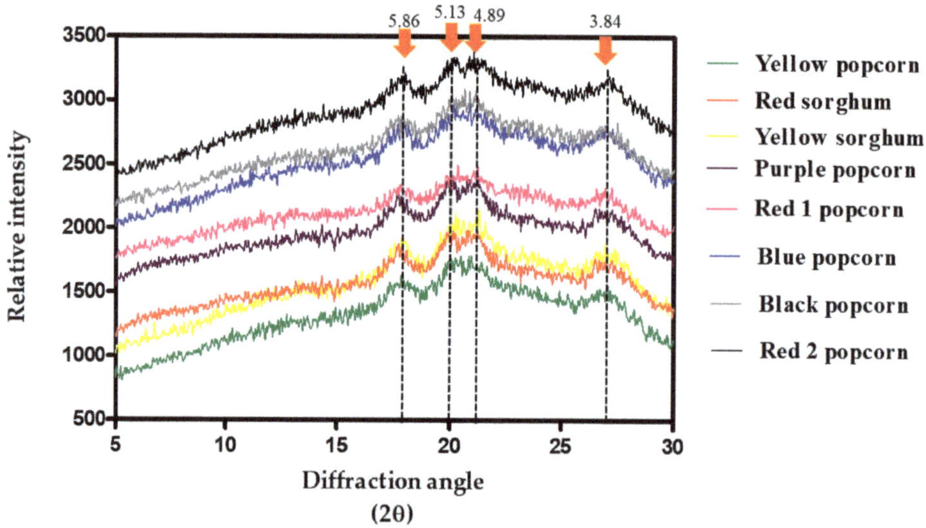

Figure 3. X-ray diffraction analysis of the evaluated nonconventional grains of sorghum and corn.

Four peaks corresponding to the crystalline structure of native starch granules were detected [36]. Strong reflections can be observed at 17.5° and 27.5° (2θ), corresponding to the interplanar spaces (d) of 5.86 and 3.84, respectively. Furthermore, a doublet at 20.5° and 21° (2θ) was detected at the interplanar spaces of 5.13 and 4.89 (d), which agrees with the structures previously reported for the whole grain flours of corn and sorghum [37,38]. No differences were observed in the X-ray diffraction patterns of the popcorn and sorghum lines. Nevertheless, yellow sorghum exhibited more defined peaks than red sorghum. The findings of the popcorn patterns were the same as those reported by Trovo et al. [39] in starch extracted from creole popcorn grains, with peaks observed at 15°,18°, 19°, and 23° at 2θ.

3.6. Morphological Assessments

Figures 4 and 5 present the micrographs of the popcorn and sorghum samples, respectively, exhibiting their soft, hard, and intermediate endosperms. Figure 4(A1–A6) presents the polyhedral structure with angular shapes of the starch granules found in the hard endosperm of popcorn grains. The size of the starch granules in these grains was approximately 10 μm. The hard and compact structures in our samples are similar to those reported by Singh et al. [35], who isolated starch granules from popcorn samples of different grain sizes. The protein matrix (PM) covered the starch granules (Figure 4(B1–B6)) in the intermediate endosperm. Surrounding the oval starch granules, the protein matrix formed the soft endosperm structures (Figure 4(C1–C6)). In the soft endosperm, the size of the starch granules was approximately 10–15 μm and was similar in all the popcorn samples. The starch structure was intact because the images taken were of half-cut grains and not flour.

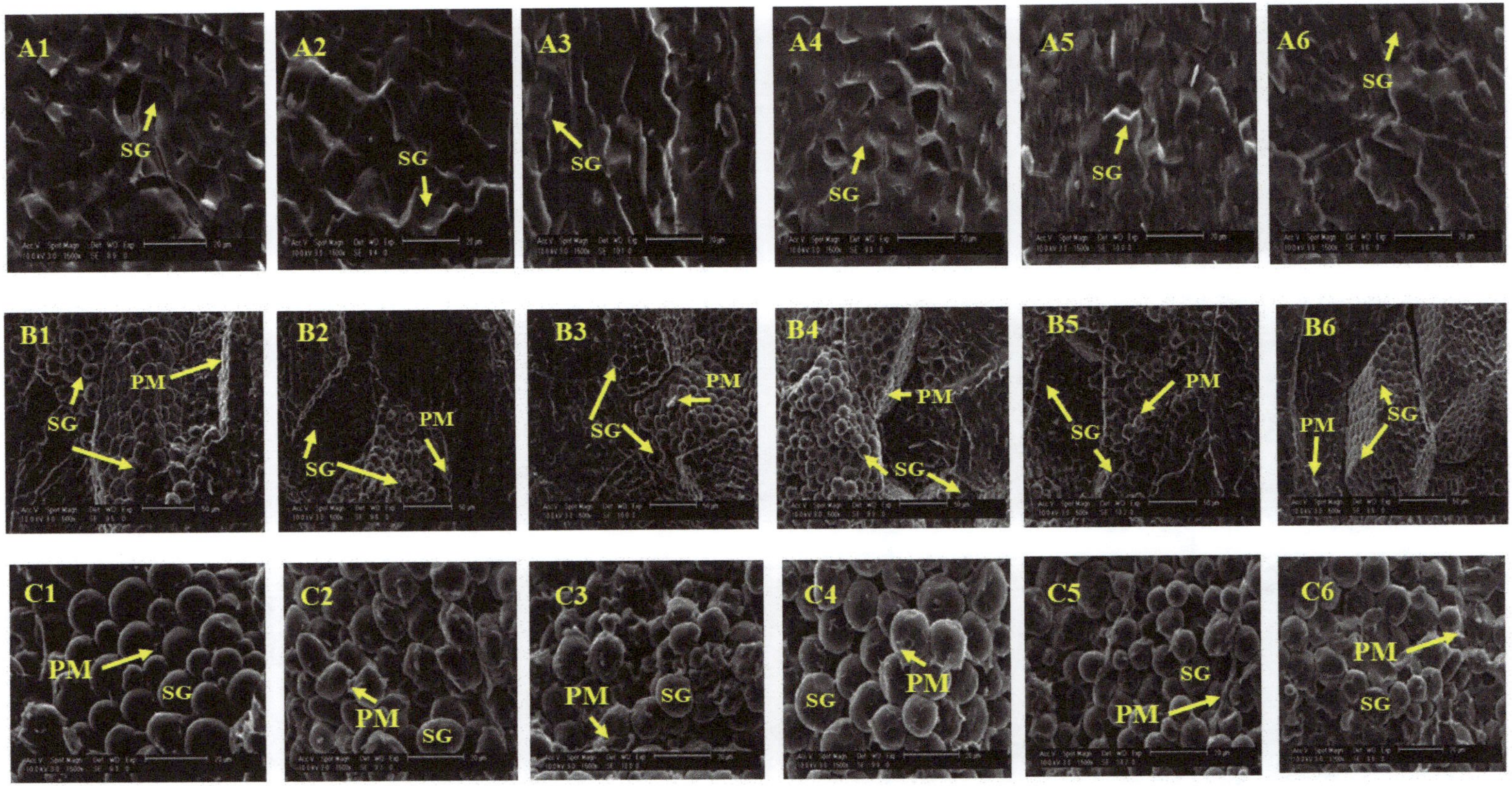

Figure 4. Micrographs of the hard (**A**) at 1500×, intermediate (**B**) at 500×, and soft endosperm (**C**) at 1500× of popcorn samples corresponding to (1) yellow popcorn, (2) purple popcorn, (3) red 1 popcorn, (4) blue popcorn, (5) black popcorn, and (6) red 2 popcorn. Abbreviations: SG, starch granules; PM, protein matrix.

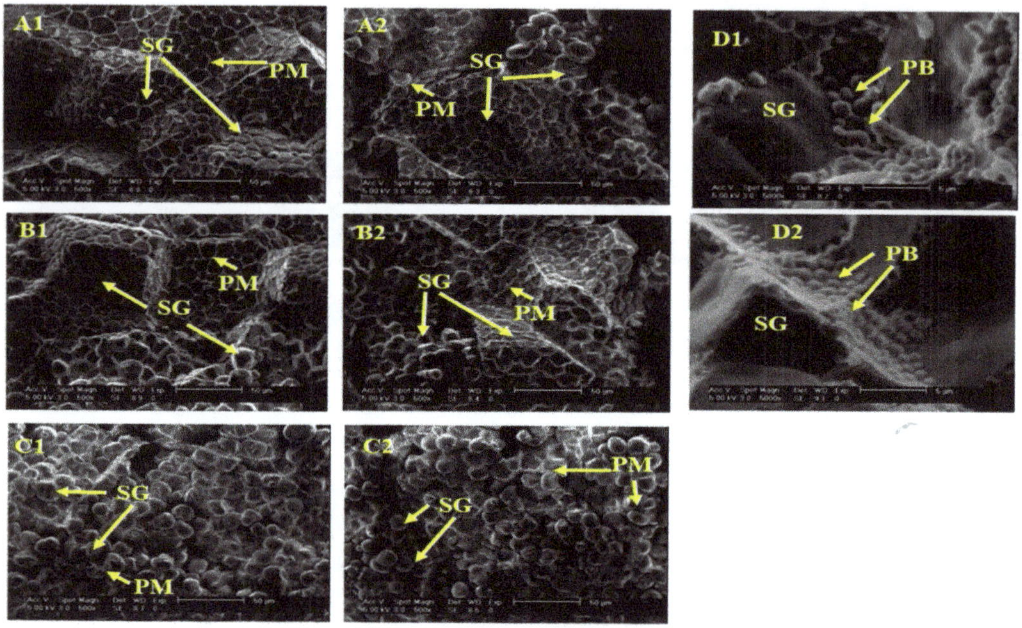

Figure 5. Micrographs of the hard endosperm (**A**) at 500×, intermediate endosperm (**B**) at 500x, soft endosperm (**C**) at 5000×, and (**D**) protein bodies at 5000× of sorghum samples corresponding to (1) red and (2) yellow sorghum. Abbreviations: SG, starch granule; PM, protein matrix; PB, protein bodies.

According to Ziegler et al. [40], popcorn grains contain 27% amylose and 73% amylopectin, and the form of the granules is spherical and polyhedral, which agrees with the morphological structures of our samples. In the soft endosperm (Figure 4(C1–C6)), some voids were observed among the granules, which are necessary for the arrangement of this grain proportion. This could be related to the expansion volume because samples of progenies with high expansion volumes had a higher proportion of compact endosperm and few voids interspersed among the granules [41]. This should be discussed as a quality parameter for popcorn in further studies.

Although no significant differences were observed in the protein content of popcorn grains, sample red 1 (Figure 4(C3)) exhibited a denser PM covering the soft endosperm. In general, the micrographic images of popcorn kernels agree with the maize type and findings reported by Cui et al. [42]. Furthermore, electron microscopy images of opaque and translucent endosperm in a popcorn hybrid from Iran and American popcorn agree with those of our samples. They demonstrate the presence of polygonal (pentagonal and hexagonal) starch granules in the translucent endosperm (hard), with the starch granules measuring 15 m in size. These structures are closely packed with no spaces among them [21], as observed in Figure 4(B1–B4). During heating, the vitreous (translucent) proportion exhibits the melting of the crystalline regions and gelatinization because water vapor is forced into the starch granules, causing further expansion [41].

Figure 5(A1,B1,C1) presents the hard, intermediate, and soft endosperm of the red sorghum grains, respectively. The compact structure of the starch granules was observed in the hard proportion (A1) with the PM cover, even when the protein content of this type of grain was the lowest (7.93%). The size of the starch granules was ~10–25 μm, and the granules had a polyhedral shape and defined limits, contrary to the structures found in the popcorn lines. Figure 5(D1) depicts the presence of multiple indentations on the grain surface caused by protein bodies and concurs with the morphological descriptions of the vitreous endosperm of sorghum lines reported by Bean et al. [43].

A study conducted on sorghum grains and changes in their morphology reported similar findings about the morphological properties of these grains using the same methodology. The shape and size of the starch were similar (i.e., polyhedral and spherical) in the hard and soft endosperm sections [24]. Evaluating the endosperm type and proportion in grains used for expanded products is important because the vitreous endosperm is the structure that primarily contributes to kernel expansion during popping [41].

4. Conclusions

This is the first study analyzing the properties of pigmented specialty popcorn and sorghum grains. According to their agronomical origin, popcorn and sorghum varieties exhibited different biophysical properties. These experiments were performed using commercial batches of specialty grains, and the results may vary when new batches are analyzed. This is expected because these biomaterials might vary during each harvesting season. Nevertheless, the first characterization of new bioproducts is always necessary for understanding more complex behaviors when the biomaterials are processed into final products. The physicochemical traits of both the grain types and varieties were similar to those given in the literature. Nevertheless, in terms of the nutraceutical features, the sorghum samples exhibited higher total phenolic content than the other varieties. Moreover, the total anthocyanin content of the red, purple, blue, and black popcorn was extremely high compared with that of the commercial grain, which was expected because of their nature. The same trend was observed in the red sorghum variety. The rheological, structural, and morphological assessments revealed consistency with the characteristics reported in other studies; however, the content of nutraceutical compounds (phenolics and anthocyanins) can influence these properties. In general, these grains have the potential to be used as functional ingredients and could be added in the cereal industry to produce low-caloric or low-glycemic foods. Further studies are required to investigate this. Full characterization of these specialty grains is crucial because these characteristics influence the functional and technological properties of their final products and derivatives.

Author Contributions: Writing—original draft preparation, methodology, formal analysis, V.T.R.-P.; resources, writing—review and editing, S.S.S.; writing—review and editing, visualization, resources, J.d.D.F.-C.; resources, visualization, W.L.R.; methodology, formal analysis, J.P.D.-V.; conceptualization, writing—review and editing, formal analysis, C.C.-H.; writing—original draft preparation, methodology, formal analysis, writing—review and editing, A.E.-A. All authors have read and agreed to the published version of the manuscript.

Funding: The APC was funded by the Institute for Obesity Research and the School of Engineering and Sciences, Tecnologico de Monterrey.

Data Availability Statement: The data used to support the findings of this study can be made available by the corresponding author upon request.

Acknowledgments: The authors wish to thank José Juan Veles-Medina from CINVESTAV-Qro and Karen Dennysse Monterroso-Morales from the School of Engineering and Sciences on campus in Toluca for their technical assistance.

Conflicts of Interest: The authors declare no conflict of interest.

References

1. Torbica, A.; Belović, M.; Popović, L.; Čakarević, J.; Jovičić, M.; Pavličević, J. Comparative Study of Nutritional and Technological Quality Aspects of Minor Cereals. *J. Food Sci. Technol.* **2021**, *58*, 311–322. [CrossRef]
2. Preciado-Ortiz, R.E.; Ochoa-Centeno, N.J.; Vázquez-Carrillo, M.G.; Santiago-Ramos, D.; Terrón-Ibarra, A.D. Grain Yield, Physical and Pasting Properties, and Anthocyanins of Non-Conventional Pigmented Corn Hybrids for Pozole End-Use Adapted to Subtropical Regions. *Appl. Food Res.* **2022**, *2*, 100180. [CrossRef]

3. Peralta-Veran, L.; Espinosa-Leal, C.; Escalante-Aburto, A.; Preciado-Ortiz, R.E.; Puente-Garza, C.A.; Serna-Saldivar, S.O.; García-Lara, S. Effects of Pozole Broth Production on Phenolic Acids and Antioxidant Activity of Specialty Maize Landraces. *J. Cereal Sci.* **2022**, *107*, 103543. [CrossRef]
4. Dudeja, I.; Gupta, M.; Mankoo, R.K.; Singh, A. Pigmented Maize: Nutritional Properties and Bioactive Profile. In *Pigmented Cereals and Millets*; Bangar, S.P., Maqsood, S., Siroha, A.K., Eds.; The Royal Society of Chemistry: London, UK, 2023; Volume 38, pp. 50–55.
5. Espitia-Hernández, P.; Chávez González, M.L.; Ascacio-Valdés, J.A.; Dávila-Medina, D.; Flores-Naveda, A.; Silva, T.; Ruelas Chacón, X.; Sepúlveda, L. Sorghum (*Sorghum bicolor* L.) as a Potential Source of Bioactive Substances and Their Biological Properties. *Crit. Rev. Food Sci. Nutr.* **2020**, *62*, 2269–2280. [CrossRef] [PubMed]
6. Ben Mrid, R.; Bouargalne, Y.; El Omari, R.; Nhiri, M. New Insights into the Therapeutic Effects of Phenolic Acids from Sorghum Seeds. *J. Rep. Pharma Sci.* **2019**, *8*, 91–101.
7. Khalid, W.; Ali, A.; Arshad, M.S.; Afzal, F.; Akram, R.; Siddeeg, A.; Kousar, S.; Rahim, M.A.; Aziz, A.; Maqbool, Z.; et al. Nutrients and Bioactive Compounds of *Sorghum bicolor* L. Used to Prepare Functional Foods: A Review on the Efficacy against Different Chronic Disorders. *Int. J. Food Prop.* **2022**, *25*, 1045–1062. [CrossRef]
8. Riaz, M.N. Snack Foods, Processing. In *Reference Module in Food Science*; Elsevier: Amsterdam, The Netherlands, 2016. [CrossRef]
9. Sergio, O. Serna-Saldivar Popcorn and Other Puffed Grains. In *Snack Foods*, 1st ed.; CRC Press: Boca Raton, FL, USA, 2022; p. 20.
10. Mohammed, R.; Are, A.K.; Bhavanasi, R.; Munghate, R.S.; Kavi Kishor, P.B.; Sharma, H.C. Quantitative Genetic Analysis of Agronomic and Morphological Traits in Sorghum, *Sorghum bicolor. Front. Plant Sci.* **2015**, *6*, 945. [CrossRef]
11. Serna-Saldivar, S.O. *Cereal Grains: Properties, Processing and Nutritional Attributes*; CRC Press: Boca Ratón, FL, USA, 2010.
12. American Organization of Analytical Chemists International (AOAC). *Official Methods 962.09, 978.02, 925.10, 923.03. Determination of Crude Fiber, Total Nitrogen, Moisture, and Ash*; AOAC: Washington, DC, USA, 2010.
13. AACC. International AACC Approved Methods of Analysis, 11th Edition—AACC Method 30-20.01. Crude Fat in Grain and Stock Feeds. Available online: https://www.cerealsgrains.org/resources/Methods/Pages/30CrudeFat.aspx (accessed on 3 June 2023).
14. FAO. Appendix XVI: Methods of Feed Analysis. Available online: https://www.fao.org/3/s4314e/s4314e0v.htm (accessed on 16 May 2023).
15. Ainsworth, E.A.; Gillespie, K.M. Estimation of Total Phenolic Content and Other Oxidation Substrates in Plant Tissues Using Folin-Ciocalteu Reagent. *Nat. Protoc.* **2007**, *2*, 875–877. [CrossRef]
16. Escalante-Aburto, A.; Ramírez-Wong, B.; Torres-Chávez, P.I.; López-Cervantes, J.; De Figueroa-Cárdenas, J.D.; Barrón-Hoyos, J.M.; Morales-Rosas, I.; García, N.P.; Gutiérrez-Dorado, R. Obtaining Ready-to-Eat Blue Corn Expanded Snacks with Anthocyanins Using an Extrusion Process and Response Surface Methodology. *Molecules* **2014**, *19*, 21066–21084. [CrossRef]
17. Escalante-Aburto, A.; Ponce-García, N.; Ramírez-Wong, B.; Santiago-Ramos, D.; Véles-Medina, J.J.; de Dios Figueroa Cárdenas, J. Effect of Extrusion Factors and Particle Size on Starch Properties of Nixtamalized Whole Blue Corn Snacks. *Starch/Staerke* **2016**, *68*, 1111–1120. [CrossRef]
18. Tian, Y.; Buriak, P.; Eckhoff, S.R. Effect of Hybrid and Physical Properties of Individual Popcorn Kernels on Expansion Volume. *Cereal Chem.* **2001**, *78*, 578–582. [CrossRef]
19. Surpam, T.; Pardeshi, I.; Rokade, H. Engineering Properties of Sorghum. *Int. J. Chem. Stud.* **2019**, *7*, 108–110.
20. Erkmen, O.; Bozoglu, T.F. (Eds.) Spoilage of Cereals and Cereal Products. In *Food Microbiology: Principles into Practice*; John Wiley & Sons: Hoboken, NJ, USA, 2016; pp. 364–375. [CrossRef]
21. Farahnaky, A.; Alipour, M.; Majzoobi, M. Popping Properties of Corn Grains of Two Different Varieties at Different Moistures. *J. Agric. Sci. Technol.* **2013**, *15*, 771–780.
22. Mawouma, S.; Condurache, N.N.; Turturică, M.; Constantin, O.E.; Croitoru, C.; Rapeanu, G. Chemical Composition and Antioxidant Profile of Sorghum (*Sorghum bicolor* (L.) Moench) and Pearl Millet (*Pennisetum glaucum* (L.) R.Br.) Grains Cultivated in the Far-North Region of Cameroon. *Foods* **2022**, *11*, 2026. [CrossRef] [PubMed]
23. Palavecino, P.M.; Penci, M.C.; Calderón-Domínguez, G.; Ribotta, P.D. Chemical Composition and Physical Properties of Sorghum Flour Prepared from Different Sorghum Hybrids Grown in Argentina. *Starch Stärke* **2016**, *68*, 1055–1064. [CrossRef]
24. Hernández-Becerra, E.; Gutierrez-Oñate, M.P.; Martinez-Soto, G.; Vega-Rojas, L.J.; Acosta-Osorio, A.A.; Contreras-Padilla, M.; Rodríguez-García, M.E. Physicochemical Characterization of Corn–Sorghum Nixtamalized Flours as a Function of the Steeping Time. *J. Food Meas. Charact.* **2016**, *10*, 434–443. [CrossRef]
25. Xu, J.; Wang, W.; Zhao, Y. Phenolic Compounds in Whole Grain Sorghum and Their Health Benefits. *Foods* **2021**, *10*, 1921. [CrossRef]
26. Shavandi, M.; Javanmard, M.; Basiri, A. Novel Popping through Infrared: Effect on Some Physicochemical Properties of Popcorn (*Zea mays* L. Var. Everta). *LWT* **2022**, *155*, 112955. [CrossRef]
27. Coco, M.G.; Vinson, J.A. Analysis of Popcorn (*Zea mays* L. Var. Everta) for Antioxidant Capacity and Total Phenolic Content. *Antioxidants* **2019**, *8*, 22. [CrossRef]
28. Bhukya, R.; Chamarthy, R.V.; Ediga, S.; Reddy, A.C.; Babu Marriboina, S.; Tonapi, V.A. Variability of Polyphenols, Antioxidant Activity and UFLC Phenolic Acid Profiles of Different Sorghum Genotypes. *Sch. Int. J. Biochem.* **2020**, *3*, 104–113. [CrossRef]
29. Rao, S.; Santhakumar, A.B.; Chinkwo, K.A.; Wu, G.; Johnson, S.K.; Blanchard, C.L. Characterization of Phenolic Compounds and Antioxidant Activity in Sorghum Grains. *J. Cereal Sci.* **2018**, *84*, 103–111. [CrossRef]

30. Rumler, R.; Bender, D.; Speranza, S.; Frauenlob, J.; Gamper, L.; Hoek, J.; Jäger, H.; Schönlechner, R. Chemical and Physical Characterization of Sorghum Milling Fractions and Sorghum Whole Meal Flours Obtained via Stone or Roller Milling. *Foods* **2021**, *10*, 870. [CrossRef] [PubMed]
31. Sang, Y.; Bean, S.; Seib, P.A.; Pedersen, J.; Shi, Y.C. Structure and Functional Properties of Sorghum Starches Differing in Amylose Content. *J. Agric. Food Chem.* **2008**, *56*, 6680–6685. [CrossRef]
32. Balet, S.; Guelpa, A.; Fox, G.; Manley, M. Rapid Visco Analyser (RVA) as a Tool for Measuring Starch-Related Physiochemical Properties in Cereals: A Review. *Food Anal. Methods* **2019**, *12*, 2344–2360. [CrossRef]
33. Paraginski, R.T.; Ziegler, V.; Peter, M.; Rockenbach, B.A.; Vanier, N.L.; Elias, M.C. Physicochemical and Sensory Properties of Popcorn Grain Stored at Different Temperatures. *Curr. Agric. Sci. Technol.* **2016**, *22*, 14–23. [CrossRef]
34. Truong, H.H.; Khoddami, A.; Moss, A.F.; Liu, S.Y.; Selle, P.H. The Potential of Rapid Visco-Analysis Starch Pasting Profiles to Gauge the Quality of Sorghum as a Feed Grain for Chicken-Meat Production. *Anim. Nutr.* **2017**, *3*, 11–18. [CrossRef]
35. Sandhu, K.S.; Singh, N.; Kaur, M. Characteristics of the Different Corn Types and Their Grain Fractions: Physicochemical, Thermal, Morphological, and Rheological Properties of Starches. *J. Food Eng.* **2004**, *64*, 119–127. [CrossRef]
36. Dome, K.; Podgorbunskikh, E.; Bychkov, A.; Lomovsky, O. Changes in the Crystallinity Degree of Starch Having Different Types of Crystal Structure after Mechanical Pretreatment. *Polymers* **2020**, *12*, 641. [CrossRef]
37. Lee, C.J.; Na, J.H.; Park, J.Y.; Chang, P.S. Structural Characteristics and In Vitro Digestibility of Malic Acid-Treated Corn Starch with Different PH Conditions. *Molecules* **2019**, *24*, 1900. [CrossRef]
38. Shaikh, F.; Ali, T.M.; Mustafa, G.; Hasnain, A. Structural, Functional and Digestibility Characteristics of Sorghum and Corn Starch Extrudates (RS3) as Affected by Cold Storage Time. *Int. J. Biol. Macromol.* **2020**, *164*, 3048–3054. [CrossRef]
39. Torovo Marues de Souza Cesar, A.L.; Gomes Cheim, L.M.; Afonso Rossignoli, P.; Rodrigues, L.J.; FOnseca da Silva, F.; Pereira Takeuchi, K.; de Morais Carvalho, D.; de Melo Faria, A.M. Physical Chemicals and Rheologicals Characterization of Corn Starch (*Zea mays* L.) Landraces Popcorn. *Res. Soc. Dev.* **2021**, *10*, e402101321394. [CrossRef]
40. Ziegler, V.; Timm, N.d.S.; Ferreira, C.D.; Goebel, J.T.; Pohndorf, R.S.; de Oliveira, M. Effects of Drying Temperature of Red Popcorn Grains on the Morphology, Technological, and Digestibility Properties of Starch. *Int. J. Biol. Macromol.* **2020**, *145*, 568–574. [CrossRef] [PubMed]
41. Freire, A.I.; De, E.; Castro, M.; Pereira, A.M.; Ranielly, R.; Cruz, P.; Machado De Souza, F.B.; Filipe, W.; Chagas, T.; Cândido De Souza, J. Amylose Content and Micromorphology of Popcorn Progenies with Different Popping Expansion Volumes. *Ciência Rural* **2020**, *50*, e20180962. [CrossRef]
42. Cui, L.; Dong, S.; Zhang, J.; Liu, P. Starch Granule Size Distribution and Morphogenesis in Maize (*Zea mays* L.) Grains with Different Endosperm Types. *AJCS* **2014**, *8*, 1560–1565.
43. Bean, S.R.; Wilson, J.D.; Moreau, R.A.; Galant, A.; Awika, J.M.; Kaufman, R.C.; Adrianos, S.L.; Ioerger, B.P. Structure and Composition of the Sorghum Grain. *Sorghum State Art Future Perspetives* **2019**, *58*, 173–214. [CrossRef]

foods

MDPI

Article

Bread Products from Blends of African Climate Resilient Crops: Baking Quality, Sensory Profile and Consumers' Perception

Stefano Renzetti [1,*], Heikki Aisala [2], Ruth T. Ngadze [3], Anita R. Linnemann [3] and Martijn W. Noort [1]

[1] Wageningen Food and Biobased Research, Wageningen University & Research, Bornse Weilanden 9, 6700 AA Wageningen, The Netherlands
[2] VTT Technical Research Centre of Finland Ltd., Tietotie 2, 02044 Espoo, Finland
[3] Food Quality and Design Group, Wageningen University and Research, Bornse Weilanden 9, 6708 WG Wageningen, The Netherlands
* Correspondence: stefano.renzetti@wur.nl

Abstract: With food insecurity rising dramatically in Sub-Saharan Africa, promoting the use of sorghum, cowpea and cassava flours in staple food such as bread may reduce wheat imports and stimulate the local economy through new value chains. However, studies addressing the technological functionality of blends of these crops and the sensory properties of the obtained breads are scarce. In this study, cowpea varieties (i.e., Glenda and Bechuana), dry-heating of cowpea flour and cowpea to sorghum ratio were studied for their effects on the physical and sensory properties of breads made from flour blends. Increasing cowpea Glenda flour addition from 9 to 27% (in place of sorghum) significantly improved bread specific volume and crumb texture in terms of instrumental hardness and cohesiveness. These improvements were explained by higher water binding, starch gelatinization temperatures and starch granule integrity during pasting of cowpea compared to sorghum and cassava. Differences in physicochemical properties among cowpea flours did not significantly affect bread properties and texture sensory attributes. However, cowpea variety and dry-heating significantly affected flavour attributes (i.e., beany, yeasty and ryebread). Consumer tests indicated that composite breads could be significantly distinguished for most of the sensory attributes compared to commercial wholemeal wheat bread. Nevertheless, the majority of consumers scored the composite breads from neutral to positive with regard to liking. Using these composite doughs, chapati were produced in Uganda by street vendors and tin breads by local bakeries, demonstrating the practical relevance of the study and the potential impact for the local situation. Overall, this study shows that sorghum, cowpea and cassava flour blends can be used for commercial bread-type applications instead of wheat in Sub-Saharan Africa.

Keywords: bread; sorghum; cowpea; cassava; sensory; food security

Citation: Renzetti, S.; Aisala, H.; Ngadze, R.T.; Linnemann, A.R.; Noort, M.W. Bread Products from Blends of African Climate Resilient Crops: Baking Quality, Sensory Profile and Consumers' Perception. *Foods* **2023**, *12*, 689. https://doi.org/10.3390/foods12040689

Academic Editors: Laura Gazza and Francesca Nocente

Received: 10 January 2023
Revised: 23 January 2023
Accepted: 2 February 2023
Published: 5 February 2023

1. Introduction

Currently, the food system in Sub-Saharan Africa (SSA) is severely challenged because of the growing urban population and climate change [1,2]. Massive urbanization is resulting in a dietary shift, diverting from the use of local crops to imported cereals associated with the Western lifestyle, largely maize and wheat [3]. Concomitantly, food production cannot keep pace with internal demand, making SSA increasingly dependent on imported crops such as wheat [4]. This issue is further exacerbated by climate change with projected reductions in wheat and maize yields in SSA [3,5] and by the wheat crisis related to the Russia–Ukraine conflict.

Indigenous African crops such as sorghum, cassava and cowpea are climate-resilient crops (CRCs) as they have enhanced tolerance to biotic and abiotic stresses [6,7]. Cowpea requires few inputs, grows in low rainfall and shade [8] and is suitable for intercropping with sorghum, reducing fertiliser use and soil erosion [9]. Promoting the valorisation of these CRCs into value-added ingredients and in the production of attractive, affordable and nutritious food such as bread-type products could improve food and nutrition security, stimulate the local economy and create new employment opportunities throughout the value chain [10,11].

From a nutritional perspective, the relative overconsumption of starchy crops in SSA is a concern for protein as well as micronutrient security [12]. Cassava is an affordable source of carbohydrates and energy, but should be combined with other indigenous crops from pulses and cereals [13]. Consumption of sorghum can positively impact human health, especially regarding disorders such as celiac disease, diabetes and obesity [14]. Tannins present in sorghum can reduce starch digestion [15,16], resulting in a low glycaemic index [17,18]. Monomeric flavonoids in sorghum showed several anti-inflammatory activities [19]. Sorghum is also rich in potassium and phosphorus and contains good levels of calcium. The legume cowpea is a rich source of protein, dietary fibre and additionally of polyphenols, vitamins and minerals [20,21]. Cowpea proteins are rich in glutamic acid, aspartic acid and lysine, which are limiting in sorghum. From this perspective, it is nutritionally beneficial to complement sorghum and cassava with cowpea in the human diet [22].

Sorghum flour has been studied for partial wheat replacement in pan breads [23], showing detrimental effects on dough properties and the quality of the composite breads with inclusions of 15% and beyond. From a sensory perspective, the inclusion of sorghum in wheat bread products was found to be acceptable up to a maximum of 30% [24,25]. Due to its gluten-free status and nutritional value, sorghum flour has been also studied for application in breads for people with celiac disease [26], often in combination with starches [26,27] and with hydrocolloids [28]. Cassava has been extensively studied for partial replacement of wheat flour in bread applications [29]. However, widespread implementation of cassava in commercial products has failed to date, due to technological challenges and poor product quality of cassava-wheat composite breads as perceived by consumers and bakers [11].

Despite the relevance for human nutrition and food security, studies on composite breads based on sorghum, cowpea and cassava are scarce. However, their combination offers opportunities to optimize the nutritional composition and technological properties of bread-type products [30], which would benefit the growing African population but potentially also the segment of the global population suffering from celiac disease. To the best of our knowledge, Renzetti and co-workers were the first to report on the use of a composite sorghum–cowpea–cassava mixture to prepare a processable dough, instead of a liquid batter, and produce tin breads (i.e., breads baked inside tins) [31]. These authors reported that (physical) texture properties of the breads could be improved by modulating cowpea flour properties, e.g., by dry-heating treatments, suggesting cowpea as a functional ingredient for both technological and nutritional purposes. Further studies were suggested to explore the implementation potential of these bread concepts, taking also the sensory aspects into account. Variations in cowpea varieties and inclusion levels may have a different contribution to the quality of the bread-type products due to differences in sensory profile [32] and in functional properties [33].

Against this background, this study evaluated the effect of variations in cowpea flour properties, namely variety and dry-heating treatment, and the level of addition (i.e., cowpea to sorghum ratio) on the physical and sensory properties of breads made from sorghum, cowpea and cassava mixtures. Two cowpea varieties were used for this purpose. Relevant physicochemical properties of the flours were analysed in order to relate to the bread properties. Descriptive sensory analysis was performed to understand the effect of variations in flours and bread properties on the intensity of the sensory attributes. Additionally, consumer studies were performed to gain insights into the perception and liking of a selected CRCs-based bread formulation as compared to commercial wheat bread. Implementation potential of the developed doughs was tested in Uganda with small bakeries making tin breads and with street vendors making chapati.

2. Materials and Methods

2.1. Materials

Red, non-tannin, King Korn superfine sorghum (locally known as mabele) meal was obtained from a local supermarket in Pretoria (South Africa). Cowpea seeds from a white (Bechuana white) and a red (Glenda) variety were sourced from Agrinawar Agricol Pty (Pretoria, South Africa) and milled as whole grains at ProCorn Mills (Edenvale, Sebenza, South Africa). Sorghum contained 10.2% protein, 11.5% dietary fibres (of which 2.3% was soluble) and 73.1% starch. Bechuana white cowpea flour (BECH) contained 23.9% protein (of which 18.6% was soluble at native pH), 20.6% dietary fibres (of which 7.5% was soluble) and 40.7% starch. Red Glenda cowpea flour (GL) contained 23.9% protein (of which 18.4% was soluble at native pH), 24.1% dietary fibres (of which 7.7% was soluble) and 39.7% starch. Dry-heated GL (GL-DH) was also tested based on the result of a recent study on the Glenda variety [31]. One treatment condition was selected to evaluate the contribution to the sensory profile, which was not previously assessed. The treatment consisted of equilibrating the flour at 50% RH and subsequently heating in an oven at 100 °C for 2 h after sealing in a heat-resistant plastic bag.

Cassava starch (93.2% starch, 0.3% protein and 2.1% soluble fibres) was supplied by DADTCO (Dutch Agricultural Development and Trading Company, Inhambane, Mozambique). Psyllium husk powder (88% dietary fibres, 3% proteins) was from Unilecithin (Sharjah, United Arab Emirates). Dry yeast (Mauripan red, AB Mauri, Dordrecht, The Netherlands), salt and sucrose (both sourced in The Netherlands for lab tests and in Uganda for implementation tests) were used for the breadmaking trials.

2.2. Methods

2.2.1. Water Binding Capacity of Native and Treated Flours

The water binding capacity (WBC) of the native and dry-heated GL (GL-DH) samples was determined in triplicate, according to a modified version of [34]. Flours (0.4 g on dry basis) were placed in 5 mL Eppendorf tubes and 3.6 g of distilled water was added during vigorous stirring. After mixing on a vortex, the samples were left to shake at room temperature for 20 min on a Multi Reax Vortex (Heidolph Instruments GmbH, Schwabach, Germany). Then, the samples were centrifuged for 10 min at 5000 G using an Avanti J-26XP High Speed Centrifuge (Beckman Coulter, Indianapolis, IN, USA). The supernatant was collected and the pellet was drained for 15 min at an angle of 45°, dried and then weighed. WBC was expressed as follows:

$$WBC\ (g/g) = \frac{\text{wet pellet (g)} - \text{dried pellet (g)}}{\text{dried pellet (g)}} \quad (1)$$

The moisture content of the pellet was measured by drying overnight in aluminium dishes in an oven at 105 °C. The filled dishes were cooled for 1 h in a desiccator before weight determination.

2.2.2. Thermal Analysis of Native and Treated Flours

Flour concentrations of 20% (on dry matter basis) in distilled water were used to measure starch gelatinization and protein denaturation with a TA Instruments type Q200 Differential Scanning Calorimeter (DSC) as earlier described [31]. Samples were measured by equilibrating at −5 °C for 5 min and then scanned to 160 °C with a rate of 5 °C/min. The onset of starch gelatinization and protein denaturation (T_{onset}), peak temperature (T_{min}) and gelatinization/denaturation enthalpy were determined using the analysis tool available in the Universal Analysis software (TA Instruments, New Castle, DE, USA). Experiments were performed in triplicate.

2.2.3. Pasting Behaviour of Native and Treated Flours

Pasting behaviour was investigated using a Rapid Visco Analyser (RVA) Super 4 (Perten, Hägersten, Sweden) as earlier described [31]. Flour or starch suspensions of 8% dry matter (dm) in water were used. Samples were subjected to a time–temperature profile. Initial stirring speed was 960 rpm at 50 °C for 60 s. Then, the stirring speed was decreased to 160 rpm while the temperature was increased to 95 °C within 3 min 42 s. Samples were then held at 95 °C for 2 min 30 s minutes and cooled to 50 °C within 3 min 48 s. Finally, samples were held at 50 °C for 2 min. All tests were performed in duplicate. Pasting temperature (PT), peak viscosity (PV), hold viscosity (HV), breakdown (BD), final viscosity (FV) and set back (SB) were obtained from the RVA measurements and expressed as centipoise (cP).

2.2.4. Bread-Making Procedure

Variations in CRCs-based bread formulations were built upon a product concept recently developed containing sorghum, cassava and cowpea [31], as shown in Table 1. Variations were designed to test the effect of cowpea flour (i.e., GL9 vs. G27), compare between varieties at highest inclusion level to maximize differences (i.e., G27 vs. BENCH27) and evaluate the effect of dry-heating treatment as compared to untreated cowpea flour (i.e., GL9 vs. GL9-DH).

Table 1. Bread dough formulations tested for baking properties and descriptive sensory and for sensory with naive consumers.

Ingredients	Formulations in Baker's %				
	GL9	GL27	BECH27	GL9-DH	BENCH9 **
Flours mixture *					
Sorghum	45.7	27.4	27.4	45.7	45.7
Cassava starch	45.7	45.7	45.7	45.7	45.7
GL	8.7	26.9			
BECH			26.9		8.7
GL-DH				8.7	
Salt	2.3	2.3	2.3	2.3	2.3
Dry yeast	5.0	5.0	5.0	5.0	5.0
Rapeseed oil	3.7	3.7	3.7	3.7	3.7
Sucrose	3.7	3.7	3.7	3.7	3.7
Psyllium flour	7.3	7.3	7.3	7.3	7.3
Water	108.7	108.7	108.7	108.7	108.7

* Sorghum, cassava and cowpea flours account together for the total flour; the remaining ingredients are expressed as percentage of the flour mixture. GL = Cowpea flour from Glenda variety; BECH = cowpea from Bechuana variety; GL-DH = dry heated cowpea flour Glenda variety. ** Formulation used only for sensory evaluation with naive consumers.

In total, about 1300 g of dry ingredients were added to a Sinmag spiral mixer (Sinmag Europe bvba, Zuienkerke, Belgium) and pre-mixed at low speed (speed I) for 1 min. Then, water was slowly added during mixing, which was performed for 5 min at speed I and for another 4 min at speed II. After mixing, the dough was divided and shaped manually, and put into three greased baking tins, each containing 700 g of dough. These tins were put in a fermentation chamber at 30 °C and 85% RH. The proofing time was defined as the time needed by 50 g of dough to reach a CO_2 production of 90 mL. The CO_2 production was determined using a Risograph (National Manufacturing, Lincoln, NE, USA). After proofing, the doughs were put in a swing oven at 180 °C for 70 min. During the first minute, steam was injected twice to regulate the moisture content. After baking, the breads were cooled at room temperature for 40 min, sealed in plastic low-density polyethylene bags and stored at room temperature until further analysis one day after baking. Baking tests were performed in triplicate. The described procedure was used for bread intended for instrumental characterization and descriptive sensory analysis.

For the naïve consumers' study, sorghum and BECH flours were first hydrated in excess water for 1.5 h in order to minimize sandiness in breadcrumbs, based on preliminary trials. After hydration, the flour and the water were combined with the rest of the ingredients in the Sinmag spiral mixer and the same breadmaking protocol was applied.

2.2.5. Instrumental Bread Quality Evaluation

Loaf volume was determined on 2 loaves from each baking test, with a rapeseed displacement according to [35]. In total, 6 measurements were performed per variation. Specific volume (SV) was calculated as loaf volume divided by loaf weight (mL/g).

Crumb texture was measured by means of Texture Profile Analysis (TPA), using a TA-XT2i Texture Analyser from Stable Micro Systems (Godalming, Surrey, UK) with a 30 kg load cell and a 75 mm compression plate and performed as previously described [35]. In total, 12 measurements were performed per bread type.

The moisture content of the bread crumb (5 g sample) was measured according to [35] by drying overnight in aluminium dishes in an oven at 105 °C. The filled dishes were cooled for 1 h in a desiccator before weight determination. In total, 6 measurements were performed per bread type.

2.2.6. Descriptive Sensory Analysis

Sensory profiling of the pan breads was conducted as generic descriptive analysis with 8 trained panellists who were regularly trained. Written informed consents were obtained from the participants prior to the evaluation. The base attribute list was developed by five trained assessors in a consensus session using previous studies as a basis [32,36,37]. This list, along with all samples, was then presented to the whole sensory panel in a consensus training session where they refined the attributes and their descriptions, discussed the intensity ranges of the samples and decided on reference products. The final sensory profile had 18 attributes that covered the odour (i.e., cereal, sweet, ryebread, beany, fermented), appearance (dark, air bubble size), tactile texture (crumbliness), taste (sour, sweet, astringent), flavour (ryebread, beany, yeasty, spicy) and mouthfeel (sandy, crumbly, moist) of the samples.

For serving, a slice of each sample was packed in closed plastic bag and presented with a 3-digit code. Water and a piece of wheat-based cream cracker were used as palate cleansers. The serving order was randomized with a Latin squares design. The samples were evaluated in duplicate in a complete block design. The attribute intensities were evaluated with a 0–10 continuous line (0 = non-perceivable and 10 = very intense). The data were collected with EyeQuestion version 5.3 (Logic8 B.V., Elst, The Netherlands).

2.2.7. Sensory Evaluation with Naive Consumers of a CRCs-Based Bread and of Wholemeal Wheat Bread

Subjects

Fifty-one participants (n = 51, 37 female, age: 19–28 years) were recruited from Wageningen University & Research campus using flyers, posters and social media. Subjects were regular consumers of bread. Other inclusion criteria (self-reported) were no allergies or intolerances to gluten, good dental health and non-smoking habits. Participants were mainly of Dutch nationality (n = 37), followed by Italian (n = 5), and the remaining 9 were each from a different nationality. A consent form was signed by all participants. Subjects received reimbursement for their participation and were naive concerning the experimental conditions and purposes.

Sensory Sessions

The sensory tests were conducted in meeting facilities at Wageningen University, equipped with desk dividers for a maximum of six participants per session. Subjects were asked to fill in a paper questionnaire. One short session was carried out to allow participants to familiarize themselves with the sensory method. An explanation brochure for the different descriptors and their definitions was provided during the test session. Mechanically sliced samples of bread (thickness 1 cm) of the two different formulations were presented to the panellists with randomized three-digit codes. The panellists received one slice of bread per formulation. Panellists were instructed to first taste the bread crumb of the two different bread samples before scoring them. Subjects were instructed to cleanse their mouth with water and have a break of at least 2 min between evaluating the samples.

Hedonic Characterization and Rate-All-That-Apply (RATA)

Participants were asked to evaluate commercial wholemeal bread (Stevig grof volkoren, Albert Heijn, Zaandam, The Netherlands) and CRCs-based bread prepared following the recipe of GL9 (Table 1), but using BECH instead of GL. Participants first evaluated overall liking of the bread using a hedonic 9-point scale ranging from "Dislike it extremely" (1) to "Like it extremely" (9). After the hedonic evaluations, subjects were asked to evaluate the samples using a RATA method with 9-box scales as previously described by [38,39]. The complete list of sensory terms, as well as their definitions, are reported in Table 2. The list of attributes was presented to the subjects, who were asked to indicate whether the specific descriptors were applicable to the assessed sample ("Yes" or "No" choice). Once an attribute was selected as applicable to the sample ("Yes" choice), then subjects had to rate the perceived intensity of the selected attribute on a 9 point-scale where "1" corresponded to low intensity and "9" to high intensity. It was clarified that a non-selection of an attribute was equivalent to a non-perception of the sensory stimulus. The order in the questionnaire of the sensory attributes was randomized within each block of attribute category (appearance, texture, and flavour) for each participant.

Table 2. List of descriptors and definitions used in the RATA test with naive consumers.

Attribute	Definition
Appearance	
Pore size	Size of holes inside a loaf
Homogeneity of pores	Observation of regular size of pores
Colour: dark	Perception of dark colour
Colour: red tone	Perception of red colour tones
Colour: yellow tone	Perception of yellow colour tones
Texture	
Hard	Related to the force required to bite
Soft	Related to the force required to bite
Dense	Tightly packed crumb structure, more closed crumb structure
Sticky	Adhering or sticking to oral cavity
Smooth	Degree of perceived smoothness of bread
Sandy	Sensation that describes presence of particles in oral cavity
Chewy	Related to the number of chews required before swallowing
Pasty	Sensation that describes the formation of a dough of the bolus
Crumbly	Easily breaking into small fragments
Dry	Degree of drying effect, amount of saliva absorbed by the sample
Moist	Amount of moisture perceived of the product
Taste	
Salty	Perception of salt
Sweet	Perception of sugar taste
Bitter	Perception of bitter taste
Sour	Perception of sour taste
Beany flavour	Having a flavour associated with cooked dry beans
Bland	Lacking taste
Tangy	Having a strong piquant flavour.
Yeasty flavour	Having a flavour associated with (dry) yeast

2.2.8. Statistical Analysis

Statistical evaluations (analysis of variance, ANOVA, with Tukey's test as post hoc test at a significance level of $p < 0.05$) for flour properties and physical properties of breads were performed with SPSS (IBM, version 25, Chicago, IL, USA). A two-way mixed model

ANOVA with samples as fixed factor and assessors as random factor was used for sensory profiling. Principal component analysis (PCA) of sensory profiling data was performed with Rstudio (RStudio version 1.1.463, Inc., Boston, MA, USA) using the PCA function of the *FactoMineR* package [40], together with correlation analysis. Averaged data over assessors and replicates were used for the PCA on sensory profiling.

For the RATA intensity scores, non-checked attributes were treated as intensity = 0, and RATA intensity scores (0–9) were treated as continuous data [38,39]. A paired sample *t*-test was performed to establish significant differences between the two bread samples for each of the listed attributes. A significance level of $p < 0.05$ was chosen. Data from RATA tests were analysed using SPSS.

3. Results and Discussion

3.1. Physicochemical Properties of Sorghum, Cowpea and Cassava Flours

Relevant physicochemical properties of the flours were studied to elucidate their contribution to the baking behaviour of the composite CRCs doughs (Table 3). GL showed the largest WBC among all flours, followed by BECH, sorghum flour and cassava starch. The WBC of dry-heated GL flour was intermediate to GL and BECH. The decrease in WBC of cowpea flour with dry-heating may be attributed to increased hydrophobicity of proteins and annealing of starch [31,41]. The main compositional difference between the two cowpea varieties was in the total dietary fibre content and particularly the insoluble part. Most likely, these compositional differences explained the WBC results, as a general correlation was observed between WBC and the dietary fibre content of the flours ($R^2 = 0.968$, $p < 0.05$).

Table 3. Physicochemical properties of the flours used in the study.

	Cassava	Sorghum	BECH	GL	GL-DH
WBC (g/g)	1.5 ± 0.1 a	2.1 ± 0.2 b	3.1 ± 0.2 c	3.7 ± 0.3 d	3.1 ± 0.2 cd
DSC parameters					
Tonset (°C)	60.1 ± 0.2 a	68.0 ± 0.2 d	67.0 ± 0.6 cd	64.6 ± 1.0 b	66.1 ± 0.5 bc
Tpeak1 (starch) (°C)	71.1 ± 0.1 a	74.4 ± 0.1 b	78.5 ± 0.1 d	76.0 ± 0.2 c	76.0 ± 0.1 c
Tpeak2 (protein) (°C)	-	-	87.4 ± 1.1	88.3 ± 0.6	87.7 ± 0.9
ΔH (kJ/mol)	17.0 ± 0.5 b	14.9 ± 1.6 b	8.9 ± 1.2 a	7.8 ± 0.5 a	8.6 ± 0.6 a
RVA parameters					
PT (°C)	70.7 ± 0.0 a	92.2 ± 0.1 e	86.6 ± 0.1 d	80.3 ± 0.1 b	82.8 ± 0.2 c
PV (cP)	2397 ± 4 e	487 ± 1 d	219 ± 3 b	277 ± 15 c	130.5 ± 1 a
HV (cP)	1094 ± 2 d	484 ± 1 c	216 ± 2 b	247 ± 21 b	129 ± 1 a
BD (cP)	1303 ± 6 c	4 ± 1 a	4 ± 1 a	30 ± 6 b	1.5 ± 1 a
FV (cP)	1471 ± 2 d	967 ± 4 c	363 ± 5 b	342 ± 13 b	174.5 ± 2 a
SB (cP)	377 ± 0 d	483 ± 2 e	147 ± 3 c	96 ± 8 b	45.5 ± 1 a

Values with different letters within each row indicated significant differences in ANOVA analysis ($p < 0.05$). GL = Cowpea flour from Glenda variety; BECH = cowpea from Bechuana variety; GL-DH = dry heated cowpea flour Glenda variety.

The DSC analysis of the flours revealed the main differences as being in their thermal behaviour (Table 3). Cassava and sorghum flour showed one main endothermic peak associated with starch gelatinization. The gelatinization temperature for cassava and sorghum starch were in agreement with ranges previously reported [42,43]. On the contrary, GL and BECH flours were characterized by two endothermic transitions with peaks appearing around 77 and 88 °C. These peaks could be associated with starch gelatinization and protein denaturation, respectively, as earlier reported [31]. Cassava showed the lowest onset of starch gelatinization (T_{onset}), while sorghum and BECH had the highest ($p < 0.05$). The T_{peak} of starch was the highest for BECH, followed by GL and GL-DH, while cassava was the lowest ($p < 0.05$). The enthalpies for starch and protein in cowpea flours could not be distinguished due to partial overlapping between the two peaks. Nevertheless, the gelatinization enthalpies of cassava and sorghum flour were significantly higher than the enthalpy for all the cowpea flours.

With regards to pasting behaviour, cassava starch showed the lowest pasting temperature while sorghum flour had the highest, followed by BECH ($p < 0.05$). Samples GL and GL-DH showed pasting temperatures that were significantly higher than cassava but lower than BECH ($p < 0.05$). Dry heating significantly increased the pasting temperature compared to the untreated GL. Paste viscosities (i.e., PV, HV and FV) were the highest for cassava starch, followed by sorghum flour, GL, BECH and GL-DH ($p < 0.05$). The paste viscosities of BECH were significantly lower than those of GL. Furthermore, dry heating of GL resulted in significant reductions in PV, HV and FV. BD was the largest for cassava starch and the lowest for sorghum, BECH and GL-DH. Sorghum flour showed the highest SB, followed by cassava starch, BECH and GL ($p < 0.05$). Dry heating significantly reduced SB compared to the untreated GL, which was in agreement with recent work on GL with similar treatments [31]. It was recently shown that changes in the pasting properties and water binding capacity of cowpea flour significantly affect the baking behaviour of bread dough made from sorghum, cowpea flour and cassava starch [31]. Therefore, differences in cowpea flour variety and concentration (in place of sorghum) were expected to modulate bread properties.

3.2. *Baking Quality of Breads Made from Blends of Cassava, Sorghum and Cowpea Flours*

Baking tests were performed to evaluate the effect of cowpea flour variety and level of addition on the baking performance of the dough (Table 4). Increasing GL content from about 9 to 27% in the dough resulted in an overall improvement in the baking performance, as indicated by the significant increase in SV, springiness and resilience and a concomitant decrease in crumb hardness. Despite the significant differences observed between the two cowpea varieties in terms of physicochemical properties (Table 3), replacing GL with BECH did not significantly affect bread properties (i.e., samples GL27 and BECH27, Table 4). Bread GL9-DH showed bread properties that were intermediate to GL9 and GL27, suggesting dry-heating may be a simple and effective technology to functionalise cowpea flour [31], although the size of the effect should be further optimized to justify the additional processing step.

Table 4. Specific volume (SV) and crumb properties of the CRCs based breads.

	GL9	GL27	BECH27	GL9-DH
SV (mL/g)	1.73 ± 0.03 a	1.82 ± 0.02 bc	1.84 ± 0.00 c	1.77 ± 0.03 ab
Crumb properties				
Moisture (%)	52.5 ± 0.1 a	52.4 ± 0.0 a	52.4 ± 0.1 a	52.5 ± 0.1 a
Hardness (N)	21.1 ± 1.7 b	16.2 ± 1.6 a	16.4 ± 1.8 a	20.6 ± 1.3 b
Springiness	0.887 ± 0.012 a	0.917 ± 0.018 b	0.915 ± 0.009 b	0.904 ± 0.010 b
Cohesiveness	0.423 ± 0.017 a	0.477 ± 0.012 b	0.462 ± 0.016 b	0.436 ± 0.008 a
Resilience	0.191 ± 0.011 a	0.225 ± 0.008 c	0.213 ± 0.010 bc	0.201 ± 0.005 ab

Values with different letters within each row indicated significant differences in ANOVA analysis ($p < 0.05$). GL9 = Bread with 9% Glenda cowpea flour; GL27 = Bread with 27% Glenda cowpea flour; BECH27 = Bread with 27% Bechuana cowpea flour; GL9-DH = Bread with 9% dry-heated Glenda cowpea flour.

Due to the lack of gluten, strain hardening is missing during fermentation and the early stages of baking with CRCs-based doughs. The mechanical resistance against gas pressure and collapse is merely provided by viscosity (or by shear modulus), as observed in cake batters [44]. From this standpoint, the differences in WBC among cassava, sorghum and cowpea flours are relevant as WBC will affect dough viscosity. A high level of cowpea flours in place of sorghum may contribute to improved dough stability during proofing and the early stages of baking, before starch gelatinization takes place, thus positively influencing bread volume.

During the baking stage with CRCs dough, fixation of the expanding foam structure is mainly related to the starch gelatinization process, due to the absence of the gluten thermo-setting mechanism. Starch gelatinization increases the viscosity and shear modulus of the batter dramatically and the swollen starch granules further support against normal forces in order to withstand collapse [45]. In bakery applications, such as cakes, where a gluten network is also absent, variations in the temperature at which starch gelatinization occurs largely determine the final volume [46]. Cowpea flours showed higher gelatinization temperatures than sorghum, which may have slightly prolonged the time available for further bubble expansion before structure setting. Additionally, the higher melting transition temperatures could also implicate a faster stabilisation of the starch paste during cooling. An optimum in viscosity is also likely to contribute to baking performance, with too high viscosity limiting expansion and too low resulting in collapse. As suggested by the RVA results, the paste viscosity was largely dominated by cassava starch. Raising the level of cowpea flour in place of sorghum or adding dry-heated cowpea flour most likely modulated paste viscosity, positively contributing to the increase in SV. Additionally, native and dry-heated cowpea flour have shown low paste breakdown due to the role of proteins around the starch granule acting as a physical barrier [31]. An increase in the amount of starch granules that maintain integrity and rigidity during baking can contribute to the continuity and strength of the starch phase upon cooling, thus resulting in improved springiness, cohesiveness and resilience [31].

3.3. Descriptive Sensory Profiling of Bread

Significant differences in appearance, odour and flavour attributes and in texture were observed among breads (Table 5). PCA analysis of the sensory profile also indicated that the first two principal components (i.e., PC_1 and PC_2) accounted for over 78% of the variance, thus providing a good representation of the differences among samples. Bread samples were differentiated in terms of texture (crumbliness, moistness) and yeasty flavour/fermented odour along the PC_1, mainly dominated by samples GL27 and GL9-DH. PC_2 was dominated by samples GL9 and BECH27, which were separated based on beany flavour, beany odour and darkness of the crumb (Figure 1A). The use of dry-heated cowpea (GL9-DH) resulted in a significant decrease in cereal odour and increased fermented odour compared to the other samples. Sample BENCH27 had the most intense beany odour and beany flavour while samples GL9 and GL9-DH, respectively, had the lowest ($p < 0.05$). Dry heating of cowpea provided bread GL9-DH with the most intense yeasty flavour. In a recent study, flatbreads made with the Bechuana variety of cowpea also showed a more intense beany odour and beany flavour compared to the Glenda variety [32]. Differences were attributed to the higher phenolic compounds in the more pigmented cowpea varieties [47,48]. Off-flavours are generated by the breakdown of polyunsaturated fatty acids by lipoxygenase to form secondary lipid oxidation products [49]. By binding to lipoxygenase present in the beans, phenolics limit the oxidation of unsaturated fatty acids during harvesting, thus controlling the beany aroma in legumes [50,51]. Flavour is one of the most important sensory attributes in terms of acceptability [52] and beany flavour considerably decreases the liking of bread enriched with legumes [53,54]. In this study, the addition of 27% cowpea flour enhanced the beany odour and flavour perception, particularly for BECH. The 9% addition of GL resulted in rather low scores for beany flavour (i.e., 2.17 on a 0-to-10-point scale), thus suggesting that such a level of inclusion may be suitable for bread applications. Thermal treatment has been reported to reduce beany flavour and increase yeasty flavour. Similar findings were recently reported for the thermal treatment of yellow pea [54]. However, thermal treatments can only partially attenuate the beany flavour [55]. The limited effects observed for sample GL9-DH may be explained by the low scores of beany flavour already attributed to sample GL9. The significant increase in yeasty and fermented flavour for sample GL9-DH may be a positive effect when associated with volatile compounds positively perceived by consumers [56] and should be further investigated in future studies.

Table 5. Sensory profile analysis of the different breads: mean scores and Tukey's post hoc groups.

Attribute	GL9	GL27	BECH27	GL9-DH	*p*-Values
Appearance					
Darkness	4.74 bc	6.28 a	3.41 c	4.94 ab	<0.001
Pore size	3.91	4.17	3.64	3.46	0.232
Odour					
Cereal odour	4.89 a	3.51 ab	4.20 ab	2.78 b	0.004
Sweet odour	2.52	2.24	2.84	3.70	0.056
Ryebread odour	3.79	3.86	2.92	3.3	0.452
Beany odour	1.67 b	3.06 ab	3.89 a	2.54 ab	0.009
Fermented odour	1.81 b	1.59 b	1.54 b	5.46 a	<0.001
Flavour/Taste					
Ryebread flavour	3.32 a	3.45 a	2.69 ab	1.91 b	0.007
Beany flavour	2.17 b	2.70 ab	4.08 a	1.94 b	0.004
Yeasty flavour	1.88 b	1.18 b	1.73 b	4.22 a	0.001
Spicy flavour	2.12	1.84	1.56	2.94	0.122
Sourness	3.94	3.95	3.06	4.03	0.265
Sweetness	1.96	2.16	2.54	2.82	0.353
Astringency	2.18	2.56	2.06	2.65	0.390
Texture					
Crumbliness tactile	6.17	5.55	5.79	5.84	0.774
Sandiness	3.64	3.06	3.01	3.26	0.642
Crumbliness mouthfeel	5.61 ab	4.56 b	5.13 ab	5.95 a	0.019
Moistness	2.99 ab	3.58 a	3.13 ab	2.55 b	0.049

Attribute intensities scored with a 0–10 continuous line scale with 0 = non-perceivable and 10 = very intense. Values with different letters within each row indicated significant differences in ANOVA post hoc analysis ($p < 0.05$). GL9 = Bread with 9% Glenda cowpea flour; GL27 = Bread with 27% Glenda cowpea flour; BECH27 = Bread with 27% Bechuana cowpea flour; GL9-DH = Bread with 9% dry-heated Glenda cowpea flour.

BECH27 had the lightest crumb and GL27 had the darkest. In a recent study on flatbreads from composite flours, breads prepared with the Glenda variety were also perceived as darker than those with the Bechuana variety. Differences were attributed to the higher concentration of anthocyanins in the seed coats of the red variety [57]. A dark colour may negatively affect the liking of bread appearance by consumers [53]. From that perspective, the BECH variety may be preferred over the GL one.

Crumbliness is an important quality aspect of bread. Crumbliness is defined as the degree to which a sample fractures into pieces during mastication [58]. In our study, sample GL9-DH showed the highest crumbliness and lowest moistness, while sample GL27 showed the lowest crumbliness and highest moistness perception ($p < 0.05$). Perception of crumbliness and moistness were significantly correlated ($R^2 = 0.95$, $p < 0.05$), with lower crumbliness scores observed with increasing moistness perception (Figure 1B). Crumbliness scores (i.e., both tactile and mouthfeel perception) were inversely related to instrumental cohesiveness and resilience (Figure 1B). However, the correlation was significant only between resilience and tactile crumbliness ($R^2 = 0.91$, $p < 0.05$). For wet soft-solids, such as protein/polysaccharide gels, crumbliness perception increases with increasing recoverable energy [59], with recoverable energy and cohesiveness both being measures of the recovery after deformation [60]. Crumbly gels also exhibit low serum/water release [59]. Whether these principles also apply to breadcrumbs remains to be proven. In commercial gluten-free bread, the perception of crumbliness was inversely related to instrumental springiness [61]. Dryness perception of commercial wheat pan bread was inversely related to both instrumental cohesiveness and springiness [62]. On the contrary, no meaningful relations were observed between bread texture and texture profile analysis in studies conducted on gluten-free bread [63] and cassava composite bread [64]. Overall, a comparison of sensory and instrumental analysis on crumb properties from this study indicates that positive changes in mechanical properties, such as increased softness and cohesiveness/resilience, may be associated with positive sensory perception, i.e., less crumbliness.

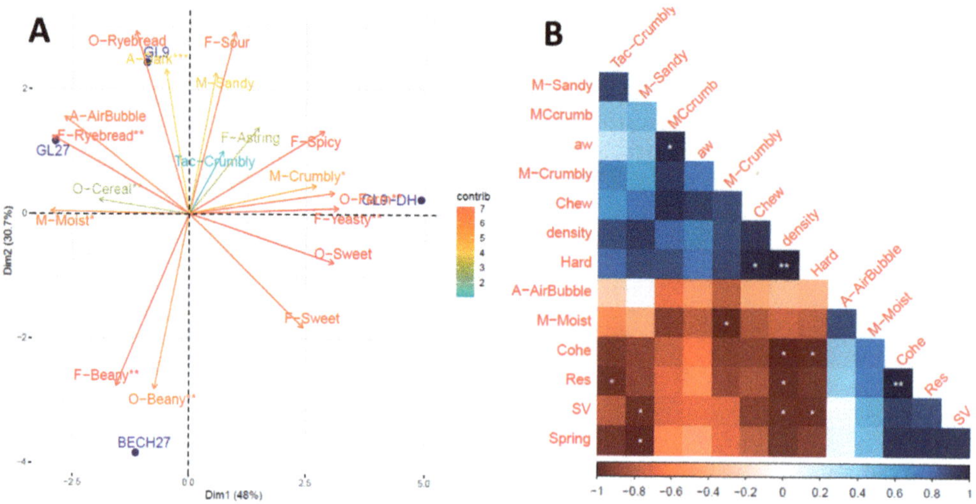

Figure 1. PCA biplot comparing the sensory attributes of the four CRCs based breads (**A**); correlation analysis between texture sensory attributes and instrumental properties of breads (**B**). Bread sample codes are explained in Table 1. Measured parameters: O-Cereal = cereal odour, O-sweet = sweet odour, O-Ryebread = rye bread odour, O-Beany = beany odour, O-Ferm = fermented odour, A-Dark = dark colour appearance, A-AirBubble = appearance air bubble size, Tac-Crumbly = crumbliness by hand (tactile), F-Sour = sourness, F-Ryebread = Rye bread flavour, F-Beany = beany flavour, F-Yeasty = yeasty flavour, F-Spicy = spicy flavour, F-sweetness = sweet taste, F-Astring = astringency, M-Sandy = sandy mouthfeel, M-Crumbly = crumbly mouthfeel, M-Moist = moistness in the mouth, SV = specific volume of bread, MCcrumb = % moisture content in the crumb, Chew = TPA chewiness, density = crumb density (g/mL), Hard = TPA hardness, Spring = TPA springiness, Cohe = TPA cohesiveness, Res = TPA resilience. For both PCA and correlation table: * $p < 0.05$, ** $p < 0.01$, *** $p < 0.001$.

Sandiness was perceived in all samples and changes in the composition of the flour blends and dry heating did not have significant effects. In preliminary trials, it was observed that both sorghum and cowpea flours contributed to sandiness. Pre-trials with sieving flours to below 200 μm or re-milling did not result in noticeable improvements (data not shown). For legumes, the hard-to-cook phenomenon is widely reported and attributed to structural and compositional changes induced by storage under hot and humid conditions, as encountered in many subtropical and tropical African countries [65]. Lignification of the cell wall contributes to increased cooking time [65] and could be one possible cause of sandiness perception in bread from this study, since the intact cowpea seeds were milled into flour. Additionally, an increase in starch crystallinity has been reported in beans during storage [66]. In cowpea flour, starch is tightly covered with protein material [67,68], which limits the water binding and swelling power of the starch [68]. From these data, it can be inferred that starch hydration during mixing and proofing may be a limiting factor during breadmaking, resulting in some crystalline starch material still being retained after baking. Sorghum starch can also contribute to this mechanism as starch granules are encapsulated by the hydrophobic kafirin [69], thus restricting the starch granules' ability to absorb water. During cooking, this protein barrier is further strengthened by the formation of protein aggregates capable of resisting the combined dissociating action of urea and reducing agents, which further limits starch accessibility [70].

3.4. Consumers Evaluation of CRCs-Based Bread and Commercial Wholemeal Wheat Bread

The overall liking and sensory perception of CRCs-based bread and commercial wholemeal wheat bread were compared in the consumers' test. The wholemeal wheat bread was chosen since the sorghum and cowpea flours were not refined. The CRCs-bread formulation for this study was formulation BENCH9 (Table 1); BECH was preferred to get a light crumb colour. The low quantity of cowpea flour was added to limit the beany odour and flavour. The CRCs bread received an average general liking of 5.0, indicating that the bread was neither liked nor disliked (Figure 2A). In particular, 47% of participants were in the group that liked the bread (scores 6–9), 12% did not like or disliked it (score = 5) and the remaining 41% did not like the bread (scores 1–4). The wheat bread received an average general liking of 6.84, meaning it was moderately liked. Differences in the overall liking of the two bread types were significant ($p < 0.05$).

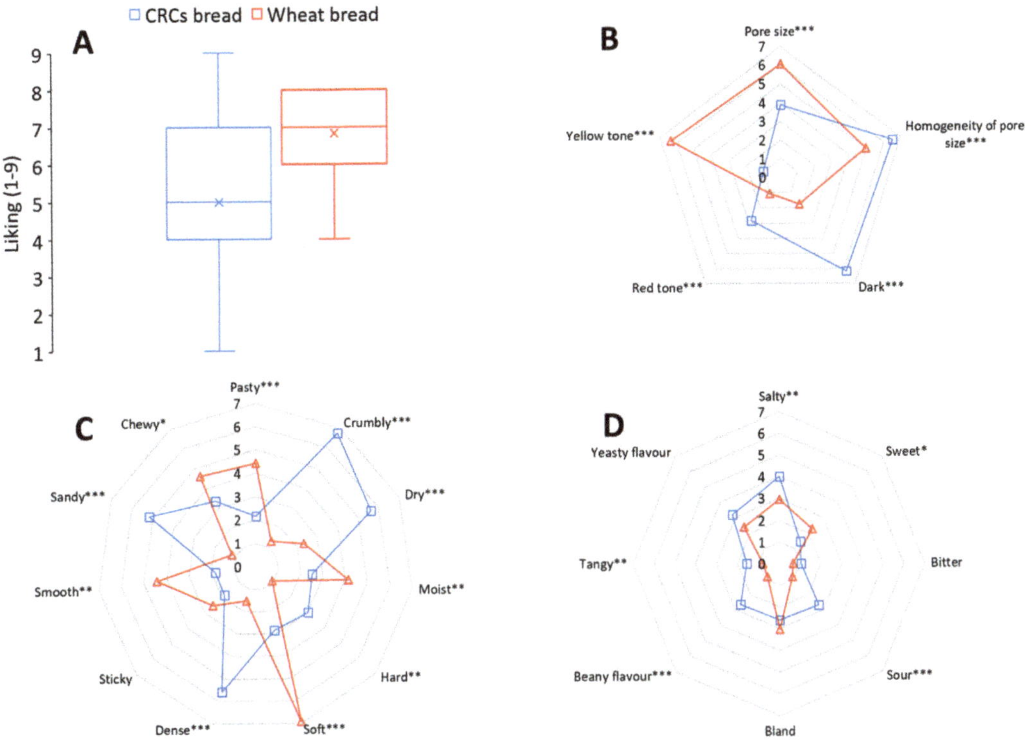

Figure 2. Overall acceptance of breads by consumers on a 1–9 scale (**A**) and comparison of the mean intensity scores for RATA test on a 0–9 point scale for attributes related to appearance (**B**), texture (**C**) and flavour (**D**). * $p < 0.05$, ** $p < 0.01$, *** $p < 0.001$.

With regards to the RATA tests, many significant differences were found for appearance, texture and taste attributes (Figure 2B–D). CRCs breadcrumbs were perceived as substantially darker and with a slightly more red tone compared to the predominant yellow tone and lighter appearance of the wheat bread. The CRCs bread had substantially smaller and more homogeneous pore size, providing a more dense appearance. The texture of CRCs breads was perceived by consumers as dry and crumbly compared to the wheat bread, which was soft, moist and chewy. Despite the fact that the wheat bread crumb was significantly softer, the hardness of the CRCs bread scored low in intensity. The CRCs bread was also perceived as sandy as compared to wheat bread, even though the latter contained bran particles. These results are in line with a recent evaluation of commercial gluten-free breads for which the texture sensations were described as hard, dry, crumbly and sandy [61]. Composite breads with sorghum were also reported to be sandy [71], which was attributed to the sorghum flour. Puerta and co-workers indicated that sandy and crumbly sensations in commercial gluten-free breads were correlated and could be both related to fragmentation of the bread crumb in the mouth as compared to wheat breads [61]. This mechanism may also contribute to the sandiness perception of the CRCs bread in this study. In our research, the sorghum and cowpea flours were eventually soaked in water for 1.5 h before use for breadmaking to minimize the perception of sandy-like particles. In preliminary evaluations, this approach seemed successful and substantially minimized sandiness perception.

The differences in flavour were related to salty, beany, tangy, sweet and sour attributes. However, the largest differences in intensity scores were limited to beany flavour and sour taste. Saltiness was more pronounced in the CRCs bread, likely due to a higher salt content than in commercial wheat bread. Even though differences in beany flavour were clearly perceived by consumers, this attribute received a low intensity score, suggesting that the chosen level of cowpea flour addition may also be suitable for white varieties such as Bechuana. The slight sourness and tanginess perceived in the CRCs bread may be considered a positive attribute, when not excessive, as they are naturally associated with sourdough breads [72].

3.5. Demonstration of Wheat Replacement in Real Life Conditions in SSA

One of the CRCs-based doughs in this study was evaluated for its implementation potential in SSA, as a means to reduce Africa's dependency on imported wheat and valorise traditional and underutilised CRCs. Chapati-type flatbreads, the most popular convenience foods produced by street vendors [11], and tin breads, a popular breakfast and lunch staple in combination with condiments [73], were explored as relevant applications currently based on refined wheat.

Chapati were tested with street vendors in the Kasanvu Slum of Kampala (Uganda), by preparing popular dishes such as *Kikomando* (chapati served with beans; Figure 3F) and *Rolex* (a chapati baked with eggs and rolled together with vegetables; Figure 4D). Due to increasing wheat and fuel prices, local vendors are currently reducing the sizes of the chapati to maintain affordable prices (communication from vendors, June 2022). The flour mixture GL9 (Table 1) without yeast was provided to the street vendors. All other ingredients and utensils were supplied by the vendor. The CRCs-based dough could be prepared manually in a bowl and shaped into small dough balls as usually performed by the vendors (Figure 3A,B). The dough balls were first flattened by hand and then with a small roller (Figure 3C). The CRCs-based chapati was baked on an open-fire heated pan with oil, rolled-up and cut into pieces to be served with beans as '*Kikomando*' (Figure 3D–F). The CRCs-based chapati was also heated together with eggs and then rolled with sliced tomatoes and served as a wrap named '*Rolex*' (Figure 4). Vendors could prepare the CRCs-based chapati quite efficiently, which is one of the most important requirements for their laborious business, with customers waiting for freshly produced food on the go. The chapati were highly rollable, which was an important quality parameter for the street vendors for their versatile use.

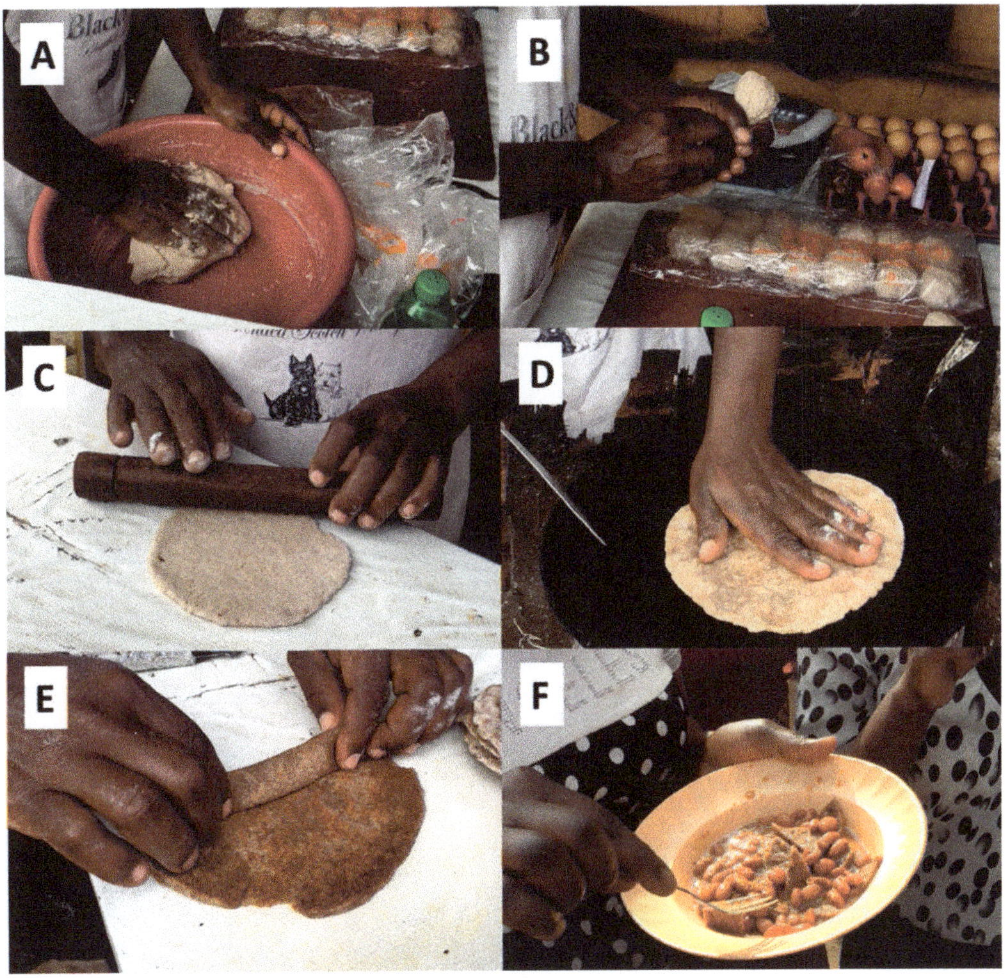

Figure 3. Main steps in the preparation of chapati by a street vendor using the CRCs-based dough GL9 (Table 1) without yeast. Dough mixing by hand in a plastic bowl (**A**), forming of dough balls by hand (**B**), sheeting with a roller (**C**), baking on a hot pan with additional oil (**D**), rolling the chapati before cutting (**E**) and serving Kikomando (chapati with beans) to the local consumers on the street (**F**).

Baking experiments for CRCs-based tin breads were also performed in Uganda in a BBROOD formal bakery in Tororo. The bakery produces and sells Western-type breads, including tin breads, which are becoming popular among the middle class in the evolving and rapidly growing urban market [11]. The dough mixing was performed with equipment available at the commercial bakery (Figure 5A). Tin breads were produced using the flour mixture GL9 (Table 1, Figure 5B). The baked breads were tasted at the BBROOD bakery shop in Muyanga (Kampala) by local customers. After tasting, about 20 people were informally asked for their feedback by the shop assistants. The customers' (consumers) responses to the bread samples were observed and noted. Most people had a neutral to positive perception of the bread (i.e., 15 out of 20). Five out of the twenty indicated that the bread was too salty. Sandiness was mentioned by only one of the consumers. Breads using sorghum, cassava and cowpea locally sourced were also successfully produced using a recipe similar to GL9 Figure 5B), suggesting the adaptability to a local situation.

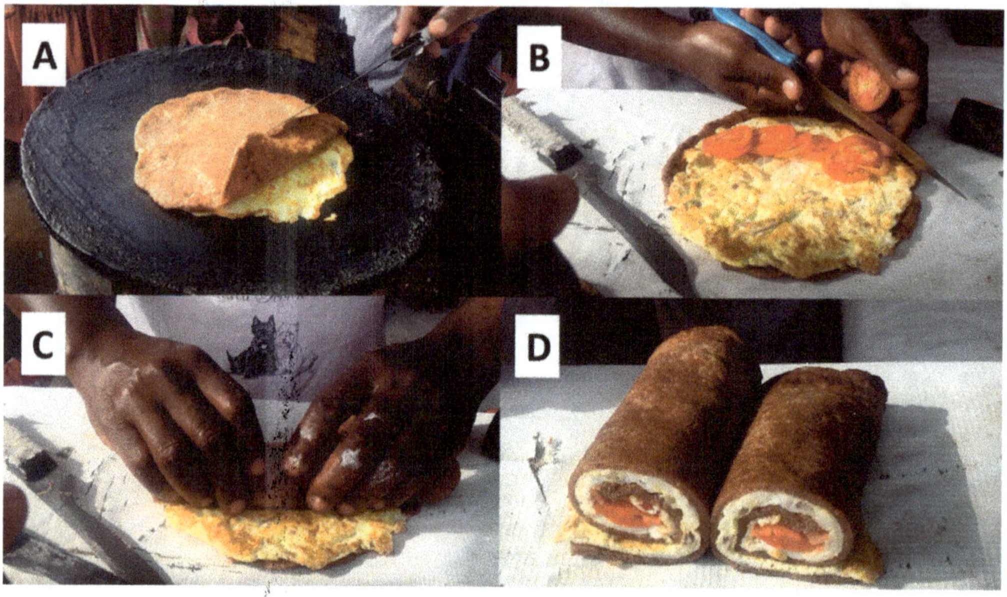

Figure 4. Preparation of a Rolex by the street vendor using the CRCs-based dough GL9 (Table 1) without yeast. After preparation and pre-baking as in Figure 3A–D, eggs are cooked on the hot plate and the chapati is added on top of the frying eggs (**A**). Once the eggs are cooked, the chapati is placed on a table and vegetables are added (**B**); the chapati is then rolled (**C**) and served to the local customers (**D**).

Figure 5. Bakers at BBROOD bakery in Tororo preparing the CRCs-based dough for tin bread baking (**A**); tin breads from the CRCs dough (formulation GL9 in Table 1) based on flours used in this study (**left**) and with flours locally sourced (**right**) (**B**).

To date, wheat replacement initiatives have not been very successful, as consumers in many SSA countries perceive composite breads as a lower quality product and therefore prefer bread made from 100% wheat flour [29,74]. On the contrary, innovations that create new markets are critical to promote the use of CRCs ingredients [75]. The bread-type products in this study could be proposed and further studied as new products, thus overcoming the major pitfall for composite wheat breads not meeting consumers expectations on shape and appearance [29].

4. Conclusions

Cowpea flour proved to be functional in modulating the baking properties of the CRCs breads. High cowpea to sorghum ratio improved specific volume and instrumental texture by enhancing softness and cohesiveness. Substantial differences in WBC and pasting properties of cowpea flour compared to sorghum flour and cassava starch could be related to these improvements. Among varieties, the red Glenda cowpea was the most functional in reducing perceived crumbliness and increasing perceived moistness, probably due to its high WBC. Additionally, the Glenda variety scored better with regards to taste, as beany flavour was most pronounced in breads with high inclusion levels of the Bechuana variety. Dry-heating of cowpea flour substantially affected its functionality, but had limited effects on bread texture. The most significant effects were observed for the perceived yeasty and fermented flavour of the bread. Sensory tests with naive consumers indicated that the CRCs bread was the most distinct from commercial wheat bread for its crumbly texture and for the beany, sour and yeasty taste. Despite that, the CRCs bread was neither liked nor disliked, while the commercial bread was only moderately liked. These blends of CRCs could be successfully used in Uganda to produce chapati and tin breads with street vendors and local bakeries, respectively. Overall, the result of this study showed that blends of African local crops can be used to fully replace wheat in bread-type products. The selection of the cowpea to sorghum ratio and cowpea variety are important for modulating their texture and taste. These results are relevant to alleviate African dependency on imported wheat, thus potentially contributing to food and nutrition security in SSA in the current conditions of climate change and geopolitical crisis.

Author Contributions: Conceptualisation, S.R.; methodology, S.R. and H.A.; formal analysis, S.R. and H.A.; writing—original draft preparation, S.R.; writing—review and editing, S.R., H.A., R.T.N., A.R.L. and M.W.N.; visualisation, S.R.; project administration, M.W.N.; funding acquisition, S.R. and M.W.N. All authors have read and agreed to the published version of the manuscript.

Funding: This work was partially funded by the LEAP-Agri project NUTRIFOODS "Innovative approaches to value-addition and commercialisation of climate-smart crops for enhanced food security and nutrition in Africa and beyond". This project has received funding from the European Union's Horizon 2020 research and innovation program under grant agreement No 727715. The project was funded in part by the Dutch Research Council NWO (W.09.03.110) under the LEAP Agri Joint Research Collaboration Program NUTRIFOODS project.

Data Availability Statement: Data available upon request to corresponding author.

Acknowledgments: The authors thank Jolanda Henket for assistance in the DSC analysis and Eric Raaijmakers for the RVA and WBC experiments, Frederique Catsman and Luuk Deckers for performing the baking experiments, Dick van der Breggen and Nicholas Kasoa from BBROOD and Lukas den Admirant from BISS bakeries for support with the tests in Uganda. The technical assistance of Mara Vlemmix in arranging the consumer test is gratefully acknowledged.

Conflicts of Interest: The authors declare no conflict of interest.

References

1. Ofori, S.A.; Cobbina, S.J.; Obiri, S. Climate Change, Land, Water, and Food Security: Perspectives From Sub-Saharan Africa. *Front. Sustain. Food Syst.* **2021**, *5*, 680924. [CrossRef]
2. Blekking, J.; Giroux, S.; Waldman, K.; Battersby, J.; Tuholske, C.; Robeson, S.M.; Siame, G. ScienceDirect the Impacts of Climate Change and Urbanization on Food Retailers in Urban Sub-Saharan Africa. *Curr. Opin. Environ. Sustain.* **2022**, *55*, 101169. [CrossRef]
3. Cairns, J.E.; Hellin, J.; Sonder, K.; Araus, J.L.; MacRobert, J.F.; Thierfelder, C.; Prasanna, B.M. Adapting Maize Production to Climate Change in Sub-Saharan Africa. *Food Secur.* **2013**, *5*, 345–360. [CrossRef]
4. Mason, N.M.; Jayne, T.S.; Shiferaw, B. Africa's Rising Demand for Wheat: Trends, Drivers, and Policy Implications. *Dev. Policy Rev.* **2015**, *33*, 581–613. [CrossRef]
5. Shew, A.M.; Tack, J.B.; Nalley, L.L.; Chaminuka, P. Yield Reduction under Climate Warming Varies among Wheat Cultivars in South Africa. *Nat Commun* **2020**, *11*, 4408. [CrossRef]

6. Acevedo, M.; Pixley, K.; Zinyengere, N.; Meng, S.; Tufan, H.; Cichy, K.; Bizikova, L.; Isaacs, K.; Ghezzi-Kopel, K.; Porciello, J. A Scoping Review of Adoption of Climate-Resilient Crops by Small-Scale Producers in Low- and Middle-Income Countries. *Nat. Plants* **2020**, *6*, 1231–1241. [CrossRef]
7. Dhankher, O.P.; Foyer, C.H. Climate Resilient Crops for Improving Global Food Security and Safety. *Plant Cell Environ.* **2018**, *41*, 877–884. [CrossRef]
8. Ndiaye, M.; Termorshuizen, A.J.; van Bruggen, A.H.C. Effect of Rotation of Cowpea (Vigna Unguiculata) with Fonio (Digitaria Exilis) and Millet (Pennisetum Glaucum) on Macrophomina Phaseolina Densities and Cowpea Yield. *Afr. J. Agric. Res.* **2008**, *3*, 37–43.
9. Chimonyo, V.G.P.; Modi, A.T.; Mabhaudhi, T. Water Use and Productivity of a Sorghum-Cowpea-Bottle Gourd Intercrop System. *Agric. Water Manag.* **2016**, *165*, 82–96. [CrossRef]
10. Raheem, D.; Dayoub, M.; Birech, R.; Nakiyemba, A. The Contribution of Cereal Grains to Food Security and Sustainability in Africa: Potential Application of UAV in Ghana, Nigeria, Uganda, and Namibia. *Urban Sci.* **2021**, *5*, 8. [CrossRef]
11. Noort, M.W.J.; Renzetti, S.; Linderhof, V.; du Rand, G.E.; Marx-Pienaar, N.J.M.M.; de Kock, H.L.; Magano, N.; Taylor, J.R.N. Towards Sustainable Shifts to Healthy Diets and Food Security in Sub-Saharan Africa with Climate-Resilient Crops in Bread-Type Products: A Food System Analysis. *Foods* **2022**, *11*, 135. [CrossRef]
12. Gaffney, J.; Bing, J.; Byrne, P.F.; Cassman, K.G.; Ciampitti, I.; Delmer, D.; Habben, J.; Lafitte, H.R.; Lidstrom, U.E.; Porter, D.O.; et al. Science-Based Intensive Agriculture: Sustainability, Food Security, and the Role of Technology. *Glob. Food Sec.* **2019**, *23*, 236–244. [CrossRef]
13. Schönfeldt, H.C.; Hall, N.G. Dietary Protein Quality and Malnutrition in Africa. *Br. J. Nutr.* **2012**, *108*, S69–S76. [CrossRef] [PubMed]
14. Pontieri, P.; Mamone, G.; de Caro, S.; Tuinstra, M.R.; Roemer, E.; Okot, J.; de Vita, P.; Ficco, D.B.M.; Alifano, P.; Pignone, D.; et al. Sorghum, a Healthy and Gluten-Free Food for Celiac Patients as Demonstrated by Genome, Biochemical, and Immunochemical Analyses. *J. Agric. Food Chem.* **2013**, *61*, 2565–2571. [CrossRef] [PubMed]
15. Amoako, D.; Awika, J.M. Polyphenol Interaction with Food Carbohydrates and Consequences on Availability of Dietary Glucose. *Curr. Opin. Food Sci.* **2016**, *8*, 14–18. [CrossRef]
16. Kan, L.; Capuano, E.; Oliviero, T.; Renzetti, S. Wheat Starch-Tannic Acid Complexes Modulate Physicochemical and Rheological Properties of Wheat Starch and Its Digestibility. *Food Hydrocoll.* **2022**, *126*, 107459. [CrossRef]
17. Zhang, G.; Hamaker, B.R. Slowly Digestible Starch: Concept, Mechanism, and Proposed Extended Glycemic Index. *Crit. Rev. Food Sci. Nutr.* **2009**, *49*, 852–867. [CrossRef]
18. Hargrove, J.L.; Greenspan, P.; Hartle, D.K.; Dowd, C. Inhibition of Aromatase and A-Amylase by Flavonoids and Proanthocyanidins from Sorghum Bicolor Bran Extracts. *J. Med. Food* **2011**, *14*, 799–807. [CrossRef]
19. Moraes, É.A.; Isabel, D.; Natal, G.; Aparecida, V.; Queiroz, V.; Eugene, R.; Roberto, P.; Oliveira, S.; Paula, D.; Benjamim, A.; et al. Sorghum Genotype May Reduce Low-Grade Inflammatory Response and Oxidative Stress and Maintains Jejunum Morphology of Rats Fed a Hyperlipidic Diet. *Food Res. Int.* **2012**, *49*, 553–559. [CrossRef]
20. Awika, J.M.; Duodu, K.G. Bioactive Polyphenols and Peptides in Cowpea (Vigna Unguiculata) and Their Health Promoting Properties: A Review. *J. Funct. Foods* **2017**, *38*, 686–697. [CrossRef]
21. Jayathilake, C.; Visvanathan, R.; Deen, A.; Bangamuwage, R.; Jayawardana, B.C.; Nammi, S.; Liyanage, R. Cowpea: An Overview on Its Nutritional Facts and Health Benefits. *J. Sci. Food Agric.* **2018**, *98*, 4793–4806. [CrossRef] [PubMed]
22. Prinyawiwatkul, W.; McWatters, K.H.; Beuchat, L.R.; Phillips, R.D. Cowpea Flour: A Potential Ingredient in Food Products. *Crit. Rev. Food Sci. Nutr.* **1996**, *36*, 413–436. [CrossRef]
23. Rumler, R.; Schönlechner, R. Effect of Sorghum on Rheology and Final Quality of Western Style Breads: A Literature Review. *Foods* **2021**, *10*, 1392. [CrossRef] [PubMed]
24. Sibanda, T.; Ncube, T.; Ngoromani, N. Rheological Properties and Bread Making Quality of White Grain Sorghum-Wheat Flour Composites. *Int. J. Food Sci. Nutr. Eng.* **2015**, *2015*, 176–182. [CrossRef]
25. Keregero, M.M.; Mtebe, K. Acceptability of Wheat-Sorghum Composite Flour Products: An Assessment. *Plant Foods Hum. Nutr.* **1994**, *46*, 305–312. [CrossRef]
26. Ari Akin, P.; Demirkesen, I.; Bean, S.R.; Aramouni, F. Sorghum Flour Application in Bread: Technological Challenges and Opportunities. *Foods* **2022**, *11*, 2466. [CrossRef]
27. Onyango, C.; Mutungi, C.; Unbehend, G.; Lindhauer, M.G. Modification of Gluten-Free Sorghum Batter and Bread Using Maize, Potato, Cassava or Rice Starch. *LWT* **2011**, *44*, 681–686. [CrossRef]
28. Schober, T.J.; Messerschmidt, M.; Bean, S.R.; Park, S.H.; Arendt, E.K. Gluten-Free Bread from Sorghum: Quality Differences among Hybrids. *Cereal Chem.* **2005**, *82*, 394–404. [CrossRef]
29. Abass, A.B.; Awoyale, W.; Alenkhe, B.; Malu, N.; Asiru, B.W.; Manyong, V.; Sanginga, N. Can Food Technology Innovation Change the Status of a Food Security Crop? A Review of Cassava Transformation into "Bread" in Africa. *Food Rev. Int.* **2018**, *34*, 87–102. [CrossRef]
30. Marchini, M.; Marti, A.; Tuccio, M.G.; Bocchi, E.; Carini, E. Technological Functionality of Composite Flours from Sorghum, Tapioca and Cowpea. *Int J. Food Sci. Technol.* **2022**, *57*, 4736–4743. [CrossRef]
31. Renzetti, S.; Heetesonne, I.; Ngadze, R.T.; Linnemann, A.R. Dry Heating of Cowpea Flour below Biopolymer Melting Temperatures Improves the Physical Properties of Bread Made from Climate-Resilient Crops. *Foods* **2022**, *11*, 1554. [CrossRef]

32. Dankwa, R.; Aisala, H.; Kayitesi, E.; de Kock, H.L. The Sensory Profiles of Flatbreads Made from Sorghum, Cassava, and Cowpea Flour Used as Wheat Flour Alternatives. *Foods* **2021**, *10*, 3095. [CrossRef]
33. Henshaw, F.O.; McWatters, K.H.; Akingbala, J.O.; Hung, Y.C. Functional Characterization of Flour of Selected Cowpea (Vigna Unguiculata) Varieties: Canonical Discriminant Analysis. *Food Chem.* **2002**, *79*, 381–386. [CrossRef]
34. Zanoletti, M.; Marti, A.; Marengo, M.; Iametti, S.; Pagani, M.A.; Renzetti, S. Understanding the Influence of Buckwheat Bran on Wheat Dough Baking Performance: Mechanistic Insights from Molecular and Material Science Approaches. *Food Res. Int.* **2017**, *102*, 728–737. [CrossRef]
35. Renzetti, S.; Theunissen, M.; Horrevorts, K. A Systematic Comparison of the Intrinsic Properties of Wheat and Oat Bran Fractions and Their Effects on Dough and Bread Properties: Elucidation of Chemical Mechanisms, Water Binding, and Steric Hindrance. *Foods* **2021**, *10*, 2311. [CrossRef] [PubMed]
36. Akin, A.P.; Miller, R.; Jaffe, T.; Koppel, K.; Ehmke, L. Sensory Profile and Quality of Chemically Leavened Gluten-Free Sorghum Bread Containing Different Starches and Hydrocolloids. *J. Sci. Food Agric.* **2019**, *99*, 4391–4396. [CrossRef]
37. Kwak, H.S.; Kim, M.J.; Kim, S.S. Sensory Profile, Consumer Acceptance, and Physicochemical Properties of Pan Bread Made with Imported or Domestic Commercial Wheat Flour. *J. Sens. Stud.* **2019**, *34*, e12487. [CrossRef]
38. Meyners, M.; Jaeger, S.R.; Ares, G. On the Analysis of Rate-All-That-Apply (RATA) Data. *Food Qual. Prefer.* **2016**, *49*, 1–10. [CrossRef]
39. Oppermann, A.K.L.; de Graaf, C.; Scholten, E.; Stieger, M.; Piqueras-Fiszman, B. Comparison of Rate-All-That-Apply (RATA) and Descriptive Sensory Analysis (DA) of Model Double Emulsions with Subtle Perceptual Differences. *Food Qual. Prefer.* **2017**, *56*, 55–68. [CrossRef]
40. Husson, A.F.; Josse, J.; Le, S.; Mazet, J.; Husson, M.F. Package 'FactoMineR'. 2022, pp. 1–106. Available online: https://cran.r-project.org/web/packages/FactoMineR/FactoMineR.pdf (accessed on 14 December 2022).
41. Phillips, R.D.; Chinnan, M.S.; Branch, A.L.; Miller, J.; McWatters, K.H. Effects of Pretreatment Properties on Functional and Nutritional of Cowpea Meal. *J. Food Sci.* **1988**, *53*, 805–809. [CrossRef]
42. Chisenga, S.M.; Workneh, T.S.; Bultosa, G.; Alimi, B.A. Progress in Research and Applications of Cassava Flour and Starch: A Review. *J. Food Sci. Technol.* **2019**, *56*, 2799–2813. [CrossRef] [PubMed]
43. Zhu, F. Structure, Physicochemical Properties, Modifications, and Uses of Sorghum Starch. *Compr. Rev. Food Sci. Food Saf.* **2014**, *13*, 597–610. [CrossRef]
44. Mizukoshi, M. Model Studies of Cake Baking-Cake Shrinkage and Shear Modulus of Cake Batter During Baking. *Cereal Chem.* **1985**, *62*, 242–246.
45. Roman, L.; Gomez, M.; Martinez, M.M. Mesoscale Structuring of Gluten-Free Bread with Starch. *Curr. Opin. Food Sci.* **2021**, *38*, 189–195. [CrossRef]
46. Renzetti, S.; van der Sman, R.G.M. Food Texture Design in Sugar Reduced Cakes: Predicting Batters Rheology and Physical Properties of Cakes from Physicochemical Principles. *Food Hydrocoll.* **2022**, *131*, 107795. [CrossRef]
47. Zia-Ul-Haq, M.; Ahmad, S.; Amarowicz, R.; De Feo, V. Antioxidant Activity of the Extracts of Some Cowpea (*Vigna unguiculata* (L.) Walp.) Cultivars Commonly Consumed in Pakistan. *Molecules* **2013**, *18*, 2005–2017. [CrossRef] [PubMed]
48. Adjei-Fremah, S.; Jackai, L.E.; Worku, M. Analysis of Phenolic Content and Antioxidant Properties of Selected Cowpea Varieties Tested in Bovine Peripheral Blood. *Am. J. Anim. Vet. Sci.* **2015**, *10*, 235–245. [CrossRef]
49. Roland, W.S.U.; Pouvreau, L.; Curran, J.; Van De Velde, F.; De Kok, P.M.T. Flavor Aspects of Pulse Ingredients. *Cereal Chem.* **2017**, *94*, 58–65. [CrossRef]
50. Khrisanapant, P.; Kebede, B.; Leong, S.Y.; Oey, I. A Comprehensive Characterisation of Volatile and Fatty Acid Profiles of Legume Seeds. *Foods* **2019**, *8*, 651. [CrossRef]
51. Karolkowski, A.; Guichard, E.; Briand, L.; Salles, C. Volatile Compounds in Pulses: A Review. *Foods* **2021**, *10*, 3140. [CrossRef]
52. Verbeke, W. Functional Foods: Consumer Willingness to Compromise on Taste for Health? *Food Qual. Prefer.* **2006**, *17*, 126–131. [CrossRef]
53. Ivanovski, B.; Seetharaman, K.; Duizer, L.M. Development of Soy-Based Bread with Acceptable Sensory Properties. *J. Food Sci.* **2012**, *77*, 71–76. [CrossRef]
54. Fahmi, R.; Ryland, D.; Sopiwnyk, E.; Aliani, M. Sensory and Physical Characteristics of Pan Bread Fortified with Thermally Treated Split Yellow Pea (*Pisum sativum* L.) Flour. *J. Food Sci.* **2019**, *84*, 3735–3745. [CrossRef] [PubMed]
55. Kotsiou, K.; Sacharidis, D.D.; Matsakidou, A.; Biliaderis, C.G.; Lazaridou, A. Impact of Roasted Yellow Split Pea Flour on Dough Rheology and Quality of Fortified Wheat Breads. *Foods* **2021**, *10*, 1832. [CrossRef]
56. Pico, J.; Bernal, J.; Gómez, M. Wheat Bread Aroma Compounds in Crumb and Crust: A Review. *Food Res. Int.* **2015**, *75*, 200–215. [CrossRef]
57. Singh, B.; Pal, J.; Kaur, A.; Singh, N. Phenolic Composition and Antioxidant Potential of Grain Legume Seeds: A Review. *Food Res. Int.* **2017**, *101*, 1–16. [CrossRef]
58. Pascua, Y.; Koç, H.; Foegeding, E.A. Food Structure: Roles of Mechanical Properties and Oral Processing in Determining Sensory Texture of Soft Materials. *Curr. Opin. Colloid Interface Sci.* **2013**, *18*, 324–333. [CrossRef]
59. van den Berg, L.; Carolas, A.L.; van Vliet, T.; van der Linden, E.; van Boekel, M.A.J.S.; van de Velde, F. Energy Storage Controls Crumbly Perception in Whey Proteins/Polysaccharide Mixed Gels. *Food Hydrocoll.* **2008**, *22*, 1404–1417. [CrossRef]

60. Nishinari, K.; Fang, Y.; Rosenthal, A. Human Oral Processing and Texture Profile Analysis Parameters: Bridging the Gap between the Sensory Evaluation and the Instrumental Measurements. *J. Texture Stud.* **2019**, *50*, 369–380. [CrossRef]
61. Puerta, P.; Laguna, L.; Villegas, B.; Rizo, A.; Fiszman, S.; Tarrega, A. Oral Processing and Dynamics of Texture Perception in Commercial Gluten-Free Breads. *Food Res. Int.* **2020**, *134*, 109233. [CrossRef] [PubMed]
62. Gambaro, A.; Varela, P.; Gimenez, A.; Aldrovandi, A.; Fiszman, S.M.; Hough, G. Textural Quality of White Pan Bread by Sensory and Instrumental Measurements. *J. Texture Stud.* **2002**, *33*, 401–413. [CrossRef]
63. Matos, M.E.; Rosell, C.M. Relationship between Instrumental Parameters and Sensory Characteristics in Gluten-Free Breads. *Eur. Food Res. Technol.* **2012**, *235*, 107–117. [CrossRef]
64. Jensen, S.; Skibsted, L.H.; Kidmose, U.; Thybo, A.K. Addition of cassava flours in bread-making: Sensory and textural evaluation. *LWT—Food Sci. Technol.* **2015**, *60*, 292–299. [CrossRef]
65. Mubaiwa, J.; Fogliano, V.; Chidewe, C.; Linnemann, A.R. Hard-to-Cook Phenomenon in Bambara Groundnut (*Vigna subterranea* (L.) Verdc.) Processing: Options to Improve Its Role in Providing Food Security. *Food Rev. Int.* **2017**, *33*, 167–194. [CrossRef]
66. Garcia, E.; Lajolo, F.M. Starch Alterations in Hard-To-Cook Beans (Phaseolus Vulgaris). *J. Agric. Food Chem.* **1994**, *42*, 612–615. [CrossRef]
67. Błaszczak, W.; Doblado, R.; Frias, J.; Vidal-Valverde, C.; Sadowska, J.; Fornal, J. Microstructural and Biochemical Changes in Raw and Germinated Cowpea Seeds upon High-Pressure Treatment. *Food Res. Int.* **2007**, *40*, 415–423. [CrossRef]
68. Adjei-Fremah, S.; Worku, M.; De Erive, M.O.; He, F.; Wang, T.; Chen, G. Effect of Microfluidization on Microstructure, Protein Profile and Physicochemical Properties of Whole Cowpea Flours. *Innov. Food Sci. Emerg. Technol.* **2019**, *57*, 102207. [CrossRef]
69. Duodu, K.G.; Nunes, A.; Delgadillo, I.; Parker, M.L.; Mills, E.N.C.; Belton, P.S.; Taylor, J.R.N. Effect of Grain Structure and Cooking on Sorghum and Maize in Vitro Protein Digestibility. *J. Cereal Sci.* **2002**, *35*, 161–174. [CrossRef]
70. Elkhalifa, A.E.O.; Bernhardt, R.; Bonomi, F.; Iametti, S.; Pagani, M.A.; Zardi, M. Fermentation Modifies Protein/Protein and Protein/Starch Interactions in Sorghum Dough. *Eur. Food Res. Technol.* **2006**, *222*, 559–564. [CrossRef]
71. Carson, L.; Setser, C.; Sun, X.S. Sensory Characteristics of Sorghum Composite Bread. *Int. J. Food Sci. Technol.* **2000**, *35*, 465–471. [CrossRef]
72. Lotong, V.; Chambers IV, E.; Chambers, D.H. Determination of the Sensory Attributes of Wheat Sourdough Bread. *J. Sens. Stud.* **2000**, *15*, 309–326. [CrossRef]
73. Viljoen, A.T.; Botha, P.; Boonzaaier, C.C. Factors Contributing to Changes in Food Practices of a Black South African Community. *J. Fam. Ecol. Consum. Sci.* **2005**, *33*, 46–62. [CrossRef]
74. Adikwu, O.; Ayoola, J.B.; Akerele, D. Factors Influencing the Use of High Quality Flour among Master Bakers in Makurdi Local Government Area, Benu State Nigeria. *FUW Trends Sci. Technol. J.* **2017**, *2*, 409–414.
75. Pereira, L.M. Cassava Bread in Nigeria: The Potential of 'Orphan Crop' Innovation for Building More Resilient Food Systems. *Int. J. Technol. Glob.* **2017**, *8*, 97–115. [CrossRef]

foods

MDPI

Article

Chemical Composition and Antioxidant Profile of Sorghum (*Sorghum bicolor* (L.) Moench) and Pearl Millet (*Pennisetum glaucum* (L.) R.Br.) Grains Cultivated in the Far-North Region of Cameroon

Saliou Mawouma [1], Nina Nicoleta Condurache [2], Mihaela Turturică [2], Oana Emilia Constantin [2], Constantin Croitoru [3] and Gabriela Rapeanu [2,*]

1 Department of Biological Sciences, Faculty of Science, University of Maroua, Maroua P.O. Box 814, Cameroon; mawouma2001@yahoo.fr
2 Faculty of Food Science and Engineering, Dunarea de Jos University of Galati, Domnească Street 111, 800201 Galati, Romania; nina.condurache@ugal.ro (N.N.C.); mihaela.turturica@ugal.ro (M.T.); oana.constantin@ugal.ro (O.E.C.)
3 Academy of Agricultural and Forestry Sciences, 61 Marasti Blvd., 011464 Bucharest, Romania; c.croitoru@sodinal.com
* Correspondence: gabriela.rapeanu@ugal.ro

Abstract: Sorghum and pearl millet are grain crops that can grow in semi-arid climates, with nutritional and bioactive properties superior to those of major cereals such as rice, wheat, and maize. However, these properties vary a lot, depending on the genetic factors, growing conditions, and place of cultivation. Four sorghum and two pearl millet grains cultivars grown in the Far-North region of Cameroon were screened for their chemical composition and antioxidant profile. The proximate and mineral analyses were performed using AOAC standard methods. The antioxidant profile was assayed spectrophotometrically and details on the phenolic compounds were investigated using HPLC. The pearl millet cultivars, especially *mouri*, showed higher contents of proteins, lipids, ash, calcium, copper, iron, and zinc. The *red* sorghum specifically exhibited the greatest amounts of total polyphenols (82.22 mg GAE/g DE), total flavonoids (23.82 mg CE/g DE), and total 3-deoxyanthocyanidin (9.06 mg/g DE). The most abundant phenolic compound was gallic acid, while the most frequent were chlorogenic and ferulic acids. The maximum antioxidant activity against DPPH was observed in *yellow-pale* sorghum (87.71%), followed by *red* sorghum (81.15%). Among the studied varieties of cereals, *mouri* pearl millet and *red* sorghum were the best sources of nutrients and bioactive compounds, respectively. Their consumption should be encouraged to tackle nutrient deficiencies and non-communicable diseases within local populations.

Keywords: sorghum; pearl millet; chemical composition; antioxidant activity; Far-North Cameroon

Citation: Mawouma, S.; Condurache, N.N.; Turturică, M.; Constantin, O.E.; Croitoru, C.; Rapeanu, G. Chemical Composition and Antioxidant Profile of Sorghum (*Sorghum bicolor* (L.) Moench) and Pearl Millet (*Pennisetum glaucum* (L.) R.Br.) Grains Cultivated in the Far-North Region of Cameroon. *Foods* **2022**, *11*, 2026. https://doi.org/10.3390/foods11142026

Academic Editors: Laura Gazza and Francesca Nocente

Received: 15 June 2022
Accepted: 6 July 2022
Published: 8 July 2022

Publisher's Note: MDPI stays neutral with regard to jurisdictional claims in published maps and institutional affiliations.

1. Introduction

Sorghum (*Sorghum bicolor* (L.) Moench) and pearl millet (*Pennisetum glaucum* (L.) R. Br.) are cereal crops belonging to the Poaceae family, which are native to Africa and were domesticated between 3000 and 5000 years ago [1]. After wheat, rice, maize, and barley, sorghum and pearl millet are the most widely produced grains on the planet [2,3]. Sorghum and pearl millet can endure a variety of environmental conditions, including low soil fertility, high temperatures, and insufficient rainfall. Sorghum and pearl millet are cultivated particularly in the semi-arid parts of Africa and Asia, where they are predominantly used for human consumption and are staple foods for the local populations [4–6]. In the Far-North region of Cameroon, as in other Sahelian parts of Africa, sorghum and pearl millet, which are consumed as gruel, rolled balls, partially cooked grains, and fermented beverages, are less expensive sources of nutrients for low-income individuals. They are nutritionally superior to the major cereals in protein, energy, vitamins, and minerals [7]. Additionally, sorghum and pearl millet are excellent sources of bioactive chemicals that help to improve non-communicable disease characteristics, such as obesity, diabetes, cardiovascular diseases, and cancer [8–10].

The pericarp of sorghum contains significant amounts of non-starch polysaccharides; phenolic chemicals such as 3-deoxyanthocyanidins, tannins, and phenolic acids; and carotenoids. The germ is composed of lipids, fat-soluble vitamins, B-complex vitamins, and minerals, whereas the endosperm is rich in carbohydrates, proteins, B-complex vitamins, and minerals [1].

Proteins, carbohydrates, dietary fiber, and minerals are all present in finger millet. Among all cereals, it contains the most calcium (344 mg/100 g). However, phytates, polyphenols, tannins, trypsin inhibitory substances, and dietary fiber are also present in millet. Phytochemicals such as dietary fiber and polyphenols are abundant in the millet seed coating, which is an edible part of the kernel [2].

The richness in dietary fibers, absence of gluten, and interesting protein and fat profiles are other properties that make these cereals very balanced food options that may help in the management of many disorders [11]. On the other hand, sorghum and pearl millet grains have a more variable nutritional and functional potential than major cereal grains [12]. Genetic factors, the growth environment, and the cultivation location all influence these variations [13]. Sorghum varieties that were resistant to biotic and abiotic stressors, for example, had higher levels of proanthocyanidins, 3-deoxyanthocyanidins, and flavan-4-ols on average than sensitive varieties [14].

An abundance of scientific studies report on the nutritional and bioactive properties of minor cereals. However, these studies generally concentrate on cultivars originating from America, Asia, and Europe, but very few African countries [15–17]. To the best of our knowledge, a comprehensive and comparative investigation of the chemical compositions of sorghum and pearl millet cultivars grown in Cameroon has not been reported. However, the characterization of local sorghum cultivars is an important step for breeding programs, nutrition policies, and the food and nutraceutical industries.

The goal of this research was to assess the nutritional and bioactive profiles of sorghum and pearl millet grain varieties that are regularly produced and consumed by locals. Moreover, the renewed interest in using sorghum and pearl millet to make value-added products for human nutrition and the lack of data on the chemical makeup of cultivars found in Cameroon's Far-North region sustained this research.

2. Materials and Methods

2.1. Chemicals

Hexane, acetone, ethanol, methanol, HPLC-grade methanol, sodium carbonate, 2,20-azino-bis (3-ethylbenzothiazoline-6-sulfonic acid) diammonium salt (ABTS), 2,2-diphenyl1-picrylhydrazyl (DPPH), Folin–Ciocalteu reagent, gallic acid solution, hydrochloric acid, sodium nitrite, aluminum chloride, sodium hydroxide, iron (III) chloride, sulfosalicylic acid, phytic acid and potassium persulfate were purchased from Sigma Aldrich (Schnelldorf, Germany). The phenolic acid (gallic acid, vanillic acid, chlorogenic acid, caffeic acid, ferulic acid) and flavonoid (catechin, epicatechin, quercetin, and kaempferol) standards were purchased from Sigma Aldrich (Schnelldorf, Germany).

2.2. Samples Preparation

Sorghum (*white, yellow-pale, yellow,* and *red*) and pearl millet (*mouri*) grains were purchased from a local market in Maroua, the principal city of the Far-North region of Cameroon. The *gawane* cultivar of pearl millet was generously supplied by the Agricultural Research Institute of Development (IRAD)'s regional branch. The grains were cleaned and sorted to remove all dirt. After sun-drying, the grains were packed in polypropylene bags and stored at room temperature.

The grains were ground in a domestic grinder (Bosch TSM6A014R, 180 W) for 30 s, and the resulting flours (particle size 250 μm) were stored at −20 °C before analyses.

2.3. *Characterization of Sorghum and Pearl Millet Flours*

2.3.1. Proximate Analysis

The moisture, lipid, protein, crude fiber, and ash contents of the flours were determined according to AOAC standard methods [11]. The carbohydrate content was determined by the difference between 100 and the total percentages of proteins, lipids, crude fibers, and ash [18].

2.3.2. Determination of Mineral Content

The mineral contents of flours were determined using an atomic absorption spectrophotometer (3400 AAS Agilent Technologies). In brief, each flour sample (about 1 g) was burnt in a calcining furnace at 500 °C. Then, the ash was dissolved in 2.5 mL nitric acid (1 N) and filtrated. The filtrate was diluted using ultrapure water before analysis.

2.3.3. Determination of Phytochemical Profile of Flours

The ultrasound-assisted extraction was performed by mixing 1 g of flour with 9 mL of 70% methanol (v/v) prepared with pure methanol and distilled water. The samples were vortexed for 5 min and then treated in an ultrasonic water bath (MRC Scientific Instruments) at 40 kHz and 30–35 °C for 30 min. Afterward, the samples were centrifuged (6000 rpm at 10 °C) for 10 min (Universal 320R Hettich Zentrifugen), followed by concentration to dryness of the supernatants with an AVC 2–18 concentrator (Christ, UK). All dried extracts were redissolved in 70% methanol (v/v) to reach a 10 mg/mL concentration for further analyses.

Total polyphenol content (TPC): The sorghum and millet flour TPC values were spectrophotometrically measured using the Folin–Ciocalteu method [19,20]. Briefly, 200 μL of the extract was mixed thoroughly with 15.8 mL of distilled water and 1 mL of Folin–Ciocalteau reagent. After 10 min, 3 mL of Na_2CO_3 20% was added to the mixture. The resultant mixture was stored at room temperature in the dark for 60 min before being measured with a Biochrom Libra S22 spectrophotometer at 765 nm. The results were expressed as milligrams of gallic acid equivalents per gram of dry flour (mg GAE/g DW) using a calibration curve (0.1–0.5 mg/mL, $R^2 = 0.984$).

Total flavonoid content (TFC): The aluminum chloride spectrophotometric method was used to determine the TFC values of sorghum and pearl millet flours [21]. Briefly, 0.25 mL of the extract was mixed with 2 mL of distilled water and 0.075 mL of 5% sodium nitrite ($NaNO_2$). After 5 min, 0.15 mL of aluminum chloride ($AlCl_3$) was added to the mixture. Six minutes later, 0.5 mL of sodium hydroxide (NaOH) 1 M was added to the mixture before being measured with a Biochrom Libra S22 spectrophotometer at 510 nm. The results were reported as milligrams of catechin equivalents per gram of dry flour (mg CE/g DW) using a calibration curve (0.1–0.5 mg/mL, $R^2 = 0.997$).

Total 3-deoxyanthocyanidin content (TDC): The absorbance values of redissolved extracts were directly read at 480 nm, and the TDC was expressed as milligrams of 3-deoxyanthocyanidin per gram of flour (mg/g DW) using the molar extinction coefficient of luteolinidin, which is 13,800 M^{-1} cm^{-1} [22].

Total carotenoid content (TCC): Carotenoids were extracted as described above but using the hexane/acetone (3:2) mixture as the solvent. The absorbance values of redissolved dried extracts were directly read at 450 nm, and the TCC was expressed as milligrams per 100 g of dry flour (mg/100 g DW) using the molar extinction coefficient 2500 M^{-1} cm^{-1} [23].

Phytate content: The phytate content was determined according to the method described by Vaintraub and Lapteva [24], with slight modifications. Briefly, 0.5 g of either sorghum or pearl millet flour was extracted for 1 h at room temperature with 10 mL of 2.4% HCl. The mixture was centrifuged for 30 min at 3000 rpm at room temperature, and the supernatant was used to calculate the phytate. Three milliliters of the supernatant was mixed with one milliliter of Wade reagent (0.03% $FeCl_3$ solution with 0.3% sulfosalicylic acid in distilled water) and centrifuged for 10 min at 3000 rpm at room temperature. Then, the absorbance was measured at 500 nm. A phytic acid standard curve (5–40 mg/mL, $R^2 = 0.980$) was used to compute the phytate concentration, and the results were represented as phytic acids in milligrams per 100 g of dry weight (mg/100 g DW).

2.3.4. Antioxidant Activity

DPPH scavenging method: The extracts' antiradical activity was tested using the stable 2,2-diphenyl-1-picrylhydrazyl radical (DPPH) compound in accordance with the manufacturer's instructions [25]. The ability of the extracts to bleach the free radical was used to examine their ability to scavenge free radicals. The blank absorbance was measured at 515 nm using a 3.9 mL DPPH solution 0.1 M (in methanol) and 0.100 mL methanol instead of the extract (*A0*). For the samples, 3.9 mL of 0.1 M DPPH solution was mixed with 0.100 mL of each extract, and afterward the mixtures were kept for 30 min at room temperature in the dark before the absorbances were recorded (*Af*). The inhibition percentage was calculated as follows:

$$\%\ Inhibition = \frac{A0 - Af}{A0} \times 100 \quad (1)$$

ABTS scavenging method: For the ABTS scavenging activity, 2.85 mL of ABTS stock solution 7 mM (in ethanol, mixed with 2.45 mM potassium persulfate), having 1.10 absorbance (*A0*), was mixed with 0.15 mL of extract solution (*Af*). After 2 h of incubation in the dark, the solution's absorbance was measured at 734 nm. The percentage of radical scavenging activity was estimated as follows:

$$\%\ Inhibition = \frac{A0 - Af}{A0} \times 100 \quad (2)$$

2.3.5. HPLC Analysis of Polyphenols

A chromatographic profile of sorghum and millet was created utilizing a Surveyor HPLC system (Finnigan Surveyor LC, Thermo Scientific, Waltham, MA, USA) using the following methodology for the preparation and separation of compounds, as described by Păcularu-Burada et al. [26]. The samples were suspended in 5 mL of 70% (*v*/*v*) methanol prior to HPLC separations. The mixtures were dissolved in an ultrasonic bath (MRC, Holon, Israel) for 45 min, and the sample supernatants were centrifuged at 6000 rpm and 4 °C for 10 min (Hettich Universal 320R, Tuttlingen, Germany) before being filtered through 0.22 m syringe filters (Merck, Darmstadt, Germany). Briefly, the elution system used was formed from 100% (*v*/*v*) methanol (solvent A) and 3% (*v*/*v*) formic acid (solvent B) and the separation was performed using a linear gradient: 0–20 min (91% B), 20–40 min (91–65% B), and 40–55 min (65–91% B). The analysis was conducted at detection wavelengths of 280 (for phenolic acids) and 320 nm (for flavonoids). The polyphenols were identified using the retention time for the commercially available standards as a guideline, and by comparison with the literature reviews.

2.4. Statistical Analysis

Unless otherwise stated, the analyses were performed in triplicate and the figures were reported as means ± standard deviation. Data were subjected to ANOVA and significant differences between means were revealed via post hoc Duncan's multiple range test ($p < 0.05$). The principal component analysis (PCA) was carried out to gain an overview of the relationships among experimental data.

3. Results and Discussion

3.1. Proximate Chemical Composition of Sorghum and Pearl Millet Flours

The proximate physicochemical contents related to the main macronutrients (proteins, lipids, carbohydrates, and fibers), moisture, and ash in sorghum and pearl millet flours are shown in Table 1.

Table 1. Proximate chemical composition of sorghum and pearl millet flours (g/100 g DW).

Samples	Moisture (%)	Proteins	Lipids	Fibers	Ash	Carbohydrates
			Sorghum Varieties			
white	9.33 ± 0.01 [a]	19.62 ± 0.01 [a]	3.49 ± 0.02 [a]	2.56 ± 0.02 [a]	1.59 ± 0.01 [a]	72.71± 0.02 [a]
yellow-pale	8.51± 0.01 [b]	23.21 ± 0.01 [b]	3.62 ± 0.01 [b]	3.39 ± 0.01 [b]	1.44 ± 0.01 [b]	68.31 ± 0.04 [b]
yellow	8.63 ± 0.01 [c]	23.78 ± 0.01 [c]	2.74 ± 0.01 [c]	3.79 ± 0.03 [c]	1.21 ± 0.01 [c]	68.45 ± 0.02 [c]
red	8.85 ± 0.01 [d]	23.51 ± 0.01 [d]	3.33 ± 0.01 [d]	4.70 ± 0.03 [d]	1.15 ± 0.01 [d]	67.28 ± 0.02 [d]
			Pearl Millet Varieties			
gawane	8.00 ± 0.01 [e]	27.85 ± 0.01 [e]	5.11 ± 0.01 [e]	5.68 ± 0.03 [e]	2.24 ± 0.01 [e]	59.09 ± 0.01 [e]
mouri	8.03 ± 0.01 [f]	32.56 ± 0.02 [f]	5.36 ± 0.01 [f]	3.72 ± 0.05 [c]	2.77 ± 0.01 [f]	55.57 ± 0.04 [f]

DW: dry weight of flour. Mean values in the same column with different superscript letters are significantly different ($p < 0.05$).

The moisture, protein, lipid, crude fiber, ash, and carbohydrate contents of the analyzed sorghum samples varied in the ranges of 8.51–9.33%, 19.62–23.78%, 2.74–3.32%, 2.56–4.70%, 1.15–1.59%, and 67.281–72.71%, respectively. As stated in Table 1, *white* sorghum was the most carbohydrate-rich cultivar with the highest moisture and ash contents. On the other hand, this cultivar had the lowest protein and fiber contents. The *yellow-pale* sorghum cultivar had the highest lipid concentration. The protein level of *yellow* sorghum was the highest, whereas its lipid content was the lowest. *Red* sorghum was determined to have the highest fiber content while having the lowest ash and carbohydrate levels. Our results are in agreement with other studies. Shegro et al. [27] and Udachan et al. [28] also reported differences in nutrient concentrations between different types of sorghum due to genetic differences. However, the concentrations identified in our study are comparable with those reported by these authors.

The carbohydrate and fiber content of pearl millet was significantly higher in the *gawane* cultivar (Table 1), whereas the protein, fat, and ash contents were significantly higher in the *mouri* cultivar ($p < 0.05$). By comparison, the pearl millet samples were higher in proteins (27.81–32.56%), lipids (5.11–5.36%), crude fibers (3.72–5.68%), and ash (2.24–2.77%) but lower in moisture (8.00–8.03%) and carbohydrates (55.57–59.09%) when compared to sorghum samples (Table 1). It is known that pearl millet has a better nutritional profile than sorghum and other major cereals, with the same findings being reported by other authors such as Ojo et al. [29].

The variations in the proximate compositions of the various samples may have been primarily due to genetic factors, since the studied cultivars were cultivated under similar climatic conditions [13]. Pearl millet cultivars, with low carbohydrate contents and high crude fiber contents, can be recommended to people suffering from metabolic syndrome, characterized by high glucose levels and hypercholesterolemia. In addition, considering the high levels of proteins and lipids, the studied pearl millet varieties are good candidates to fight protein-energy malnutrition in children.

3.2. The Mineral Content of Sorghum and Pearl Millet Flours

The mineral contents of the studied cereals are detailed in Table 2.

Table 2. Macro-element (mg/100 g DW) and trace element contents of sorghum and pearl millet flours (mg/100 g DW).

Samples	Ca	Na	K	Mg	P
		Sorghum Varieties			
white	11.20 ± 0.08^{a}	4.55 ± 0.03^{c}	328.70 ± 0.89^{d}	130.47 ± 0.13^{a}	256.74 ± 1.04^{a}
yellow-pale	12.91 ± 0.09^{b}	3.98 ± 0.13^{a}	313.39 ± 8.31^{c}	149.11 ± 0.46^{b}	311.37 ± 0.13^{b}
yellow	11.90 ± 0.01^{c}	3.94 ± 0.01^{a}	314.34 ± 1.10^{c}	139.35 ± 0.03^{c}	279.73 ± 0.76^{c}
red	10.81 ± 0.03^{d}	4.21 ± 0.01^{b}	278.68 ± 0.21^{a}	145.69 ± 0.63^{d}	301.77 ± 0.35^{d}
		Pearl Millet Varieties			
gawane	13.66 ± 0.09^{e}	4.48 ± 0.05^{c}	302.52 ± 1.36^{b}	132.47 ± 0.21^{e}	266.03 ± 0.90^{e}
mouri	15.67 c $\pm 0.30^{f}$	3.96 ± 0.03^{a}	307.06 ± 1.92^{bc}	142.48 ± 0.40^{f}	292.66 ± 0.12^{f}

DW: dry weight of flour. Mean values in the same column with different superscript letters are significantly different ($p < 0.05$).

As shown in Table 2, *white* sorghum was the cultivar with the highest sodium and potassium levels, while having the lowest levels of magnesium and phosphorus. The *yellow-pale* sorghum cultivar had the highest calcium, magnesium, and phosphorus concentrations of all of the cultivars studied, but the lowest sodium concentration was found for the *yellow* sorghum cultivar. The lowest calcium and potassium concentrations were found in *red* sorghum. While *gawane* millet had a high sodium content, *mouri* pearl millet had the greatest calcium, magnesium, and phosphorus levels. No significant differences were observed between *gawane* and *mouri* pearl millet flours in the potassium concentrations ($p > 0.05$). By comparison, as already seen in Table 2, pearl millet presented a significantly higher calcium content than sorghum ($p < 0.05$).

The obtained results are comparable to data reported earlier for sorghum genotypes by authors such as Chavan et al. [30]. Other studies have reported pearl millet containing higher amounts of minerals compared to sorghum [31]. The cultivar with the lowest levels of copper, iron, and zinc was discovered to be *white* sorghum (Table 3). The copper and manganese concentrations in the *yellow-pale* sorghum were the highest of all the varieties evaluated. *Yellow* sorghum had the highest iron content but the lowest manganese content. *Red* sorghum also had a high copper content, with no significant difference from *yellow-pale* sorghum ($p > 0.05$). *Red* sorghum was also discovered to be the most zinc-rich cultivar. Although *gawane* pearl millet had the highest amounts of copper and zinc, *mouri* had the highest iron and manganese levels (Table 3).

Table 3. Macro-element (mg/100 g DW) and trace element contents of sorghum and pearl millet flours (mg/100 g DW).

Samples	Cu	Fe	Mn	Zn	Samples
		Sorghum Varieties			
White	0.12 ± 0.07^{a}	2.75 ± 0.15^{a}	1.48 ± 0.05^{a}	1.34 ± 0.01^{a}	*White*
yellow-pale	0.25 ± 0.07^{c}	3.15 ± 0.08^{b}	1.69 ± 0.01^{b}	1.71 ± 0.01^{b}	*yellow-pale*
yellow	0.21 ± 0.08^{b}	3.28 ± 0.07^{c}	1.40 ± 0.02^{c}	1.38 ± 0.03^{c}	*yellow*
red	0.32 ± 0.08^{c}	3.07 ± 0.01^{d}	1.56 ± 0.01^{d}	2.13 ± 0.06^{d}	*red*
		Pearl Millet Varieties			
Gawane	0.69 ± 0.03^{e}	4.45 ± 0.01^{e}	0.54 ± 0.01^{e}	2.78 ± 0.02^{e}	*Gawane*
Mouri	0.59 ± 0.06^{d}	4.92 ± 0.04^{f}	0.92 ± 0.01^{f}	1.97 ± 0.01^{f}	*Mouri*

DW: dry weight of flour. Mean values in the same column with different superscript letters are significantly different ($p < 0.05$).

As far as trace elements are concerned, copper, iron, and zinc contents were higher ($p < 0.05$) in pearl millet cultivars compared to sorghum. Only manganese was more abundant in sorghum. Many studies reported pearl millet as a better source of minerals than the major cereals, especially iron [32]. The stated variations in the mineral contents of the studied cultivars can be explained by genetic factors and the soil composition [33]. Indeed, the soil characteristics are not homogeneous in the Far-North region of Cameroon [34]. Pearl millet grains can be used to prepare various nutrient-dense food products, effectively fighting mineral deficiency in children and women.

3.3. *Phytochemicals Profile of Sorghum and Pearl Millet Flours*

The phytochemical composition of the extracts derived from sorghum and pearl millet was determined. Table 4 shows the concentrations of TFC, TPC, TDC, TCC, and phytates.

Table 4. Phytochemicals content of sorghum and pearl millet flours.

Samples	TPC (mg GAE/g DE)	TFC (mg CE/g DE)	TDC (mg/g DE)	TCC (mg/100 g DE)	Phytates (mg/100 g DW)
		Sorghum Varieties			
white	22.48 ± 0.75^{a}	7.14 ± 0.34^{a}	1.60 ± 0.03^{a}	0.99 ± 0.10^{a}	330.44 ± 19.59^{a}
yellow-pale	33.96 ± 0.80^{b}	5.18 ± 0.64^{b}	1.04 ± 0.05^{b}	0.94 ± 0.02^{a}	391.00 ± 18.95^{b}
yellow	21.91 ± 0.93^{a}	19.97 ± 0.52^{c}	1.20 ± 0.02^{b}	0.74 ± 0.02^{b}	389.91 ± 24.57^{b}
red	82.22 ± 3.29^{c}	23.82 ± 1.27^{d}	9.06 ± 0.32^{c}	0.66 ± 0.03^{c}	223.33 ± 12.24^{c}
		Pearl Millet Varieties			
gawane	17.36 ± 0.44^{a}	9.23 ± 0.10^{e}	0.74 ± 0.01^{d}	0.52 ± 0.03^{d}	384.93 ± 18.28^{b}
mouri	19.15 ± 0.56^{a}	8.85 ± 0.06^{e}	1.01 ± 0.05^{b}	0.53 ± 0.01^{d}	273.60 ± 15.54^{d}

TPC: Total Polyphenols Content; TFC: Total Flavonoids Content; TDC: Total 3-Deoxyanthocyanidin Content; TCC: Total Carotenoids Content; GAE: Gallic Acid Equivalent; CE: Catechin Equivalent; DW: dry weight of flour; DE: dry weight of extract; Mean values in the same column with different superscript letters are significantly different ($p < 0.05$).

The phytochemical profile showed significant variations among the studied cultivars. According to Table 4, *red* sorghum was the richest cultivar in total polyphenols, total flavonoids, and total 3-deoxyanthocyanidin. However, the lowest phytate contents were noticed in *red* sorghum. One of the elements determining the content and profile of flavonoids is the color of the sorghum grains [35,36]. Sorghum grains contain flavonoids in the form of 3-deoxyanthocyanidins [12,32]. Polyphenols are the main bioactive compounds of sorghum and are present in all cultivars of this cereal crop [37]. *White* sorghum was the richest cultivar in total carotenoids. A recent study conducted in Poland on sorghum grains also revealed the white genotype to have the highest content in carotenoids [37]. These findings suggest that the pigmentation of the external coat of sorghum cultivars is not an indicator of the abundance of carotenoids, as it is the case with many fruits and vegetables.

The *mouri* pearl millet was the richest source of total polyphenols and TDC, while *gawane* showed the highest phytate content. In terms of the TFC and TCC, no significant differences were observed between the two cultivars of pearl millet ($p > 0.05$).

In the present study, the analyzed compounds were globally found in higher amounts in sorghum varieties compared to pearl millet. However, polyphenols and phytates are also known as antinutritional factors since they form insoluble complexes with minerals such as iron, zinc, and calcium, reducing their bioavailability [38].

3.4. *Antioxidant Activity of Sorghum and Pearl Millet Flours*

The radical scavenging activities of sorghum and pearl millet flour varieties are presented in Table 5, with DPPH and ABTS being used as free radicals.

Table 5. Antioxidant activity of sorghum and millet extracts.

Samples	DPPH (%)	ABTS (%)
	Sorghum Cultivars	
white	73.18 ± 5.26^{b}	95.02 ± 5.51^{a}
yellow-pale	93.14 ± 4.46^{c}	92.65 ± 6.76^{a}

Table 5. *Cont.*

Samples	DPPH (%)	ABTS (%)
yellow	64.09 ± 3.29 [a]	98.14 ± 5.48 [a]
red	86.43 ± 5.03 [c]	95.77 ± 3.97 [a]
	Pearl Millet Cultivars	
gawane	70.55 ± 3.62 [ab]	90.64 ± 4.48 [a]
mouri	73.27 ± 5.36 [b]	89.24 ± 1.64 [a]

Mean values in the same column with different superscript letters are significantly different ($p < 0.05$).

The values from Table 5 reveal that the sorghum varieties were high in DPPH antioxidant activity compared to the pearl millet cultivars. The highest antioxidant activity was for *yellow-pale* sorghum (93.14%), followed by *red* sorghum (86.43%). Punia et al. [39] found *red* sorghum to exhibit the highest antioxidant activity among five varieties cultivated in India. Another recent study carried out in the Mediterranean zone also identified *red* sorghum to have high antioxidant potential [40]. However, it can be noticed that no sorghum variety with a yellowish pericarp was used in these two previous studies.

The antioxidant activity levels of pearl millet flours tested against DPPH radical were more than two-fold higher than the result obtained by Gull et al. (31.80%) in a pearl millet variety grown in India [41]. In addition to genetic factors, the observed difference may be attributed to the local harsh and stressful climatic conditions, which could have boosted the synthesis of antioxidant phytochemicals.

In terms of ABTS, no significant differences were observed in the inhibition activity levels of the sorghum and pearl millet flours ($p > 0.05$). The antioxidant properties of cereal grains are attributed to their polyphenols and flavonoids, which act as free radical scavenging agents and protect against oxidative stress within the human body [42].

3.5. High-Performance Liquid Chromatography Analysis

Figure 1 illustrates the chromatographic profile of sorghum and millet flour varieties. At 320 nm, 13 compounds were identified: caffeic acid, chlorogenic acid, ferulic acid, gallic acid, p coumaric acid, protocatechuic acid, sinapic acid, syringic acid, and vanillic acid. Catechin, epicatechin, quercetin, and kaempferol were the flavonoid compounds that were separated.

Table 6 shows the concentrations of bioactive compounds identified in sorghum and pearl millet varieties.

The polyphenolic extracts of sorghum and pearl millet revealed different concentrations of each bioactive compound in the analysis. It can be seen from Figure 1 and Table 6 that the main compounds identified were gallic acid, chlorogenic acid, and ferulic acid. Chlorogenic acid, caffeic acid, p-coumaric acid, ferulic acid, and sinapic acid were the hydroxycinnamic acids measured (Figure 1), with the different levels among the genotypes (Table 6) attributed to the cultivars and the growth conditions and environment they were exposed to [39]. Among them, the most frequent phenolic acids identified were chlorogenic acid and ferulic acid. Ferulic acid was higher in *red* and *yellow* sorghum while chlorogenic acid was higher in *yellow* sorghum and *mouri* pearl millet. Similar results were obtained in previous studies [40,43].

The hydroxybenzoic acids identified were gallic acid, protocatechuic acid, vanillic acid, and syringic acid (Figure 1). Vanillic acid was most prominent in *yellow* sorghum and was lacking in *white* sorghum.

As indicated in Table 6, *red* sorghum had a more considerable phenolic compound diversity than the other samples, followed by *gawane* pearl millet. In their studies, Ghinea et al. also identified that sorghum bicolor grains exhibited a high diversity of compounds such as caffeic acid, chlorogenic acid, epicatechin, p-coumaric acid, daidzein, rutin, hyperoside, quercetin, naringenin, and genistein [44]. Another study by Hong et al. found a variety of polyphenolic compounds isolated from sorghum extracts, including caffeic acid, coumaric acid, ellagic acid, ferulic acid, gallic acid, sinapic acid, syringic acid, vanillic acid, apigenin, catechin, chrysin, eriodictyol, luteolin, naringenin, and quercetin [45].

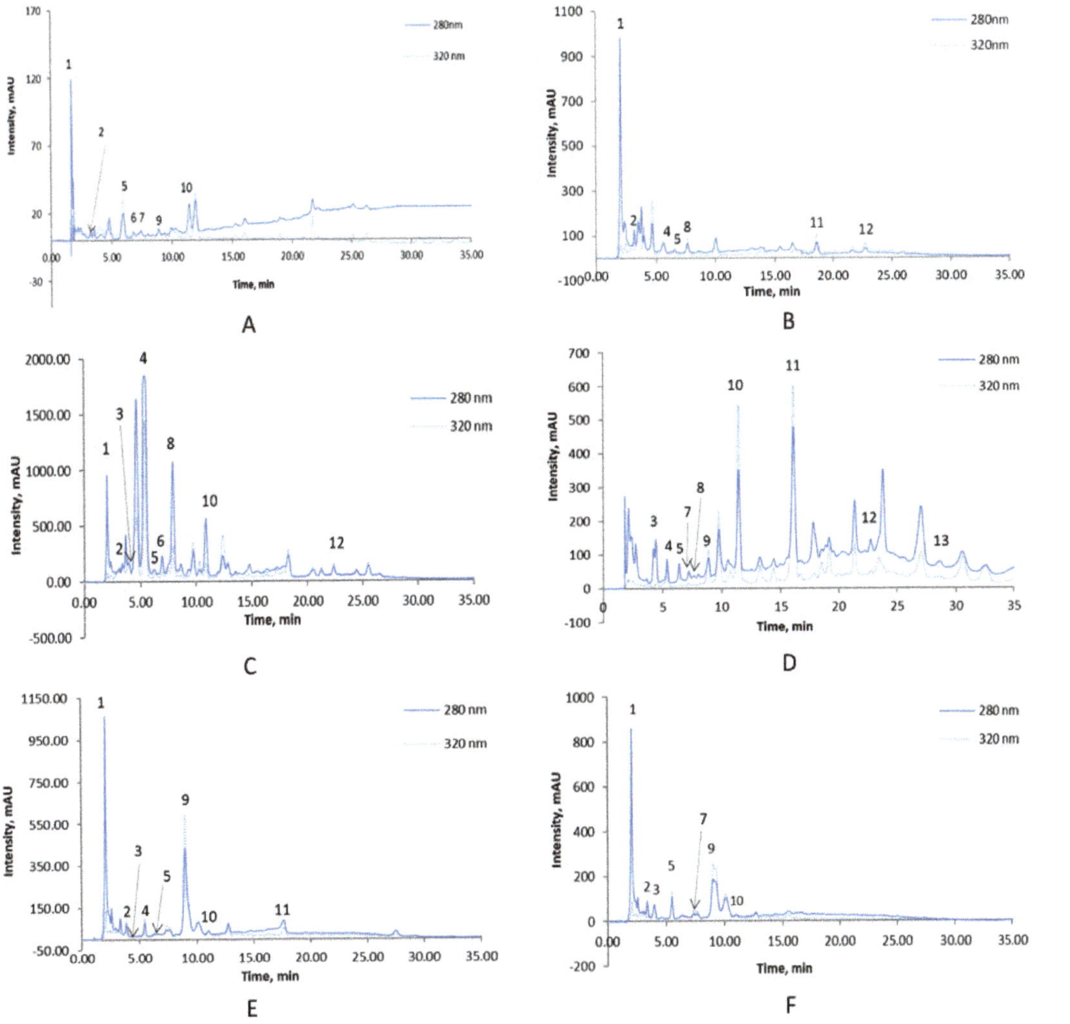

Figure 1. Chromatographic profile of sorghum and pearl millet phenols detected at 280 nm and 320 nm: peak 1—gallic acid; peak 2—protocatechuic acid; peak 3—catechin; peak 4—vanillic acid; peak 5—chlorogenic acid; peak 6—epicatechin; peak 7—caffeic acid; peak 8—syringic acid; peak 9—p coumaric acid; peak 10—ferulic acid; peak 11—sinapic acid; peak 12—quercetin; 13—kaempferol; (**A**)—*white* sorghum; (**B**)—*yellow-pale* sorghum; (**C**)—*yellow* sorghum; (**D**)—*red* sorghum; (**E**)—*gawane* millet' (**F**)—*mouri* millet.

Table 6. The concentrations of compounds detected in sorghum and pearl millet cultivars.

Bioactive Compounds Identified (µg/mL)	Sorghum Cultivars			Pearl Millet Cultivars		
	White	*Yellow-Pale*	*Yellow*	*Red*	*Gawane*	*Mouri*
Gallic Acid	115.11 ± 2.00 [c]	170.01 ± 0.80 [b]	104.73 ± 0.90 [d]	ND	185.79 ± 0.70 [a]	165.59 ± 0.10 [b]
Catechin	ND	ND	NQ	87.41 ± 0.90 [a]	12.65 ± 0.60 [c]	75.73 ± 0.30 [b]
Vanillic Acid	ND	21.34 ± 0.7	548.65 ± 1.40 [b]	18.24 ± 0.04 [a]	20.27 ± 0.20 [b]	ND
Chlorogenic Acid	10.11 ± 0.10 [f]	22.37 ± 0.11 [d]	59.36 ± 0.09 [a]	32.71 ± 0.08 [c]	19.06 ± 0.07 [e]	34.61 ± 0.12 [b]
Epicatechin	ND	ND	114.80 ± 2.69 [a]	ND	ND	ND
Caffeic Acid	7.42 ± 0.04 [a]	ND	ND	4.72 ± 0.01 [b]	ND	4.32 ± 0.05 [c]
Ferulic Acid	2.73 ± 0.22 [d]	5.11 ± 0.07 [c]	55.96 ± 0.17 [a]	34.16 ± 0.49 [b]	NQ	NQ
Quercetin	ND	ND	ND	53.85 ± 0.74 [a]	ND	ND
Kaempferol	ND	ND	ND	11.49 ± 0.10 [a]	ND	ND

ND: not detected; NQ: not quantified. Mean values in the same column with different superscript letters are significantly different ($p < 0.05$).

3.6. Principal Components Analysis (PCA) of Experimental Data

A principal component analysis was carried out to determine and visualize the relationships between the different sorghum and pearl millet cultivars and the studied parameters. The eigenvalues were 10.57, 5.35, 3.13, 1.71, and 1.24 for factors F1 to F5, respectively. The first two principal components or factors (F1 and F2) together explained 72.96% of the total original variance in the data set. A biplot projection of the observations (cultivars) and measured variables on the plane defined by F1 and F2 is shown in Figure 2.

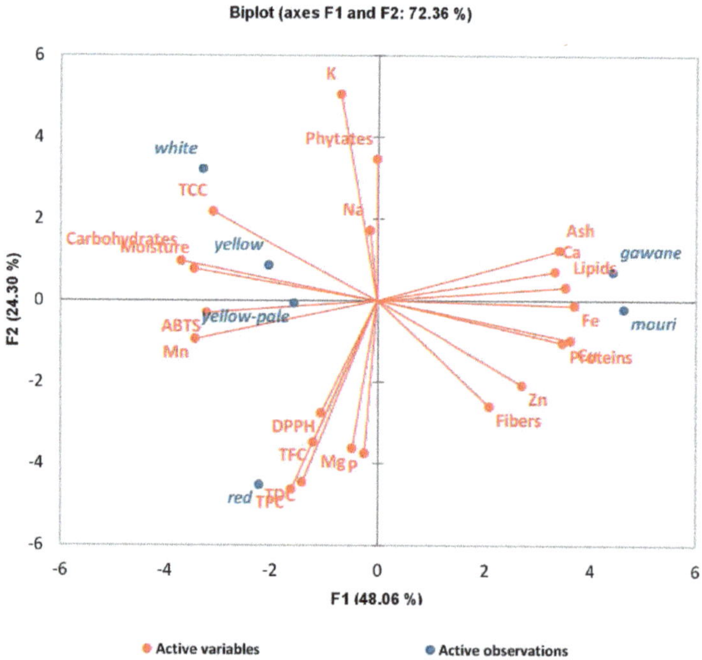

Figure 2. Principal components analysis of the experimental data.

The first principal component F1, which explained 48.06% of the total experimental variability, aggregated all of the proximate analysis parameters, trace elements, and calcium. The location of *gawane* and *mouri* pearl millet close to proteins, lipids, and trace elements such as copper (Cu), iron (Fe), and zinc (Zn) clearly indicates that these cultivars are better sources of nutrients compared to sorghum. The tight positive correlation between the proteins and the above-mentioned trace elements may be due to the mineral-binding ability of some amino acid side chains. Additionally, our findings suggest a possible competitive binding process among divalent cations favorable to calcium, copper, iron, and zinc. *Yellow-pale* and *yellow* sorghum are characterized by high carbohydrate, carotenoid, and manganese (Mn) contents, which have a strong negative correlation with the majority of nutrients. The carotenoids may be the main contributors to the ABTS antioxidant activity observed in the studied samples.

The second principal component F2, which explained 24.30% of the total experimental variability, clustered phytochemicals with antioxidant properties (TDC, TFC, TPC), phytates, and macro-elements such as magnesium (Mg), phosphorus (P), potassium (K), and sodium (Na). Phytates negatively correlated with other phytochemicals. There is a strong positive correlation between the grouped phytochemicals, which are synthesized in the context of a physiological adaptation of the plant to environmental stress. Additionally, it can be deduced by the position of *red* sorghum being close to TDC, TFC, TPC, and DPPH that it had the best antioxidant profile. The independent relationship between trace elements and phytochemicals such as polyphenols and phytates is a paradoxal finding. In fact, these two compounds are known to be divalent cations chelators [46].

The principal component analysis clearly segregated pearl millet cultivars (especially *mouri*) and *red* sorghum as the major sources of nutrients and bioactive compounds, respectively. This implies that recommending their consumption will depend on the type of nutritional challenges faced. *Mouri* pearl millet seems to be suitable for addressing protein-energy and micronutrients deficiencies, while *red* sorghum could be useful in managing non-communicable diseases.

4. Conclusions

This study analyzed the chemical composition and antioxidant profile of four sorghum and two pearl millet cultivars grown and consumed in the Far-North region of Cameroon. The physicochemical and mineral analyses revealed a global nutritional superiority of pearl millet cultivars, especially *mouri*, which exhibited high amounts of proteins and trace elements. The phytochemicals and antioxidant activity were noticeably higher in colored cultivars of sorghum (*red* and *yellow*). *Red* sorghum had a more considerable phenolic compound diversity than the other samples. The most abundant phenolic component was gallic acid, while ferulic acid was the most dominant. The studied cereal crops can be considered health-promoting tools for local populations, and their consumption should be encouraged to tackle nutrient deficiencies and non-communicable diseases. However, further investigations are required to identify adequate processing methods that best preserve the nutritional and functional properties mentioned above.

Author Contributions: Conceptualization: S.M. and G.R.; methodology and formal analysis: S.M., N.N.C., M.T. and O.E.C.; resources: C.C.; original draft preparation and editing: S.M. and O.E.C.; supervision and review: G.R. All authors have read and agreed to the published version of the manuscript.

Funding: This research was funded by AUF (Agence Universitaire de la Francophonie) through a postdoctoral fellowship. The APC was supported by a grant from the Romanian Ministry of Research and Innovation, funding number CNFIS-FDI-2022-0205.

Institutional Review Board Statement: Not applicable.

Informed Consent Statement: Not applicable.

Data Availability Statement: Data is contained within the article.

Acknowledgments: The Integrated Center for Research, Expertise, and Technological Transfer in the Food Industry is acknowledged for providing technical support.

Conflicts of Interest: The authors declare no conflict of interest.

References

1. de Morais Cardoso, L.; Pinheiro, S.S.; Martino, H.S.D.; Pinheiro-Sant'Ana, H.M. Sorghum (*Sorghum bicolor* L.): Nutrients, bioactive compounds, and potential impact on human health. *Crit. Rev. Food Sci. Nutr.* **2017**, *57*, 372–390. [CrossRef] [PubMed]
2. Devi, P.B.; Vijayabharathi, R.; Sathyabama, S.; Malleshi, N.G.; Priyadarisini, V.B. Health benefits of finger millet (*Eleusine coracana* L.) polyphenols and dietary fiber: A review. *J. Food Sci. Technol.* **2014**, *51*, 1021–1040. [CrossRef] [PubMed]
3. Saxena, R.; Vanga, S.K.; Wang, J.; Orsat, V.; Raghavan, V. Millets for Food Security in the Context of Climate Change: A Review. *Sustainability* **2018**, *10*, 2228. [CrossRef]
4. Afify, A.E.-M.M.R.; El-Beltagi, H.S.; El-Salam, S.M.A.; Omran, A.A. Biochemical changes in phenols, flavonoids, tannins, vitamin E, β–carotene and antioxidant activity during soaking of three white sorghum varieties. *Asian Pac. J. Trop. Biomed.* **2012**, *2*, 203–209. [CrossRef]
5. Dillon, S.L.; Shapter, F.M.; Henry, R.J.; Cordeiro, G.; Izquierdo, L.; Lee, L.S. Domestication to Crop Improvement: Genetic Resources for Sorghum and Saccharum (Andropogoneae). *Ann. Bot.* **2007**, *100*, 975–989. [CrossRef]
6. Elkhalifa, A.E.O.; Schiffler, B.; Bernhardt, R. Effect of fermentation on the functional properties of sorghum flour. *Food Chem.* **2005**, *92*, 1–5. [CrossRef]
7. Li, J.; Chen, Z.; Guan, X.; Liu, J.; Zhang, M.; Xu, B. Optimization of germination conditions to enhance hydroxyl radical inhibition by water-soluble protein from stress millet. *J. Cereal Sci.* **2008**, *48*, 619–624. [CrossRef]
8. Gupta, N.; Srivastava, A.K.; Pandey, V.N. Biodiversity and Nutraceutical Quality of Some Indian Millets. *Proc. Natl. Acad. Sci. India Sect. B Boil. Sci.* **2012**, *82*, 265–273. [CrossRef]
9. Lee, H.-S.; Santana, Á.L.; Peterson, J.; Yucel, U.; Perumal, R.; De Leon, J.; Lee, S.-H.; Smolensky, D. Anti-Adipogenic Activity of High-Phenolic Sorghum Brans in Pre-Adipocytes. *Nutrients* **2022**, *14*, 1493. [CrossRef]
10. Woo, H.J.; Oh, I.T.; Lee, J.Y.; Jun, D.Y.; Seu, M.C.; Woo, K.S.; Nam, M.H.; Kim, Y.H. Apigeninidin induces apoptosis through activation of Bak and Bax and subsequent mediation of mitochondrial damage in human promyelocytic leukemia HL-60 cells. *Process Biochem.* **2012**, *47*, 1861–1871. [CrossRef]
11. Vila-Real, C.; Pimenta-Martins, A.; Maina, N.; Gomes, A.; Pinto, E. Nutritional Value of African Indigenous Whole Grain Cereals Millet and Sorghum. *Nutr. Food Sci. Int. J.* **2017**, *4*, 555628. [CrossRef]
12. Ragaee, S.; Abdel-Aal, E.-S.M.; Noaman, M. Antioxidant activity and nutrient composition of selected cereals for food use. *Food Chem.* **2006**, *98*, 32–38. [CrossRef]
13. Taleon, V.; Dykes, L.; Rooney, W.L.; Rooney, L.W. Effect of genotype and environment on flavonoid concentration and profile of black sorghum grains. *J. Cereal Sci.* **2012**, *56*, 470–475. [CrossRef]
14. Dicko, M.H.; Gruppen, H.; Barro, C.; Traore, A.S.; van Berkel, W.J.H.; Voragen, A.G.J. Impact of Phenolic Compounds and Related Enzymes in Sorghum Varieties for Resistance and Susceptibility to Biotic and Abiotic Stresses. *J. Chem. Ecol.* **2005**, *31*, 2671–2688. [CrossRef] [PubMed]
15. Obadina, A.; Ishola, I.O.; Adekoya, I.O.; Soares, A.G.; de Carvalho, C.W.P.; Barboza, H.T. Nutritional and physico-chemical properties of flour from native and roasted whole grain pearl millet (*Pennisetum glaucum* [L.] R. Br.). *J. Cereal Sci.* **2016**, *70*, 247–252. [CrossRef]
16. Ghimire, B.-K.; Seo, J.-W.; Yu, C.-Y.; Kim, S.-H.; Chung, I.-M. Comparative Study on Seed Characteristics, Antioxidant Activity, and Total Phenolic and Flavonoid Contents in Accessions of *Sorghum bicolor* (L.) Moench. *Molecules* **2021**, *26*, 3964. [CrossRef]
17. Kardeş, Y.M.; Kaplan, M.; Kale, H.; Yılmaz, M.F.; Karaman, K.; Temizgül, R.; Akar, T. Biochemical composition of selected lines from sorghum (*Sorghum bicolor* L.) landraces. *Planta* **2021**, *254*, 26. [CrossRef]
18. Horwitz, W.; Latimer, G.W. *Official Methods of Analysis of AOAC International*; AOAC International: Rockville, ML, USA, 2005.
19. Cheok, C.Y.; Chin, N.L.; Yusof, Y.A.; Talib, R.A.; Law, C.L. Optimization of total monomeric anthocyanin (TMA) and total phenolic content (TPC) extractions from mangosteen (*Garcinia mangostana* Linn.) hull using ultrasonic treatments. *Ind. Crops Prod.* **2013**, *50*, 1–7. [CrossRef]
20. Turturică, M.; Stănciuc, N.; Bahrim, G.; Râpeanu, G. Effect of thermal treatment on phenolic compounds from plum (*prunus domestica*) extracts—A kinetic study. *J. Food Eng.* **2016**, *171*, 200–207. [CrossRef]
21. Dewanto, V.; Wu, X.; Adom, K.K.; Liu, R.H. Thermal Processing Enhances the Nutritional Value of Tomatoes by Increasing Total Antioxidant Activity. *J. Agric. Food Chem.* **2002**, *50*, 3010–3014. [CrossRef]
22. Kumar, V.G.; Viswanathan, R.; Malathi, P.; Nandakumar, M.P.; Sundar, A.R. Differential Induction of 3-deoxyanthocyanidin Phytoalexins in Relation to Colletotrichum falcatum Resistance in Sugarcane. *Sugar Tech* **2015**, *17*, 314–321. [CrossRef]
23. de Carvalho, L.M.J.; Gomes, P.B.; de Oliviera Godoy, R.L.; Pacheco, S.; do Monte, P.H.F.; de Carvalho, J.L.V.; Nutti, M.R.; Neves, A.C.L.; Vieira, A.C.R.A.; Ramos, S.R.R. Total carotenoid content, α-carotene and β-carotene, of landrace pumpkins (*Cucurbita moschata* Duch): A preliminary study. *Food Res. Int.* **2012**, *47*, 337–340. [CrossRef]
24. Vaintraub, I.A.; Lapteva, N.A. Colorimetric determination of phytate in unpurified extracts of seeds and the products of their processing. *Anal. Biochem.* **1988**, *175*, 227–230. [CrossRef]
25. Castro-Vargas, H.I.; Rodríguez-Varela, L.I.; Ferreira, S.R.S.; Parada-Alfonso, F. Extraction of phenolic fraction from guava seeds (*Psidium guajava* L.) using supercritical carbon dioxide and co-solvents. *J. Supercrit. Fluids* **2010**, *51*, 319–324. [CrossRef]
26. Păcularu-Burada, B.; Turturică, M.; Rocha, J.M.; Bahrim, G.-E. Statistical Approach to Potentially Enhance the Postbiotication of Gluten-Free Sourdough. *Appl. Sci.* **2021**, *11*, 5306. [CrossRef]

27. Shegro, A.; Shargie, N.G.; Van Biljon, A.; Labuschagne, M.T. Diversity in starch, protein and mineral composition of sorghum landrace accessions from Ethiopia. *J. Crop Sci. Biotechnol.* **2012**, *15*, 275–280. [CrossRef]
28. Udachan, I.; Sahoo, A.K.; Hend, G.M. Extraction and characterization of sorghum (*Sorghum bicolor* L. Moench) starch. *Int. Food Res. J.* **2012**, *19*, 315–319.
29. Iyabo, O.O.; Ibiyinka, O.; Abimbola Deola, O. Comparative study of nutritional, functional and anti-nutritional properties of white sorghum bicolor (*Sorghum*) and *Pennisetum glaucum* (pearl millet). *Int. J. Eng. Technol. Manag. Res.* **2018**, *5*, 151–158. [CrossRef]
30. Chavan, U.D.; Patil, J.V.; Shinde, M.S. Nutritional and roti quality of sorghum genotypes. *Indones. J. Agric. Sci.* **2016**, *10*, 80–87. [CrossRef]
31. Songre-Ouattara, L.T.; Bationo, F.; Parkouda, C.; Dao, A.; Bassole, I.H.N.; Diawara, B. Qualité des grains et aptitude à la transformation: Cas des variétés de *Sorghum bicolor*, *Pennisetumg laucum* et *Zea mays* en usage en Afrique de l'Ouest. *Int. J. Biol. Chem. Sci.* **2015**, *9*, 2819–2832. [CrossRef]
32. Dube, M.; Nyoni, N.; Bhebhe, S.; Maphosa, M.; Bombom, A. Pearl millet as a sustainable alternative cereal for novel value-added products in sub-saharan africa: A review. *Agric. Rev.* **2021**, *42*, 240–244. [CrossRef]
33. Obilana, A.B.; Manyasa, E. Millets. In *Pseudocereals and Less Common Cereals: Grain Properties and Utilization Potential*; Belton, P.S., Taylor, J.R.N., Eds.; Springer: Berlin/Heidelberg, Germany, 2002; pp. 177–217. [CrossRef]
34. Tsozué, D.; Noubissie, N.M.M.; Mamdem, E.L.T.; Basga, S.D.; Oyono, D.L.B. Effects of environmental factors and soil properties on soil organic carbon stock in a natural dry tropical area of Cameroon. *Soil* **2021**, *7*, 677–691. [CrossRef]
35. Awika, J.M.; Rooney, L.W.; Waniska, R.D. Anthocyanins from black sorghum and their antioxidant properties. *Food Chem.* **2005**, *90*, 293–301. [CrossRef]
36. Dykes, L.; Seitz, L.M.; Rooney, W.L.; Rooney, L.W. Flavonoid composition of red sorghum genotypes. *Food Chem.* **2009**, *116*, 313–317. [CrossRef]
37. Dykes, L.; Rooney, L.W. Sorghum and millet phenols and antioxidants. *J. Cereal Sci.* **2006**, *44*, 236–251. [CrossRef]
38. Przybylska-Balcerek, A.; Frankowski, J.; Stuper-Szablewska, K. The influence of weather conditions on bioactive compound content in sorghum grain. *Eur. Food Res. Technol.* **2020**, *246*, 13–22. [CrossRef]
39. Punia, H.; Tokas, J.; Malik, A.; Satpal; Sangwan, S. Characterization of phenolic compounds and antioxidant activity in sorghum [*Sorghum bicolor* (L.) Moench] grains. *Cereal Res. Commun.* **2021**, *49*, 343–353. [CrossRef]
40. Pontieri, P.; Pepe, G.; Campiglia, P.; Merciai, F.; Basilicata, M.G.; Smolensky, D.; Calcagnile, M.; Troisi, J.; Romano, R.; Del Giudice, F.; et al. Comparison of Content in Phenolic Compounds and Antioxidant Capacity in Grains of White, Red, and Black Sorghum Varieties Grown in the Mediterranean Area. *ACS Food Sci. Technol.* **2021**, *1*, 1109–1119. [CrossRef]
41. Gull, A.; Prasad, K.; Kumar, P. Physico-chemical, functional and antioxidant properties of millet flours. *J. Agric. Eng. Food Technol.* **2015**, *2*, 73–75.
42. Kumari, D.; Madhujith, T.; Chandrasekara, A. Comparison of phenolic content and antioxidant activities of millet varieties grown in different locations in Sri Lanka. *Food Sci. Nutr.* **2016**, *5*, 474–485. [CrossRef]
43. Coulibaly, A.; Kouakou, B.; Chen, J. Phytic Acid in Cereal Grains: Structure, Healthy or Harmful Ways to Reduce Phytic Acid in Cereal Grains and Their Effects on Nutritional Quality. *Am. J. Plant Nutr. Fertil. Technol.* **2011**, *1*, 1–22. [CrossRef]
44. Van Hung, P. Phenolic Compounds of Cereals and Their Antioxidant Capacity. *Crit. Rev. Food Sci. Nutr.* **2016**, *56*, 25–35. [CrossRef] [PubMed]
45. Ghinea, I.O.; Mihaila, M.D.I.; Blaga, G.-V.; Avramescu, S.M.; Cudalbeanu, M.; Isticioaia, S.-F.; Dinica, R.M.; Furdui, B. HPLC-DAD Polyphenolic Profiling and Antioxidant Activities of *Sorghum bicolor* during Germination. *Agronomy* **2021**, *11*, 417. [CrossRef]
46. Hong, S.; Pangloli, P.; Perumal, R.; Cox, S.; Noronha, L.E.; Dia, V.P.; Smolensky, D. A Comparative Study on Phenolic Content, Antioxidant Activity and Anti-Inflammatory Capacity of Aqueous and Ethanolic Extracts of Sorghum in Lipopolysaccharide-Induced RAW 264.7 Macrophages. *Antioxidants* **2020**, *9*, 1297. [CrossRef]

foods

MDPI

Article

Investigations on Functional and Thermo-Mechanical Properties of Gluten Free Cereal and Pseudocereal Flours

Iuliana Banu and Iuliana Aprodu *

Faculty of Food Science and Engineering, Dunarea de Jos University of Galati, 111 Domneasca Str, 800008 Galati, Romania; iuliana.banu@ugal.ro
* Correspondence: iuliana.aprodu@ugal.ro

Abstract: Seven commercial gluten-free (rice, oat, sorghum, foxtail millet, amaranth, quinoa, and buckwheat) flours were investigated in this study from the point of view of thermo-mechanical properties and solvent retention capacity (SRC). Each flour was used to prepare doughs with specific water absorption (WA) to get a consistency of 1.1 Nm (WA1) and doughs with WA2 levels higher than 85% to ensure a sufficient amount of water in the system for allowing the hydration of all components of the flours. Different correlations were established between proteins, ash, pentosans, damaged starch, and amylose contents on the one hand, and the capacity of the flour samples to retain different solvents such as sucrose, sodium carbonate and $CaCl_2$ on the other hand. Although no significant correlation was found between the protein content of the flours and lactic acid-SRC, the mechanical weakening of the protein was significantly correlated with lactic acid-SRC for both tested WA levels. The doughs with WA1 had higher starch gelatinization and hot gel stability values compared to the corresponding dough systems with a higher water amount. Moreover, lower starch retrogradation and setback torques were obtained in the case of the dough prepared with higher amounts of water.

Keywords: gluten-free flours; solvent retention capacity; Mixolab; dough consistency

Citation: Banu, I.; Aprodu, I. Investigations on Functional and Thermo-Mechanical Properties of Gluten Free Cereal and Pseudocereal Flours. *Foods* **2022**, *11*, 1857. https://doi.org/10.3390/foods11131857

Academic Editors: Laura Gazza and Francesca Nocente

Received: 16 May 2022
Accepted: 21 June 2022
Published: 23 June 2022

1. Introduction

The most suitable flour for obtaining gluten free baked products is rice flour. Rice is widely recognized as a hypoallergenic cereal with high nutritional value [1]. The proteins of both white and brown rice mainly consist of glutenin fraction, while the albumin, globulin, and gliadin fractions are in small quantities [1].

Generally, rice flour is blended with other grain flours to improve the functionality and nutritional properties of the final products [2].

In addition to rice, a large number of grains can be used to obtain gluten-free flour, such as the group of cereals named coarse cereals, which includes oat, sorghum, millet, and buckwheat, and the minor grain-like cereals, such as quinoa and amaranth. Beyond the gluten free property, every grain mentioned above is characterized by particular nutritional constituents.

Oats are recommended for their high content of β-glucans, which are components that have all the properties that are specific to water-soluble dietary fibers and are used as a healthy food ingredient [3,4]. Yue et al. [5] reported a high proportion of 7S globulin fraction in oat proteins.

Quinoa has high-quality proteins with a balanced amino acid content [6] and high levels of vitamin E that assures high stability of quinoa lipids during storage [7]. The quinoa proteins consist of 11S globulin fraction (37%), 2S albumin fraction (35%), while the prolamine fraction represents about 0.5–7% [8].

As well, amaranth is a good source of high-quality proteins [9], having a high content of methionine, cysteine, and lysine [10]. The distribution of protein fractions is closer to pulses than cereals and the digestibility of the proteins is high [10]. The proteins are mainly formed from albumins and globulins (50–60%) [9].

Buckwheat has proteins with a well-balanced amino acid composition and large amounts of flavonoids, rutin, and quercetin with good antioxidant activity [11]. The main protein fractions found in buckwheat are globulins (up 50%) and albumins (about 25%) [11].

Sorghum is rich in polyphenols and phytosterols [12], and the protein fractions mainly consist of kafirins [13].

Foxtail millet contains high levels of protein and fiber [14]. The main protein fractions from foxtail millet are prolamins (up to 60% of the total protein content) and glutelins, which are rich in essential amino acids [15]. Foxtail millet has been listed among protein sources with good potential for replacing animal proteins in different types of products. It has been reported that foxtail millet proteins display bioactive effects that are promising for the efficient management of different human chronic diseases [15].

In order to obtain gluten-free baked products with high overall quality, it is necessary to know the functionality of gluten-free flour constituents and the rheological properties of the dough. Starting from this, the objective of the study was to compare the physicochemical and functional properties of seven gluten-free flours as well as the thermo-mechanical properties of the dough systems.

2. Materials and Methods

2.1. Materials

Seven commercial gluten-free grain flours purchased from the Galati market (Romania) were used: rice flour (Solaris Plant SRL, Romania), oat flour (Sano Vita, Romania), sorghum flour (origin Hungary, distributed by Adams Vision SRL Tg Mures, Romania), foxtail millet flour (distributed by La Finestra sul Cielo Vilareggia, Italy), amaranth flour (Adams Vision SRL, Tg Mures, Romania), quinoa flour (Vitanescu Maricel, Romania), and buckwheat flour (distributed by SC Prifan Distribution SRL, Romania).

2.2. Proximate Analyses and Physical Properties

The chemical composition of the flour samples was determined as follows: moisture content by SR ISO 712:2005 [16], protein content using the semimicro-Kjeldahl method (Raypa Trade, R Espinar, SL, Barcelona, Spain), and the nitrogen-to-protein conversion factor of 5.95 for rice flours; 6.25 for oat, foxtail millet, buckwheat, and quinoa flours; 5.75 for sorghum flour; and 5.85 for amaranth flour. The fat content was determined through ether extraction using Soxhlet method (SER-148; VELP Scientifica, Usmate Velate (MB), Italy). The crude fiber content was determined by Fibretherm Analyser (C. Gerhardt GmbH & Co. KG, Königswinter, Germany). The total pentosans content was determined using the method described by Delcour et al. [17], and the ash content was determined by SR ISO 2171/2002 [16]. The starch content was estimated by subtracting 100 g of products from the average contents of the components that were determined experimentally. The Amylose/Amylopectin Assay Kit (Megazyne International Ireland Ltd. Wicklow, Ireland) was used to determine the amylose contents of the flours.

The damaged starch content was quantified using the AACC Method 76-31.01 [18] and the Starch Damage Assay Kit (Megazyme International Ireland Ltd. Wicklow, Ireland).

The fineness module was determined by sieving the flour samples through a 400, 315, 160, and 125 μm mesh [19].

2.3. Solvent Retention Capacity

The solvent retention capacity (SRC) profile was determined to be in agreement with the AACC Method 56-11.02 [18] when the percentage of solvents retained by the flour samples upon centrifugation for 15 min at 1000× g. The following solvents were tested: water (W-SRC), 5% sodium carbonate (SC-SRC), 50% sucrose (S-SRC), 5% lactic acid (LA-SRC) (AACC International, 2000), and 1 M CaCl2 (Ca-SRC) [3]. The SRC values were reported at moisture basis (14%).

2.4. Thermo-Mechanical Properties

The thermo-mechanical properties of the flours were determined through the Chopin+ protocol using the Mixolab device (Chopin Technology, Villeneuve La Garenne, France). To better understand the evolution of dough during thermal and mixing constraints, two water absorption (WA) values were considered when running the Chopin+ protocol on each of the tested flours. WA1 was needed to obtain dough with a maximum torque C1 of 1.1 Nm, except for sorghum and buckwheat, for which it was not possible to reach the targeted dough consistency and WA2 of 85%. Oat flour was the only sample for which the C1 of 1.1 Nm was achieved for WA1 of 85%. The following torques were registered in the case of the Mixolab tests performed at both WA levels: maximum C1 torque at initial mixing, consistency of the dough after 8 min of mixing at constant temperature of 30 °C (CS), C2 showing dough changes at heating caused by protein weakening, C3 associated to starch gelatinization, C4 provided information on the stability of the hot gel, and C5 registered the cooling phase when starch retrogradation occurred [20]. Further thermo-mechanical indicators were calculated as follows: mechanical weakening of the proteins $MWP = (C1 - CS)/C1 \times 100$, strength of the protein network while heating the dough (C1-C2), intensity of starch gelatinization (C3-C2), breakdown torque (C3-C4), and setback torque (C5-C4) [21].

2.5. Statistical Analysis

Triplicate measurements were performed, and the results are presented as the average ± standard deviation values. The significant differences among samples were assessed using the Minitab 19 software (Minitab Inc., State College, PA, USA) through the one-way ANOVA with a 95% confidence interval, after assessing the normality and variance equality conditions. The Tukey method was selected for the post-hoc analysis when p values lower than 0.05 were indicated by ANOVA analysis. The Pearson's correlation was calculated to identify the potential relationships between the SRC of the flour and dough characteristics.

3. Results and Discussion

3.1. Proximate Compositions and Physical Properties of Gluten-Free Flours

The proximate composition of the gluten-free flours is shown in Table 1. The protein content varied from 6.21% in rice flour to 13.98% in quinoa flour. Overall, higher protein contents were found in pseudocereals, i.e., quinoa, amaranth, and buckwheat, compared to cereals, i.e., rice, millet, sorghum, and oat.

The highest contents of starch were registered in rice, sorghum, and oat flour, while millet flour had the lowest starch content. The fiber content ranged from 16.33% in millet flour to 3.72% in sorghum flour. However, oat flour had the highest pentosans content of 5.13%, while rice and amaranth flour had the lowest values of 1.41–1.48%. Amaranth, millet, and quinoa flour had the highest fat (6–5.30%) and ash (2.94–2.41%) content, while rice flour had the lowest fat (2.14%) and ash (1.51%) content.

The damaged starch content ranged between 1.58%, in the case of buckwheat flour, and 5.29%, in the case of oat flour. The starch damage is the result of ripping, rubbing, shearing, and cutting forces acting on the grains during the milling process [3], but the extent of the damage also depends on the endosperm structure [22,23]. Therefore, even if oat and quinoa flour had close values for the fineness module—2.26% and 2.25%, respectively—they had significantly different damaged starch contents of 5.29% and 2.71%, respectively (Table 1).

Table 1. Proximate compositions and fineness modules of the gluten free flours.

Component	Flours						
	Rice	Oat	Sorghum	Millet	Buckwheat	Quinoa	Amaranth
Moisture, %	11.28 ± 0.03 [b]	10.9 ± 0.05 [c]	8.16 ± 0.01 [e]	10.91 ± 0.03 [c]	11.28 ± 0.02 [b]	10.25 ± 0.02 [d]	11.69 ± 0.03 [a]
Ash, %	1.51 ± 0.01 [f]	1.42 ± 0.01 [g]	1.61 ± 0.01 [e]	2.68 ± 0.02 [b]	1.88 ± 0.01 [d]	2.41 ± 0.01 [c]	2.94 ± 0.01 [a]
Protein, %	6.21 ± 0.04 [f]	10.91 ± 0.07 [d]	9.81 ± 0.02 [e]	9.85 ± 0.02 [e]	11.60 ± 0.03 [c]	13.98 ± 0.02 [a]	13.59 ± 0.02 [b]
Fat, %	2.14 ± 0.03 [g]	3.88 ± 0.03 [d]	3.18 ± 0.02 [e]	5.72 ± 0.02 [b]	2.67 ± 0.03 [f]	5.30 ± 0.02 [c]	6.00 ± 0.02 [a]
Crude fiber, %	6.60 ± 0.02 [d]	7.19 ± 0.02 [c]	3.72 ± 0.05 [f]	16.33 ± 0.06 [a]	10.22 ± 0.03 [b]	5.31 ± 0.02 [e]	6.70 ± 0.03 [d]
Pentosans, %	1.48 ± 0.02 [f]	5.13 ± 0.03 [a]	3.71 ± 0.02 [c]	4.45 ± 0.02 [b]	3.56 ± 0.01 [d]	2.22 ± 0.03 [e]	1.41 ± 0.01 [g]
Starch, %	83.54 ± 0.05 [a]	76.60 ± 0.11 [c]	81.68 ± 0.08 [b]	65.42 ± 0.06 [g]	73.63 ± 0.06 [d]	73.00 ± 0.06 [e]	70.77 ± 0.02 [f]
Damaged starch, %	4.40 ± 0.05 [b]	5.29 ± 0.04 [a]	3.79 ± 0.03 [d]	3.20 ± 0.02 [e]	1.58 ± 0.02 [g]	2.71 ± 0.02 [f]	3.96 ± 0.01 [c]
Amylose, %	31.32 ± 0.30 [a]	27.64 ± 0.26 [b]	21.79 ± 0.20 [d]	12.77 ± 0.25 [f]	23.52 ± 0.36 [c]	10.92 ± 0.26 [g]	17.90 ± 0.35 [e]
Fineness module	2.85 ± 0.05 [a]	2.26 ± 0.05 [c]	1.55 ± 0.05 [e]	1.87 ± 0.03 [d]	2.36 ± 0.05 [b,c]	2.25 ± 0.05 [c]	2.46 ± 0.05 [b]

Means from the same row not sharing a superscript letter are significantly different ($p < 0.05$).

3.2. Solvent Retention Capacity of Gluten-Free Flours

SRC was initially developed to define the functional profile of wheat flour to allow for the prediction of the baking performance of flour [18]. In the last few years, SRC has been also used for characterizing different gluten-free flours [24,25].

The SRC values of the gluten-free flours investigated in the present study are reported in Table 2. The W-SRC varied from 87.00% to 126.34%, with the lowest value being registered for quinoa flour, while the highest was for amaranth flour. However, the W-SRC values of all investigated flours are much higher than those indicated by the AACC method 56-11.02 [18] for the wheat flour recommended for cookies (W-SRC below 51%) or sponge and dough bread (W-SRC below 57%).

Table 2. Solvent retention capacity of gluten-free flours.

SRC	Flours						
	Rice	Oat	Sorghum	Millet	Buckwheat	Quinoa	Amaranth
W-SRC, %	101.96 ± 0.48 [e]	115.23 ± 0.50 [c]	115.61 ± 0.44 [c]	107.28 ± 0.54 [d]	121.06 ± 0.41 [b]	87.00± 0.36 [f]	126.34 ± 0.57 [a]
Ca-SRC, %	142.82 ± 0.20 [a]	133.25 ± 0.25 [b]	131.06 ± 0.48 [c]	118.74 ± 0.25 [e]	122.52 ± 0.28 [d]	104.16 ± 0.30 [g]	117.75 ± 0.31 [f]
SC-SRC, %	116.52 ± 0.50 [b]	122.62 ± 0.47 [a]	106.28 ± 0.20 [d]	96.52 ± 0.30 [e]	94.00 ± 0.30 [f]	96.56 ± 0.23 [e]	109.40 ± 0.36 [c]
LA-SRC, %	132.29 ± 0.26 [b]	124.99 ± 0.34 [d]	126.40 ± 0.36 [c]	119.32 ± 0.20 [e]	134.72 ± 0.37 [a]	114.81 ± 0.20 [f]	131.83 ± 0.32 [b]
S-SRC, %	125.00 ± 0.36 [f]	145.41 ± 0.37 [a]	136.40 ± 0.36 [c]	142.06 ± 0.31 [b]	135.11 ± 0.35 [d]	130.15 ± 0.22 [e]	117.08 ± 0.19 [g]

W-SRC—water retention capacity; Ca-SRC—$CaCl_2$ solvent retention capacity; Na-SRC—NaCl solvent retention capacity; SC-SRC—sodium carbonate solvent retention capacity; LA-SRC—lactic acid solvent retention capacity; Su-SRC—sucrose solvent retention capacity. Means from the same row not sharing a superscript letter are significantly different ($p < 0.05$).

SC-SRC ranged from 94.00% to 122.62%. According to Kweon et al. [26], SC-SRC is related to the content of damaged starch, which is easily soluble in Na_2CO_3 solution with a pH above the pKa of the starch hydroxyl groups. Indeed, oat flour, having the highest level of damaged starch (5.29%), exhibited the highest SC-SRC value, while buckwheat flour, with the lowest value of damaged starch (1.58%), presented the lowest SC-SRC value (Table 2). In agreement with the findings of Kweon et al. [26], the content of damaged starch for the gluten-free flours was significantly correlated (R^2 of 0.938 and $p < 0.01$) with SC-SRC, confirming the high swelling ability of the damaged starch when placed in contact with Na_2CO_3 solution. In addition, a significant correlation (R^2 of 0.758 and $p < 0.05$) was found between the ash content (Table 1) and SC-SRC (Table 2) of the investigated gluten-free flours.

Oat flour had the highest S-SRC value of 145.41% among all investigated gluten-free flours. In addition, as indicated in Table 2, oat flour had the highest pentosans content. In fact, a significant correlation (R^2 of 0.964 of $p < 0.01$) was found between pentosans content and S-SRC.

LA-SRC provides information on gluten functionality, being particularly related to glutenin characteristics. Anyway, the presence of high amounts of bran particles, which have good swelling ability in lactic acid solution, might interfere with the accurate interpretation of the LA-SRC of whole flours [27]. If in the case of wheat flour the LA-SRC varied generally between 100–115% [27], in case of the gluten-free flour investigated in our study, the LA-SRC varied from 114.81% to 134.72%. The correlation (R^2 of 0.308 and $p < 0.05$) between the protein content and LA-SRC was not significant.

A significant correlation (R^2 of 0.758 and $p < 0.05$) was found between the ash content of gluten-free flours and Ca-SRC. Additional correlations were registered between the protein contents and Ca-SRC (R^2 of 0.852 and $p < 0.05$), and between the amylose content and Ca-SRC (R^2 of 0.920 and $p < 0.01$). On the other hand, in the case of oat flour, different authors reported significant correlations between Ca-SRC and β-glucan, with an R^2 of 0.615 ($p < 0.01$) [4] and R^2 of 0.82 ($p < 0.01$), respectively [3]. Additionally, Zhang et al. [4] reported a significant correlation between Ca-SRC and the molecular weight of β-glucan of oat flour (R^2 of 0.366 and $p < 0.05$). As indicated by Guo et al. [28] and Yamazaki et al. [29], the water retention capacity of β-glucans is favored upon binding metal ions like Ca^{2+} in a solution with pH that is regulated from neutral to acidic.

3.3. The Thermo-Mechanical Properties

The Mixolab device was designed for the investigation of wheat dough properties during the dual constraints of kneading and temperature. If in the case of the wheat flour bread the dough consistency of 1.1 ± 0.05 Nm is a benchmark, in the case of gluten-free flours, this dough consistency is no longer a necessary target, given the different technology for preparing bread in the absence of gluten in the system. Cappa et al. [30] appreciated that, in the case of gluten-free formulas, a lower dough consistency is preferred. For this reason, two experimental set-ups were considered in the present study, which look for the investigation of gluten-free-flour-based dough rheology at specific water absorption levels that are needed to obtain a dough consistency of 1.1 ± 0.05 Nm (WA1) in the case of each investigated flour (Table 3), and at the same water absorption of 85% (WA2), which is chosen in such a manner as to assure a dough consistency value below 1.1 Nm (Table 4). In Figure 1, the Mixolab curves are depicted, showing substantial differences between the thermo-mechanical profiles of the investigated gluten-free flours. The particularities of the thermo-mechanical behavior of the gluten-free doughs are derived from the differences in the chemical composition and hydration ability of the flour components during kneading, and the further dough behavior during heating and cooling.

Table 3. The thermo-mechanical properties of gluten-free flours at specific water absorption (WA) levels required to obtain doughs with the maximum consistency C1 of 1.1 ± 0.05 Nm.

Parameters	Flours				
	Rice	Oat	Quinoa	Amaranth	Millet
WA, %	66.0	85.0	62.1	61.0	61.9
C1, Nm	1.08 ± 0.03 b	1.09 ± 0.01 b	1.15 ± 0.01 a	1.08 ± 0.01 b	1.04 ± 0.01 c
CS, Nm	1.06 ± 0.03 a	1.03 ± 0.01 a	0.83 ± 0.01 b	1.06 ± 0.01 a	0.76 ± 0.01 c
C2, Nm	0.68 ± 0.01 a	0.67 ± 0.01 a	0.22 ± 0.01 c	0.41 ± 0.01 b	0.15 ± 0.01 d
C3, Nm	2.31 ± 0.01 a	2.18 ± 0.01 b	1.60 ± 0.02 c	0.51 ± 0.01 d	nd
C4, Nm	2.04 ± 0.02 b	1.17 ± 0.02 d	1.35 ± 0.01 c	0.49 ± 0.01 e	2.67 ± 0.01 a
C5, Nm	3.33 ± 0.04 b	1.73 ± 0.02 d	1.92 ± 0.01 c	0.81 ± 0.01 e	3.54 ± 0.01 a
MWP, %	1.85 ± 0.05 c	5.50 ± 0.05 b	27.83 ± 0.24 a	1.85 ± 0.01 c	26.93 ± 1.43 a
C1-C2, Nm	0.40 ± 0.03 c	0.42 ± 0.02 c	0.93 ± 0.01 a	0.67 ± 0.02 b	0.89 ± 0.02 a
C3-C2, Nm	1.63 ± 0.01 a	1.51 ± 0.01 b	1.38 ± 0.03 c	0.10 ± 0.00 d	nd
C3-C4, Nm	0.27 ± 0.03 b	1.01 ± 0.02 a	0.25 ± 0.03 b	0.02 ± 0.01 c	nd
C5-C4, Nm	1.29 ± 0.04 a	0.56 ± 0.00 c	0.57 ± 0.02 c	0.32 ± 0.02 d	0.87 ± 0.01 b

Means from the same row not sharing a superscript letter are significantly different ($p < 0.05$); nd—not detected; MWP—mechanical weakening of the proteins.

Table 4. The thermo-mechanical properties of gluten-free flours at a water absorption of 85% used for obtaining doughs.

Parameters	Flours						
	Rice	Oat	Quinoa	Amaranth	Millet	Sorghum	Buckwheat
C1, Nm	0.11 ± 0.01 [f]	1.09 ± 0.01 [b]	0.81 ± 0.01 [c]	0.14 ± 0.01 [f]	0.21 ± 0.02 [e]	0.41 ± 0.01 [d]	4.19 ± 0.01 [a]
CS, Nm	0.10 ± 0.01 [d]	1.03 ± 0.01 [b]	0.06 ± 0.01 [e]	0.09 ± 0.01 [d]	0.04 ± 0.01 [e]	0.24 ± 0.01 [c]	3.68 ± 0.01 [a]
C2, Nm	0.09 ± 0.01 [b]	0.67 ± 0.01 [a]	0.01 ± 0.01 [d]	0.08 ± 0.01 [b,c]	0.01 ± 0.01 [d]	0.06 ± 0.01 [c]	nd
C3, Nm	1.64 ± 0.02 [c]	2.18 ± 0.01 [a]	0.80 ± 0.02 [d]	0.28 ± 0.01 [e]	1.60 ± 0.02 [c]	1.85 ± 0.01 [b]	nd
C4, Nm	1.36 ± 0.01 [d]	1.17 ± 0.02 [e]	0.43 ± 0.02 [f]	0.31 ± 0.01 [g]	1.42 ± 0.01 [c]	1.87 ± 0.02 [a]	1.53 ± 0.01 [b]
C5, Nm	1.98 ± 0.01 [d]	1.73 ± 0.01 [e]	0.42 ± 0.01 [g]	0.51 ± 0.02 [f]	2.15 ± 0.00 [c]	2.77 ± 0.02 [a]	2.28 ± 0.02 [b]
MWP, %	9.14 ± 0.83 [e,f]	5.50 ± 0.05 [f]	92.60 ± 1.14 [a]	35.84 ± 2.57 [d]	81.14 ± 2.98 [b]	41.48 ± 1.01 [c]	12.17 ± 0.45 [e]
C1-C2, Nm	0.02 ± 0.01 [e]	0.42 ± 0.02 [b]	0.80 ± 0.01 [a]	0.06 ± 0.01 [e]	0.20 ± 0.03 [d]	0.35 ± 0.02 [c]	nd
C3-C2, Nm	1.55 ± 0.02 [b,c]	1.51 ± 0.01 [c]	0.79 ± 0.03 [d]	0.20 ± 0.01 [e]	1.59 ± 0.03 [b]	1.79 ± 0.00 [a]	nd
C3-C4, Nm	0.28 ± 0.01 [c]	1.01 ± 0.02 [a]	0.37 ± 0.03 [b]	−0.03 ± 0.02 [e]	0.18 ± 0.01 [d]	−0.02 ± 0.01 [e]	nd
C5-C4, Nm	0.62 ± 0.00 [c]	0.56 ± 0.01 [d]	−0.01 ± 0.01 [f]	0.20 ± 0.03 [e]	0.73 ± 0.01 [b]	0.90 ± 0.00 [a]	0.75 ± 0.01 [b]

Means from the same row not sharing a superscript letter are significantly different ($p < 0.05$); nd—not detected; MWP—mechanical weakening of the proteins.

As can be seen from Table 3, the water absorption needed to obtain dough with 1.1 ± 0.05 Nm varied in large limits. Moreover, in the case of sorghum and buckwheat flour, it was not possible to reach 1.1 ± 0.05 Nm during kneading at constant temperature (30 °C). Torbica et al. [31] highlighted the importance of the amount of water used for preparing gluten-free dough. They reported the higher water requirements for preparing the oat flour-based dough. After analyzing the results presented in Table 3, one can see that, among the seven investigated gluten-free flours, the highest water absorption was registered for oat flour. Our observations regarding the behavior of the sorghum flour comply with the findings of Torbica et al. [31], who failed to obtain dough with a consistency of 1.1 Nm. The sorghum-flour-based dough was very firm and remained attached to the arms of the mixer in such a manner that the device could not record the consistency values.

In order to compare the strength of the dough during kneading, MWP values were calculated (Table 4). The low MTW values are associated with a high value of the torque after 8 min of kneading, which means there is a higher stability for dough during kneading. Doughs prepared with rice, amaranth, and oat flour exhibited higher resistance during kneading compared to the millet and quinoa doughs. These results can be explained by the presence of different types of protein fractions that are present in the gluten-free flours and their particular behavior during kneading. The main proteins found in the rice flour are glutenins [1], while for the oat flour, globulins are the most abundant fraction [5]. An important additional factor that influences the C1 values is the pentosans content (5.13% in oat flour and 1.48% in rice flour).

As the temperature rises, the dough consistency decreases until it reaches the C2 value. The rice and oat doughs had (C1-C2) values close to those of wheat dough, while for the amaranth, quinoa, and millet doughs, the (C1-C2) values were much higher. The same C2 value of 0.67 Nm was registered for the oat flour at both tested WA levels, whereas for rice flour, C2 decreased from 0.68 to 0.09 Nm when WA increased from 66% to 85% (Tables 3 and 4). Even if quinoa, amaranth, and millet flour are able to form doughs with C1 of 1.1 ± 0.05 Nm at similar WA levels of 61–62.1% (Table 3), the C2 values varied significantly ($p < 0.05$). Amaranth flour presented a C2 value that was about two times higher than quinoa flour, while the lowest C2 value was registered for millet flour, suggesting the weakness of the protein network during heating. In addition to the higher protein contents in quinoa and amaranth flour compared to millet flour, the protein fractions prevailing in quinoa and amaranth flour, consisting of albumins and globulins, have good solubility in water and dilute salt solutions [32]—unlike prolamins and glutelins, which are mainly found in millet flour and have poor solubility [33].

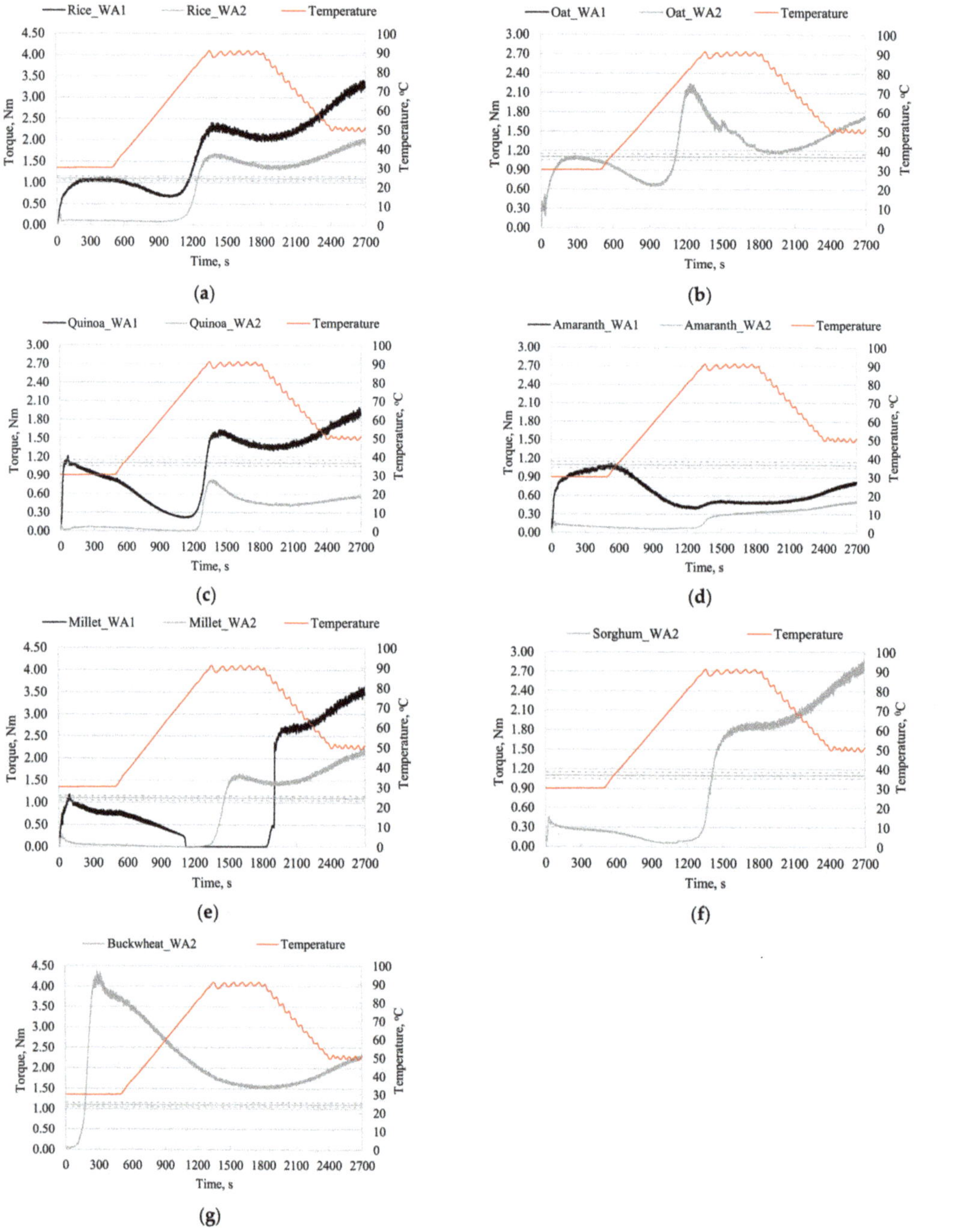

Figure 1. Mixolab curves of the dough samples prepared with rice (**a**), oat (**b**), quinoa (**c**), amaranth (**d**), millet (**e**), sorghum (**f**), and buckwheat (**g**) flour at different water absorption (WA) levels: WA1 necessary to obtain a maximum torque of 1.1 ± 0.05 Nm and WA2 of 85%. Note: For the oat flour, WA1 and WA2 had the same value of 85%.

When comparing the C2 of rice and amaranth flour-based doughs, Hadnadev et al. [20] noted that the lower weakening of rice flour proteins is due to mechanical and thermal constraints, whereas the high weakening observed for amaranth flour, which had a higher protein content, was assigned to the lower protein quality.

Doughs prepared with WA 85% can be distributed in three groups based on the behavior during kneading at a constant temperature (30 °C) and while heating up to 50–55 °C: (i) oat dough characterized by a Mixolab curve (Figure 1b) was similar to those specific to wheat flour; (ii) rice (Figure 1a), quinoa (Figure 1c), amaranth (Figure 1d), millet (Figure 1e), and sorghum (Figure 1f) dough with C1 below 1.1 $\pm$ 0.05 Nm and C2 values falling in a very narrow range of 0.01–0.09 Nm; and (iii) buckwheat dough with a Mixolab curve having C1 over 4.50 Nm and lacking C2, with the dough consistency being in a continuous decrease during heating from 30 °C to 50–55 °C (Table 4, Figure 1g). For gluten-free flour from group (ii), the water amount from the dough system appears to be too high with respect to the requirements for the chemical components of the flour, while in the case of buckwheat flour, the amount of water used for preparing the dough appeared to be too low.

MWP was significantly correlated with the LA-SRC for both tested WA levels: WA1 needed to obtain C1 of 1.1 $\pm$ 0.05 Nm (R^2 of 0.891, $p < 0.05$) and WA2 of 85% (R^2 of 0.719 and $p < 0.05$).

Additional correlations were established between the various solvent retention capacities of the gluten-free flours and the thermo-mechanical properties of the corresponding doughs, which depended on the WA level. For instance, for WA1, the C2 (R^2 of 0.941 and $p < 0.01$), (C2-C1) (R^2 of 0.943 and $p < 0.01$), and MWP (R^2 of 0.776 and $p < 0.05$) were significantly correlated with SC-SRC. Moreover, for WA1, the Ca-SRC was significantly correlated with (C1-C2) (R^2 of 0.968 and $p < 0.01$), while for WA2, Ca-SRC was significantly correlated with MWP (R^2 of 0.629 and $p < 0.05$). According to Codină et al. [34], calcium ions decrease the softening degree of the dough during kneading. For wheat flour, Ca^{2+} was reported to improve protein solubility and to favor the overall hydration capacity [35]. When factoring in the role played by wheat flour starch, the destabilization effect, which is associated in particular with the damaged starch, should be considered. Given the existence of high spaces between the amylopectin chains in the damaged starch of wheat flour, the binding of Ca^{2+} is facilitated, thereby favoring the increase of the water absorption values of the doughs.

Finally, (C1-C2) was correlated with LA-SRC (R^2 of 0.684 and $p < 0.05$) when the WA2 of 85% was used, suggesting that the ability of the gluten-free flours to retain the lactic acid solution might provide information on the weakening behavior of the proteins.

As the temperature rises from 50–55 °C to 90 °C, the protein's contribution to the dough consistency decreases and the starch properties become more important. Higher starch gelatinization (C3) and hot gel stability (C4) values were observed for the doughs prepared using WA1, which needed to obtain C1 of 1.1 $\pm$ 0.05 Nm, compared to WA2 of 85% (Tables 3 and 4). The use of a higher WA level of 85% appeared to benefit the dough by improving the structure of the dough prepared with millet, oat, and rice, respectively. Sorghum, buckwheat, and millet formed stronger starch networks than rice and oat when the WA2 of 85% was used.

In the case of quinoa and amaranth flour, the dough with WA2 had a very low maximum consistency C3 and starch retrogradation (C5-C4) (Table 4) compared to the corresponding dough samples prepared with WA1. The Mixolab curve indicated an atypical behavior of the amaranth flour-based dough at 95 °C and while cooling at 50 °C compared to other investigated flour samples. Similar results were reported by Inglett et al. [36], who obtained low values for the maximum viscosity, and the viscosity remained constant even after cooling to 50 °C.

Starch behavior is influenced by the particularities of the starch structure; more specifically, it is influenced by the length of the amylose and amylopectin chains and the ratio between the two macromolecules [37]. Quinoa and amaranth have amylose contents of

10.92% and 17.96%, respectively. Although millet has an intermediate amylose content of 12.77%, a different starch retrogradation behavior was noticed, which was likely the result of differences in the botanical source of the starch. It should also be noted that quinoa, amaranth, and millet had a lower content of starch and higher content of lipids compared to the other investigated flours. These observations comply with previous findings that indicate that lipids can complex amylose, thereby causing a reduction in the peak viscosity [21,38]. On the other hand, rice flour, which has the highest amount of carbohydrates among all investigated flours (Table 1), had maximum peak torque (C3) and gelatinization intensity (C3-C2) values that prevail over those of other flours when the doughs were prepared using WA1, which was needed to obtain C1 of 1.1 $\pm$ 0.05 Nm.

The dough systems prepared with a higher amount of water (WA2) presented a lower starch retrogradation (C5) compared to the corresponding doughs with WA1. A better bread-making performance of the flours with a low C5 value was suggested by Ekpa et al. [39], who also related these parameters with a slow staling process. The increase of the water level used to prepare the dough, from WA1 to WA2, also resulted in a decrease of the setback torques (C5-C4) (Tables 3 and 4). In agreement with Ekpa et al. [39], this decrease might result in the improvement of the shelf life of bread.

4. Conclusions

Significant correlations were found between the solvent retention capacity of gluten-free flours and the thermo-mechanical properties of the doughs prepared at two different hydration levels. A significant correlation was found at lower hydration levels between the mechanical weakening of the proteins and the LA-SRC. At a high water absorption of 85%, the strength of the protein network while heating the dough was correlated with LA-SRC, but no correlation could be established at a lower water absorption level when the dough had C1 of 1.1 $\pm$ 0.05 Nm. The starch behavior at high temperatures highly depended on the amount of water used to prepare the dough systems. The gluten-free dough systems with a higher water absorption presented higher values of starch gelatinization and hot gel stability. The high amount of water in the dough system also resulted in the decrease of starch retrogradation and setback torques, a situation that can be associated with the increase of bread shelf life.

Author Contributions: Conceptualization, I.A. and I.B.; methodology, I.B.; validation, I.A.; formal analysis, I.B.; investigation, I.B. and I.A.; writing—original draft preparation, I.B.; writing -review and editing, I.A.; supervision, I.A. All authors have read and agreed to the published version of the manuscript.

Funding: This research received no external funding.

Institutional Review Board Statement: Not applicable.

Informed Consent Statement: Not applicable.

Data Availability Statement: Data is contained within the article.

Conflicts of Interest: The authors declare no conflict of interest.

References

1. Cao, X.; Wen, H.; Li, C.; Gu, Z. Differences in functional properties and biochemical characteristics of congenetic rice proteins. *J. Cereal Sci.* **2009**, *50*, 184–189. [CrossRef]
2. Badiu, E.; Aprodu, I.; Banu, I. Trends in the development of gluten-free bakery products. *Nnals Univ. Dunarea De Jos Galati Fasc. VI-Food Technol* **2014**, *38*, 21–36.
3. Niu, Q.; Pu, Y.; Li, X.; Ma, Z.; Hu, X. Solvent Retention Capacities of Oat Flour. *Int. J. Mol. Sci.* **2017**, *18*, 590. [CrossRef] [PubMed]
4. Zhang, K.; Li, X.; Ma, Z.; Hu, Z. Solvent retention capacity of oat flour: Relationship with oat β-glucan content and molecular weight. *Food Hydrocoll.* **2019**, *93*, 19–23. [CrossRef]
5. Yue, J.; Gu, Z.; Zhu, Z.; Yi, J.; Ohm, J.B.; Chen, B.; Rao, J. Impact of defatting treatment and oat varieties on structural, functional properties, and aromatic profile of oat protein. *Food Hydrocoll.* **2021**, *112*, 106368. [CrossRef]
6. Agrawal, R.S. Quinoa—Supergrain of the future: A Review. *Pharma Innov.* **2018**, *7*, 249–251.

7. Ng, S.C.; Anderson, A.; Coker, J.; Ondrus, M. Characterization of lipid oxidation products in quinoa (*Chenopodium quinoa*). *Food Chem.* **2007**, *101*, 185–192. [CrossRef]
8. Dakhili, S.; Abdolalizadeh, L.; Hosseini, S.M.; Shojaee-Aliabadi, S.; Mirmoghtadaie, L. Quinoa protein: Composition, structure and functional properties. *Food Chem.* **2019**, *299*, 125161. [CrossRef]
9. Joshi, D.C.; Sood, S.; Hosahatti, R.; Kant, L.; Pattanayak, A.; Kumar, A.; Yadav, D.; Stetter, M.G. From zero to hero: The past, present and future of grain amaranth breeding. *Theor. Appl. Genet.* **2018**, *131*, 1807–1823. [CrossRef]
10. Narwade, S.; Pinto, S. Amaranth—A Functional Food. *Concepts Dairy Vet. Sci.* **2018**, *1*, 000112.
11. Torbica, A.; Hadnađev, M.; Hadnađev, T.D. Rice and buckwheat flour characterisation and its relation to cookie quality. *Food Res. Int.* **2012**, *48*, 277–283. [CrossRef]
12. Fu, J.; Zhang, Y.; Hu, Y.; Zhao, G.; Tang, Y.; Zou, L. Concise review: Coarse cereals exert multiple beneficial effects on human health. *Food Chem.* **2020**, *325*, 126761. [CrossRef] [PubMed]
13. Hamaker, B.R.; Bugusu, B.A. Overview: Sorghum protein and food quality. Department of Food Science. Purdue University and the INTSORMIL CRSP West Lafayette, Indiana, USA (20 May 2003). In Proceedings of the Afripro-Workshop on the Proteins of Sorghum and Millets: Enhancing Nutritional and Functional Properties for Africa, Indiana, Pretoria, South Africa, 2–4 April 2003.
14. Sharma, N.; Niranjan, K. Foxtail millet: Properties, processing, health benefits, and uses. *Food Rev. Int.* **2018**, *34*, 329–363. [CrossRef]
15. Sachdev, N.; Goomer, S.; Singh, L.R. Foxtail millet: A potential crop to meet future demand scenario for alternative sustainable protein. *J. Sci. Food Agr.* **2021**, *101*, 831–842. [CrossRef] [PubMed]
16. SR ISO 712:2005; SR ISO 2171/2002. Romanian Standards Catalog for Cereal and Milling Products Analysis; ASRO: Bucharest, Romania, 2008.
17. Delcour, J.A.; Vanhamel, S.; De Geest, C. Physico-Chemical and Functional Properties of Rye Nonstarch Polysaccharides. I. Colorimetric Analysis of Pentosans and Their Relative Monosaccharide Compositions in Fractionated (Milled) Rye Products. *Cereal Chem.* **1989**, *66*, 107–111.
18. AACC International. *Approved Methods of Analysis*, 11th ed.; Methods 56-11.02 and 76-31.01; American Association of Cereal Chemists International: St. Paul, MN, USA, 2000.
19. Godon, B.; Wilhm, C. *Primary Cereal Processing A Comprehensive Sourcebook*; VCH: New York, NY, USA, 1994; pp. 129–130.
20. Dubat, A.; Boinot, N. *Mixolab Applications Handbook. Rheological and Enzymes Analyses*; Chopin Technology: Villenueve, France, 2012; p. 14.
21. Hadnadev, T.D.; Torbica, A.; Hadnadev, M. Rheological properties of wheat flour substitutes/alternative crops assessed by Mixolab. *Procedia Food Sci.* **2011**, *1*, 328–334. [CrossRef]
22. Barrera, G.; Perez, G.; Ribotta, P.; Leon, A. Influence of damaged starch on cookie and bread-making quality. *Eur. Food Res. Technol.* **2007**, *225*, 1–7. [CrossRef]
23. Topin, V.; Radjai, F.; Dellene, J.Y.; Sadoudi, A.; Mabille, F. Wheat endosperm as a cohesive granular material. *J. Cereal Sci.* **2008**, *47*, 347–356. [CrossRef]
24. Collar, C.; Angioloni, A. Pseudocereals and teff in complex breadmaking matrices: Impact on lipid dynamics. *J. Cereal Sci.* **2014**, *59*, 145–154. [CrossRef]
25. Mariotti, M.; Lucisano, M.; Pagani, M.A.; Ng, P.K.W. Effects of dispersing media and heating rates on pasting profiles of wheat and gluten-free samples in relation to their solvent retention capacities and mixing properties. *LWT Food Sci. Technol.* **2016**, *66*, 201–210. [CrossRef]
26. Kweon, M.; Slade, L.; Levine, H. Solvent retention capacity (SRC) testing of wheat flour: Principles and value in predicting flour functionality in different wheat-based food processes and in wheat breeding—A review. *Cereal Chem.* **2011**, *88*, 537–552. [CrossRef]
27. Wang, N.; Hou, G.G.; Kweon, M.; Lee, B. Effects of particle size on the properties of whole-grain soft wheat flour and its cracker baking performance. *J. Cereal Sci.* **2016**, *69*, 187–193. [CrossRef]
28. Guo, X.; Hu, G.; Liu, S. Anti-nutritive role of oat β-glucan and application of oat β-glucanase in feed. *Jiangxi Feed* **2001**, *2*, 11–13.
29. Yamazaki, E.; Murakami, K.; Kurita, O. Easy preparation of dietary fiber with the high water-holding capacity from food sources. *Plant Foods Hum. Nutr.* **2005**, *60*, 17–23. [CrossRef]
30. Cappa, C.; Lucisano, M.; Mariotti, M. Influence of Psyllium, sugar beet fibre and water on gluten-free dough properties and bread quality. *Carbohyd. Polym.* **2013**, *98*, 1657–1666. [CrossRef]
31. Torbica, A.; Belović, M.; Tomić, J. Novel breads of non-wheat flours. *Food Chem.* **2019**, *282*, 134–140. [CrossRef]
32. Alonso-Miravalles, L.; O'Mahony, J. Composition, Protein Profile and Rheological Properties of Pseudocereal-Based Protein-Rich Ingredients. *Foods* **2018**, *7*, 73. [CrossRef]
33. Akharume, F.; Santra, D.; Adedeji, A. Physicochemical and functional properties of proso millet storage protein fractions. *Food Hydrocoll.* **2020**, *108*, 105497. [CrossRef]
34. Codină, G.G.; Zaharia, D.; Stroe, S.G.; Ropciuc, S. Influence of calcium ions addition from gluconate and lactate salts on refined wheat flour dough rheological properties. *CYTA J. Food* **2018**, *16*, 884–891. [CrossRef]
35. Sehn, G.A.R.; Nogueira, A.C.; Almeida, E.L.; Chang, Y.K.; Steel, C.J. Fortification of wheat dough with calcium and magnesium ions affects empirical rheological properties. *Cereal Chem.* **2015**, *92*, 405–410. [CrossRef]

36. Inglett, G.E.; Chen, D.; Liu, S.X. Physical properties of gluten-free sugar cookies made from amaranth-oat composites. *LWT Food Sci. Technol.* **2015**, *63*, 214–220. [CrossRef]
37. Aprodu, I.; Banu, I. Milling, functional and thermo-mechanical properties of wheat, rye, triticale, barley and oat. *J. Cereal Sci.* **2017**, *77*, 42–48. [CrossRef]
38. Zaidul, I.S.M.; Yamauchi, H.; Kim, S.; Hashimotom, N.; Noda, T. RVA study of mixtures of wheat flour and potato starches with different phosphorus contents. *Food Chem.* **2007**, *102*, 1105–1111. [CrossRef]
39. Ekpa, O.; Palacios-Rojas, N.; Rosales, A.; Renzetti, S.; Fogliano, V.; Linnemann, A. Genotype selection influences the quality of gluten-free bread from maize. *LWT Food Sci. Technol.* **2020**, *125*, 109214. [CrossRef]

foods MDPI

Article

Chemical Composition, Fatty Acid and Mineral Content of Food-Grade White, Red and Black Sorghum Varieties Grown in the Mediterranean Environment

Paola Pontieri [1,*], Jacopo Troisi [2], Matteo Calcagnile [3], Scott R. Bean [4], Michael Tilley [4], Fadi Aramouni [4], Antonio Boffa [1], Giacomo Pepe [5], Pietro Campiglia [5], Fabio Del Giudice [6], Alberto L. Chessa [7], Dmitriy Smolensky [4], Mariarosaria Aletta [8], Pietro Alifano [3] and Luigi Del Giudice [1]

1 Istituto di Bioscienze e BioRisorse-UOS Napoli-CNR c/o Dipartimento di Biologia, Sezione di Igiene, 80134 Napoli, Italy; boffa83@gmail.com (A.B.); luigi.delgiudice@ibbr.cnr.it (L.D.G.)
2 Theoreosrl, Spin Off of the University of Salerno, Department of Medicine and Surgery, Via Degli Ulivi, 3, Montecorvino Pugliano, 84090 Salerno, Italy; troisi@theoreosrl.com
3 Dipartimento di Scienze e Tecnologie Biologiche e Ambientali, Università del Salento, 73100 Lecce, Italy; matteo.calcagnile@unisalento.it (M.C.); pietro.alifano@unisalento.it (P.A.)
4 USDA-ARS, CGAHR, Manhattan, KS 66502, USA; scott.bean@usda.gov (S.R.B.); michael.tilley@usda.gov (M.T.); fadi.aramouni@usda.gov (F.A.); dmitriy.smolensky@usda.gov (D.S.)
5 Department of Pharmacy, School of Pharmacy, University of Salerno, 84084 Fisciano, Italy; gipepe@unisa.it (G.P.); pcampiglia@unisa.it (P.C.)
6 Bioteam Laboratory, Via Girolamo Santacroce, 80129 Napoli, Italy; felicita24@libero.it
7 Sorghum Breeder, Fernando Camino N° 15 P4 F, 29016 Málaga, Spain; alberto.chessa@outlook.com
8 DCSRSI SPR BIBLIOTECA, 80131 Napoli, Italy; mariarosaria.aletta@igb.cnr.it
* Correspondence: paola.pontieri@ibbr.cnr.it

Citation: Pontieri, P.; Troisi, J.; Calcagnile, M.; Bean, S.R.; Tilley, M.; Aramouni, F.; Boffa, A.; Pepe, G.; Campiglia, P.; Del Giudice, F.; et al. Chemical Composition, Fatty Acid and Mineral Content of Food-Grade White, Red and Black Sorghum Varieties Grown in the Mediterranean Environment. *Foods* **2022**, *11*, 436. https://doi.org/10.3390/foods11030436

Academic Editors: Laura Gazza and Francesca Nocente

Received: 29 December 2021
Accepted: 28 January 2022
Published: 2 February 2022

Abstract: Grain sorghum (*Sorghum bicolor*) is a gluten-free cereal grown around the world and is a food staple in semi-arid and subtropical regions. Sorghum is a diverse crop with a range of pericarp colour including white, various shades of red, and black, all of which show health-promoting properties as they are rich sources of antioxidants such as polyphenols, carotenoids, as well as micro- and macro-nutrients. This work examined the grain composition of three sorghum varieties possessing a range of pericarp colours (white, red, and black) grown in the Mediterranean region. To determine the nutritional quality independent of the contributions of phenolics, mineral and fatty acid content and composition were measured. Minor differences in both protein and carbohydrate were observed among varieties, and a higher fibre content was found in both the red and black varieties. A higher amount of total saturated fats was found in the white variety, while the black variety had a lower amount of total unsaturated and polyunsaturated fats than either the white or red varieties. Oleic, linoleic, and palmitic were the primary fatty acids in all three analysed sorghum varieties. Significant differences in mineral content were found among the samples with a greater amount of Mg, K, Al, Mn, Fe, Ni, Zn, Pb and U in both red and black than the white sorghum variety. The results show that sorghum whole grain flour made from grain with varying pericarp colours contains unique nutritional properties.

Keywords: sorghum; pericarp; nutrition; grain; proximate composition; minerals; lipid composition

1. Introduction

Sorghum (*Sorghum bicolor* (L.) Moench) is a widely consumed cereal staple in regions of Africa and Asia [1–8] and is the fifth leading cereal crop in the world, after the crops wheat, maize, rice, and barley [9]. The United States is the number one producer and exporter of sorghum, generating roughly 20% of total production and near 80% of total sorghum exports from 2001–2003 [10]). Where sorghum has been traditionally a basic food staple, it has also been used in several food products and in some cases health food items [8,11,12]. Sorghum does not contain peptide sequences that are toxic to persons with celiac disease, as are found in wheat, barley, and rye, and is therefore a safe food for celiac patients [13–15]. With increasing interest related to the unique properties of sorghum, its value as a food in helping to improve human health and to prevent disease has generated increasing research [1,2,4,11,15–17]. Specifically, increased research attention has focussed on the diverse content of phenolic compounds present in sorghum, which is a unique attribute among cereal grains [2]. These phenolic compounds have been shown to have various properties, e.g., inhibiting cancer cell growth [17], and while more research is needed on the health benefits of sorghum, consumption of whole grain sorghum may have the potential to help reduce health problems such as heart disease, diabetes, and obesity [16].

A current trend worldwide is a considerable preference for foods that have additional health benefits beyond basic nutrition. Research has continued to demonstrate that sorghum whole grains have numerous human health benefits, especially as related to antioxidant activity of phenolic compounds present in the outer layers of the grain [18,19]. The free radical scavenging activity of sorghum phenolic compounds has been related to beneficial health attributes, including anti-microbial properties [20], reduced oxidative stress [18], anti-inflammatory properties [21] and anti-cancer activity [17,22–25], thereby adding value to sorghum grains and its increasing human consumption [26]. The beneficial activities of sorghum for human health have been attributed mainly to the phenolic compounds found in sorghum grain and which are well known to vary with pericarp colour. While much of the research related to sorghum phenolic compounds and potential health benefits has been conducted using whole sorghum bran, or crude extracts from sorghum grain/bran, e.g., [6,17,18,20,21], numerous types of polyphenols have been identified in sorghum with examples including, flavonoids, hydroxybenzoic acids and hydroxycinnamic acids with specific levels varying according to both genetics and environment [24,27]. Several varieties of sorghum exist with a wide range of pericarp colour, and which can be classified based on the pigmentation of the pericarp [28]. In particular, research has shown that total phenolic content and antioxidant activity in sorghum are correlated with the pericarp thickness and colour, and sorghum with darker and thicker pericarp had greater levels of phenolic compounds and increased antioxidant activity [28,29]. Highly pigmented sorghum may therefore be desirable for use in human foods with improved human health attributes.

Substantial research has been conducted with the aim of developing the cultivation of sorghum lines in the Mediterranean area for use in production of human food products [8,30–32]. With that overall goal, the focus of this research was to compare the nutritional composition of sorghum varieties that differed in pericarp colour to (1) determine how nutritional properties other than phenolic content varied and (2) identify varieties with improved nutritional characteristics in addition to phenolic content and thus provide greater potential health value for consumers. Additionally, this research adds to the body of knowledge on sorghum grain nutrient composition, especially for sorghum grown outside the major sorghum producing regions.

2. Materials and Methods

2.1. Sorghum Cultivars

The sorghum varieties along with seed sources used in this research are shown in Table 1. In 2019, sorghum production was conducted in San Bartolomeo in Galdo (BN) in the Fortore area, which is in the Campania Region of southern Italy (41°25′ N, 15°01′ E and 597 m a.s.l.). The soil in this region is predominantly clay loam, deep and with a good water holding capacity. The milling was carried out starting from 1 month from the harvest of the sorghum grain, which was stored in a dry environment at 16 °C.

Table 1. List of sorghum varieties.

Variety Colour	Variety Name	Source	Supplied by
White sorghum	DSM 3-410	Richardson Seeds Ltd.	M. Malin
Red sorghum	DSM IF-41912	Richardson Seeds Ltd.	M. Malin
Black sorghum	DSM 212-2311	Richardson Seeds Ltd.	M. Malin

2.2. Flour Sample Preparation

Flour samples were produced from approximately 1 kg of grain samples that were milled using a two-roll mill (Chopin Moulin CD1; Chopin S.A., Villeneuve la Garenne, France) and subsequently were sieved using a planetary sieve (Buhler AG, Uzwil, Switzerland) with a screen size of 120 μm^2.

2.3. Moisture

Moisture was determined according to the method described by Pontieri et al. [31]. Briefly, a ceramic capsule was accurately weighed after a complete desiccation at 100 °C in vacuum-packed (25 mm Hg) conditions using an oven (ISCO mod. NSV9035) and chilled at room temperature in a silica gel dryer. Then, an accurately weighed aliquot of flour samples (about 2 g) was placed in the desiccated ceramic capsule. The humidity was removed from the sample, by keeping it in the same temperature and pressure conditions for about five hours, until a constant weight was achieved. The moisture content was estimated by the weight loss.

2.4. Ash

To measure total ash, sorghum grain samples (ca. 3 g each) were weighed into broad, shallow ashing dishes and incinerated at ~550 °C, after which the dishes were placed in a desiccator to cool and then weighed after coming to room temperature [33].

2.5. Protein Content

Nitrogen content was measured using the Kjeldahl method [34] with total protein content determined with a conversion factor of 6.25. Sorghum grain samples (2 g each) were analysed with a Mineral Six Digester and an Auto Disteam semi-automatic distilling unit (International PBI, Milan, Italy).

2.6. Total Lipid Content

Total lipid content was measured as described by Pontieri et al. [30]. Briefly, approximately 3 g of grain was ground with liquid nitrogen using a mortar and pestle and lyophilized with the FTS-System Flex-DryTM instrument. The ground whole meal was then extracted using a Soxhlet apparatus with chloroform ($CHCl_3$) for 4 h. Extracts were then dried with a rotary evaporator to obtain the crude extracts, which were subsequently weighed to determine the amount of extracted fat.

2.7. Gas Chromatography of Fatty Acids

Esterification of fatty acids from the crude extracts and subsequent gas chromatographic analysis of the fatty acid methyl esters was carried out as described previously [30,31]. Briefly, solid sorghum fat was melted in an oven at 50 °C to determinate its composition. A drop of fat was transferred into a 1.5 mL-vial. One ml of hexane and 100µL of 2N KOH methanolic solution were added. The vial was vortexed for 5 min, and then left under static conditions for 5 min, to enable a complete stratification of the hexanic portion, which contained the methyl ester of the fatty acids. Chromatographic separation was achieved using a GC-2010 (Shimadzu, Kyoto, Japan) equipped with a DB-Wax (Phenomenex, Torrance, CA, USA), 30 m length, 0.25 mm internal diameter, 0.25 µm film thickness column. The GC conditions were as follows: carrier gas, He; pressure, 75 kPa; injector temperature, 220 °C;

FID temperature, 250 °C; and oven program, 170 °C for 8 min, 2°C/min to 185 °C for 10 min, 1 °C/min to 190 °C for 12 min, 10 °C/min to 240 °C for 5 min.

2.8. Carbohydrates

Carbohydrate content was determined by subtraction as the amount of material left after accounting for moisture, ash, protein, and fat content [35].

2.9. Fibre

Fibre was determined according to the AOAC [36] method. Briefly, fibre was determined as the loss, after incineration, of the sample digested in an acidic environment by H_2SO_4 (0.255 N), followed by an alkaline digestion with NaOH (0.223 N). Digestion was obtained with an automatic digestor (Velp Scientific mod. FIWE3, Usmate Velate, Monza e Brianza, Italy).

2.10. Total Minerals Determination

The determination of the mineral elements of interest was performed according to Tenore et al. [37] as described by Pontieri et al. [38].

Briefly, for each sample, the ash content was solubilized using ultrapure water (18 MΩ, produced using a Millipore Direct-Q UV3 water purifier) based HNO_3 (Ultrapure, Sigma Aldrich, St. Louis, MO, USA) 5% solution. The solution was filtered using ash-free regenerated cellulose filters. All chemicals were of the highest commercially available purity grade. No glass (flask, pipettes, etc.) was used for any operation. Before use, all plastic containers were cleaned using 10% ultra-pure grade HNO_3 for at least 24 h, and then rinsed copiously with ultra-pure water before use.

Element quantification was performed using quadrupole inductively coupled plasma mass spectrometry, ICP-QMS (820-MS, Bruker Daltonics, Billerica, MA). The operational parameters were: Plasma flow: 18 L/min, Auxiliary flow: 1.8 L/min, Sheath Gas: 0.14 L/min, Nebulizer flow: 0.98 L/min, RF power: 1.40 kW, Pump rate: 4 rpm, Stabilization delay: 20 s, First Extraction Lens: −40 volts, Second Extraction Lens: −166 volts, Third Extraction Lens: −234 volts, Corner Lens: −208 volts, Mirror Lens left: 29 volts, Mirror Lens right: 26 volts, Mirror Lens bottom: 30 volts; CRI parameters: Skimmer Gas: H_2 at 50 mL/min, Sample Gas: He at 10 mL/min; dwell time, 10,000 μs; no. of scan replicate: 10, no. replicate for sample: 5. High purity He (99.9999% He, SALDOGAS Srl, Naples, Italy) and H_2 (99.9999% H_2, produced by the DBS H_2 generator PGH2-300) were used, in order to minimize the potential problems caused by unidentified reactive contaminant species in the cell. Calibration solutions were prepared from multi-elemental standard stock solutions of 20.00 mg/L. Calibration curves were obtained using 9 calibration solutions. Reagent blanks containing ultra-pure water were additionally analysed to control the purity of the reagents and laboratory equipment. Standards and blanks were subjected to the same treatment as the samples. A mixed solution of internal standard (^{6}Li, ^{45}Sc, ^{72}Ge, ^{89}Y, ^{103}Rh ^{159}Tb, ^{165}Ho, ^{209}Bi) 10 μg/L was on-line aspired with a T union with the sample and standard solution.

2.11. ELISA Assay

The RIDASCREENR standard test kit [RIDASCREEN R Gliadin (Art. No R7001) R-Biopharm AG] sandwich ELISA based method was used to determine the presence of protein sequences reactive to gliadins in sorghum flour samples [39] following the manufacturer's instructions. Commercial gliadin standard 16–18% N (Sigma Aldrich, Milan, Italy) was used as control.

2.12. Statistical Analysis

With the exception of total lipids analysis, which was performed in triplicate, all analyses were performed in quintuples (n = 5) (technical replicates), and the results are presented as the mean ± SD. Data distributions were evaluated by means of Shapiro–Wilk test. As all data was not normally distributed, differences in means were investigated using the non-parametric Mann–Whitney U test. Analysis of variance (ANOVA) was used to assess if the different values were statistically significant or not. The Tukey post-hoc test was used to identify which samples were different. False discovery rate (FDR) corrected p-value was used to manage the multiple comparisons.

3. Results

3.1. Nutrient Composition

The chemical composition of white, red, and black sorghum varieties developed in the USA but produced in Southern Italy is shown in Table 2. The table also reports the recommended daily dose (RDA) according to the European legislation [40]. Minor variations in both protein and carbohydrate were observed among the three coloured sorghum varieties analysed, while a higher fibre content was found in both the red and black varieties ($p < 0.05$).

Table 2. Nutritional values of white, red, and black sorghum varieties. Abbreviation: Recommended Daily dose (RDA).

Parameter	White	Red	Black	RDA
Moisture (%)	11.86 ± 0.06	11.92 ± 0.04 *	11.44 ± 0.09 §	
Ash (%)	1.22 ± 0.04	1.44 ± 0.05 *	1.88 ± 0.06 *§	
Total proteins (%)	6.14 ± 0.10	6.85 ± 0.07 *	7.28 * ± 0.09 §	50 g/day
Fats (%)	2.23 ± 0.05	2.00 ± 0.04 *	1.55 * ± 0.03 §	70 g/day
Total carbohydrates (%)	73.17 ± 0.27	71.32 ± 0.30 *	70.07 * ± 0.39 §	260 g/day
Sugars (%)	0.67 ± 0.05	0.63 ± 0.06	0.77 ± 0.06	90 g/day
Fibres (%)	5.37 ± 0.14	6.46 ± 0.29 *	7.78 ± 0.24 *§	

FDR corrected p-value < 0.05 comparing to white sorghum was indicated as *, while comparing to red sorghum as §.

3.2. Fatty Acid Composition of Total Lipids

The percentages of total fatty acids, also aggregated as saturated, mono-unsaturated and polyunsaturated fats, of white, red and black sorghum varieties are shown in Table 3. Greater levels of total saturated fats (* $p < 0.05$) was found in the white variety than in the red and black varieties, while the black variety had a lesser amount of total unsaturated and polyunsaturated fats (* $p < 0.05$) than both the white and red varieties.

Table 3. Fatty acid content (g per 100 g raw fat) of white, red, and black sorghum varieties.

Fatty Acid	White	Red	Black
Myristic acid	0.013 ± 0.000	0.012 ± 0.000	0.036 ± 0.000 *§
Palmitic acid	18.633 ± 0.001	17.322 ± 0.01 *	12.769 ± 0.001 *§
Palmitoleic acid	0.824 ± 0.002	0.792 ± 0.002	0.690 ± 0.001 *§
Margaric acid	0.064 ± 0.534	0.065 ± 0.537	0.099 ± 0.385 *§
Margaroleic acid	0.063 ± 0.447	0.061 ± 0.421	0.067 ± 0.0438 *§
Stearic acid	2.226 ± 0.613	2.236 ± 0.598	1.234 ± 0.599 *§
Oleic acid	37.62 ± 0.031	42.655 ± 0.029 *	40.178 ± 0.018 *§
Linoleic acid	35.707 ± 0.062	33.985 ± 0.058	42.084 ± 0.052 *§
Linolenic acid	2.051 ± 0.087	1.958 ± 0.081	2.084 ± 0.091 *§
Arachidic acid	0.435 ± 0.026	0.374 ± 0.025 *	0.214 ± 0.028 *§
Eicosenoic acid	0.302 ± 0.023	0.274 ± 0.021 *	0.220 ± 0.022 *§
Behenic acid	0.072 ± 0.021	0.061 ± 0.019 *	0.027 ± 0.023 *§
Lignoceric acid	0.203 ± 0.015	0.188 ± 0.013 *	0.232 ± 0.018 *§
Erucic acid	0.019 ± 0.015	0.018 ± 0.013	0.065 ± 0.014 *§
Saturated fats	0.52 ± 0.05	0.41 ± 0.04 *	0.22 ± 0.03 *§
Monounsaturated fats	0.85 ± 0.02	0.89 ± 0.01	0.64 ± 0.02 *§
Polyunsaturated fats	0.86 ± 0.07	0.71 ± 0.02 *	0.69 ± 0.02 *

FDR corrected p-value < 0.05 comparing to white sorghum was indicated as *, while comparing to red sorghum as §.

Oleic, linoleic, and palmitic, were the primary fatty acids in all three of the sorghum varieties analysed, which is in agreement with previously reported results [31,41,42]. The percentage of palmitic acid in the black sorghum variety was slightly lower than both the white and red varieties, while the percentage of linoleic acid was slightly higher in the black variety than in the white and red varieties. Finally, the percentage of oleic acid was comparable between the three varieties of sorghum.

3.3. Mineral Content

Levels of minerals from the three sorghum varieties are reported in Table 4. Statistical analysis was not performed on the mineral content due to the number of minerals tested. However, the levels of macro-elements followed the sequence K > Mg > Ca > Na in all three varieties analysed. Micro-element content followed the sequence Fe > Zn > Al > Mn > Cr > Ni > Cu > Ba > Mo > Pb > Co > Sn > Ag > As > Se > V > Be > Tl in the white variety, while the content of micro-elements followed the sequence Fe > Zn > Al > Mn > Ni > Cu > Cr > Ba > Mo > Pb > Co > Sn > Ag > As > Se > V > Be > Tl in both the red and black varieties analysed. The white variety had a lower element content than that of both the red and black varieties, with K, Fe and Sb were the most abundant macro-element, micro-element, and trace element in all analysed varieties, except Hg which was the most abundant trace element in the white variety. The potassium and sodium content of the samples varied from 26.89 to 35.66 g kg^{-1} and 0.42 to 0.54 g kg^{-1}, respectively, with the potassium content of the samples ranging from about 64-fold to 66-fold higher than that of sodium. Therefore, the K:Na ratio was higher than the recommended ratio 5.0 [43] for the human diet. The fact that the sorghum hybrids all contained a high K:Na ratio suggests that sorghum could be used to modulate sodium-related health problems. In fact, diets with a higher K:Na ratio are recommended for certain health conditions such as [44].

Table 4. Elements content in sorghum varieties. Abbreviation: Recommended Daily dose (RDA).

Metal	Unit	White	Red	Black	RDA
K	g/Kg	26.89 ± 0.62	32.02 ± 0.68 *	35.66 ± 0.61 *§	2.0 g/day
Mg	g/Kg	8.69 ± 0.35	12.86 ± 0.22 *	16.93 ± 0.41 *§	0.375 g/day
Ca	g/Kg	1.25 ± 0.03	2.16 ± 0.03 *	2.88 ± 0.08 *§	0.8 g/day
Na	g/Kg	0.42 ± 0.04	0.43 ± 0.01	0.54 ± 0.01 *§	
Fe	mg/Kg	346.91 ± 1.35	578.75 ± 1.42 *	655.15 ± 1.37 *§	14 mg/day
Zn	mg/Kg	180.21 ± 0.86	250.47 ± 5.34 *	284.35 ± 7.59 *§	10 mg/day
Al	mg/Kg	54.59 ± 0.54	179.01 ± 5.43 *	200.01 ± 4.68 *§	
Mn	mg/Kg	49.81 ± 1.22	79.44 ± 2.58 *	98.68 ± 2.53 *§	2 mg/day
Cr	mg/Kg	31.17 ± 1.13	43.54 ± 1.55 *	53.74 ± 0.61 *§	0.04 mg/day
Ni	mg/Kg	29.32 ± 0.51	40.13 ± 0.78 *	49.91 ± 1.46 *§	
Cu	mg/Kg	24.11 ± 0.49	31.83 ± 0.88 *	35.56 ± 0.83 *§	1 mg/day
Ba	mg/Kg	4.63 ± 0.14	6.46 ± 0.25 *	8.00 ± 0.08 *§	
Mo	mg/Kg	1.15 ± 0.03	1.62 ± 0.02 *	2.05 ± 0.05 *§	0.05 mg/day
Pb	mg/Kg	0.57 ± 0.06	1.39 ± 0.04 *	1.61 ± 0.06 *§	
Co	mg/Kg	0.50 ± 0.02	0.96 ± 0.01 *	1.07 ± 0.01 *§	
Sn	mg/Kg	0.17 ± 0.01	0.31 ± 0.01 *	0.39 ± 0.01 *§	
Ag	mg/Kg	0.17 ± 0.01	0.30 ± 0.01 *	0.34 ± 0.01 *§	
As	mg/Kg	0.63 ± 0.01	0.23 ± 0.01 *	0.28 ± 0.01 *§	
Se	mg/Kg	0.08 ± 0.01	0.05 ± 0.01 *	0.07 ± 0.01 *§	0.055 mg/day
V	mg/Kg	<0.01	<0.01	<0.01	
Be	mg/Kg	<0.01	<0.01	<0.01	
Tl	mg/Kg	<0.01	<0.01	<0.01	
Sb	µg/Kg	38.62 ± 0.90	64.69 ± 1.10 *	79.80 ± 2.01 *§	
Hg	µg/Kg	61.56 ± 3.08	50.81 ± 2.06 *	62.70 ± 2.20 §	
Cd	µg/Kg	11.86 ± 0.20	32.90 ± 0.68 *	36.93 ± 0.86 *§	
U	µg/Kg	3.14 ± 0.05	5.54 ± 0.13 *	6.21 ± 0.12 *§	

FDR corrected *p*-value < 0.05 comparing to white sorghum was indicated as *, while comparing to red sorghum as §.

3.4. Immunochemical Evidence for the Absence of Gluten in Coloured Sorghum Varieties

Immunochemical measurement of gliadin concentration in the sorghum flour from all samples tested showed that gluten levels in all sorghum cultivars were less than 5 ppm (the detectable limit) (Table 5) and are at levels substantially below the 20 mg/kg (ppm) threshold recommended as safe for celiac patients [39].

Table 5. Measurement of gliadin (as ppm) in flours by using sandwich R5 enzyme-linked immunosorbent assay (ELISA).

Variety	Type	Content (ppm) [2]
White	Sorghum	<5
Red	Sorghum	<5
Black	Sorghum	<5
Gliadin standard [1]	Wheat	56

[1] Gliadin standard from wheat (Sigma). [2] Mean values from 3 measurements.

4. Discussion

As it has been reported that pericarp colour of sorghum grain may vary due to both genotype environmental factors [42,45,46], in this work we compared both the chemical composition and the content of fatty acids and the mineral content of three coloured varieties of sorghum grown in the Mediterranean environment of Southern Italy. The search for varieties of sorghum developed in the USA that have high functional and nutraceutical properties when grown in the Mediterranean area will stimulate the use of sorghum for human use as a health food in European countries; it may encourage European farmers to produce sorghum, as it is a drought tolerant plant very well suited to environmental changes [8].

The composition profiles of white, red, and black food-grade sorghum varieties developed in the USA, and grown in Southern Italy, were overall similar with slight differences in both protein and carbohydrate percentages. The higher fibre content found in the red and black varieties suggests that this variety may have health benefits in addition to those conferred from just phenolic compounds. The black sorghum also had slightly higher total protein levels and less total fat, which could be minor benefits for use of black sorghum flour in human food products.

The quantities of the total saturated and mono-unsaturated fats of both the white and red varieties were similar and higher than those of the black variety, while the red and black varieties had similar quantities of total polyunsaturated fats but lower than that of the white variety. Thus, the black variety analysed in this research may have a slight nutritional advantage related to consumption of saturated fat relative the other two varieties. Oleic, linoleic, and palmitic were the primary fatty acids in all the sorghum varieties. Unsaturated fatty acids are important for human nutrition, as they are major components of biological membranes and play a role in modulating the fluidity of membranes. Additionally, unsaturated fatty acids do not have cholesterogenic properties (unlike saturated fatty acids), and reduce the risk of thrombosis, due to anti-aggregating activity of blood lipoprotein particles. Because of these features, unsaturated fatty acids are strongly recommended to lower the risk of atherosclerosis [4,11,16]. The sorghum samples analysed in this work all contained some levels of unsaturated fatty acids and could supplement other plant-based sources of unsaturated fats in human diets.

The content of each macro-element followed the sequence K > Mg > Ca > Na in all three coloured sorghum varieties analysed with the primary mineral being K, followed by Mg, which is consistent with the literature [38,47–49]. Furthermore, the concentrations of the above four macro-elements were higher in the red and black sorghum varieties than in the white sorghum variety, confirming previous works whose results indicate that the mineral content of sorghum was affected by both genetic and environmental factors [38]. With regards to macro-element content, this research reported a K:Na ratio greater than what is recommended in the human diet for all sorghum varieties analysed [43]. An improved K:Na ratio may improve bone health, lessen muscle loss, and moderate other chronic diseases such as hypertension and stroke [44]. In addition to the above, the magnesium content in the sorghum varieties was greater than typically found in corn (on average, 0.47 g kg^{-1}) and wheat flour (on average, 0.25 g kg^{-1}) [50]. Because each of the three types of coloured sorghum varieties analysed have high magnesium content, these sorghum varieties may be good sources of magnesium. Magnesium is an important macro-element because it is required for the function of many enzyme systems and therefore human metabolism [50].

The content of micro-elements followed the sequence Fe > Zn > Al > Mn > Cr > Ni > Cu > Ba > Mo > Pb > Co > Sn > Ag > As > Se > V >Be > Tl in the white variety analysed, while the content of micro-elements followed the sequence Fe > Zn > Al > Mn > Ni > Cu > Cr > Ba > Mo > Pb > Co > Sn > Ag > As > Se > V > Be > Tl in both red and black varieties analysed. The differences in the concentrations of some micro-elements between the white sorghum variety and both red and black sorghum varieties reported above could be affected by the sorghum variety, soil conditions and the state of plant maturity at harvest [38]. The most abundant micro-element was Fe in all three sorghum varieties analysed, confirming the data reported in the literature [38,46,49]. The latter is an essential micro-element in human nutrition, and Fe-deficiency is a major public health threat worldwide [6]. The expanding production of sorghum for human use in the US [11] and in Mediterranean countries [8], suggests the use of this cereal for healthy nutrition. Thus, identifying sorghum varieties with the highest levels of Fe is beneficial when identifying sorghum varieties for production in Europe.

The concentrations of trace element content followed the sequence Hg > Sb > Cd > U in the white variety, while it followed the sequence Sb > Hg > Cd > U in both red and black varieties. Importantly, with regards to the trace elements Sb, Hg, Cd, U, their concentration in the three sorghum hybrids analysed in this study did not exceed the maximum permitted by Regulation (CE) n. 41/2009.

Regarding the micro-elements content, the results reported in the present study show high content of both Fe and Zn in all sorghums. The latter two elements are essential micro-elements in human nutrition, and Fe and Zn deficiencies are worldwide public health issues [6].

Furthermore, in this work, the sorghum varieties developed in the USA and grown in the Mediterranean environment were also analysed immunochemically to measure the concentration of gliadin to verify previous reports on safety of sorghum for people with celiac disease. As shown in Table 5, the results indicated that the gluten levels in all sorghum cultivars were less than 5 mg/kg (below detectable limits) which is below the 20 mg/kg level proposed as a safe level for celiac patients [39] and agrees with previous results [13–15].

5. Conclusions

Consumers worldwide have increasingly expressed interest in both functional and nutraceutical foods due to the additional health benefits provided through their consumption. Substantial research has been focused on identifying the mechanisms associated with the disease prevention or therapeutic potential of such foods. One example of a functional and nutraceutical food that has received increased research attention is sorghum grain. It is well known that sorghum is a genetically diverse crop—that diversity extends to the presence of phenolic content and composition, and results in phenotypic expression in sorghum grain with a range of pericarp colours. Sorghum has been studied for several potential human health benefits, including the role of sorghum phenolic compounds present in types of sorghum that vary in pericarp colour. The present study supports the continued strategy of evaluating sorghum with a range of pericarp colour not only for the properties of their phenolic compounds, but also for additional nutritional properties such as protein and carbohydrate contents, levels of unsaturated fatty acids and minerals. Sorghum varieties developed for production in the USA and grown in the Mediterranean region demonstrate the feasibility of producing a range of different sorghums that vary in polyphenolic content and the high antioxidant capacity of the compound eriodictyol-O-hexoside isolated from the red sorghum variety, a flavonoid very important for human health due to its ability to fight free radicals with high efficiency [51]. The current research provides valuable information on nutrient composition of sorghum and supports the growing research on the unique health benefits of sorghum whole grain consumption. This research also shows that sorghum varying in pericarp colour and in associated phenolic compounds [50] can also vary in overall nutrient composition.

Cereals have long been consumed by humans and are staple foods providing a primary source of carbohydrates, proteins, B vitamins and minerals for a substantial portions of the world's population; this is especially so where sorghum is consumed as the primary food source. Sorghum also contains a variety of phytochemicals which may, in addition to basic nutrition, provide some of the health benefits seen in populations consuming primarily plant food-based diets [47]. The fact that the nutritional composition was similar between the same varieties of sorghum grown in the USA and in the Mediterranean area is confirmation that it is possible to utilize sorghum for human use in Europe.

Author Contributions: Conceptualization, P.P., J.T., P.A., L.D.G.; Resources (cultivation of the three varieties in the field), A.B., A.L.C.; writing—original draft preparation, S.R.B., M.T., F.A., D.S., L.D.G., P.P.; writing—review and editing, F.D.G., M.A.; visualization, M.C., G.P., P.C. All authors have read and agreed to the published version of the manuscript.

Funding: The research was supported by both MIUR- PON03PE_00060_2, Decreto di Concessione del 27/06/2014, Progetto 2 "Progettazione, sviluppo e produzione di cibi funzionali e/o arricchiti", (OR4: Farine funzionali e prodotti da forno per celiaci ed intolleranti al glutine) to P. Pontieri and by both CNR-DISBA project "NutrAge" (project nr. 7022) and CNR project FOE-2019 DBA.AD003.139. Part of this work was supported by USDA-ARS (project nr. 3020-3440-002).

Institutional Review Board Statement: Not applicable.

Informed Consent Statement: Not applicable.

Data Availability Statement: All the data are reported in the paper.

Acknowledgments: The authors are grateful to Francesco Salamini for helpful discussion and critical reading of the manuscript. Thanks also to Matthew Malin for a generous gift of the food-grade white, red and black coloured sorghum varieties. The technical assistance of both Federico Gomez Paloma and Concetta Porzio is acknowledged. Names are necessary to report factually on available data; however, the U.S. Department of Agriculture neither guarantees nor warrants the standard of the product and use of the name by the U.S. Department of Agriculture implies no approval of the product to the exclusion of others that may also be suitable.

Conflicts of Interest: The authors declare no conflict of interest. Mention of trade names or commercial products in this publication is solely for the purpose of providing specific information and does not imply recommendation or endorsement by the U.S. Department of Agriculture. USDA is an equal opportunity provider and employer.

References

1. Anglani, C. Sorghum for human food: A review. *Plant Food Hum. Nutr.* **1998**, *52*, 85–89. [CrossRef]
2. Awika, J.M.; Rooney, L.W. Sorghum phytochemicals and their potential aspects on human health. *Phytochemistry* **2004**, *65*, 1199–1221. [CrossRef]
3. Kresovich, S.; Barbazuk, B.; Bedell, J.A. Toward sequencing the sorghum genome. A US National Science Foundation-sponsored Work Report. *Plant Physiol.* **2005**, *138*, 1898–1902.
4. Dicko, M.H.; Gruppen, H.; Traoré, A.S.; Voragen, A.G.J.; van Barkel, W.J.H. Sorghum grain as human food in Africa: Relevance of content of starch and amylase activities. *Afr. J. Biotechnol.* **2006**, *5*, 384–395.
5. Reddy, B.V.S.; Ramesh, S.; Sanjana-Reddy, P.; Ashok-Kumar, A. Genetic enhancement for drought tolerance in sorghum. *Plant Breed. Rev.* **2009**, *31*, 189–222.
6. Ashok-Kumar, A.; Reddy, B.V.S.; Sahrawat, K.L.; Ramaiah, B. Combating micronutrient malnutrition: Identification of commercial sorghum cultivars with high grain iron and zinc. *J. SAT Agric. Res.* **2010**, *8*, 1–5.

7. Elhassan, M.S.M.; Emmambux, M.N.; Hays, D.B.; Peterson, G.C.; Taylor, J.R.N. Novel biofortified sorghum lines with combined waxy (high amylopectin) starch and high protein digestibility traits: Effects on endosperm and flour properties. *J. Cereal Sci.* **2015**, *65*, 132–139. [CrossRef]
8. Pontieri, P.; Del Giudice, L. Sorghum: A Novel and Healthy Food. In *The Encyclopedia of Food and Health*; Caballero, B., Finglas, P., Toldrà, F., Eds.; Elsevier: Amsterdam, The Netherlands, 2016; pp. 33–42.
9. FAO. FAOSTAT. World Crops Website. Available online: www.fao.org/faostat/en/#data/QC (accessed on 30 March 2019).
10. USDA (United States Department of Agriculture) Foreign Agriculture Division. 2003. Available online: www.fas.usda.gov/psd (accessed on 30 March 2019).
11. Taylor, J.R.N.; Schober, T.J.; Bean, S.R. Novel food and non-food uses for sorghum and millets. *J. Cereal Sci.* **2006**, *44*, 252–271. [CrossRef]
12. Awika, J.M. Chapter 3-sorghum: Its Unique Nutritional and Health-Promoting Attributes. In *Gluten-Free Ancient Grains*; Taylor, J.R.N., Awika, J., Eds.; Woodhead Publishing: Sawston, UK, 2017; pp. 21–54.
13. Kasarda, D.D. Grains in relation to celiac disease. *Cereal Foods World* **2001**, *46*, 209–210.
14. Ciacci, C.; Maiuri, L.; Caporaso, N.; Bucci, C.; Del Giudice, L.; Massardo, D.R.; Pontieri, P.; Di Fonzo, N.; Bean, S.R.; Ioerger, B.; et al. Celiac Disease: In Vitro and In Vivo Safety and Palatability of Wheat-Free Sorghum Food Products. *Clin. Nutr.* **2007**, *26*, 799–805. [CrossRef]
15. Pontieri, P.; Mamone, G.; De Caro, S.; Tuinstra, M.R.; Roemer, E.; Okot, J.; De Vita, P.; Ficco, D.B.; Alifano, P.; Pignone, D.; et al. Sorghum, a healthy and gluten-free food for celiac patients as demonstrated by genome, biochemical and immunochemical analyses. *J. Agric. Food Chem.* **2013**, *61*, 2565–2571. [CrossRef]
16. Stefoska-Needham, A.; Beck, E.J.; Johnson, S.K.; Tapsell, L.C. Sorghum: An underutilized cereal whole grain with the potential to assist in the prevention of chronic disease. *Food Rev. Int.* **2015**, *31*, 401–437. [CrossRef]
17. Smolensky, D.; Rhodes, D.; McVey, D.S.; Fawver, Z.; Perumal, R.; Herald, T.; Noronha, L. High-polyphenol sorghum bran extract inhibits cancer cell growth through ROS induction, cell cycle arrest, and apoptosis. *J. Med. Food* **2018**, *21*, 990–998. [CrossRef]
18. Khan, I.; Yousif, A.M.; Johnson, S.K.; Gamlath, S. Acute effect of sorghum flourcontaining pasta on plasma total polyphenols, antioxidant capacity and oxidative stress markers in healthy subjects: A randomised controlled trial. *Clin. Nutr.* **2015**, *34*, 415–421. [CrossRef]
19. Khoddami, A.; Truong, H.H.; Liu, S.Y.; Roberts, T.H.; Selle, P.H. Concentrations of specific phenolic compounds in six red sorghums influence nutrient utilisation in broiler chickens. *Anim. Feed Sci. Technol.* **2015**, *210*, 190–199. [CrossRef]
20. Kil, H.Y.; Seong, E.S.; Ghimire, B.K.; Chung, I.M.; Kwon, S.S.; Goh, E.J.; Heo, K.; Kim, M.J.; Lim, J.D.; Lee, D.; et al. Antioxidant and antimicrobial activities of crude sorghum extract. *Food Chem.* **2009**, *115*, 1234–1239. [CrossRef]
21. Burdette, A.; Garner, P.L.; Mayer, E.P.; Hargrove, J.L.; Hartle, D.K.; Greenspan, P. Anti-inflammatory activity of select sorghum (*Sorghum bicolor*) brans. *J. Med. Food* **2010**, *13*, 879–887. [CrossRef]
22. Awika, J.M.; Yang, L.Y.; Browning, J.D.; Faraj, A. Comparative antioxidant, antiproliferative and phase II enzyme inducing potential of sorghum (*Sorghum bicolor*) varieties. *LWT-Food Sci. Technol.* **2009**, *42*, 1041–1046. [CrossRef]
23. Wu, L.; Huang, Z.H.; Qin, P.Y.; Yao, Y.; Meng, X.J.; Zou, J.Q.; Zhu, K.; Ren, G.X. Chemical characterization of a procyanidin-rich extract from sorghum bran and its effect on oxidative stress and tumor inhibition in vivo. *J. Agric. Food Chem.* **2011**, *59*, 8609–8615. [CrossRef]
24. Rao, S.; Santhakumar, A.B.; Chinkwo, K.A.; Wu, G.; Johnson, S.K.; Blanchard, C.L. Characterization of phenolic compounds and antioxidant activity in sorghum grains. *J. Cereal Sci.* **2018**, *84*, 103–111. [CrossRef]
25. de Morais Cardoso, L.; Pinheiro, S.S.; Martino, H.S.D.; Pinheiro-Sant'Ana, H.M. Sorghum (*Sorghum bicolor* L.): Nutrients, bioactive compounds, and potential impact on human health. *Crit. Rev. Food Sci. Nutr.* **2017**, *57*, 372–390. [CrossRef]
26. Francis, N.; Rao, S.; Blanchard, C.; Santhakumar, A. Black Sorghum Phenolic Extract Regulates Expression of Genes Associated with Oxidative Stress and Inflammation in Human Endothelial Cells. *Molecules* **2019**, *24*, 3321. [CrossRef]
27. Wu, G.; Johnson, S.K.; Bornman, J.F.; Bennett, S.J.; Clarke, M.W.; Singh, V.; Fang, Z. Growth temperature and genotype both play important roles in sorghum grain phenolic composition. *Sci. Rep.* **2016**, *6*, 21835. [CrossRef]
28. Dykes, L.; Rooney, L.W.; Waniska, R.D.; Rooney, W.L. Phenolic compounds and antioxidant activity of sorghum grains of varying genotypes. *J. Agric. Food Chem.* **2005**, *53*, 6813–6818. [CrossRef]
29. Xiong, Y.; Zhang, P.; Johnson, S.; Luo, J.; Fang, Z. Comparison of the phenolic contents, antioxidant activity and volatile compounds of different sorghum varieties during tea processing. *J. Sci. Food Agric.* **2020**, *100*, 978–985. [CrossRef]
30. Pontieri, P.; Di Maro, A.; Tamburino, R.; De Stefano, M.; Tilley, M.; Bean, S.R.; Roemer, E.; De Vita, P.; Alifano, P.; Del Giudice, L.; et al. Chemical composition of selected food-grade sorghum varieties grown under typical mediterranean conditions. *Maydica* **2010**, *55*, 139–143.
31. Pontieri, P.; Di Fiore, R.; Troisi, J.; Bean, S.R.; Roemer, E.; Okot, J.; Alifano, P.; Pignone, D.; Del Giudice, L.; Massardo, D.R. Chemical composition and fatty acid content of white food sorghums grown in different environments. *Maydica* **2011**, *56*, 1–7.
32. Pontieri, P.; De Vita, P.; Boffa, A.; Tuinstra, M.R.; Bean, S.R.; Krishnamoorthy, G.; Miller, C.; Roemer, E.; Alifano, P.; Pignone, D.; et al. Yield and morpho-agronomical evaluation of food-grade white sorghum hybrids grown in Southern Italy. *J. Plant Interact.* **2012**, *3*, 49–55. [CrossRef]
33. Association of Analytical Chemists Official Method, 923. 03. Ash of flour, direct method. *J. AOAC Inter.* **1923**, *7*, 132.

34. Association of Analytical Chemists Official Method, 920.87. Protein (total) in flour. 1920. Available online: http://www.aoacofficialmethod.org/index.php?main_page=product_info&cPath=1&products_id=2282 (accessed on 25 January 2021).
35. Arienzo, M.; De Martino, A.; Capasso, R.; Di Maro, A.; Parente, A. Analysis of carbohydrates and amino acids in vegetable waste waters by ion chromatography. *Phytochem. Anal.* **2003**, *14*, 74–82. [CrossRef]
36. Association of Analytical Chemists Official Method, 962.09. Fiber (Crude) in Animal Feed and Pet Food. In *Official Methods of Analysis AOC International*, 16th ed.; Cunniff, P., Ed.; AOAC: Rockville, MD, USA, 1995.
37. Tenore, G.C.; Troisi, J.; Di Fiore, R.; Basile, A.; Novellino, E. Chemical composition, antioxidant and antimicrobial properties of Rapa Catozza Napoletana (*Brassica rapa* L. var. rapa DC.) seed meal, a promising protein source of Campania region (southern Italy) horticultural germplasm. *J. Sci. Food Agric.* **2012**, *92*, 1716–1724. [CrossRef]
38. Pontieri, P.; Troisi, J.; Di Fiore, R.; Di Maro, A.; Bean, S.R.; Tuinstra, M.R.; Roemer, E.; Boffa, A.; Del Giudice, F.; Pizzolante, G.; et al. Mineral content in grains of seven food-grade sorghum hybrids grown in a Mediterranean environment. *Aust. J. Crop Sci.* **2014**, *8*, 1550–1559.
39. Valdés, I.; García, E.; Llorente, M.; Méndez, E. Innovative approach to low-level gluten determination in foods using a novel sandwich enzyme-linked immunosorbent assay protocol. *Eur. J. Gastroenterol. Hepatol.* **2003**, *15*, 465–474. [CrossRef]
40. Regulation (EU) No 1169/2011 of the European Parliament and of the Council of 25 October 2011 "on the provision of food information to consumers, amending Regulations (EC) No 1924/2006 and (EC) No 1925/2006 of the European Parliament and of the Council, and Repealing Commission Directive 87/250/EEC, Council Directive 90/496/EEC, Commission Directive 1999/10/EC, Directive 2000/13/EC of the European Parliament and of the Council, Commission Directives 2002/67/EC and 2008/5/EC and Commission Regulation (EC) No 608/2004". Available online: https://eur-lex.europa.eu/legal-content/IT/TXT/?uri=celex%3A32011R1169 (accessed on 25 January 2021).
41. Osagie, A.U. Total lipids of sorghum grain. *J. Agric. Food Chem.* **1987**, *35*, 601–604. [CrossRef]
42. Serna-Saldivar, S.O.; Rooney, L.W. Structure and Chemistry of Sorghum and Millets. In *Sorghum and Millets: Chemistry and Technology*; Dendy, D.A.V., Ed.; American Association of Cereal Chemists: St. Paul, MN, USA, 1995.
43. Szentmihalyi, K.; Kéry, A.; Then, M.; Lakatos, B.; Sándor, Z.; Vinkler, P. Potassium-sodium ratio for the characterisation of medicinal plant extracts with diuretic activity. *Phytother. Res.* **1998**, *12*, 163–166. [CrossRef]
44. Arbeit, M.L.; Nicklas, T.A.; Berenson, G.S. Considerations of dietary sodium/potassium/energy ratios of selected foods. *J. Am. Coll. Nutr.* **1992**, *11*, 210–222. [CrossRef]
45. Girard, A.L.; Awika, J.M. Sorghum polyphenols and other bioactive components as functional and health promoting food ingredients. *J. Cereal Sci.* **2018**, *84*, 112–124. [CrossRef]
46. Taleon, V.; Dykes, L.; Rooney, W.L.; Rooney, L.W. Effect of genotype and environment on flavonoid concentration and profile of black sorghum grains. *Cereal Sci.* **2012**, *56*, 470–475. [CrossRef]
47. Nutrition Foundation Task Force. Plants: Diet. and Health. In *The Report of the British Nutrition Foundation Task Force*; Goldberg, G., Ed.; Blackwell Science: Oxford, UK, 2003.
48. Afify, A.M.R.; El-Beltagi, H.S.; Abd El-Salam, S.M.; Omran, A.A. Effect of soaking, cooking, germination and fermentation processing on proximate analysis and mineral content of three white sorghum varieties (*Sorghum bicolor* L. Moench). *Not. Bot. Horti Agrobot. Cluj-Napoca* **2012**, *40*, 92–98.
49. Jambunathan, R. Improvement of the nutritional quality of sorghum and pearl millet. *Food Nutr. Bull.* **1980**, *2*, 11–16. [CrossRef]
50. Saxholt, E.; Christensen, A.T.; Møller, A.; Hartkopp, H.B.; Hess-Ygil, K.; Hels, O.H. Danish Food Composition Databank, revision 7. Department of Nutrition, National Food Institute, Technical University of Denmark: Kongens Lyngby, Denmark, 2008.
51. Pontieri, P.; Pepe, G.; Campiglia, P.; Merciai, F.; Basilicata, M.G.; Smolensky, D.; Calcagnile, M.; Troisi, J.; Romano, R.; Del Giudice, F.; et al. Comparison of content in phenolic compounds and antioxidant capacity in grains of white, red and black sorghum varieties grown in Mediterranean area. *ACS Food Sci. Technol.* **2021**, *1*, 1109–1119. [CrossRef]

foods

Article

Identification and Quantification of Selected Benzoxazinoids and Phenolics in Germinated Spelt (*Triticum spelta*)

Andrej Živković [1], Dejan Gođevac [2], Blaž Cigić [1], Tomaž Polak [1] and Tomaž Požrl [1,*]

[1] Department of Food Science and Technology, Biotechnical Faculty, University of Ljubljana, SI-1111 Ljubljana, Slovenia; andrej.zivkovic@bf.uni-lj.si (A.Ž.); blaz.cigic@bf.uni-lj.si (B.C.); tomaz.polak@bf.uni-lj.si (T.P.)

[2] Institute of Chemistry, Technology and Metallurgy, National Institute of the Republic of Serbia, University of Belgrade, 11000 Belgrade, Serbia; dejan.godjevac@ihtm.bg.ac.rs

[*] Correspondence: tomaz.pozrl@bf.uni-lj.si; Tel.: +386-1-3203716

Abstract: In this study, we investigated the effects of germination on the secondary metabolite composition in spelt grains. Germination significantly increased the content of various metabolites in free and bound forms. Benzoxazinoids were the most important compounds in the free fraction of the 96 h germinated grains (MBOA content as the predominant compound was 277.61 ± 15.29 μg/g DW). The majority of phenolic acids were present in the bound fraction, with *trans*-ferulic acid as the main component, reaching 753.27 ± 95.87 μg/g DW. The often neglected *cis*-isomers of phenolic acids accounted for about 20% of the total phenolic acids. High levels of apigenin di-C-glycosides were found in spelt grains, and the schaftoside content was most affected by germination, increasing threefold. The accumulation of secondary metabolites significantly increased the antioxidant activity of germinated spelt. According to the results of this study, the content of most bioactive compounds was highest in spelt grains after 96 h of germination. These data suggest that germinated spelt could potentially be valuable for the production of functional foods.

Keywords: spelt; germination; benzoxazinoids; *cis*-isomers; schaftoside; free and bound fractions

Citation: Živković, A.; Gođevac, D.; Cigić, B.; Polak, T.; Požrl, T. Identification and Quantification of Selected Benzoxazinoids and Phenolics in Germinated Spelt (*Triticum spelta*). *Foods* **2023**, *12*, 1769. https://doi.org/10.3390/foods12091769

Academic Editors: Laura Gazza and Francesca Nocente

Received: 31 March 2023
Revised: 13 April 2023
Accepted: 23 April 2023
Published: 24 April 2023

1. Introduction

Spelt (*Triticum spelta* L.) is primitive wheat that is a distant cousin of common wheat (*Triticum aestivum* L.). Along with einkorn (*Triticum monococcum* L.) and emmer (*Triticum turgidum* L.), spelt is considered an ancient wheat that has remained unchanged over a very long period of time. Compared to common wheat, ancient wheats are more resistant to disease, require less nitrogen fertilization, and are generally better adapted to harsh growing conditions. Products from spelt and other ancient cereals are reported to be better tolerated by individuals with intolerances or allergies to modern wheat varieties [1]. Recent evidence from in vitro, in vivo, and clinical studies suggests that the consumption of ancient wheat products has antioxidant and anti-inflammatory effects. In addition, ancient cereals and their products have a lower glycemic index than other grains [2].

As a result of these findings and its image as a "healthier and more natural" cereal compared to modern wheat varieties, spelt is gaining popularity in both conventional and organic agriculture and thus commercial interest in the food industry.

Germination processes are a traditional method for improving the nutrient profile of grains and offer a practical way to naturally biotransform grains. It is considered a "green food" engineering method to accumulate natural bioactive compounds in seeds and sprouts that can be consumed as functional foods [3]. Germination is initiated by increasing the moisture content of the grain to 43–45% by soaking in water [4]. After initiation, storage macromolecules are degraded by newly synthesized enzymes, and these reactions lead to the development of new highly bioactive compounds through de novo synthesis and transformation, thus increasing the nutritional value and health-promoting effects of germinated grains [5]. Germination increases various metabolites (polyphenols, alkylresorcinols, vitamins) and many other less known groups of secondary metabolites. Other benefits of germination include removal or reduction of antinutritional compounds (e.g., phytates) and enrichment with dietary fiber [3,6,7].

In the literature, phenolic compounds are the most reported type of bioactive compounds in cereals, and they generally occur in free and bound forms. However, the total phytochemical content in whole grains is often underestimated since most studies determine only the content of free phenolics. The free form of phenolic compounds accounts for only a small portion of the phenolics in grains [8]. The majority of phenolics in cereals are bound to cell wall materials, such as lignin, cellulose, proteins, and arabinoxylan and can be released only by alkaline or enzymatic hydrolysis [9]. Consequently, bound phenolic compounds can survive gastrointestinal digestion to reach the colon intact, where they may provide a favorable antioxidant environment for intestinal microbiota [10]. This might partly explain the positive health effect of whole-grain consumption, as demonstrated by epidemiological studies [11]. In addition to phenolic acids, there are other, often neglected compounds found in cereal grains, such as benzoxazinoids and apigenin di-C-glucosides (mainly schaftoside and isoschaftoside). It is suggested that these compounds could be additional contributing factors to the health benefits of whole grains.

Benzoxazinoids are nitrogen-containing secondary metabolites found mainly in the vegetative parts of Poaceae plants, such as rye, wheat, triticale, and maize. They are usually divided into three groups according to their structure: benzoxazolinones, lactams, and hydroxamic acids. Benzoxazinoids are mostly analyzed because of their importance in plant physiology as allelochemicals for defense against predators and infection [12]; however, to the best of our knowledge, there is no information about dynamic changes in benzoxazinoids during germination of spelt grains or in spelt grains whatsoever.

Recent studies have found that benzoxazinoids are present not only in the vegetative parts of young plants but also in mature cereal grains. Considerable amounts of benzoxazinoids are found in fermented beverages made from wheat or rye malt [13]. With the significant dietary intake of various whole grain cereals and cereal products, the potential health-promoting effects of benzoxazinoids have come into focus.

There are still no conclusive data on the health effects of these compounds in humans [14]; however, recent studies on benzoxazinoids have reported their pharmacological and health-promoting properties, including anti-inflammatory, anticancer, antimicrobial, appetite suppressant, and reproductive system stimulant effects [15]. Animal and human studies have demonstrated that dietary benzoxazinoids are absorbed and metabolized in mammals [16]. Quantitative analysis of benzoxazinoid metabolism in a rat model revealed that the bioavailability of various benzoxazinoids based on their urinary excretion levels varied from <1 to 21% [17]. The pharmacokinetics of benzoxazinoids in plasma and urine have shown that benzoxazinoid levels are dose-dependent, and it takes approximately 3 h to reach the highest plasma levels. After consumption, most benzoxazinoids and their metabolic derivatives are excreted slowly in the urine [18].

Flavonoids are another group of compounds present in cereal seeds and represent a large family of plant polyphenolic compounds that act as UV filters and colorants, serve to defend against pathogens, and are of great interest to human health. Schaftoside and isoschaftoside are flavonoid di-C-glycosides that possess a variety of biological activities, including antidiabetic, antihypertensive, hepatoprotective, anti-inflammatory, and antioxidant activities in mammals, with potential for applications as drugs or dietary supplements [19,20]. Because of the various health benefits of compounds in cereal grains, understanding the dynamic changes in bioactive compounds in cereals, both in free and bound forms, during germination is highly important [21]. However, limited information is available on the dynamic changes in benzoxazinoids and apigenin di-C-glycosides during the first stages of germination.

The present investigation reveals the effect of germination on the quantitative contribution of these substances to the total nutritional value of spelt grains. Therefore, the main objective of this study was to study and characterize the dynamic changes in the composition and content of selected phenolics, benzoxazinoids, and apigenin di-C-glycosides in free and bound forms of spelt grains at different stages of germination. The second objective was to quantify often neglected cis isomers of phenolic acids in the bound fraction of spelt extracts. Finally, we evaluated the effect of germination on the total phenolic content and antioxidant activity. Our goal was to provide information that can contribute to the implementation of germinated spelt grains for the production of new functional food products.

2. Materials and Methods

2.1. Materials

Throughout this work, we used the »Ostro« cultivar of common spelt (*Triticum spelta* L.) grown in organic growth conditions that were kindly supplied by Rangus mill (Šentjernej, Slovenia). Methanol, hydrochloric acid, sodium bicarbonate, sodium hydroxide, 1,1-diphenyl-2-picrylhydrazyl (DPPH), and 2,2′-azino-bis (3-ethylbenzothiazolin-6-sulfonic acid diammonium salt) (ABTS) were purchased from Sigma-Aldrich (Steinheim, Germany). Manganese dioxide was from Kemika (Zagreb, Croatia) and Folin–Ciocalteu (FC) reagent was from Merck (Darmstadt, Germany). The analytical standards of 6-methoxy-2-benzoxazolinone (MBOA), 2-benzoxazolinone (BOA), ferulic acid, p-coumaric acid, and a mixture of *cis*/*trans* isomers of ferulic acid were from Sigma-Aldrich (Steinheim, Germany). Schaftoside and isoschaftoside were from Biosynth (Bratislava, Slovakia). All of the standards used were analytical or HPLC grade. All aqueous solutions were prepared using Milli-Q purified water (Merck Millipore, Bedford, MA, USA).

2.2. Germination Method

Before germination, we prepared spelt samples by removing foreign materials and damaged grains. Disinfection of the grains was performed by soaking the samples in 50 °C water for 5 min [22]. The soaking time was 8 h in water, with a 15 min aeration period every hour. After soaking, the grains were placed in a thin layer on perforated metal trays. The trays were placed in a growth chamber with a humidifier to ensure high humidity (relative humidity, >95%) and germinated at 20 °C. Germinated seeds were harvested at 12, 24, 36, 48, 72, and 96 h after the start of soaking. Prior to analysis, moisture content in all samples was determined using a modified AACC method 44-19.01, and results were expressed on a dry weight basis.

2.3. Extraction of Free Phenolic Compounds

The extraction of free phenolic compounds was carried out according to the method previously reported by Živković et al. [7]. Briefly, 1 g of ground grains was mixed with 3.0 mL 70% aqueous methanol, and the mixture was shaken in the dark at room temperature for 40 min at 200 rpm (EV-403; Tehtnica Železniki, Železniki, Slovenia). After centrifugation at 8709× *g* for 8 min at 10 °C (Avanti JXN-26; Beckman Coulter, Krefeld, Germany), the supernatant was removed and stored, and the extraction was repeated twice more. The 3 supernatants were pooled, diluted to 10 mL with 70% aqueous methanol, filtered using 0.45-μm pore size syringe filters (Chromafil A-45/25; Macherey-Nagel, Düren, Germany), and stored at 2 °C until determination of total phenolic content (TPC) and antioxidative activity (AA) analysis within 24 h.

2.4. Extraction of Bound Phenolic Compounds

After methanol extraction, the solid residues were hydrolyzed with sodium hydroxide, as described previously by Živković et al. [7]. Briefly, 20 mL of 2 M NaOH was added to the reaction tube, and the mixture was shaken in the dark at room temperature for 4 h at 200 rpm (Tehtnica Železniki EV-403, Slovenia). The hydrolyzed mixture was acidified to pH 3.2 to 3.4 by the addition of 3.5 mL of concentrated formic acid. After centrifugation at 8709× *g* for 8 min at 10 °C (Avanti JXN-26; Beckman Coulter, Krefeld, Germany), the supernatant was removed and filtered through 0.45-µm pore size syringe filters (Chromafil A-45/25; Macherey-Nagel, Düren, Germany) and stored at 2 °C until determination of total phenolic content (TPC) and antioxidative activity (AA) analysis within 24 h.

2.5. Total Phenolic Content (TPC)

The TPC of the crude grain extracts was determined using the Folin–Ciocalteu (FC) reagent according to Živković et al. [7]. A total of 100 microliters of extract was dispensed into 2.0 mL microcentrifuge tubes and mixed with 1.3 mL Milli-Q water and 0.3 mL diluted FC reagent (reagent:water, 1:2). After 5 min, 0.3 mL 20% (*w*/*v*) aqueous Na_2CO_3 was added. After 1 h at room temperature, the absorbances were measured at 765 nm (UV-Vis spectrophotometer; Model 8453; Agilent Technologies, Santa Clara, CA, USA). The measurements were compared with a standard curve of a Trolox solution, and TPC was expressed as mg Trolox equivalents (TE) per g dry weight of the grain sample (mg TE/g DW). Trolox was used as a standard because it exchanges the same number of electrons in FC, ABTS, and DPPH assays [23], which allows a direct comparison of the relative efficiency of extracted phenolic compounds in FC and antioxidant assays.

2.6. DPPH Radical Scavenging Activity

The DPPH radical scavenging activity [24] of the grain extracts was determined according to a method described previously [7]. A total of 50 microliters of each extract was mixed with 250 µL of acetic buffer, 0.7 mL of 70% aqueous methanol, and 1 mL of a 0.2 mM methanol solution of DPPH to give a final volume of 2 mL. The absorbance of the mixture was measured after 1 h at 517 nm (UV-Vis spectrophotometer; Model 8453; Agilent Technologies, Santa Clara, CA, USA). The measurement was compared to a standard curve of a Trolox solution, and the radical scavenging activity was expressed as mg Trolox equivalents per g dry matter (mg TE/g DW).

2.7. ABTS Radical Cation Scavenging Activity

The ABTS radical scavenging activities of the grain extracts were determined according to a method described previously [7]. A total of 50 microliters of each extract was mixed with 0.5 mL 0.325 M phosphate buffer, 1.0 mL of diluted ABTS radical cation solution, and 0.45 mL Milli-Q water to give a final volume of 2 mL. The mixture was shaken and left in the dark for 1 h. The absorbance was measured after 1 h at 734 nm (UV-Vis spectrophotometer; Model 8453; Agilent Technologies, CA, USA). The measurement was compared to a standard curve of a Trolox solution, and the radical scavenging activity was expressed as mg TE/g DW.

2.8. Purification of Extracts

Crude grain extracts were purified using 100 mg Strata-X RP cartridges (Phenomenex, Torrance, CA, USA) according to a previously described method [7]. Briefly, 30 mL of the diluted crude methanol extracts (extract:water, 1:9) or 3.0 mL of the hydrolyzed extracts were applied to the SPE cartridges, washed with 4.0 mL of Milli-Q water, and dried with a flow of air. The compounds bound to the cartridges were eluted with 2.0 mL of 70% (*v*/*v*) aqueous methanol. The resulting extracts were filtered through syringe filters with a pore size of 0.20 µm (Chromafil Xtra-20/13; cellulose acetate; Macherey-Nagel, Düren, Germany) and then stored at −80 °C until liquid chromatography–mass spectrometry analysis (LC-MS).

2.9. Liquid Chromatography–Mass Spectrometry Analysis

For separation and quantification of each compound in spelt extracts, reversed-phase LC-MS analysis was used. The LC system used (1100 chromatography system; Agilent Technologies, CA, USA) included a thermostated autosampler (G1330B), a thermostated column compartment (G1316A), a diode array detector (G1315B), and a binary pump (1312A). The LC system was coupled with a mass spectrometer (Quattro micro API; Waters, Milford, MA, USA). Chromatographic separation was carried out using a C18 column (2.7 μm, 150 mm × 2.1 mm; Ascentis Express) with a C18 guard column (2.7 μm, 5 mm × 2.1 mm; Ascentis Express; Supelco, Bellefonte, PA, USA). The conditions used were as follows: column temperature, 35 °C; injection volume, 2 μL; and mobile phase flow rate, 320 μL/min. The components of the mobile phase were 0.1% aqueous formic acid (solution A) and acetonitrile (solution B). The mobile phase gradient was programmed as follows (%B): 0–4 min, 10%; 4–18 min, 10–60%; 18–18.2 min, 60–80%; 18.2–20 min, 80%; 20–20.2 min, 80–10%; and 20.2–26 min, 10%. Detection was performed with scanning diode array spectra from 240 nm to 650 nm.

The mass spectrometer was operated in negative ionization mode, and the operating conditions were as follows: electrospray capillary voltage, 3.5 kV; cone voltage, 20 V; extractor voltage, 2 V; source block temperature, 100 °C; desolvation temperature, 350 °C; cone gas flow rate, 30 L/h, and desolvation gas flow rate, 350 L/h. The data signals were acquired and processed on a PC using MassLynx software (V4.1 2005; Waters Corporation, Milford, MA, USA). Compared to previously determined calibration curves, identification of the individual compounds was achieved by comparing their retention times and both the spectroscopic and mass spectrometric data, with quantification according to peak areas.

The compound corresponding to peak 16 in the LC-MS chromatograms was isolated by repetitive semipreparative chromatography runs. The chromatography conditions and gradient were the same as specified previously in the main experiment.

2.10. NMR Spectroscopy

NMR spectra were recorded on a Bruker Avance III 500 NMR spectrometer with a proton NMR frequency of 500.26 MHz and a 5 mm BBO probe head using standard pulse sequences. Methanol-d4 was used as the solvent, and spectra were recorded at 298 K. The spectra were referenced to the residual proton signal of methanol-d4. Chemical shifts were given in δ (ppm), and coupling constants were given in Hz.

2.11. Statistical Analysis

All experiments were carried out in triplicate using a complete randomization method. All spelt extracts were prepared in duplicate. Data were presented as mean ± standard deviation (SD) for three analyses for each extract. Results were subjected to two-way comparison ANOVA, and significance of differences between means was determined using Tukey's Multiple Comparison Tests. Data analysis was performed using SPSS Statistics software (version 24; IBM, New York, NY, USA). Statistical significance was defined at the level of $p < 0.05$.

3. Results and Discussion

3.1. Effect of Germination on Total Phenolic Content and Antioxidant Activity

The changes in the content of free and bound phenolic compounds at the different germination stages are shown in Table 1. Our results show that germination induced dynamic changes in free, bound, and total phenolic compounds in spelt. Germination had a significant effect on the content of free phenolic compounds ($p < 0.05$), which increased from 1.17 mg TE/g DW in nongerminated grains to 4.57 mg TE/g DW at the end of the 96 h germination period. Bound phenolic compounds were the predominant form in the nongerminated grains and accounted for approximately 72.0% of the TPC on a dry weight basis. This is consistent with results previously reported for TPC in nongerminated spelt [25,26]. It was found that germination increases the TPC of both free and bound phenolic compounds in spelt grains, so the next objective was to evaluate the dynamic changes in antioxidant capacity of the free and bound fractions of germinated spelt. The spelt extracts were evaluated for their scavenging activity against the stable free radicals DPPH and ABTS. The radical scavenging activity of DPPH and ABTS radicals in germinated spelt extracts was expressed as milligrams of Trolox equivalents per gram dry weight (mg TE/g DW). The results are summarized in Table 1. With both assays, the lowest AA was measured in the free fraction of grains prior to germination (Table 1). Similar values of AA in nongerminated spelt were reported by Yilmaz et al. [26]. In the same study, the levels of AA measured by the ABTS assay were 6–8-fold higher than the levels of AA measured by the DPPH method. As seen from our results in Table 1, similar differences were found between the values measured by the DPPH method and the ABTS values. The differences in the measured antioxidant capacity between the two assays can be explained by the different reactivities (Figure S1) of the compounds present in the spelt extract toward the free radicals ABTS and DPPH [27].

Table 1. Total phenolic content (FC) and antioxidant activities (DPPH, ABTS) for the free and bound extraction fractions of the spelt extracts during germination.

Analysis	Measure	Germination Time (h)						
		Nongerminated	12	24	36	48	72	96
		Total phenolic content (mg TE/g dry weight)						
FC	Free	1.17 ± 0.08 [a]	1.39 ± 0.06 [ab]	1.47 ± 0.07 [ab]	1.76 ± 0.11 [b]	2.40 ± 0.15 [c]	3.12 ± 0.28 [d]	4.57 ± 0.57 [e]
	Bound	3.01 ± 0.16 [a]	3.12 ± 0.24 [ab]	3.35 ± 0.28 [ab]	3.45 ± 0.57 [ab]	3.69 ± 0.29 [b]	4.34 ± 0.20 [c]	4.54 ± 0.40 [c]
	Total	4.18 ± 0.18 [a]	4.51 ± 0.29 [a]	4.82 ± 0.30 [a]	5.21 ± 0.59 [ab]	6.09 ± 0.41 [b]	7.46 ± 0.46 [c]	9.11 ± 0.96 [d]
		Antioxidant activity (mgTE/g dry weight)						
DPPH	Free	0.36 ± 0.03 [a]	0.43 ± 0.05 [ab]	0.50 ± 0.05 [b]	0.61 ± 0.04 [c]	0.72 ± 0.06 [d]	0.92 ± 0.07 [e]	1.13 ± 0.09 [f]
	Bound	1.34 ± 0.07 [a]	1.31 ± 0.05 [a]	1.42 ± 0.04 [a]	1.67 ± 0.02 [b]	1.80 ± 0.06 [bc]	1.96 ± 0.08 [c]	2.14 ± 0.19 [d]
	Total	1.70 ± 0.07 [a]	1.74 ± 0.09 [a]	1.92 ± 0.09 [a]	2.28 ± 0.04 [b]	2.52 ± 0.11 [b]	2.88 ± 0.14 [c]	3.27 ± 0.28 [d]
ABTS	Free	2.22 ± 0.12 [a]	2.72 ± 0.06 [b]	2.89 ± 0.12 [b]	3.34 ± 0.16 [c]	3.95 ± 0.13 [d]	4.80 ± 0.06 [e]	6.14 ± 0.56 [f]
	Bound	9.33 ± 0.19 [a]	9.41 ± 0.34 [a]	9.69 ± 0.32 [a]	10.43 ± 0.48 [a]	11.66 ± 0.96 [b]	13.09 ± 0.67 [c]	13.98 ± 1.05 [c]
	Total	11.55 ± 0.22 [a]	12.13 ± 0.39 [a]	12.58 ± 0.40 [ab]	13.77 ± 0.45 [b]	15.61 ± 0.98 [c]	17.89 ± 0.69 [d]	20.12 ± 1.61 [e]

Data are means ± SD from three independent replicates. Means with different letters in rows indicate statistically significant differences between the different stages of germination ($p < 0.05$).

The antioxidant activity in both free and bound fractions gradually increased during the observed 96 h germination period. These results are in agreement with previous reports in other cereals, such as rice [28], wheat [29], and buckwheat [7]. As seen from the results of TPC and AA of the germinated spelt extracts, the ratio between the measured values in the free and bound fractions changed during the germination process (Figure 1). This difference is most pronounced for values obtained by the FC method. Free phenolic compounds in nongerminated spelt extracts accounted for 28% of the total phenolic content, while this ratio increased to 50% in extracts of spelt germinated for 96 h. The change in the ratio between free and bound phenolics was also measured by the DPPH and ABTS assays but not as much as by the FC assay. This may be explained by the accumulation of newly synthesized compounds in the germinated spelt and their different reactivities in the FC, DPPH, and ABTS assays. According to the profile of compounds from LC-MS analysis, the major constituents in the free fractions of germinated spelt were benzoxazinoids. The specific reactivities of BOA and MBOA toward the FC, DPPH, and ABTS reagents (Figure S1) were analyzed, and the results showed that MBOA had a high affinity for the FC reagent and almost no affinity for either ABTS or DPPH. Differences in the reactivity of MBOA and probably other benzoxazinoids to FC, DPPH, and ABTS assays can explain the difference in the ratio between the measured values of free and bound fractions in nongerminated and germinated spelt extracts.

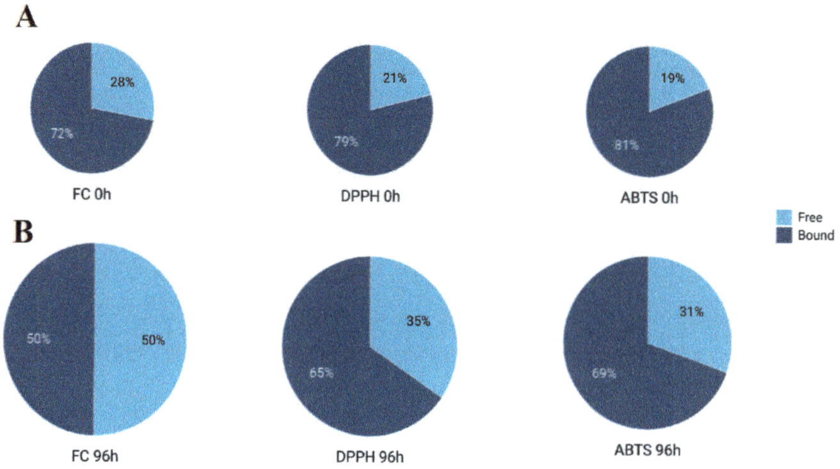

Figure 1. Ratio between values of free and bound fractions measured by FC, DPPH, and ABTS assays in nongerminated spelt (**A**) and 96 h germinated spelt (**B**). An increase in plot area represents a relative increase of measured values during 96 h of germination.

3.2. Phenolic Characterization by Liquid Chromatography–Mass Spectrometry

LC-MS analysis of the extracts of the raw and germinated grains (i.e., sprouts) revealed the presence of several compounds in free and bound forms. The changes in the profile of the compounds of germinated spelt at different stages of germination are shown in Table 2, and the representative chromatograms of the detected components are shown in Figure 2. The results show large differences between the compounds in germinated and nongerminated spelt.

To identify some of the detected compounds, we used chromatographic separation to isolate a selected peak (peak 16) and NMR spectroscopy for structural identification. The isolated peak was identified by NMR spectroscopy as 6-methoxy-2-benzoxazolinone (MBOA) (Figures S3–S5). Based on the identified compound, another benzoxazinoid, 2-benzoxazolinone (BOA, peak8), was identified by comparing UV-Vis spectra (Figure S2), MS data, and retention times with the commercial standard. Since standards for other benzoxazinoids were not commercially available, Peak 5 was characterized based on UV-Vis spectra (Figure S2) and MS data and tentatively identified as 2-hydroxy-1,4-benzoxazin-3-one (HBOA) and was expressed as MBOA equivalents (μg/g extract). We also detected several unidentified compounds in the free fraction. Peaks 2 (m/z 388.2), 4 (418.2), 6 (m/z 594.5), and 14 (m/z 432.4) had UV-Vis spectrum profiles similar to that of HBOA (Figure S1) and similar to UV-Vis spectra of other lactams and hydroxamic acids in the literature (λmax = 264–266 nm) [30–32]. We can assume that these compounds may be related to benzoxazinoids, more specifically to lactams, hydroxamic acids, or their methyl derivatives, but due to a lack of literature data and no available commercial standards, we cannot confirm this hypothesis. MBOA was detected 24 h after soaking, and during 48 to 96 h germination, its content gradually increased to maximum values of 277 μg/g DW. BOA also increased during germination, but the concentrations were much lower than those of MBOA. The content of HBOA was strongly affected by germination and reached 219.65 μg/g DW at the end of the germination period. This strong increase in benzoxazinoids in the early stages of germination is consistent with previous studies of metabolic synthesis of benzoxazinoids in rye [33] in which genes responsible for benzoxazinoid synthesis showed the highest expression levels 24–30 h after the onset of germination. Although there are no available data yet on the biosynthesis of benzoxazinoids in spelt, we can assume that pathways similar to those in other Poaceae plants are initiated during germination.

Table 2. Contents of the individual bioactive compounds (μg/g DW) in the germinating spelt seeds.

Compound	Content of Benzoxazinoids and Phenolics (μg/g DW) during Germination (h) for the Nongerminated and Germinated Spelt Seeds						
	Nongerminated	12	24	36	48	72	96
Free fraction							
Schaftoside	13.58 ± 1.54^{b}	9.62 ± 1.22^{a}	12.3 ± 0.52^{b}	9.21 ± 0.55^{a}	12.89 ± 1.40^{b}	18.53 ± 0.58^{c}	53.69 ± 2.65^{d}
Schaftoside isomer 1	46.78 ± 5.41^{bc}	39.8 ± 5.20^{ab}	47.94 ± 2.04^{c}	35.08 ± 1.75^{a}	46.82 ± 7.44^{bc}	45.51 ± 1.71^{bc}	47.48 ± 1.56^{c}
Schaftoside isomer 2	91.28 ± 15.26^{b}	83.38 ± 15.77^{ab}	92.97 ± 3.97^{b}	71.30 ± 3.00^{a}	89.71 ± 9.43^{b}	85.20 ± 5.56^{ab}	90.42 ± 3.38^{b}
BOA	ND	ND	4.13 ± 1.32^{a}	11.88 ± 1.33^{b}	34.67 ± 3.00^{d}	19.77 ± 4.41^{c}	20.49 ± 0.86^{c}
MBOA	ND	ND	6.98 ± 2.55^{a}	38.78 ± 5.97^{b}	111.52 ± 10.38^{c}	181.05 ± 29.94^{d}	277.61 ± 15.29^{e}
HBOA	ND	ND	ND	14.97 ± 6.37^{a}	26.05 ± 5.72^{a}	130.08 ± 30.88^{b}	219.65 ± 46.01^{c}
trans-ferulic acid	1.90 ± 0.19^{a}	1.90 ± 0.39^{a}	1.63 ± 0.36^{a}	2.06 ± 0.46^{a}	2.05 ± 0.37^{a}	1.90 ± 0.18^{a}	3.00 ± 0.70^{b}
cis-ferulic acid	0.96 ± 0.40^{ab}	1.27 ± 0.33^{b}	0.95 ± 0.33^{ab}	1.14 ± 0.47^{ab}	1.32 ± 0.32^{b}	0.52 ± 0.13^{a}	0.52 ± 0.11^{a}
trans-p-Coumaric acid	ND	ND	0.97 ± 0.19^{a}	1.34 ± 0.14^{ab}	1.13 ± 0.09^{a}	1.12 ± 0.14^{a}	1.59 ± 0.20^{b}
Bound fraction							
trans-ferulic acid	359.92 ± 9.21^{a}	406.61 ± 12.03^{a}	419.48 ± 11.44^{ab}	439.96 ± 32.99^{ab}	489.16 ± 42.94^{b}	580.89 ± 38.23^{c}	753.27 ± 95.87^{d}
cis-ferulic acid	76.69 ± 7.51^{a}	97.29 ± 14.07^{a}	93.46 ± 22.90^{a}	110.44 ± 27.16^{ab}	140.38 ± 13.47^{bc}	150.84 ± 17.75^{c}	203.66 ± 29.30^{d}
trans-p-Coumaric acid	16.87 ± 1.75^{a}	17.21 ± 0.58^{a}	18.44 ± 0.81^{a}	20.18 ± 2.41^{a}	25.36 ± 1.07^{a}	50.05 ± 3.69^{b}	119.77 ± 15.42^{c}
cis-p-Coumaric acid	1.59 ± 0.36^{a}	1.68 ± 0.23^{a}	1.73 ± 0.22^{a}	1.69 ± 0.28^{a}	2.33 ± 0.29^{ab}	3.41 ± 0.56^{b}	9.18 ± 1.56^{c}

Data are means ± SD from three independent replicates. Means with different letters in rows indicate statistically significant differences between contents in the different stages of germination ($p < 0.05$); not detected (ND).

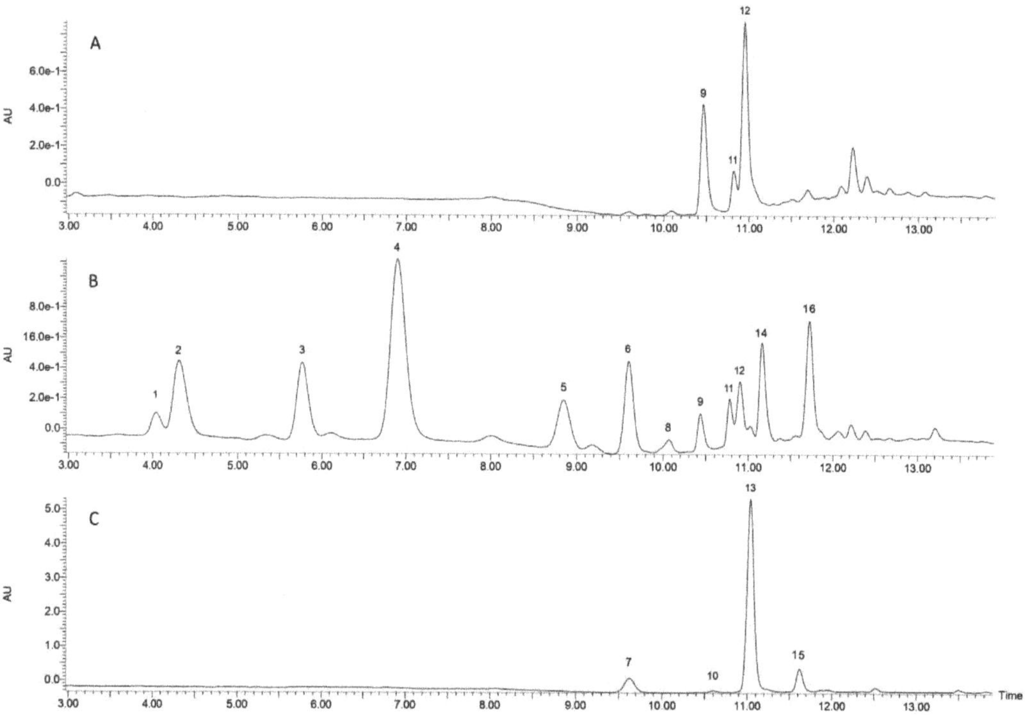

Figure 2. Chromatograms obtained through LC-MS analysis of (**A**) free fraction of nongerminated spelt, (**B**) free fraction of 96 h germinated spelt, and (**C**) bound fraction of 96 h germinated spelt. Peaks: 1–unidentified, (*m*/*z* 534.3); 2–unidentified, (*m*/*z* 388.2); 3–unidentified, (*m*/*z* 134.2); 4–unidentified, (*m*/*z* 418.2); 5–HBOA; 6–unidentified, (*m*/*z* 594.5); 7–*trans* p-coumaric acid; 8-BOA; 9–schaftoside structural isomer 1; 10–cis p-coumaric acid; 11–schaftoside; 12–schaftoside structural isomer 2; 13–*trans* ferulic acid; 14–unidentified, (*m*/*z* 432.4); 15–cis ferulic acid; 16–MBOA.

Two phenolic acids were detected in methanol extracts but at very low concentrations. In nongerminated grains, ferulic acid was the only phenolic compound detected (1.9 and 0.96 μg/g DW for *trans* and *cis* isomers, respectively). In germinated grains, *trans*-p-coumaric acid was also detected, with the highest concentration reached at the end of germination (1.59 μg/g DW).

Characterization of the methanol extracts in the grains before germination showed a significant content of a compound with an *m*/*z* of 563.5 (peaks 9, 11, and 12). Based on retention times and fragmentation pattern matching with a commercial standard (Table S1), the compounds were identified as apigenin-di-C-glucosides (schaftoside and its structural isomers). Literature data concerning schaftoside and its isomers in wheat and cereals are relatively scarce [34], and to the best of our knowledge, there is no information about dynamic changes in apigenin-di-C-glucosides during germination. Of the three apigenin di-C glucosides detected in nongerminated spelt, schaftoside was detected at the lowest concentration (13.58 μg/g DW), but it was most affected by germination, reaching 53.69 μg/g DW at the end of the 96 h germination period. Although the content of most compounds in spelt increased during germination, the main compounds in raw grains (structural isomers of schaftoside) were not significantly affected by the germination process. Flavonoids in plant tissues are associated with protection against UV light, and their content usually increases when the plant is exposed to UV radiation [35]. Since the germination process in our experiment was conducted under dark conditions, it is possible that there was no activation of the photoreceptors responsible for the induction of UV-protective flavonoid synthesis [36].

A higher concentration of phenolic compounds was detected in the bound fraction of spelt grain extracts. As expected from the literature data [37], the most abundant phenolic compounds in the bound fraction were *trans*-ferulic acid and *trans*-p-coumaric acid. Significant accumulation of bound phenolic compounds during germination was also observed. This confirms the conclusions reached in the literature [38,39] that during germination, the content of bound phenolics increased gradually. This increase coincides with the growth of the seedling and the development of new tissue. Previous studies reported high levels of bound phenolics in leaves and other tissues of cereal plants [40], so this increase can be explained by the growth of tissues (shoot and radicle) rich in bound phenolics. The content of *trans*-ferulic acid increased significantly and reached 753 μg/g DW after 96 h of germination, which corresponds to an increase of 110% compared to raw grains. *Trans*-p-coumaric acid, which was also present in high concentrations in the bound fraction, showed a significant increase during germination ($p < 0.05$), reaching 119.77 μg/g DW (610% increase) after 96 h of germination. In addition to *trans*-ferulic acid and *trans*-p-coumaric acid, two other peaks were detected in the bound fraction (peaks 10 and 15). The MS analysis of the samples showed that Peak 10, eluted 1 min after *trans*-p-coumaric acid, had the same m/z ratio as *trans*-p-coumaric acid (m/z 163). The unknown compound showed the same fragmentation pattern as *trans*-p-coumaric acid, so we can assume that the peak occurring after *trans*-p-coumaric acid is the corresponding *cis*-isomer. Peak 15 was confirmed to be *cis*-ferulic acid, according to the retention time of the commercial standard of the ferulic acid isomer mixture and MS data analysis. A similar conclusion was reached by another study [41], where secondary peaks of p-coumaric, caffeic, and ferulic acid were noticed. The two *cis*-isomers were quantified using the calibration curve of their respective *trans*-isomers. The levels of *cis*-isomers were also significantly increased after germination and were 165% and 477% higher than the levels of *cis*-ferulic acid and *cis*-p-coumaric acid in nongerminated grains, respectively. Our results provide a new perspective on phenolic acid content in cereals. Most of the works on bound phenolic content in cereals did not mention the existence of *cis*-stereoisomers of phenolic acids due to the lack of effective separation methods. Only a few papers mention the separation and identification of *cis*-stereoisomers in food samples [42,43]. In the present study, *cis*-ferulic acid accounted for approximately 20% of the total ferulic acid content in the spelt samples, which is consistent with the results reported by Tang et al. [42]. The proportion of *cis*-p-coumaric acid was lower and accounted for approximately 8% of the total p-coumaric acid content. This proportion of *cis*-stereoisomers of phenolic acids in cereals opens new questions about the possible physiological functions of *cis*-stereoisomers in biological systems.

According to the data in the present study, germination of the spelt grains had significant effects on the profile of secondary metabolites, as well as the levels of individual compounds in germinated grains. These results provide important information on the nutraceutical quality of germinated spelt grains.

4. Conclusions

The germination process resulted in important changes in the composition of spelt grains. The total phenolic content, antioxidant activity, and secondary metabolite content were significantly increased during germination. Ferulic and p-coumaric acids (*cis* and *trans* forms combined) were the major phenolic acids in spelt grains, and their total content increased from 457.93 ± 12.03 μg/g DW in nongerminated spelt to 1090.99 ± 101.99 μg/g DW in germinated spelt. Benzoxazinoids and apigenin-di-C-glucosides are often neglected compounds in cereals, and germination strongly affects their content in spelt grains, as the sum of the three quantified benzoxazinoids reached a concentration of 517.75 ± 48.49 μg/g DW in germinated spelt, while no benzoxazinoids were detected in nongerminated spelt. Among apigenin-di-C-glucosides, only schaftoside was significantly affected (nearly four-fold increase during germination). According to the results of the present study, the content of most bioactive compounds was highest in spelt grains after 96 h of germination. Obtained data are promising for the high-value application of germinated spelt in functional foods (e.g., enriched baked goods, whole seed flowers, ready-to-eat snacks, etc.), but further studies on the health benefits of spelt secondary metabolites are essential to better understand their health-promoting effects on humans. Overall, germinated edible grains and sprouts rich in bioactive compounds can be considered as an important raw material for the production of functional foods that have a positive impact on the prevention of some chronic diseases.

Supplementary Materials: The following supporting information can be downloaded at: https://www.mdpi.com/article/10.3390/foods12091769/s1, Table S1. Characteristics of the phenolic compounds in germinated spelt extracts as analyzed by LC-MS; Figure S1. Specific reactivities of selected compounds toward FC, DPPH, and ABTS reagents; Figure S2. UV spectrum of selected compounds in germinated spelt extracts; Figure S3. Structure of 6-Methoxy-2-benzoxazolinone (MBOA); Figure S4. ^{1}H NMR spectrum of MBOA; Figure S5. NOESY spectrum of MBOA; Figure S6. HSQC spectrum of MBOA.

Author Contributions: Conceptualization, A.Ž. and T.P. (Tomaž Požrl); methodology, A.Ž., T.P. (Tomaž Požrl), B.C. and T.P. (Tomaž Polak); software, T.P. (Tomaž Polak) and D.G.; validation, A.Ž., T.P. (Tomaž Polak) and B.C.; formal analysis, A.Ž.; investigation, A.Ž., T.P. (Tomaž Polak) and D.G.; resources, T.P.(Tomaž Požrl); data curation, A.Ž. and T.P. (Tomaž Polak); writing—original draft preparation, A.Ž.; writing—review and editing, T.P. (Tomaž Požrl), B.C. and T.P. (Tomaž Polak); visualization, A.Ž.; supervision, T.P. (Tomaž Požrl); funding acquisition, T.P. (Tomaž Požrl). All authors have read and agreed to the published version of the manuscript.

Funding: The work was financially supported by research programs funded by the Slovenian Research Agency (P4-0234).

Institutional Review Board Statement: Not applicable.

Data Availability Statement: The data presented in this study are available on request from the corresponding author.

Conflicts of Interest: The authors declare no conflict of interest.

References

1. Molberg, Ø.; Uhlen, A.K.; Jensen, T.; Flæte, N.S.; Fleckenstein, B.; Arentz-Hansen, H.; Raki, M.; Lundin, K.E.A.; Sollid, L.M. Mapping of gluten T-cell epitopes in the bread wheat ancestors: Implications for celiac disease. *Gastroenterology* **2005**, *128*, 393–401. [CrossRef] [PubMed]
2. Şerban, L.R.; Păucean, A.; Man, S.M.; Chiş, M.S.; Mureşan, V. Ancient wheat species: Biochemical profile and impact on sourdough bread characteristics—A review. *Processes* **2021**, *9*, 2008. [CrossRef]
3. Gan, R.Y.; Lui, W.Y.; Wu, K.; Chan, C.L.; Dai, S.H.; Sui, Z.Q.; Corke, H. Bioactive compounds and bioactivities of germinated edible seeds and sprouts: An updated review. *Trends Food Sci. Technol.* **2017**, *59*, 1–14. [CrossRef]
4. Muñoz-Insa, A.; Selciano, H.; Zarnkow, M.; Becker, T.; Gastl, M. Malting process optimization of spelt (*Triticum spelta* L.) for the brewing process. *LWT-Food Sci. Technol.* **2013**, *50*, 99–109. [CrossRef]
5. Hübner, F.; Arendt, E.K. Germination of Cereal Grains as a Way to Improve the Nutritional Value: A Review. *Crit. Rev. Food Sci. Nutr.* **2013**, *53*, 853–861. [CrossRef] [PubMed]
6. Herchi, W.; Bahashwan, S.; Sebei, K.; Ben Saleh, H.; Kallel, H.; Boukhchina, S. Effects of germination on chemical composition and antioxidant activity of flaxseed (*Linum usitatissimum* L.) oil. *Grasas Aceites* **2015**, *66*, e057. [CrossRef]
7. Živković, A.; Polak, T.; Cigić, B.; Požrl, T. Germinated Buckwheat: Effects of Dehulling on Phenolics Profile and Antioxidant Activity of Buckwheat Seeds. *Foods* **2021**, *10*, 740. [CrossRef]
8. Li, L.; Shewry, P.R.; Ward, J.L. Phenolic acids in wheat varieties in the healthgrain diversity screen. *J. Agric. Food Chem.* **2008**, *56*, 9732–9739. [CrossRef]
9. Bei, Q.; Liu, Y.; Wang, L.; Chen, G.; Wu, Z. Improving free, conjugated, and bound phenolic fractions in fermented oats (*Avena sativa* L.) with Monascus anka and their antioxidant activity. *J. Funct. Foods* **2017**, *32*, 185–194. [CrossRef]
10. Zhang, B.; Zhang, Y.; Li, H.; Deng, Z.; Tsao, R. A review on insoluble-bound phenolics in plant-based food matrix and their contribution to human health with future perspectives. *Trends Food Sci. Technol.* **2020**, *105*, 347–362. [CrossRef]
11. Del Rio, D.; Rodriguez-Mateos, A.; Spencer, J.P.E.; Tognolini, M.; Borges, G.; Crozier, A. Dietary (poly)phenolics in human health: Structures, bioavailability, and evidence of protective effects against chronic diseases. *Antioxid. Redox Signal.* **2013**, *18*, 1818–1892. [CrossRef]

12. Schulz, M.; Marocco, A.; Tabaglio, V.; Macias, F.A.; Molinillo, J.M.G. Benzoxazinoids in Rye Allelopathy–From Discovery to Application in Sustainable Weed Control and Organic Farming. *J. Chem. Ecol.* **2013**, *39*, 154–174. [CrossRef] [PubMed]
13. Pihlava, J.M.; Kurtelius, T. Determination of benzoxazinoids in wheat and rye beers by HPLC-DAD and UPLC-QTOF MS. *Food Chem.* **2016**, *204*, 400–408. [CrossRef]
14. Prinz, S.; Schauberger, D.; Bauer, I.M.; Knasmueller, S.; Kopp, B. Aneugenic 2,4-dihydroxy-7-methoxy-1,4-benzoxazin-3-one (DIMBOA) and 2,4-dihydroxy-1,4-benzoxazin-3-one (DIBOA) in sprouts of *Triticum aestivum* cultivars—A "safety health food"? *Food Chem.* **2010**, *121*, 973–979. [CrossRef]
15. Adhikari, K.B.; Tanwir, F.; Gregersen, P.L.; Steffensen, S.K.; Jensen, B.M.; Poulsen, L.K.; Nielsen, C.H.; Høyer, S.; Borre, M.; Fomsgaard, I.S. Benzoxazinoids: Cereal phytochemicals with putative therapeutic and health-protecting properties. *Mol. Nutr. Food Res.* **2015**, *59*, 1324–1338. [CrossRef] [PubMed]
16. Beckmann, M.; Lloyd, A.J.; Haldar, S.; Seal, C.; Brandt, K.; Draper, J. Hydroxylated phenylacetamides derived from bioactive benzoxazinoids are bioavailable in humans after habitual consumption of whole grain sourdough rye bread. *Mol. Nutr. Food Res.* **2013**, *57*, 1859–1873. [CrossRef]
17. Adhikari, K.B.; Lærke, H.N.; Mortensen, A.G.; Fomsgaard, I.S. Plasma and urine concentrations of bioactive dietary benzoxazinoids and their glucuronidated conjugates in rats fed a rye bread-based diet. *J. Agric. Food Chem.* **2012**, *60*, 11518–11524. [CrossRef]
18. Jensen, B.M.; Adhikari, K.B.; Schnoor, H.J.; Juel-Berg, N.; Fomsgaard, I.S.; Poulsen, L.K. Quantitative analysis of absorption, metabolism, and excretion of benzoxazinoids in humans after the consumption of high- and low-benzoxazinoid diets with similar contents of cereal dietary fibres: A crossover study. *Eur. J. Nutr.* **2017**, *56*, 387–397. [CrossRef]
19. Dang, J.; Paudel, Y.N.; Yang, X.; Ren, Q.; Zhang, S.; Ji, X.; Liu, K.; Jin, M. Schaftoside Suppresses Pentylenetetrazol-Induced Seizures in Zebrafish via Suppressing Apoptosis, Modulating Inflammation, and Oxidative Stress. *ACS Chem. Neurosci.* **2021**, *12*, 2542–2552. [CrossRef] [PubMed]
20. Zhou, K.; Wu, J.; Chen, J.; Zhou, Y.; Chen, X.; Wu, Q.; Xu, Y.; Tu, W.; Lou, X.; Yang, G.; et al. Schaftoside ameliorates oxygen glucose deprivation-induced inflammation associated with the TLR4/Myd88/Drp1-related mitochondrial fission in BV2 microglia cells. *J. Pharmacol. Sci.* **2019**, *139*, 15–22. [CrossRef]
21. Polonskiy, V.; Loskutov, I.; Sumina, A. Biological role and health benefits of antioxidant compounds in cereals. *Biol. Commun.* **2020**, *65*, 53–67. [CrossRef]
22. Watts, J.E.; De Villiers, O.T.; Watts, L. Sterilization of wheat seeds for tissue culture purposes. *S. Afr. J. Bot.* **1993**, *59*, 641–642. [CrossRef]
23. Abramovič, H.; Grobin, B.; Ulrih, N.P.; Cigić, B. Relevance and standardization of in vitro antioxidant assays: ABTS, DPPH, and Folin–Ciocalteu. *J. Chem.* **2018**, *2018*, 4608405. [CrossRef]
24. Brand-Williams, W.; Cuvelier, M.E.; Berset, C. Use of a free radical method to evaluate antioxidant activity. *LWT-Food Sci. Technol.* **1995**, *28*, 25–30. [CrossRef]
25. Sayed, E.; Abdel-Aal, M.; Rabalski, I. Bioactive Compounds and their Antioxidant Capacity in Selected Primitive and Modern Wheat Species. *Open Agric. J.* **2008**, *2*, 7–14. [CrossRef]
26. Yilmaz, V.A.; Brandolini, A.; Hidalgo, A. Phenolic acids and antioxidant activity of wild, feral and domesticated diploid wheats. *J. Cereal Sci.* **2015**, *64*, 168–175. [CrossRef]
27. Mathew, S.; Emilia, T.; Zainul, A.; Zakaria, A. Reactivity of phenolic compounds towards free radicals under in vitro conditions. *J. Food Sci. Technol.* **2015**, *52*, 5790–5798. [CrossRef]
28. Cho, D.H.; Lim, S.T. Changes in phenolic acid composition and associated enzyme activity in shoot and kernel fractions of brown rice during germination. *Food Chem.* **2018**, *256*, 163–170. [CrossRef] [PubMed]
29. Cevallos-Casals, B.A.; Cisneros-Zevallos, L. Impact of germination on phenolic content and antioxidant activity of 13 edible seed species. *Food Chem.* **2010**, *119*, 1485–1490. [CrossRef]
30. Dixon, D.P.; Sellars, J.D.; Kenwright, A.M.; Steel, P.G. The maize benzoxazinone DIMBOA reacts with glutathione and other thiols to form spirocyclic adducts. *Phytochemistry* **2012**, *77*, 171–178. [CrossRef]
31. Ma, X.; Lin, H.; Yong, Y.; Ju, X.; Li, Y.; Liu, X.; Yu, Z.; Wujin, C.; She, Y.; Zhang, J.; et al. Molecularly imprinted polymer-specific solid-phase extraction for the determination of 4-hydroxy-2(3H)benzoxazolone isolated from Acanthus ilicifolius Linnaeus using high-performance liquid chromatography-tandem mass spectrometry. *Front. Nutr.* **2022**, *9*, 2581. [CrossRef]
32. Otaka, J.; Subbarao, G.V.; Ono, H.; Yoshihashi, T. Biological nitrification inhibition in maize—Isolation and identification of hydrophobic inhibitors from root exudates. *Biol. Fertil. Soils* **2022**, *58*, 251–264. [CrossRef]
33. Tanwir, F.; Dionisio, G.; Adhikari, K.B.; Fomsgaard, I.S.; Gregersen, P.L. Biosynthesis and chemical transformation of benzoxazinoids in rye during seed germination and the identification of a rye Bx6-like gene. *Phytochemistry* **2017**, *140*, 95–107. [CrossRef]
34. Zou, Y.; Yang, M.; Zhang, G.; He, H.; Yang, T. Antioxidant Activities and Phenolic Compositions of Wheat Germ as Affected by the Roasting Process. *JAOCS J. Am. Oil Chem. Soc.* **2015**, *92*, 1303–1312. [CrossRef]
35. Siipola, S.M.; Kotilainen, T.; Sipari, N.; Morales, L.O.; Lindfors, A.V.; Robson, T.M.; Aphalo, P.J. Epidermal UV-A absorbance and whole-leaf flavonoid composition in pea respond more to solar blue light than to solar UV radiation. *Plant Cell Environ.* **2015**, *38*, 941–952. [CrossRef] [PubMed]
36. Casal, J.J. Photoreceptor signaling networks in plant responses to shade. *Annu. Rev. Plant Biol.* **2013**, *64*, 403–427. [CrossRef]

37. Mencin, M.; Mikulic-Petkovsek, M.; Veberič, R.; Terpinc, P. Development and Optimisation of Solid-Phase Extraction of Extractable and Bound Phenolic Acids in Spelt (*Triticum spelta* L.) Seeds. *Antioxidants* **2021**, *10*, 1085. [CrossRef] [PubMed]
38. Mencin, M.; Abramovič, H.; Jamnik, P.; Mikulič Petkovšek, M.; Veberič, R.; Terpinc, P. Abiotic stress combinations improve the phenolics profiles and activities of extractable and bound antioxidants from germinated spelt (*Triticum spelta* L.) seeds. *Food Chem.* **2020**, *344*, 128704. [CrossRef] [PubMed]
39. Žilić, S.; Basić, Z.; Hadži-Tašković Šukalović, V.; Maksimović, V.; Janković, M.; Filipović, M. Can the sprouting process applied to wheat improve the contents of vitamins and phenolic compounds and antioxidant capacity of the flour? *Int. J. Food Sci. Technol.* **2014**, *49*, 1040–1047. [CrossRef]
40. Hosseinian, F.S.; Mazza, G. Triticale bran and straw: Potential new sources of phenolic acids, proanthocyanidins, and lignans. *J. Funct. Foods* **2009**, *1*, 57–64. [CrossRef]
41. Istasse, T.; Jacquet, N.; Berchem, T.; Haubruge, E.; Nguyen, B.K.; Richel, A. Extraction of honey polyphenols: Method development and evidence of cis isomerization. *Anal. Chem. Insights* **2016**, *2016*, 49–57. [CrossRef]
42. Tang, Y.; Hao, J.; Fan, C.; Cao, X. Preparative separation of high-purity trans- and cis-ferulic acid from wheat bran by pH-zone-refining counter-current chromatography. *J. Chromatogr. A* **2021**, *1636*, 461772. [CrossRef] [PubMed]
43. Tian, W.; Wang, F.; Xu, K.; Zhang, Z.; Yan, J.; Yan, J.; Tian, Y.; Liu, J.; Zhang, Y.; Zhang, Y.; et al. Accumulation of Wheat Phenolic Acids under Different Nitrogen Rates and Growing Environments. *Plants* **2022**, *11*, 2237. [CrossRef] [PubMed]

foods

MDPI

Article

Cooking Quality and Chemical and Technological Characteristics of Wholegrain Einkorn Pasta Obtained from Micronized Flour

Laura Gazza *, Elena Galassi, Francesca Nocente, Chiara Natale and Federica Taddei

CREA-Research Center for Engineering and Agro-Food Processing, Via Manziana 30, 00189 Rome, Italy
* Correspondence: laura.gazza@crea.gov.it

Abstract: The increased demand for healthier foods, the recognition of dry pasta as an ideal carrier of functional ingredients, and the current interest for ancient wheats such as einkorn motivated the present research. Two varieties of *Triticum monococcum*, namely cv Norberto and the free-threshing cv Hammurabi, were milled by ultra-fine milling process (micronization) to produce wholegrain spaghetti. Einkorn pasta was assessed in terms of technological and biochemical properties and cooking and sensorial quality and compared to durum wheat semolina pasta. Wholewheat einkorn pasta showed a threefold increase in total dietary fibre content as well as in total antioxidant capacity in comparison to the control. The level of resistant starch in cv Norberto resulted significantly higher respect to semolina and einkorn cv Hammurabi pasta. Despite the very weak einkorn gluten network, the sensory and instrumental assessment of pasta quality highlighted that einkorn spaghetti presented good sensorial properties related to their technological quality, in particular, for the overall judgment and firmness. Cultivar Hammurabi emerged as the preeminent compromise on the basis of technological performances together with chemical and sensorial aspects.

Keywords: minor cereals; wholegrain pasta; micronization; einkorn cv Hammurabi; einkorn cv Norberto

Citation: Gazza, L.; Galassi, E.; Nocente, F.; Natale, C.; Taddei, F. Cooking Quality and Chemical and Technological Characteristics of Wholegrain Einkorn Pasta Obtained from Micronized Flour. *Foods* **2022**, *11*, 2905. https://doi.org/10.3390/foods11182905

Academic Editor: Carla Brites

Received: 29 July 2022
Accepted: 16 September 2022
Published: 19 September 2022

1. Introduction

Dried pasta is the symbol of Italian food, and thanks to its low cost, versatility, easy preparation, nutritional value, long shelf-life, and pleasant organoleptic attributes, it is the second most consumed staple food worldwide. All these properties make pasta an ideal carrier of functional ingredients, exerting human health beneficial effects. Consequently, in the last years, innovative pasta formulations have been developed by either the replacement or the enrichment of semolina with functional ingredients from plant or animal origin or by the use of alternative raw materials such as minor cereals, gluten-free cereals, or neglected species as ancient wheats [1,2]. The current interest for ancient, hulled wheats such as einkorn, emmer, and spelt has been motivated by the increased demand for healthier foods concurrently to the urgent need of a more sustainable agricultural production system [3]. Indeed, ancient wheats, traditionally cultivated under low-input conditions and not subjected to modern breeding or selection, have retained the genetic diversity of useful traits such as disease tolerance, adaptability to climate changes, and enhanced nitrogen and water use efficiency [4], making them suitable candidates to be employed for a "regenerative agriculture". Moreover, the superior nutritional quality of ancient wheats in terms of protein, minerals, and antioxidant compounds content and less negative health effects concerning gluten digestibility when compared with the modern varieties [5–7] have contributed to their comeback in large scale agriculture [3]. The hulled wheat einkorn, *Triticum monococcum* L. subsp. *monococcum* ($2n = 2x = 14$, A^mA^m), was the most ancient wheat species to be cultivated until the Neolithic period for thousand years, and progressively, it was replaced by free-threshing and high-yielding wheat species [8]. Nowadays, its cultivation is limited to marginal areas of Europe, Turkey, Caucasus, and Morocco, and recently, it has been re-introduced thanks to its adaptation to poor soils and low-inputs agriculture, tolerance and resistance to pests and diseases, good technological and organoleptic properties, and for its peculiar nutritional value [8–10]. The higher nutritional quality of einkorn with respect to bread and durum wheat lies in the higher amount of proteins, essential fatty acids, microelements, and antioxidant compounds such as carotenoids (particularly lutein), tocols, phytosterols, conjugated polyphenols, and alkylresorcinols [4,9–11]. Moreover, low β-amylase and lipoxygenase activities preserve antioxidants degradation during einkorn processing [9,12]. Although the *T. monococcum* gluten content is similar to modern tetraploid and hexaploid wheats, its gliadin and glutenin allele composition is characterized by an excess of gliadins over glutenins [13]. This protein composition makes the gluten network less polymerized and then more digestible by gastro-intestinal enzymes, resulting in a low content of immunostimulatory peptides toxic to people affected by gluten-related disorders [7,14,15]. The weakness of the gluten in *T. monococcum* was confirmed by its poor bread-making properties though einkorn accessions with a suitable bread-making quality have been identified [16–19]. Nevertheless, einkorn wheat flour resulted as suitable for the manufacturing of baking products such as cookies, pastries, and unleavened bread [20]. Concerning the einkorn pasta-making aptitude, only few studies have been performed to compare the quality of einkorn flour respect to durum wheat semolina. Brandolini et al. [21] found that pasta obtained from einkorn refined flour exhibited a lower firmness and cooking loss and a higher nutritional value. Similar results were observed in pasta from pregerminated or decorticated einkorn, einkorn–egg albumen, and einkorn–whole egg pasta [22]. Analysis of the structure of einkorn pasta revealed a less compact structure and a lower rate of starch hydrolysis compared to durum wheat pasta [23,24]. In spite of the increasing consumer demand for wholegrain pasta, studies on wholewheat einkorn pasta have not been yet reported. Hence, in this work, two varieties of *T. monococcum*, i.e., cvs Norberto and the free-threshing Hammurabi, were milled by ultra-fine milling process to produce 100% wholegrain einkorn spaghetti. Einkorn pasta-making aptitude in terms of chemical and technological properties and cooking and sensorial quality was assessed and compared to durum wheat semolina pasta.

2. Materials and Methods

2.1. Plant Material and Milling Process

Two einkorn cultivars—one naked, Hammurabi, and one hulled, Norberto—were grown by Horta® at organic small farms in Marche Region, Central Italy. De-hulled einkorn kernels were obtained by two consecutive cycles in a bench micro-thresher (Marelli SpA, Milan, Italy).

Micronization was applied on the intact, no-tempered kernels of einkorn cultivars in the KMX-500 device (Separ Microsystem, Brescia, Italy) at a frequency of 170 Hz to produce micronized wholewheat flours (85% of particles with size < 120 μm). Durum wheat cv San Carlo, grown at the CREA-IT experimental field of Montelibretti (Rome, Italy), was milled in the pilot plant (Buhler MLU 202, Uzwil, Switzerland) to recover semolina and used as control.

2.2. Rheological and Technological Analyses

Wholewheat einkorn flours and semolina were analysed with the Chopin Alvgraph (Chopin, Villeneuve La Garenne, France) according to the manufacturer's instructions under conditions as described by the standard AACC method 54-30.02 [25]. The SDS sedimentation test was performed according to the standard method AACC 56-70.01 [26]. The AACC 56-81B method [27] was used for the assessment of the falling number (FN), using the Perten Falling Number System 1500 (Stockholm, Sweden). Gluten index (GI) determination was conducted with the Glutomatic 2200 (Perten Instruments) according to AACC method 38-12 [28].

2.3. Pasta-Making Process

Pasta formulations from micronized flours of cvs Hammurabi and Norberto were produced. To achieve an appropriate consistency of the doughs for extrusion, 2 kg of micronized flours were hydrated in the kneading machine to reach a level of 32% humidity. The pasta-making process was performed using a pilot plant consisting of: (i) an extruder (NAMAD, Rome, Italy) with a capacity up to 20 kg/h, equipped with a screw (45 cm in length, 4.5 cm in diameter), which ended with a Teflon-coated die consisting of 164 holes, 1.80 mm diameter, to produce spaghetti shape (1.65 mm diameter), and (ii) an experimental dryer (AFREM, Lyon, France). Extrusion conditions were applied following the procedure already reported by Nocente et al. [29] both for einkorn and semolina pasta production. The moisture content of dried pasta was 12.5%. Pasta samples were stored at room temperature until analyses.

2.4. Chemical Characterization and Total Antioxidant Capacity of Cooked Pasta

All results are expressed as dry weight (dw), and the moisture content was determined using the thermo balance (Sartorius MA 40, Goettingen, Germany) at 120 °C. All analytical determinations were made in triplicate on cooked (Section 2.5) and freeze-dried pasta.

Protein content of pasta samples was measured by micro-Kjeldhal nitrogen analysis (ICC 105/2 method) [30], using as the conversion factor N $\times$ 5.7. Resistant starch (RS) content was determined according to the Official Method 2002.02 [31], using Resistant Starch Assay Kit (Megazyme, Bray, Ireland). Total dietary fibre (TDF) content was measured using an enzymatic-gravimetric kit for fibre determination (Bioquant, Merck, Darmstadt, Germany) according to the Official Method 991.43 [32]. Ash content was determined by the AACC 08-01.01 method [33]. Enzymatic method (AACC International Method No. 32.32) [34] was used for the determination of fructooligosaccharides (FOS). Total antioxidant capacity (TAC) was ascertained according to [35].

2.5. Cooking Quality and Pasta Colour

The cooking test was performed according to the AACC method 66-50.01 [36], adding 100 g of dried spaghetti to 1 L of boiling tap water until reaching the optimal cooking time (OCT); the time it took for the centre core of the pasta to disappear was determined by squeezing it between two plates. Water absorption (WA), total organic matter (TOM), and cooking loss (CL) were determined as already reported by Nocente et al. [37]. Firmness of cooked spaghetti was determined in compliance to the AACC 66-50.01 method [36], using the Texture Analyzer TA.XT plus (Stable Micro System, Ltd., Surrey, UK) and the Texture Exponent 32 (Texture Technologies Corporation, Scarsdale, NY, USA) software.

Pasta colour was measured by Tristimulus Colorimeter, Chroma Meter CR-400 (Konica Minolta, Osaka, Japan), using the CIE-Lab colour space coordinates L* (lightness), a* (red/green value), and b* (yellow/blue value) and the D65 illuminant.

2.6. Sensory Test

Sensory evaluation was focused on sensory texture quality traits and assessed, according to D'Egidio et al. [38], by a panel of five trained assessors, who are food technicians of our 'Cereal Food Processing Lab' in Rome. The technical panel evaluated three spaghetti textural characteristics: stickiness, which consists in the material adhering to the cooked pasta surface; firmness, which indicates the resistance to chewing by the teeth; and bulkiness, which is the degree of jamming among the spaghetti strands. The tasting was carried out by the technical panellists independently and separately. Water was provided to the tasters between samples. Each sensorial parameter was scored from 10 to 100; the overall judgment (SJ) was calculated as the arithmetic mean of the scores of each parameter [38].

2.7. Statistical Analysis

Results were reported as mean $\pm$ standard deviation. One-way ANOVA was performed with MSTATC program (Michigan State University, East Lansing, MI, USA); Duncan multiple range test for post hoc comparison of means was applied to compute significant differences ($p \leq 0.05$) for each analysed parameter.

3. Results and Discussion

3.1. Chemical Characterization of Cooked Pasta

The protein content of pasta from cv Hammurabi was on average 19.1 g/100 g, almost one percentual point higher than pasta samples from cv Norberto (Table 1). Significantly higher protein contents were observed in einkorn pasta in comparison with those reported about the durum wheat semolina pasta used as control, confirming the very high protein content of *T. monococcum* species also on organic agricultural management [39].

Table 1. Chemical traits and total antioxidant capacity of einkorn cv Hammurabi and cv Norberto and semolina cooked pasta.

	Proteins	RS	TDF	FOS	TAC	Ash
	(g/100 g)	(g/100 g)	(g/100 g)	(g/100 g)	(mmol TEAC/kg)	(g/100 g)
Hammurabi	19.10 ± 0.07 [a]	0.276 ± 0.002 [c]	10.1 ± 0.3 [a]	1.11 ± 0.03 [a]	69.7 ± 0.5 [a]	2.59 ± 0.01 [a]
Norberto	18.3 ± 0.2 [b]	0.80 ± 0.02 [a]	10.03 ± 0.08 [a]	1.3 ± 0.2 [a]	64.2 ± 0.5 [b]	2.26 ± 0.03 [b]
Semolina	13.3 ± 0.2 [c]	0.382 ± 0.005 [b]	3.6 ± 0.3 [b]	1.29 ± 0.02 [a]	46.8 ± 0.5 [c]	0.708 ± 0.001 [c]

Results are reported as dry weight and expressed as mean ± standard deviation for three replications. Within the same column, values with different letters indicate significant differences determined by Duncan's test ($p \leq 0.05$). RS, resistant starch; TDF, total dietary fibre; FOS, fructooligosaccharides; TAC, total antioxidant capacity; TEAC, trolox equivalent antioxidant capacity.

Pasta from cv Norberto showed a significantly higher content of resistant starch at 0.80 g/100 g on average, with respect to semolina pasta, +110% and even up to +190% if compared with cv Hammurabi (Table 1). Rotondi Aufiero et al. [40] observed high levels of RS in einkorn pasta made with cv Hammurabi digested in vitro when compared to commercial pasta, suggesting that einkorn pasta may be characterized by a lower glycaemic index. Several promising health benefits of RS have been proven, such as prevention from colon and cardiovascular diseases, reduction of blood glucose levels and insulin, and prebiotic effect [41].

The amount of TDF in einkorn pasta samples were increased of almost threefold respect to durum wheat, with the mean content of TDF in semolina pasta being 3.6 g/100 g (Table 1). Noticeable, 100 g of einkorn pasta samples analysed in this study provided more than 6 g total dietary fibre, corresponding to around 40% of the RDA for an adult (25 g/die; EFSA [42]), so it could be defined as "high in fibre" [43].

Results relative to ash content revealed a threefold increment in spaghetti obtained from einkorn wholewheat flours (Table 1) when compared to pasta produced from durum semolina (0.71 g/100 g); these data represent the greater mineral content of monococcum grains with respect to durum wheat kernels [9]. However, einkorn wholewheat pasta stayed largely above the Italian legal limits for durum wholewheat pasta (1.8 g/100 g) [44].

The level of TAC was significantly higher (+43%, on average) in einkorn pasta than in pasta control (Table 1), mainly in cv Hammurabi. In *T. monococcum*, the total antioxidant capacity was always higher than in durum wheat [10], likely due to the presence of higher amounts of antioxidants compounds, mainly tocols and carotenoids, in *T. monococcum* [45].

Fructooligosaccharides can be used as fermentable substrates for probiotic microorganisms, hence providing prebiotic effects linked to several health benefits, including prevention of digestion diseases, reduction of cholesterol and blood pressure, and anticancer effects [46]. In wheat, the FOS level is maximum in kernels at the milky stage; thereafter, their concentration swiftly reduces [47]. In einkorn spaghetti, FOS content turned out to be 1.2 g/100 g on average (Table 1), which was not significantly different from pasta control (1.29 g/100 g). Brandolini et al. [48] reported an average fructan concentration in kernels of four einkorn genotypes of 1.9 g/100 g. Such values might seem quite low, but wheat provides about 70% of fructans in the Western diets [49].

3.2. Rheological and Technological Parameters

Variation in total protein content alone does not adequately explain the variation in wheat processing quality since which storage proteins are expressed is an important factor as well. The gluten index (GI) is a measurement of wheat proteins that provides a simultaneous determination of gluten quality and quantity [50]. Indeed, GI is a criterion defining whether the gluten quality is weak (GI < 30%), normal (GI = 30–80%), or strong (GI > 80%). As shown in Table 2, despite a significantly higher protein content, wholewheat flour from einkorn cv Hammurabi presented an extremely weak gluten network, whereas cv Norberto can be classified as flour of normal strength. This gluten quality parameter had a bulk of effects on technological and rheological aspects besides consequences on gluten digestibility [7,14,15]. The low gluten index accounted both for the low SDS sedimentation values of Hammurabi flour, which was on average less than half of the sedimentation volume value registered for einkorn Norberto, and for the low W and P/L parameters (Table 2).

Table 2. Rheological and technological parameters of einkorn cv Hammurabi and cv Norberto wholewheat flours and durum wheat semolina.

	GI	SDS	W	P/L	FN
	(%)	(mL)	(J × 10^{-4})		(sec″)
Hammurabi	0 ^{c}	24.7 ± 0.7 ^{c}	44.0 ± 3.6 ^{c}	2.5 ± 0.1 ^{a}	463″ ± 10 ^{b}
Norberto	52 ± 2 ^{b}	58.5 ± 0.7 ^{a}	84 ± 4 ^{b}	1.6 ± 0.4 ^{b}	417″ ± 11 ^{c}
Semolina	84 ± 3 ^{a}	37.5 ± 0.7 ^{b}	227 ± 21 ^{a}	1.8 ± 0.1 ^{b}	483″ ± 2 ^{a}

Results are reported as mean ± standard deviation for three replications. Within the same column, values with different letters indicate significant differences determined by Duncan's test ($p \leq 0.05$). GI, gluten index; SDS, SDS sedimentation volume test; FN, falling number.

The FN is commonly used for assessing the baking quality of wheat flour in relation to the amylase activity. However, Sjoberg et al. [51] referred to low pasta-making aptitude wheat varieties as those with falling number of less than 300 s. The low FN value, besides the risk of an over darkening of the pasta, may affect its cooking quality parameters, mainly stickiness, due to excessive starch degradation. In the present study, the falling number levels in all flour samples showed FN over 400 sec (Table 2) even if einkorn wholegrain was reported to have a higher alpha-amylase activity than in white flours [52], hence meeting the specifications for the production of pasta in regard to this parameter.

3.3. Cooking Quality Parameters and Pasta Colour

The diameter of dry spaghetti was similar for all samples: in the range of 1.52–1.66 mm (Table 3). The variation of the diameter observed in different area of the spaghetti might be imputed to the coarse surface due to the high content of fibre particles (Table 1) observed in wholegrain einkorn pasta and also to the weak gluten net of monococcum pasta samples (Table 2). The poor gluten matrix also accounted for decreased cooking time observed in einkorn spaghetti, in particular in the Hammurabi sample, with respect to semolina pasta (10′30″ on average). The reduction in cooking time was also due to a lower water absorption (WA) for einkorn pasta. In fact, a significant reduction of water absorption was detected in einkorn pasta, mainly in Hammurabi (Table 3), with respect to the control (148.6 g), as previously observed in other bran-enriched foods [53,54], likely because of the fibre present in einkorn pasta that absorbs a lesser quantity of water with respect to the starch.

Hammurabi wholegrain spaghetti presented the highest level of organic matter on their surface (Table 3). Moreover, the increased TOM values might be due to the high content of fibre, which could disarrange the starch/gluten network, resulting in more starch released over pasta cooking [54]. High quantities of organic matter is an index of poor cooking quality; nevertheless, TOM values between 2.1 and 1.4 g/100 g correspond to good-quality pasta [55], and all the pasta samples valued in the present study fell into this range.

Table 3. Cooking, textural properties, and colour indices of einkorn cv Hammurabi and cv Norberto and semolina pasta.

	Spaghetti Diameter (mm)	OCT (min′ s″)	WA (g)	TOM (g)	CL (g/100 g)	Firmness (kg)		Colour	
							(b*)	(100-L)	(a*)
Hammurabi	1.52–1.64	7′ 00″ ± 5″ c	128.21 ± 0.08 c	2.06 ± 0.01 a	10.7 ± 0.3 a	0.33 ± 0.02 b	22.4 ± 0.8 c	59.8 ± 0.5 a	12.1 ± 0.3 a
Norberto	1.56–1.66	7′ 30″ ± 5″ b	137.99 ± 0.09 b	1.7 ± 0.1 b	7.9 ± 0.1 b	0.48 ± 0.04 a	28.0 ± 0.7 a	56.3 ± 0.5 b	10.8 ± 0.2 b
Semolina	1.53–1.60	10′ 30″ ± 5″ a	148.6 ± 0.2 a	1.64 ± 0.04 b	3.67 ± 0.02 c	0.276 ± 0.005 b	25.4 ± 0.2 b	38.2 ± 0.1 c	1.25 ± 0.08 c

Results are expressed as mean ± standard deviation for three replications. Within the same column, values with different letters indicate significant differences determined by Duncan's test ($p \leq 0.05$). OCT, optimal cooking time; WA, water absorption; TOM, total organic matter; CL, cooking loss; L, lightness.

Einkorn pasta resulted in increased cooking loss compared with the control (Table 3). The highest cooking loss value was for Hammurabi pasta sample, whereas the sample from Norberto had significantly ($p \leq 0.05$) lower cooking loss. The higher cooking loss in einkorn pasta compared with durum semolina (3.67 g/100 g) might be attributed to a weaker protein gluten network [56], especially in cv Hammurabi with a close to null gluten index (Table 2).

Cooked spaghetti firmness, as revealed by the TA.XT instrument analysis, was significantly ($p \leq 0.05$) higher in cv Norberto compared both to wholegrain Hammurabi and to semolina pasta control (Table 3); the improved spaghetti firmness of cv Norberto could be ascribed to the very high resistant starch content of this cultivar (Table 1), as already observed by Marti et al. [57] and Taddei et al. [58].

As expected, the presence of bran in einkorn spaghetti determined high brown and red indices; nevertheless, a very high yellow index was found in wholegrain einkorn spaghetti (Table 3), likely as a consequence of the large amount of yellow

Pigments have been reported for einkorn flour by several studies [9,12,21,45,48]. The difference in the b* value between spaghetti from cv Hammurabi and cv Norberto is noticeable also in cooked pasta (Figure 1).

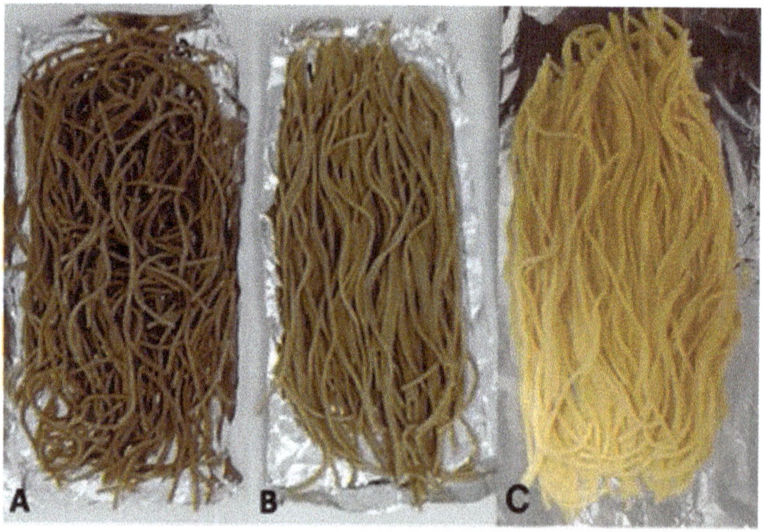

Figure 1. Wholegrain einkorn, namely cv Hammurabi (**A**) and cv Norberto (**B**), and semolina (**C**) cooked spaghetti.

3.4. Sensory Evaluation of Cooked Pasta

Firmness, stickiness, and bulkiness of spaghetti are the sensory parameters related to the most to their technological quality and are those that spaghetti consumers mainly take into consideration. The highest scores for stickiness (80), firmness (65), and overall judgment (72) were revealed, as expected, in the semolina pasta control (Table 4). The lowest firmness score was found in Hammurabi wholegrain pasta (55) followed by Norberto sample (60), which were both in the range considered sufficient (>40 and ≤60) for semolina pasta sensorial quality standard (Table 4). Lower stickiness and bulkiness indices were observed in einkorn pasta (75 for Hammurabi for both parameters) and in Norberto (60 for the two indices); these results could be related to the weak gluten network of wholewheat flour from einkorn cultivars, which is unable to counteract the release of starch upon pasta cooking.

Table 4. Sensory assessment of einkorn cv Hammurabi and cv Norberto and semolina cooked pasta.

	Firmness	Stickiness	Bulkiness	Global Sensorial Judgment
Hammurabi	55^{c}	75^{b}	75^{a}	68^{b}
Norberto	60^{b}	60^{c}	60^{c}	60^{c}
Semolina	65^{a}	80^{a}	70^{b}	72^{a}

Results are expressed as mean for five replications. Within the same column, values with different letters indicate significant differences determined by Duncan's test ($p \leq 0.05$). Firmness: absent (≤20), rare (>20 and ≤40), sufficient (>40 and ≤60), good (>60 and ≤80), very good (>80 and ≤100); bulkiness and stickiness: very high (≤20), high (>20 and ≤40), rare (>40 and ≤60), almost absent (>60 and ≤80), absent (>80 and ≤100); Global Sensorial Judgment: scarce (<55), sufficient (≥55 and <65), good (≥65 and <75), very good (≥75).

Concerning the global sensorial judgment, wholewheat einkorn pasta from Norberto reached the acceptability limit of 55, whereas the Hammurabi sample showed a "good" (68) quality of spaghetti in the same class of quality of durum semolina pasta used as control in this study (Table 4).

4. Conclusions

The paucity of studies carried out on wholegrain einkorn pasta, in contrast with the growing interest in whole-meal pasta formulated from ancient species of wheat, drove this research. The results of this study indicated that wholewheat einkorn pasta showed a notable rise in TDF content and in TAC levels with respect to the control. The level of RS in cv Norberto is very interesting also in light of the renewed importance for this nutritional parameter. Despite the very weak einkorn gluten network, the sensory and instrumental assessment of pasta quality highlighted that einkorn spaghetti demonstrated good sensorial properties related to texture, mainly for the overall judgment and firmness. Nevertheless, cv Hammurabi turned out to be the preeminent option considering both the technological performances and the chemical and sensorial aspects.

In formulating food products starting from unconventional raw materials, such as the new species of cereal addressed in this study, attention should always be paid to the genotype choice, as suggested by the differences observed between pasta obtained from cv Norberto and cv Hammurabi. Further studies should be considered to more fully evaluate the sensory and taste analysis and also involving a panel of regular consumers of whole-meal pasta obtained from minor cereals or ancient wheat varieties.

Author Contributions: Conceptualization, F.N., F.T. and L.G.; methodology, F.N., F.T., E.G. and L.G.; validation, F.N., F.T. and E.G.; formal analysis, E.G. and F.T.; investigation, L.G., C.N., F.T., F.N. and E.G.; resources, L.G.; data curation, F.N., F.T., E.G. and L.G.; writing—original draft preparation, F.N. and L.G.; writing—review and editing, F.N., F.T., E.G., C.N. and L.G.; visualization, F.N. and C.N.; supervision, L.G.; project administration, L.G.; funding acquisition, L.G. All authors have read and agreed to the published version of the manuscript.

Funding: This research was funded by Progetto GOMM, Regione Marche, Grant n. B78I18001060005.

Informed Consent Statement: Not applicable.

Data Availability Statement: The data presented in this study are available in this article.

Acknowledgments: The authors would like to thank Ester Gosparini, Roberto Mortaro, Alessandra Arcangeli, and Loriana Sereni of CREA-IT of Rome for their technical assistance and Matteo Ruggeri of Horta® for providing einkorn kernels.

Conflicts of Interest: The authors declare no conflict of interest. The funders had no role in the design of the study; in the collection, analyses, or interpretation of data; in the writing of the manuscript, or in the decision to publish the results.

References

1. Romano, A.; Ferranti, P.; Gallo, V.; Masi, P. New ingredients and alternatives to durum wheat semolina for a high quality dried pasta. *Curr. Opin. Food Sci.* **2021**, *41*, 249–259. [CrossRef]
2. Dziki, D. Current trends in enrichment of wheat pasta: Quality, nutritional value and antioxidant properties. *Processes* **2021**, *9*, 1280. [CrossRef]
3. Longin, C.F.H.; Würschum, T. Back to the future–tapping into ancient grains for food diversity. *Trends Plant Sci.* **2016**, *21*, 731–737. [CrossRef] [PubMed]
4. Geisslitz, S.; Scherf, K.A. Rediscovering ancient wheats. *Cereal Foods World* **2020**, *65*, 2. [CrossRef]
5. Shewry, P.R. Do ancient types of wheat have health benefits compared with modern bread wheat? *J. Cereal Sci.* **2018**, *79*, 469–476. [CrossRef]
6. Dinu, M.; Whittaker, A.; Pagliai, G.; Benedettelli, S.; Sofi, F. Ancient wheat species and human health: Biochemical and clinical implications. *J. Nutr. Biochem.* **2017**, *52*, 1–9. [CrossRef]
7. Picascia, S.; Camarca, A.; Malamisura, M.; Mandile, R.; Galatola, M.; Cielo, D.; Gazza, L.; Mamone, G.; Auricchio, S.; Troncone, R.; et al. In celiac disease patients the *in vivo* challenge with the diploid *Triticum monococcum* elicits a reduced immune response compared to hexaploid wheat. *Mol. Nutr. Food Res.* **2020**, *64*, 1901032. [CrossRef]
8. Zaharieva, M.; Monneveux, P. Cultivated einkorn wheat (*Triticum monococcum* L. subsp. *monococcum*): The long life of a founder crop of agriculture. *Genet. Resour. Crop Ev.* **2014**, *61*, 677–706.
9. Hidalgo, A.; Brandolini, A. Nutritional properties of einkorn wheat (*Triticum monococcum* L.). *J. Sci. Food Agr.* **2014**, *94*, 601–612. [CrossRef]
10. Ciccoritti, R.; Taddei, F.; Gazza, L.; Nocente, F. Influence of kernel thermal pre-treatments on 5-n-alkylresorcinols, polyphenols and antioxidant activity of durum and einkorn wheat. *Eur. Food Res. Technol.* **2020**, *247*, 353–362. [CrossRef]
11. Suchowilska, E.; Wiwart, M.; Kandler, W.; Krska, R. A comparison of macro- and microelement concentrations in the whole grain of four Triticum species. *Plant Soil Environ.* **2012**, *58*, 141–147. [CrossRef]
12. Hidalgo, A.; Brandolini, A. Kinetics of carotenoids degradation during the storage of einkorn (*Triticum monococcum* L. ssp. *monococcum*) and bread wheat (*Triticum aestivum* L. ssp. *aestivum*) flours. *J. Agric. Food Chem.* **2008**, *56*, 11300–11305. [PubMed]
13. Geisslitz, S.; Longin, C.F.H.; Scherf, K.A.; Koehler, P. Comparative study on gluten protein composition of ancient (einkorn, emmer and spelt) and modern wheat species (durum and common wheat). *Foods* **2019**, *8*, 409. [CrossRef]
14. Iacomino, G.; Di Stasio, L.; Fierro, O.; Picariello, G.; Venezia, A.; Gazza, L.; Ferranti, P.; Mamone, G. Protective effects of ID331 *Triticum monococcum* gliadin on in vitro models of the intestinal epithelium. *Food Chem.* **2016**, *212*, 537–542. [CrossRef] [PubMed]
15. Di Stasio, L.; Picascia, S.; Auricchio, R.; Vitale, S.; Gazza, L.; Picariello, G.; Gianfrani, C.; Mamone, G. Comparative analysis of in vitro digestibility and immunogenicity of gliadins proteins from durum and einkorn wheat. *Front. Nutr.* **2020**, *7*, 56. [CrossRef]
16. Saponaro, C.; Pogna, N.E.; Castagna, R.; Pasquini, M.; Cacciatori, P.; Redaelli, R. Allelic variation at the *Gli-A^{m}1*, *Gli-A^{m}2* and *Glu-A^{m}1* loci and bread-making quality in diploid wheat *Triticum monococcum*. *Genet. Res. Camb.* **1995**, *66*, 127–137. [CrossRef]
17. Borghi, B.; Castagna, R.; Corbellini, M.; Heun, M.; Salamini, F. Breadmaking quality of einkorn wheat (*Triticum monococcum* ssp. *monococcum*). *Cereal Chem.* **1996**, *73*, 208–214.
18. Brandolini, A.; Hidalgo, A. Einkorn (*Triticum monococcum*) flour and bread. In *Flour and Breads and Their Fortification in Health and Disease Prevention*; Preedy, V.R., Watson, R.R., Patel, V.B., Eds.; Academic Press: London, UK, 2011; pp. 79–88.
19. Geisslitz, S.; Wieser, H.; Scherf, K.A.; Koehler, P. Gluten protein composition and aggregation properties as predictors for bread volume of common wheat, spelt, durum wheat, emmer and einkorn. *J. Cereal Sci.* **2018**, *83*, 204–212. [CrossRef]
20. Corbellini, M.; Empilli, S.; Vaccino, P.; Brandolini, A.; Borghi, B.; Heun, M.; Salamini, F. Einkorn characterization for bread and cookie production in relation to protein subunit composition. *Cereal Chem.* **1999**, *76*, 727–733. [CrossRef]
21. Brandolini, A.; Lucisano, M.; Mariotti, M.; Hidalgo, A. A study on the quality of einkorn (*Triticum monococcum* L. ssp. *monococcum) pasta. J. Cereal Sci.* **2018**, *82*, 57–64. [CrossRef]
22. Hidalgo, A.; Alamprese, C.; Marti, A.; Galli, S.; Terno, A.B.; Brandolini, A. Nutritional and technological properties of non-traditional einkorn (*Triticum monococcum*) wheat pasta. *LWT* **2020**, *133*, 109932. [CrossRef]
23. Pasini, G.; Greco, F.; Cremonini, M.; Brandolini, A.; Consonni, R.; Gussoni, M. Structural and nutritional properties of pasta from *Triticum monococcum* and *Triticum durum* species. A combined 1H NMR, MRI and digestibility study. *J. Agr. Food Chem.* **2015**, *63*, 5072–5082. [CrossRef] [PubMed]
24. La Gatta, B.; Rutigliano, M.; Rusco, G.; Petrella, G.; Di Luccia, A. Evidence for different supramolecular arrangements in pasta from durum wheat (*Triticum durum*) and einkorn (*Triticum monococcum*) flours. *J. Cereal Sci.* **2017**, *73*, 76–83. [CrossRef]

25. American Association of Cereal Chemists. 54-30.02 Alveograph method for soft and hard wheat flour. In *Approved Methods of Analysis*, 11th ed.; AACC International: St. Paul, MN, USA, 2010.
26. American Association of Cereal Chemists. 56-70.01 Sodium Dodecyl Sulfate Sedimentation Test for Durum Wheat. In *Approved Methods of Analysis*, 11th ed.; AACC International: St. Paul, MN, USA, 2010.
27. American Association of Cereal Chemists. 56-81B Determination of falling number. In *Approved Methods of Analysis*, 11th ed.; AACC International: St. Paul, MN, USA, 2010.
28. American Association of Cereal Chemists. 38-12, Wet Gluten, Dry Gluten, Water-Binding Capacity, and Gluten Index. In *Approved Methods of Analysis*, 11th ed.; AACC International: St. Paul, MN, USA, 2010.
29. Nocente, F.; Taddei, F.; Galassi, E.; Gazza, L. Upcycling of brewers' spent grain by production of dry pasta with higher nutritional potential. *LWT* **2019**, *114*, 108421. [CrossRef]
30. International Association for Cereal Science and Technology. *ICC Standard Methods (Methods No. 105/2)*; ICC: Vienna, Austria, 1994.
31. Association of Official Analytical Chemists. *Official Methods of Analysis 2002.02, Resistant Starch in Starch and Plant Materials*; AOAC: Gaithersburg, MD, USA, 2002.
32. Association of Official Analytical Chemists. *Official Methods of Analysis 991.43*, 16th ed.; Cunniff, P., Ed.; AOAC: Gaithersburg, MD, USA, 1995.
33. American Association of Cereal Chemists. 08-01.01 Ash. In *Approved Methods of Analysis*, 11th ed.; AACC International: St. Paul, MN, USA, 2010.
34. American Association of Cereal Chemists. 32.32.01 Measurement of total fructans in foods by an enzymatic/spectrophotometric method. In *Approved Methods of Analysis*, 11th ed.; AACC International: St. Paul, MN, USA, 2010.
35. Martini, D.; Taddei, F.; Nicoletti, I.; Ciccoritti, R.; Corradini, D.; D'Egidio, M.G. Effects of genotype and environment on phenolic acids content and total antioxidant capacity in durum wheat. *Cereal Chem.* **2014**, *91*, 310–317. [CrossRef]
36. American Association of Cereal Chemists. 66-50.01 Pasta and noodle cooking quality-firmness. In *Approved Methods of Analysis*, 11th ed.; AACC International: St. Paul, MN, USA, 2010.
37. Nocente, F.; Natale, C.; Galassi, E.; Taddei, F.; Gazza, L. Using einkorn and tritordeum brewers' spent grain to increase the nutritional potential of durum wheat pasta. *Foods* **2021**, *10*, 502. [CrossRef]
38. D'Egidio, M.G.; Mariani, B.M.; Nardi, S.; Novaro, P.; Cubadda, R. Chemical and technological variables and their relationships: A predictive equation for pasta cooking quality. *Cereal Chem.* **1990**, *67*, 275–281.
39. Bencze, S.; Makádi, M.; Aranyos, T.J.; Földi, M.; Hertelendy, P.; Mikó, P.; Bosi, S.; Negri, L.; Drexler, D. Re-introduction of ancient wheat cultivars into organic agriculture—Emmer and einkorn cultivation experiences under marginal conditions. *Sustainability* **2020**, *12*, 1584. [CrossRef]
40. Rotondi Aufiero, V.; Di Stasio, L.; Maurano, F.; Accardo, F.; Ferranti, P.; Mamone, G.; Rossi, M.; Mazzarella, G. Beneficial effects of a *T. monococcum* wheat cultivar on diabetes incidence evaluated in non-obese diabetic mice and after in vitro simulated gastroduodenal digestion. *Int. J. Food Sci. Nutr.* **2022**, *73*, 327–335. [CrossRef]
41. Kolaric, L.; Minarovicova, L.; Laukova, M.; Karovicova, J.; Kohajdova, Z. Pasta noodles enriched with sweet potato starch: Impact on quality parameters and resistant starch content. *J Texture Stud.* **2020**, *51*, 464–474. [CrossRef]
42. Official Journal of the European Union. *REGULATION (EC) No 1924/2006 of the European Parliament and of the Council of 20 December 2006 on Nutrition and Health Claims Made on Foods*; Official Journal of the European Union: Brussels, Belgium, 2006.
43. Regulation (UE). N. 1047/2012 UE Commission. 8 November 2012. Available online: https://eur-lex.europa.eu/legal-content/IT/TXT/PDF/?uri=CELEX:32012R1047&from=BG (accessed on 28 June 2022).
44. Italian Presidential Decree n.187. Regulation for the Revision of the Legislation on the Production and Marketing of Flour and Pasta Dishes, Pursuant to Article 50 of the Law of February 22, 1994, n. 146. 9 February 2001. Available online: https://www.politicheagricole.it/flex/cm/pages/ServeAttachment.php/L/IT/D/e%252Fe%252F2%252FD.42f2f8869ef2c1b3a2e1/P/BLOB%3AID%3D2772/E/pdf?mode=download (accessed on 24 June 2022).
45. Hidalgo, A.; Brandolini, A.; Pompei, C.; Piscozzi, R. Carotenoids and tocols of einkorn wheat (*Triticum monococcum* ssp. *monococcum* L.). *J. Cereal Sci.* **2006**, *44*, 182–193. [CrossRef]
46. Tomomatsu, H. Health effects of oligosaccharides. *Food Tech.* **1994**, *48*, 61–65.
47. Paradiso, A.; Cecchini, C.; Greco, E.; D'Egidio, M.G.; De Gara, L. Variation in fructooligosaccharide contents during plant development and in different cultivars of durum wheat. *Plant. Biosyst.-Int. J. Deal All Asp. Plant. Biol.* **2008**, *142*, 656–660. [CrossRef]
48. Brandolini, A.; Hidalgo, A.; Plizzari, L.; Erba, D. Impact of genetic and environmental factors on einkorn wheat (*Triticum monococcum* L. subsp. *monococcum*) polysaccharides. *J. Cereal Sci.* **2011**, *53*, 65–72. [CrossRef]
49. Moshfegh, A.J.; Friday, J.E.; Goldman, J.P.; Chug Ahuja, J.K. Presence of inulin and oligofructose in the diets of the Americans. *J. Nutr.* **1999**, *129*, 1407–1411. [CrossRef]
50. Cubadda, R.; Carcea, M.; Pasqui, L.A. Suitability of the gluten index method for assessing gluten strength in durum wheat and semolina. *Cereal Foods World* **1992**, *37*, 866–869.
51. Sjoberg, S.M.; Carter, A.H.; Steber, C.M.; Garland-Campbell, K.A. Unraveling complex traits in wheat: Approaches for analyzing genotype × environment interactions in a multienvironment study of falling numbers. *Crop Sci.* **2020**, *60*, 3013–3026. [CrossRef]
52. Brandolini, A.; Hidalgo, A.; Plizzari, L. Storage-induced changes in einkorn (*Triticum monococcum* L.) and breadwheat (*Triticum aestivum* L. ssp. aestivum) flours. *J. Cereal Sci.* **2010**, *51*, 205–212. [CrossRef]

53. Brennan, M.A.; Merts, I.; Monro, J.; Woolnough, J.; Brennan, C.S. Impact of guar and wheat bran on the physical and nutritional quality of extruded breakfast cereals. *Starch* **2008**, *60*, 248–256. [CrossRef]
54. Aravind, N.; Sissons, M.; Egan, N.; Fellows, C.M. Effect of insoluble dietary fibre addition on technological, sensory, and structural properties of durum wheat spaghetti. *Food Chem.* **2012**, *130*, 299–309. [CrossRef]
55. D'Egidio, M.G.; De Stefanis, E.; Fortini, S.; Galterio, G.; Nardi, S.; Sgrulletta, D.; Bozzini, A. Standardization of cooking quality analysis in macaroni and pasta products. *Cereal Foods World* **1982**, *27*, 367–368.
56. Foschia, M.; Peressini, D.; Sensidoni, A.; Brennan, M.A.; Brennan, C.S. How combinations of dietary fibres can affect physicochemical characteristics of pasta. *LWT* **2015**, *61*, 41–46. [CrossRef]
57. Marti, A.; Seetharaman, K.; Pagani, M.A. Rice-based pasta: A comparison between conventional pasta-making and extrusion-cooking. *J. Cereal Sci.* **2010**, *52*, 404–409. [CrossRef]
58. Taddei, F.; Galassi, E.; Nocente, F.; Gazza, L. Innovative milling processes to improve the technological and nutritional quality of parboiled brown rice pasta from contrasting amylose content cultivars. *Foods* **2021**, *10*, 1316. [CrossRef] [PubMed]

foods

Article

Ancient Caucasian Wheats: A Contribution for Sustainable Diets and Food Diversity

Francesca Nocente, Elena Galassi, Federica Taddei, Chiara Natale and Laura Gazza *

CREA—Research Center for Engineering and Agro-Food Processing, Via Manziana 30, 00189 Rome, Italy; francesca.nocente@crea.gov.it (F.N.); elena.galassi@crea.gov.it (E.G.); federica.taddei@crea.gov.it (F.T.); chiara.natale@crea.gov.it (C.N.)
* Correspondence: laura.gazza@crea.gov.it

Abstract: Through the centuries, the domestication and modern breeding of wheat led to a significant loss of genetic variation in the cultivated gene pool with a consequent decrease in food diversity. Current trends towards low-input and sustainable agriculture call for the revitalization and exploitation of ancient wheats, which represent a reservoir of biodiversity useful to ensure sustainable wheat production in the context of climate change and low-input farming systems. Ancient Caucasian wheat species, such as the hulled wheats *Triticum timopheevii* (tetraploid A^uA^uGG) and *Triticum zhukovskyi* (hexaploid $A^uA^uA^mA^mGG$), are still grown to a limited extent in the Caucasus for the production of traditional foods. These Caucasian wheats were grown in Italy and were analyzed for physical, nutritional and technological characteristics and compared to durum wheat. Both Caucasian species revealed a high protein content (on average 18.5%) associated with a low gluten index, mainly in *T. zhukovskyi*, and test weight values comparable to commercial wheats. The total antioxidant capacity was revealed to be the double of that in durum wheat, suggesting the use of ancient Caucasian wheats for the production of healthy foods. Finally, the technological and rheological results indicated that Caucasian wheats could be potential raw material for the formulation of flat breads, biscuits and pasta.

Keywords: *Triticum timopheevii*; *Triticum zhukovskyi*; food diversity; minor cereals; sustainable diets; ancient wheat

Citation: Nocente, F.; Galassi, E.; Taddei, F.; Natale, C.; Gazza, L. Ancient Caucasian Wheats: A Contribution for Sustainable Diets and Food Diversity. *Foods* **2022**, *11*, 1209. https://doi.org/10.3390/foods11091209

Academic Editor: Cristina Martínez-Villaluenga

Received: 17 March 2022
Accepted: 19 April 2022
Published: 21 April 2022

1. Introduction

Through the centuries, domestication and modern breeding made only three cereal species, rice, corn and wheat, provide almost 60% of the energy intake of the planet's population [1]. The narrow focus of modern agriculture on intensive selection has led to a significantly reduced genetic diversity among wheat cultivars, since only few genotypes are cultivated on a large scale. The need for food diversification as well as the current demand for nutritionally healthy food products have driven a renewed interest in ancient wheats such as emmer, spelt and einkorn because of their desirable nutritional and putative health-beneficial traits [2,3]. Consequently, some neglected species and old varieties have been reintroduced in agriculture, having been recognized as interesting raw materials for the production of niche products. A superior quality, with reference to protein content, minerals and antioxidant compounds, along with minor adverse health effects in terms of allergy, intolerance and sensitivity, were observed in ancient wheats compared with the modern varieties [3–9]. Ancient Caucasian wheat species, such as the hulled wheats *Triticum timopheevii* (Zhuk.) Zhuk. subsp. *timopheevii* (tetraploid A^uA^uGG) and *Triticum zhukovskyi* Menabde et Erizian (hexaploid $A^uA^uA^mA^mGG$), investigated in the present study, have not been subjected to an extensive breeding activity, representing a reservoir of genes which could contribute to extending the biodiversity of cultivated wheats in order to better face climate fluctuations and biotic and abiotic stress. These two species were probably domesticated in Southern Turkey and Northern Syria and then transferred to Georgia, where they were cultivated as a mixture in a population called *Zanduri* which also comprises the diploid *Triticum monococcum* var. *hornemannii* (diploid A^mA^m) [10]. The genome analysis revealed that *T. zhukovskyi* originated from the hybridization of *T. timopheevii* with *T. monococcum* [11,12]. Wild *timopheevii* (Zhuk.) Zhuk. is also a primary genetic relative and gene donor to emmer wheat (*T. turgidum* subsp. *dicoccon* (Schrank) Thell.) and to common wheat (*T. aestivum* L.) [13,14]. It is worth noting that these ancient wheats are characterized by an immunity to the prevalent wheat diseases such as rusts, powdery mildew and *Fusarium* head blast, as well as a tolerance to salt and excessive humidity; additionally, they are well adapted to cool environments [13,15–18]. Their cultivation is currently limited to marginal areas for the production of traditional foods, particularly flat breads, and for feed, whereas straw is made into mats, carpets, baskets and is used for packing material [16].

To prevent the loss of Caucasian ancient wheat as an indispensable raw material for the preparation of typical foods and artifacts, a request for their inscription in the List of Intangible Cultural Heritage in Need of Urgent Safeguarding of UNESCO (United Nations Educational, Scientific, and Cultural Organization) was proposed in 2019 by the Minister of Environment, Protection and Agriculture of Georgia [19].

The reintroduction of the large-scale cultivation of undervalued cereal species, beyond showing acceptable agronomic performances, comes with the identification of feasible products (flours, breads, pasta, biscuits, beverages) appreciated by consumers and constituting a source of health-promoting bioactives.

Comparative studies on the grain quality of several ancient wheat species revealed a higher total phenolic and ferulic acids content in *T. thimopheevii* with respect to other ancient and common wheat varieties that were analyzed, along with a high antioxidant activity, balanced iron and zinc content and high protein content [16,20,21].

Considering the rising demand for ancient and undervalued crops in developed countries [22] and the paucity of scientific literature data about the nutritional and technological characteristics of these ancient species, the Caucasian wheats *T. thimopheevii* and *T. zhukovskyi*, grown in Italy, were analyzed in this work. The aim was to investigate both their capacity to be processed into foodstuff and their health-promoting potential, with a view to contributing to the sustainability, the resilience and the biodiversity of agrosystems and to fostering food diversification in the context of healthy and sustainable diets, pillars of the European '*Farm to Fork strategy*' action plan [23].

2. Materials and Methods

2.1. Plant Material

T. timopheevii (accession Lonigo, Figure 1A) and *T. zhukovskyi* (accession Far 75, Figure 1B) were grown in 2020 in Montelibretti, Rome (Italy), at the experimental fields of the Research Center for Engineering and Agro-Food Processing (CREA-IT). The reference material was the *T. durum* cv San Carlo, largely used in Italy for pasta production. Each accession was grown in 10 m^2 plots in randomized blocks with three replicates. The agronomic practices were those typical for durum wheat production in the selected area [24]. Immediately after harvest, the spikes from Caucasian wheats were threshed, and dehulled kernels were obtained by two subsequent steps using a bench micro-thresher (Marelli SpA, Milan, Italy); combined samples of grains from the three replicates were stored at 4 °C.

Figure 1. Ears, hulled and dehulled kernels of (**A**) *T. timopheevii* and (**B**) *T. zhukovskyi*.

2.2. Grain Physical Analyses

The methods ISO 520:2010 [25] and ISO 7971-1:2009 [26] were used to determine the thousand kernel weight (TKW) and test weight (TW), respectively. The hardness index (HI) of the kernel was performed on 300 kernel samples by the Perten SKCS 4100 (Perten, Springfield, IL, USA), following the manufacturer's operating procedure. The instrument was set at a range of hardness values between −40 and +120. The kernel length, width and thickness were recorded for 30 random kernels from each species using a calliper, and the average values were reported.

2.3. Chemical Characterization

All samples were milled to wholemeal flour using a laboratory mill (Cyclotec, FOSS, Hillerod, Denmark) at a 0.5 or 1.0 mm sieve, depending on the requirements of each analysis. All analyses were performed in triplicate. The sample moisture was measured using a thermobalance (Sartorius MA 40, Goettingen, Germany) at 120 °C just before the chemical analyses in order to express all data as dry weight (dw). Protein content was measured by micro-Kjeldhal nitrogen analysis according to the ICC 105/2 method [27], using as the conversion factor N × 5.7. The total and resistant starch (TS and RS) content was determined by enzymatic method using the Megazyme (Bray, Ireland) kits K-TSTA and K-RSTAR according to McCleary et al. [28] and McCleary et al. [29], respectively. The content of total dietary fiber (TDF) was measured using an enzymatic kit for fiber determination (Bioquant, Merck, Darmstadt, Germany) according to the AOAC Official Method 991.42 [30]. Protein, TS, RS and TDF content were expressed as percentage w/w. The total antioxidant capacity (TAC) was determined according to Ciccoritti et al. [31]. The total soluble phenolic content (TSPC) was determined using the Folin–Ciocalteau method as reported by Menga et al. [32], and the results were expressed as milligrams of ferulic acid equivalents per gram (mg FAE/g). Ash content was determined according to the approved method AACC 08-01.01 [33].

2.4. Rheological and Technological Tests

Semolina from durum and Caucasian wheats was obtained by Buhler MLU 202 mill (Utzwill, Switzerland). The total milling yield was considered as the percentage of the weight of semolina and flour fractions obtained from 100 g of kernels. The dry gluten content and gluten index were determined with the Glutomatic 2200 apparatus (Perten) according to the method ICC 158 [34]. Alveograph parameters (W, P and L) of semolina were obtained by Chopin Alveograph (Chopin, Villeneuve La Garenne, France) according to the manufacturer's instructions. The SDS sedimentation test was assessed according to the standard method AACC 56-70.01 [33]. The AACC 56-81B method [33] was used for the determination of the falling number (FN) using the Perten 1500 system. Semolina color was evaluated by a Tristimulus colorimeter (ChromaMeter CR-400, Minolta, Milan, Italy) equipped with a D65 illuminant, using the CIELab color space coordinate b* (yellowness), a* (redness) and L* (lightness); brownness was expressed as 100-L*.

2.5. Statistical Analysis

Replicated results were expressed as mean ± standard deviation. A one-way analysis of variance was performed with MSTATC program (Michigan State University, East Lansing, MI, USA), followed by the Duncan multiple range test for a post-hoc comparison of means, applied to assess significant differences ($p \leq 0.05$) for each considered parameter.

3. Results and Discussion

3.1. Physical Kernel Traits

Thousand kernel weight (TKW) and test weight (TW) are the main technological parameters indicating grain quality and play a large role in flour yield at milling [35]. The TKW values of de-hulled kernels were very similar in the Caucasian wheats, and they resulted in almost half of those of *T. durum* (Table 1). The TKW values were comparable to those obtained from the ancient wheats einkorn, spelt and emmer [36], but they were lower than those observed as the mean of more than 50 *T. timopheevii* accessions by Mikò et al. [37] and by Relina et al. [20], who found TKW values ranging from 33 to 39 g. These differences could be due to the agronomic practices, growing environment and genotypes used in the different studies. Similarly, no differences were observed between *T. timopheevii* and *T. zhukovskyi* for the TW values, which resulted in being statistically lower ($p \leq 0.05$) than those observed in durum wheat (Table 1).

Table 1. Physical kernel traits of the two ancient Caucasian wheats and *T. durum* cv San Carlo.

	Thousand Kernel Weight (g)	Test Weight (kg/hL)	Hardness Index	Kernel Dimensions		
				Length (mm)	Width (mm)	Thickness (mm)
T. timopheevii accession Lonigo	28.0 ± 0.4 ^{b}	72.2 ± 0.1 ^{b}	83 ± 15 ^{a}	8.7 ± 0.6 ^{b}	2.3 ± 0.1 ^{c}	2.4 ± 0.2 ^{b}
T. zhukovskyi accession Far 75	27.7 ± 0.4 ^{b}	72.0 ± 0.5 ^{b}	85 ± 17 ^{a}	8.9 ± 0.8 ^{a}	2.7 ± 0.2 ^{b}	2.5 ± 0.1 ^{b}
T. durum cv San Carlo	56.2 ± 0.3 ^{a}	84.3 ± 0.3 ^{a}	84 ± 12 ^{a}	8.1 ± 0.7 ^{c}	3.7 ± 0.4 ^{a}	3.5 ± 0.5 ^{a}

Results are expressed as mean ± standard deviation for three replications. Within the same column, values with different letters indicate significant differences determined by Duncan's test ($p \leq 0.05$).

The kernel dimensions of Caucasian *Triticum* were significantly lower than those of durum wheat (Table 1), suggesting that the small kernel size of Caucasian wheats affected the kernel weight more than the TW, as already observed by Wang and Fu [38]. However, the TW value of 72 kg/hL, found in the two ancient wheats, met the current TW requirement for the No. 4 wheat class (TW ≥ 71 kg/hL) of Canada Western Amber Durum (CWAD) [39], whereas durum wheat cv San Carlo fell into the No. 1 CWAD class (TW ≥ 80 kg/hL) [39]. The mean values of 72 kg/hL of TW have also been reported for the ancient hulled wheats einkorn, spelt and emmer [40].

Endosperm texture in wheat exerts a strong indirect impact on a bulk of technological and rheological quality traits including flour yield, dough rheological properties, bread volume and crumb structure [41]. Almost all tetraploid cereal species are characterized by an extra-hard kernel texture with an SKCS hardness index (HI) > 80 [42], mainly due to the lack of expression of puroindolines proteins. Both *T. timopheevii* and *T. zhukovskyi* revealed a very hard kernel texture (HI > 80, Table 1), comparable to that of durum wheat. These results agree with Relina et al. [20] who classified the *T. timopheevii* kernels as hard-textured.

It is worth noting that even if the physical traits of Caucasian kernels showed significantly lower values than durum wheat (Table 1), their milling yield was satisfactory (61% and 70%, in *T. timopheevii* and *T. zhukovskyi*, respectively) and comparable to that of durum cv San Carlo (69%).

3.2. Chemical and Nutritional Traits

Besides their nutritional properties, proteins are important for the processing capacity of cereals, especially for the texture of poor-gluten quality foods. The whole wheat flour of *T. timopheevii* showed a significantly higher protein content (20.1%) than both *T. zhukovskyi* (16.9%) and durum wheat (14.3%) (Table 2).

Table 2. Chemical and nutritional traits of the two ancient Caucasian wheats and *T. durum* cv San Carlo.

	Protein (%)	Total Starch (%)	TDF (%)	Ash (%)	TAC (mmol TEAC/kg)	TSPC (mg FAE/g)
T. timopheevii accession Lonigo	20.1 ± 0.8 [a]	62.2 ± 0.19 [b]	9.3 ± 0.2 [c]	2.13 ± 0.01 [a]	87.4 ± 0.5 [b]	0.94 ± 0.05 [b]
T. zhukovskyi accession Far 75	16.92 ± 0.03 [b]	62.0 ± 0.3 [b]	9.6 ± 0.2 [b]	1.96 ± 0.02 [b]	89.7 ± 0.3 [a]	0.997 ± 0.005 [b]
T. durum cv San Carlo	14.3 ± 0.5 [c]	65.0 ± 0.8 [a]	12.3 ± 0.3 [a]	1.65 ± 0.01 [c]	44.1 ± 0.3 [c]	1.19 ± 0.04 [a]

Results are reported as dry weight and expressed as mean ± standard deviation for three replications. Within the same column, values with different letters indicate significant differences determined by Duncan's test ($p \leq 0.05$). TDF = total dietary fiber; TAC = total antioxidant capacity; TEAC = trolox equivalent antioxidant capacity; TSPC = total soluble phenolic content; FAE = ferulic acid equivalents.

A higher protein content in hulled ancient wheats with respect to modern wheat varieties was also observed in previous works [43–45], suggesting that the hulled wheat species have a better potential than modern wheat varieties for using nitrogen [43] and could therefore be considered as suitable crops for low input agriculture. However, one should take into consideration that the high protein content in ancient wheats is also ascribable to their low agronomic yield. As a consequence of the higher protein content, Caucasian wheats presented a lower total starch content than *T. durum* [46]. In any case, the very high protein and total starch content of about 62% make these wheats a valuable alternative raw material for producing highly nutritious cereal foods. The quantification of RS, i.e., the fraction of the starch that cannot be digested by human gastrointestinal enzymes, revealed, in all species, a RS content lower than the limit of 2% required for an adequate accuracy of the method used [29]. However, the method allowed for the discernment of a statistically different RS content between durum wheat (0.26%) and Caucasian wheats (0.17%). Dietary fiber is the main bioactive component of wheat grain, due to its health benefits in colon cancer prevention, prebiotic activity and modulation of blood glucose and insulin levels [47]. Durum wheat cv San Carlo had a significantly higher level of TDF when compared to both Caucasian wheats (Table 2). Generally, flours made from smaller kernels have a higher percentage of fiber; however, a lower content of dietary fiber in ancient wheat species has been reported in several studies related to the comparison between ancient and modern wheats [2,22,48]. Both *T. timopheevii* and *T. zhukovskyi* resulted in higher levels of minerals, as suggested by the significantly higher ash content (Table 2). A mean value of the ash content of 2% was also reported in spelt, einkorn and emmer [40,49]. The higher ash values in Caucasian wheats resulted from a higher share of outer kernel layers compared to durum wheat due to the smaller size of the grains. An adequate intake of minerals is an important contribution to human health, even if a higher content of minerals does not mean an improved uptake and bio-accessibility and kernels may also contain toxic metals [45].

Currently, antioxidant activity is the most common in vitro parameter that is used to assess or predict the potential benefits of phytochemical compounds. The level of TAC was significantly higher in *T. zhukovskyi* (+103%) and *T. timopheevii* (+98%) than in durum wheat cv San Carlo (Table 2). A higher antioxidant activity in *T. timopheevii* compared to durum wheat was also observed by Relina et al. [20]. The highest TAC level in ancient Caucasian wheats could not be ascribed to the presence of a major phenolics content compared to *T. durum*, since their TSPC was statistically lower than in the modern wheat cultivar (Table 2). Data on the phenolics content of ancient wheats usually [50] showed that wild tetraploid wheat ancestors had the lowest phenolic content, and, even if contradictory data are present in the literature, wild wheats do not seem to possess valuable characteristics for the improvement of TPC in wheat [48]. Hence, the very high level of TAC found in ancient Caucasian grains cannot be explained by their level of TSPC but rather by the occurrence of other bioactive compounds, such as carotenoids. This hypothesis should be confirmed by further studies; in any case, as *T. zhukovskyi* possesses the einkorn A^m genome, it can be assumed that it shares a high lutein content, einkorn being indicated as the wheat with the highest level of lutein [48,51]. Moreover, the higher yellow index (b*) shown by Caucasian wheats' semolina, as reported in the following section, could reinforce this assumption.

3.3. Technological and Rheological Traits

Because of their poor-gluten quality, ancient wheats result in less structured doughs with a low elasticity and high extensibility [43]. The SDS-sedimentation test is one of the most useful single small-scale tests for screening for gluten strength and consequently for pasta-cooking and bread-making quality in durum wheat [52]. Significant differences ($p \leq 0.05$) in SDS values (Table 3) were observed between the two ancient Caucasian wheats; in particular, *T. zhukovskyi* was considered as 'poor gluten quality', having an SDS value <30 mL, whereas 'good gluten quality' could be ascribed to *T. timopheevii*, which presented an SDS value in the range of 30–40 mL [53].

Table 3. Technological and rheological traits and semolina color of the two ancient Caucasian wheats and *T. durum* cv San Carlo.

	SDS Sedimentation Volume (mL)	Gluten Index (%)	Dry Gluten Content (%)	Alveograph Parameters		Falling Number (s)	Color		
				W	P/L		Yellow Index (b*)	Brown Index (100-L*)	Red Index (a*)
T. timopheevii accession Lonigo	34.5 ± 0.7 ᵇ	34 ± 1 ᵇ	17.13 ± 0.07 ᵃ	29 ± 15 ᵇ	1.2 ± 0.7 ᵃᵇ	467 ± 1 ᵇ	29.2 ± 0.2 ᵃ	15.4 ± 0.2 ᵃ	−2.69 ± 0.09 ᵃ
T. zhukovskyi accession Far 75	22.5 ± 0.7 ᶜ	1.3 ± 0.6 ᶜ	15.3 ± 0.2 ᵇ	9 ± 8 ᵇ	0.8 ± 0.1 ᵇ	476 ± 8 ᵃ	27.7 ± 0.2 ᵇ	15.6 ± 0.2 ᵃ	−2.23 ± 0.09 ᵇ
T. durum cv San Carlo	37.5 ± 0.7 ᵃ	93 ± 1 ᵃ	10.5 ± 0.1 ᶜ	227 ± 21 ᵃ	1.8 ± 0.1 ᵃ	483 ± 2 ᵃ	22.1 ± 0.2 ᶜ	14.9 ± 0.5 ᵇ	−2.3 ± 0.2 ᵇ

Results are expressed as mean ± standard deviation for three replications. Within the same column, values with different letters indicate significant differences determined by Duncan's test ($p \leq 0.05$).

These results were in agreement with the gluten index values found in *T. zhukovskyi* and in *T. timopheevii* (Table 3). Indeed, according to the standard quality classes UNI 10709 [54] and UNI 10940 [55], *T. zhukovskyi* fell into the worst quality class, showing values slightly >1, whereas *T. timopheevii* showed a gluten index about three-fold lower than that recorded in durum wheat, falling into the quality class III. Despite the low gluten index, both Caucasian semolina showed a gluten content that was significantly higher than durum wheat (Table 3), due to the higher protein content (Table 2). It is worth noting that in *T. timopheevii* and *T. zhukovskyi*, the gluten content accounted for 85% and 90% of the total protein content, respectively, whereas in durum wheat cv San Carlo, it accounted for 73%.

Alveograph P and W values are indicators of dough elasticity and strength, respectively, and the L value is the indicator of dough extensibility. As expected, the poor quality of glutenin Caucasian wheat affected the rheological quality of semolina, as demonstrated by the W and P/L alveograph values (Table 3). The highest W value was observed in *T. durum* cv San Carlo, which met the requirements for the UNI 10709 [54] and UNI 10940 [55] standard quality class II, followed by *T. timopheevii* and *T. zhukovskyi*, which presented non-classifiable values (W < 100). The P/L ratio is a measurement of the balance between the elasticity and extensibility of dough and, with some exceptions, is higher than 1.0 in durum wheat [56], reflecting the tenacious and inextensible dough properties of this wheat species well. *T. timopheevii* showed a P/L value >1, similar to durum wheat cv San Carlo, whereas in *T. zhukovskyi* the low alveograph P value resulted in a significantly lower P/L ratio when compared to *T. timopheevii* and durum wheat. These results suggested that flours deriving from Caucasian wheats could be more suitable for being processed into pasta, flat breads and unleavened products than into traditional bread and baked products that require long leavening and processing.

The falling number (FN) is used to assess the baking quality of wheat flour in relation to the amylolytic enzymes activity, with which it is negatively correlated. FN values higher than 400 s were observed in the three analyzed species (Table 3), indicating a scarce amylolytic activity and, consequently, a poor bread-making performance in terms of crumb texture and low loaf volume. These data reinforced the idea, supported by alveograph tests, that Caucasian flours are optimal for being processed into pasta or flat breads, as already reported for einkorn, emmer and spelt wheat [57].

Kernel and milling products' color is an important factor in anticipating the end-product color quality; it is used in the durum grain trade, and the higher the b* value, the more intense the yellow coloring of the sample. Elevated values of the b* parameter (Table 3) were found in Caucasian wheats' semolina, mainly in *T. timopheevii*, which presented a higher b* value (+32%) than that of durum wheat semolina. On the contrary, the brown (100-L*) and red (a*) indexes, even if statistically different, were very similar in the three wheat species (Table 3).

4. Conclusions

The exploitation of ancient wheat species, besides playing a key role in plant breeding as a reservoir of useful genes, could contribute to providing new raw materials for the production of health-promoting foods, while increasing the agro-food biodiversity. The assessment of grain physical parameters, products' feasibility, flours' technological and rheological quality, and the presence of some health-promoting molecules revealed the ancient Caucasian wheats to be a valuable option for the entire supply chain, from farm to fork, meeting the main requirements that are used to evaluate the suitability of wheat for food production. Indeed, *T. timopheevii* and *T. zhukovskyi*, despite having a seed weight that was about half that of durum wheat, showed an excellent milling yield and an acceptable test weight, which suggests a promising use for processing. The technological and rheological parameters identified the Caucasian wheats as a potential raw material for the formulation of flat breads or biscuits, while the very high protein content could result in a good pasta-making capacity. Finally, the very high TAC level recorded in these wheats could satisfy the increasing demand for healthier and high-quality foods, encouraging the introduction of novel raw materials and products into diets, in developed countries as well. Future work will be necessary to evaluate the GxE effect on agronomical, nutritional and technological parameters and to investigate the most suitable technological processes and food.

Author Contributions: Conceptualization, F.N. and L.G.; methodology, F.N., F.T., E.G. and L.G.; validation, F.N., F.T. and E.G.; formal analysis, E.G.; investigation, C.N., F.T., F.N. and E.G.; resources, L.G.; data curation, F.N., F.T., E.G. and L.G.; writing—original draft preparation, F.N. and L.G.; writing—review and editing, F.N., F.T., E.G., C.N. and L.G.; visualization, C.N.; supervision, L.G.; project administration, L.G.; funding acquisition, F.N. and L.G. All authors have read and agreed to the published version of the manuscript.

Funding: This research was supported by Progetto RGV-FAO (MIPAAF, Italy D.M. 20380/2017).

Data Availability Statement: The data presented in this study are available in this article.

Acknowledgments: The authors would like to thank Ester Gosparini and Loriana Sereni of CREA-IT of Rome for their technical assistance.

Conflicts of Interest: The authors declare no conflict of interest. The funders had no role in the design of the study; in the collection, analyses, or interpretation of data; in the writing of the manuscript, or in the decision to publish the results.

References

1. Food and Agriculture Organization of the United Nation (FAO). Available online: https://www.fao.org/3/u8480e/u8480e07.htm (accessed on 2 February 2022).
2. Arzani, A.; Ashraf, M. Cultivated Ancient Wheats (*Triticum* spp.): A Potential Source of Health-Beneficial Food Products. *Compr. Rev. Food Sci. Food Saf.* **2017**, *16*, 477–488. [CrossRef] [PubMed]
3. Shewry, P.R. Do ancient types of wheat have health benefits compared with modern bread wheat? *J. Cereal Sci.* **2018**, *79*, 469–476. [CrossRef] [PubMed]
4. Dinu, M.; Whittaker, A.; Pagliai, G.; Benedettelli, S.; Sofi, F. Ancient wheat species and human health: Biochemical and clinical implications. *J. Nutr. Biochem.* **2017**, *52*, 1–9. [CrossRef] [PubMed]
5. Brandolini, A.; Hidalgo, A.; Moscaritolo, S. Chemical composition and pasting properties of einkorn (*Triticum monococcum* L. subsp. *monococcum*) whole meal flour. *J. Cereal Sci.* **2008**, *47*, 599–609. [CrossRef]
6. Shewry, P.R.; Hawkesford, M.J.; Piironen, V.; Lampi, A.M.; Gebruers, K.; Boros, D.; Andersson, A.A.M.; Aman, P.; Rakszegi, M.; Bedo, Z.; et al. Natural Variation in Grain Composition of Wheat and Related Cereals. *J. Agric. Food Chem.* **2013**, *61*, 8295–8303. [CrossRef] [PubMed]
7. Molberg, O.; Uhlen, A.K.; Jensen, T.; Flaete, N.S.; Fleckenstein, B.; Arentz-Hansen, H.; Raki, M.; Lundin, K.E.; Sollid, L.M. Mapping of gluten T-cell epitopes in the bread wheat ancestors: Implications for celiac disease. *Gastroenterology* **2005**, *128*, 393–401. [CrossRef]
8. Spaenij-Dekking, L.; Kooy-Winkelaar, Y.; van Veelen, P.; Drijfhout, J.W.; Jonker, H.; van Soest, L.; Smulders, M.J.; Bosch, D.; Gilissen, L.J.; Koning, F. Natural variation in toxicity of wheat: Potential for selection of nontoxic varieties for celiac disease patients. *Gastroenterology* **2005**, *129*, 797–806. [CrossRef]
9. Picascia, A.; Camarca, M.; Malamisura, R.; Mandile, M.; Galatola, M.; Cielo, D.; Gazza, L.; Mamone, G.; Auricchio, S.; Troncone, R.; et al. In celiac disease patients the in vivo challenge with the diploid *Triticum monococcum* elicits a reduced immune response compared to hexaploid wheat. *Mol. Nutr. Food Res.* **2020**, *64*, 1901032. [CrossRef]
10. Mori, N.; Kondo, Y.; Ishii, T.; Kawahara, T.; Valkoun, J.; Nakamura, C. Genetic diversity and origin of timopheevi wheat inferred by chloroplast DNA fingerprinting. *Breed. Sci.* **2009**, *59*, 571–578. [CrossRef]
11. Dvořák, J.; Terlizzi, P.D.; Zhang, H.B.; Resta, P. The evolution of polyploid wheats: Identification of the A genome donor species. *Genome* **1993**, *36*, 21–31. [CrossRef]
12. Matsuoka, Y. Evolution of Polyploid Triticum Wheats under Cultivation: The Role of Domestication, Natural Hybridization and Allopolyploid Speciation in their Diversification. *Plant Cell Physiol.* **2011**, *52*, 750–764. [CrossRef] [PubMed]
13. Zair, W.; Magos Brehm, J. Triticum timopheevii. In *The IUCN Red List of Threatened Species*; IUCN: Gland, Switzerland, 2017.
14. Vincent, H.; Wiersema, J.; Kell, S.; Fielder, H.; Dobbie, S.; Castaneda-Alvarez, N.P.; Guarino, L.; Eastwood, R.; León, B.; Maxted, N. A prioritized crop wild relative inventory to help underpin global food security. *Biol. Conserv.* **2013**, *167*, 265–275. [CrossRef]
15. Devi, U.; Grewal, S.; Yang, C.Y.; Hubbart-Edwards, S.; Scholefield, D.; Ashling, S.; Burridge, A.; King, I.P.; King, J. Development and characterisation of interspecific hybrid lines with genome-wide introgressions from *Triticum timopheevii* in a hexaploid wheat background. *BMC Plant Biol.* **2019**, *19*, 183. [CrossRef] [PubMed]
16. Jorjadze, M.; Berishvili, T.; Shatberashvili, E. The ancient wheats of Georgia and their traditional use in the southern part of the country. *Emir. J. Food Agric.* **2014**, *26*, 192–202. [CrossRef]
17. Brown-Guedira, G.L.; Gill, B.S.; Bockus, W.W.; Cox, T.S.; Hatchett, J.H.; Leath, S.; Peterson, C.J.; Thomas, J.B.; Zwer, P.K. Evaluation of a collection of wild Timopheevii wheat for resistance to disease and arthropod pests. *Plant Dis.* **1996**, *80*, 928–933. [CrossRef]
18. Järve, K.; Jakobson, I.; Enno, T. Tetraploid wheat species *Triticum timopheevii* and *Triticum militinae* in common wheat improvement. *Acta Agron. Hung.* **2002**, *50*, 463–477. [CrossRef]
19. Intagible Cultural Heritage UNESCO. Available online: https://ich.unesco.org/doc/src/47213-EN.doc (accessed on 15 February 2022).
20. Relina, L.I.; Boguslavskyi, R.L.; Vecherska, L.A.; Didenko, S.Y.; Golik, O.V.; Sheliakina, T.A.; Pozdniakov, V.V. Grain quality of tetraploid wheat *Triticum timopheevii* (zhuk.) zhuk. *Plant Breed. Seed Prod.* **2018**, *114*, 106–119. [CrossRef]
21. Engert, N.; Honermeier, B. Characterization of grain quality and phenolic acids in ancient wheat species (*Triticum* sp). *J. Appl. Bot. Food Qual.* **2012**, *84*, 33.
22. Zamaratskaia, G.; Gerhardt, K.; Wendin, K. Biochemical characteristics and potential applications of ancient cereals-An underexploited opportunity for sustainable production and consumption. *Trends Food Sci. Technol.* **2021**, *107*, 114–123. [CrossRef]
23. The EU Farm to Fork Strategy for a Fair, Healthy and Environmentally-Friendly Food System. Available online: https://ec.europa.eu/food/system/files/2020-05/f2f_action-plan_2020_strategy-info_en.pdf (accessed on 2 February 2022).
24. Quaranta, F.; Amoriello, T.; Aureli, G.; Belocchi, A.; D'Egidio, M.G.; Fornara, M.; Melloni, S.; Desiderio, E. Grain yield, quality and deoxynivalenol (DON) contamination of durum wheat (*Triticum durum* Desf.): Results of national networks in organic and conventional cropping systems. *Ital. J. Agric.* **2010**, *4*, 353–366. [CrossRef]
25. International Organization for Standardization (ISO 2010). *Cereals and Pulses-Determination of the Mass of 1000 Grains*; Method 520:2010; ISO: Geneva, Switzerland, 2010; p. 10.
26. International Organization for Standardization (ISO 2009). *Determination of Bulk Density, Called Mass per Hectolitre-Part 1: Reference Method*; Method 7971-1:2009; ISO: Geneva, Switzerland, 2009; p. 8.

27. International Association for Cereal Science and Technology. *ICC Standard Methods (Methods No. 105/2)*; ICC: Vienna, Austria, 2003.
28. McCleary, B.V.; Gibson, T.S.; Lugford, D.C. Measurement of total starch in cereal products by amyloglucosidase-α-amylase method: Collaborative study. *J. AOAC Int.* **1997**, *80*, 571–579. [CrossRef]
29. McCleary, B.V.; McNally, M.; Rossiter, P. Measurement of resistant starch by enzymatic digestion and selected plant materials: Collaborative study. *J. AOAC Int.* **2002**, *5*, 1103–1111. [CrossRef]
30. Association of Official Analytical Chemists. *Official Methods of Analysis 991*, 16th ed.; Cunniff, P., Ed.; AOAC: Gaithersburg, MD, USA, 1995; p. 42.
31. Ciccoritti, R.; Taddei, F.; Nicoletti, I.; Gazza, L.; Corradini, D.; D'Egidio, M.G.; Martini, D. Use of bran fractions and debranned kernels for the development of pasta with high nutritional and healthy potential. *Food Chem.* **2017**, *225*, 77–86. [CrossRef] [PubMed]
32. Menga, V.; Amato, M.; Phillips, T.D.; Angelino, D.; Morreale, F.; Fares, C. Gluten-free pasta incorporating chia (*Salvia hispanica* L.) as thickening agent: An approach to naturally improve the nutritional profile and the in vitro carbohydrate digestibility. *Food Chem.* **2017**, *221*, 1954–1961. [CrossRef] [PubMed]
33. American Association of Cereal Chemists. *Approved Methods of Analysis*, 11th ed.; AACC International: St. Paul, MN, USA, 2009.
34. International Association for Cereal Science and Technology. *ICC Standard Methods (Methods No. 158)*; ICC: Vienna, Austria, 1995.
35. Dexter, J.E.; Marchylo, B.A. Recent Trends in Durum Wheat Milling and Pasta Processing: Impact on Durum Wheat Quality Requirements. In Proceedings of the International Workshop on Durum Wheat, Semolina and Pasta Quality: Recent Achievements and New Trends, Montpellier, France, 27 November 2000; Abeccassis, J., Autran, J.C., Feillet, P., Eds.; Institut National de la Recherche: Montpellier, France, 2001; pp. 139–164.
36. Belcar, J.; Sobczyk, A.; Sobolewska, M.; Stankowski, S.; Gorzelany, J. Characteristics of Technological Properties of Grain and Flour from Ancient Varieties of Wheat (Einkorn, Emmer and Spelt). *Acta Univ. Cibiniensis Ser. E Food Technol.* **2020**, *24*, 269–278. [CrossRef]
37. Mikó, P.; Megyeri, M.; Molnár-Láng, M.; Kovács, G. Characterization of *Triticum timopheevii* Zhuk. gene bank accessions for the development of synthetic amphiploid wheat lines. *Acta Agron. Hung.* **2013**, *61*, 113–121. [CrossRef]
38. Wang, K.; Fu, B.X. Inter-relationships between test weight, thousand kernel weight, kernel size distribution and their effects on durum wheat milling, semolina composition and pasta processing quality. *Foods* **2020**, *9*, 1308. [CrossRef]
39. Canadian Grain Commission. Wheat: Export Grade Determinants Tables for Canada Western Amber Durum (CWAD) Wheat. 2020. Available online: https://www.grainscanada.gc.ca/en/grain-quality/official-graingrading-guide/04-wheat/export-grade-determinants/cwad-en.html (accessed on 12 February 2022).
40. Kulathunga, J.; Reuhs, B.L.; Zwinger, S.; Simsek, S. Comparative study on kernel quality and chemical composition of ancient and modern wheat species: Einkorn, emmer, spelt and hard red spring wheat. *Foods* **2021**, *10*, 761. [CrossRef]
41. Tsilo, T.J.; Hareland, G.A.; Chao, S.; Anderson, J.A. Genetic mapping and QTL analysis of flour color and milling yield related traits using recombinant inbred lines in hard red spring wheat. *Crop Sci.* **2011**, *51*, 237–246. [CrossRef]
42. Gazza, L.; Conti, S.; Taddei, F.; Pogna, N.E. Molecular characterization of puroindolines and their encoding genes in *Aegilops ventricosa*. *Mol. Breed.* **2006**, *17*, 191–200. [CrossRef]
43. Geisslitz, S.; Longin, C.F.H.; Scherf, K.A.; Koehler, P. Comparative study on gluten protein composition of ancient (einkorn, emmer and spelt) and modern wheat species (durum and common wheat). *Foods* **2019**, *8*, 409. [CrossRef] [PubMed]
44. De Santis, M.A.; Giuliani, M.M.; Giuzio, L.; De Vita, P.; Lovegrove, A.; Shewry, P.R.; Flagella, Z. Differences in gluten protein composition between old and modern durum wheat genotypes in relation to 20th century breeding in Italy. *Europ. J. Agric.* **2017**, *87*, 19–29. [CrossRef] [PubMed]
45. Rachon, L.; Bobryk-Mamczarz, A.; Kiełtyka-Dadasiewicz, A. Hulled Wheat Productivity and Quality in Modern Agriculture Against Conventional Wheat Species. *Agriculture* **2020**, *10*, 275. [CrossRef]
46. Hucl, P.; Chibbar, R.N. Variation for starch concentration in spring wheat and its repeatability relative to protein concentration. *Cereal Chem.* **1996**, *73*, 756–758.
47. Prasadi, V.P.N.; Joye, I.J. Dietary Fibre from Whole Grains and Their Benefits on Metabolic Health. *Nutrients* **2020**, *12*, 3045.
48. Shewry, P.R.; Hey, S. Do "ancient" wheat species differ from modern bread wheat in their contents of bioactive components? *J. Cereal Sci.* **2015**, *65*, 236–243. [CrossRef]
49. Serban, L.R.; Păucean, A.; Man, S.M.; Chis, M.S.; Mureşan, V. Ancient Wheat Species: Biochemical Profile and Impact on Sourdough Bread Characteristics—A Review. *Processes* **2021**, *9*, 2008. [CrossRef]
50. Laddomada, B.; Durante, M.; Mangini, G.; D'Amico, L.; Lenucci, M.S.; Simeone, R.; Piarulli, L.; Mita, G.; Blanco, A. Genetic variation for phenolic acids concentration and composition in a tetraploid wheat (*Triticum turgidum* L.) collection. *Genet. Resour. Crop Evol.* **2017**, *64*, 587–597. [CrossRef]
51. Hidalgo, A.; Brandolini, A.; Pompei, C.; Piscozzi, R. Carotenoids and tocols of einkorn wheat (*Triticum monococcum* ssp. *monococcum L.)*. *J. Cereal Sci.* **2006**, *44*, 182–193. [CrossRef]
52. Peña, R.J. Durum wheat for pasta and bread-making. Comparison of methods used in breeding to determine gluten quality-related parameters. In *Durum Wheat Improvement in the Mediterranean Region: New Challenges*; Serie A: Séminaires Méditerranéennes; CIHEAM: Zaragoza, Spain, 2000; pp. 423–430.

53. AbuHammad, W.A.; Elias, E.M.; Manthey, F.A.; Alamri, M.S.; Mergoum, M.A. Comparison of methods for assessing dough and gluten strength of durum wheat and their relationship to pasta cooking quality. *Int. J. Food Sci. Technol.* **2012**, *47*, 2561–2573. [CrossRef]
54. UNI Italian Organization for Standardization. *Durum Wheat Products for Pasta-Making—Definition, Characteristics and Quality Grades*; NumberUNI10709; UNI: Milano, Italy, 1998.
55. UNI Italian Organization for Standardization. *Durum Wheat Products for Pasta-Making—Definition, Characteristics and Quality Grades*; NumberUNI10940; UNI: Milano, Italy, 2001.
56. Quaglia, G.B. Other durum wheat products. In *Durum Wheat: Chemistry and Technology*; Fabriani, G., Lintas, C., Eds.; AACC: St Paul, MN, USA, 1988; pp. 263–274.
57. Bobryk-Mamczarz, A.; Kiełtyka-Dadasiewicz, A.; Rachoń, L. Usefulness of Hulled Wheats Grown in Polish Environment for Wholegrain Pasta-Making. *Foods* **2021**, *10*, 458. [CrossRef] [PubMed]

foods

MDPI

Article

Utilisation of Amaranth and Finger Millet as Ingredients in Wheat Dough and Bread for Increased Agro-Food Biodiversity

Calvin Onyango [1,*], Susan Karenya Luvitaa [1], Kibet Lagat [1], Alexandra Hüsken [2], Inga Smit [2] and Marcus Schmidt [2]

1 Food Technology Division, Kenya Industrial Research and Development Institute, Nairobi P.O. Box 30650-00100, Kenya; skalenya@gmail.com (S.K.L.); jlagat78@gmail.com (K.L.)
2 Department of Safety and Quality of Cereals, Max Rubner-Institut (MRI), Federal Research Institute of Nutrition and Food, Schuetzenberg 12, 32756 Detmold, Germany; alexandra.huesken@mri.bund.de (A.H.); inga.smit@mri.bund.de (I.S.); marcus.schmidt@mri.bund.de (M.S.)
* Correspondence: calonyango@yahoo.com

Abstract: Amaranth and finger millet are important food security crops in Africa but show poor bread making ability, even in composite wheat breads. Malting and steaming are promising approaches to improve composite bread quality, which have not been fully explored yet. Therefore, in this study, wheat was blended with native, steamed or malted finger millet or amaranth in the ratio of 70:30. Wheat/native amaranth (WHE-NAM) and wheat/malted amaranth (WHE-MAM) had longer dough development times and higher dough stabilities, water absorption capacities and farinograph quality numbers than wheat/steamed amaranth (WHE-SAM), wheat/native finger millet (WHE-NFM), wheat/steamed finger millet (WHE-SFM) or wheat/malted finger millet (WHE-MFM). The WHE-NAM and WHE-MAM breads had lower crumb firmness and chewiness, higher resilience and cohesiveness and lighter colours than WHE-NFM, WHE-SFM and WHE-MFM. Starch and protein digestibility of composite breads were not different ($p > 0.05$) from each other and ranged between 95–98% and 83–91%, respectively. Composite breads had higher ash (1.9–2.5 g/100 g), dietary fibre (5.7–7.1 g/100 g), phenolic acid (60–122 mg/100 g) and phytate contents (551–669 mg/100 g) than wheat bread (ash 1.6 g/100 g; dietary fibre 4.5 g/100 g; phenolic acids 59 mg/100 g; phytate 170 mg/100 g). The WHE-NAM and WHE-MAM breads possessed the best crumb texture and nutritional profile among the composite breads.

Keywords: amaranth; bread; dough; finger millet; wheat

Citation: Onyango, C.; Luvitaa, S.K.; Lagat, K.; Hüsken, A.; Smit, I.; Schmidt, M. Utilisation of Amaranth and Finger Millet as Ingredients in Wheat Dough and Bread for Increased Agro-Food Biodiversity. *Foods* **2022**, *11*, 911. https://doi.org/10.3390/foods11070911

Academic Editors: Laura Gazza and Francesca Nocente

Received: 27 February 2022
Accepted: 21 March 2022
Published: 22 March 2022

Publisher's Note: MDPI stays neutral with regard to jurisdictional claims in published maps and institutional affiliations.

1. Introduction

Finger millet (*Eleusine coracana*) and amaranth (*Amaranthus cruentus*) are important food security crops in sub-Saharan Africa because they are high-yielding crops, even under adverse agro-ecological environments. In addition, they are valuable sources of energy and proteins. However, they have limited utilization in industrial food product development. One technique to increase consumption of these crops is by incorporating them in ready-to-eat foods such as bread [1–3].

Partial substitution of wheat with non-wheat flours improves the nutritional quality of bread, promotes consumption of underutilized crops and increases sensory diversity of bread [1–3]. Unfortunately, composite bread has lower volume and harder crumb compared to wheat bread because the non-wheat flour dilutes gluten and the gluten matrix cannot develop properly due to interference by non-wheat flour constituents, such as dietary fibre [3–5]. These envelop the gluten proteins, limiting the formation of a network.

The major strategies used to manage the negative effects of non-wheat flours in composite dough and bread include using wheat flour with high protein content [5,6] and limiting the amount of non-wheat flour to about 30–40% *w*/*w* [2,7,8]. In addition, vital gluten, ascorbic acid, emulsifiers, enzymes and hydrocolloids [2,9,10] can be added to composite dough to compensate for gluten dilution and support development of the gluten matrix. Amaranth albumin proteins also improve rheological properties of dough by interacting with gluten proteins through disulphide bonds [11]. Bread with added amaranth albumin proteins has higher volume and better crumb texture compared to wheat bread [12].

The quality of composite bread can also be improved by modifying non-wheat flours prior to blending them with wheat. Guardianelli et al. [13] found that germinated amaranth improves elasticity and viscosity of composite dough, while Mlakar et al. [14] found that composite dough made from wheat and amaranth whole-grain flour had higher stability and strength compared to wheat dough. However, these two studies did not report on the impact of amaranth flours on the quality of composite bread. Tosi et al. [15] reported that low levels (4% flour-weight-basis) of defatted hyperproteic amaranth flour has no negative impact on specific volume of bread. Composite dough containing extruded finger millet is less firm and more extensible than dough containing unextruded finger millet [16]. The resulting bread has higher volume and better crumb texture than bread containing unextruded finger millet [16]. Other examples of modified cereals that have been used to improve volume and crumb texture of composite bread are germinated brown rice flour [17] and fermented sorghum [18]. There is still a lack of studies on the impact of finger millet on the quality of composite bread. It is a native African crop with remarkable resilience against heat and drought stress combined with high storage stability and good nutritional values. Thus, incorporation of finger millet into various food products should be studied more intensely. Onyango et al. [1] reported that composite bread containing hydrothermally treated finger millet had softer crumb and higher volume compared to composite bread containing native finger millet. The use of steaming or malting to improve the bread making abilities of amaranth and finger millet has not been studied yet. However, it was found that composite bread made with boiled malt flour has better crumb texture and lower degree of staling compared with composite bread made with native sorghum flour [19]. Based on these results, malting and steaming appear as promising tools to improve the quality of composite wheat bread. Hence, it was the aim of this study to close this knowledge gap by comparing the effect of steamed or malted finger millet and amaranth on the rheological properties of dough and physico-chemical quality of bread. These results are an important contribution towards an optimized utilisation of the nutritionally and economically valuable crops amaranth and finger millet.

2. Materials and Method

2.1. Modification of Finger Millet

Native finger millet (NFM) and amaranth (NAM) grains were purchased in Busia County, Kenya. Steamed finger millet (SFM) and amaranth (SAM) were prepared by washing the grains before steeping them in water (1:5 w/v) for 24 h at 24 ± 1 °C. After steeping, excess water was drained through a filter cloth before the grains were placed in a stainless-steel container, covered with an aluminium sheet and steamed in an autoclave (Biobase Co., Ltd., Shandong, China) at 100 °C for 20 min. Malted finger millet (MFM) and amaranth (MAM) were prepared using a modified method by Hugo et al. [19]. The grains were washed and steeped as described for SAM and SFM and excess water was removed. The grains were then spread on woven polypropylene cloth, which was spread on perforated aluminium tray for 48 h at 24 ± 1 °C. The tray was loosely covered with another woven polypropylene cloth. Twice daily, water was sprinkled on the grains before they were gently mixed. After malting, the grains were steamed, as described for SAM and SFM. The steamed and malted grains were dried to 12 ± 2% moisture content in an electric oven (Memmert GmbH + Co. KG., Schwabach, Germany) set at 60 °C over a period of 48 h. The grains were milled using a Bauermeister universal turbo laboratory (UTL) grinder fitted with 500 μm sieve (Bauermeister Maschinenfabrik GmbH, Hamburg-Altona, Germany).

2.2. Characterization of Flours

Protein (N × 5.75 for wheat; N × 6.25 for finger millet and amaranth, respectively), lipid and ash contents of flours were determined on dry-weight basis according to ICC standard methods No., 105/2, 136 and 104/1, respectively [20,21]. Total and digestible starch and phytate contents were measured using K-RAPRS and K-PHYT kits, respectively (Megazyme Int. Ireland Ltd., Wicklow, Ireland). Soluble, insoluble and total dietary fibre contents were measured using K-TDFR-100A kit from Megazyme Int. (Wicklow, Ireland).

Free soluble sugars were determined following the procedure described by Schmidt and Sciurba [22] with some modifications. In brief, 1.00 ± 0.01 g of sample was combined with 2.0 mL methanol and homogenized. After adding 20 mL of deionized water (80 °C), the suspension was homogenized by ultrasonication (BANDELIN Sonoplus, Berlin, Germany) for 2 × 15 s at room temperature. After centrifugation (5 min, 1700× *g*, 20 °C), the supernatant was transferred to a 100 mL volumetric flask and the hot water extraction was repeated twice. Proteins were removed from the combined supernatants by adding 500 µL of Carrez I (15% *w*/*v*) and Carrez II (32% *w*/*v*), respectively. After adjusting to volume, solids were removed by centrifugation (10 min, 3000× *g*, 20 °C) and the supernatant was filtered (0.45 µm) into a HPIC vial. For analysis of the sample extracts, high-performance anion exchange chromatography (HPAEC, Dionex ICS 5000+, Sunnyvale, CA, USA) with pulsed amperometric detection (PAD) was used. The system was equipped with a CarboPac PA 1 guard column and a CarboPac PA1 analytical column (4 × 250 mm), both operated at 25 °C. The mobile phase consisted of (A) 100 mM sodium hydroxide solution and (B) 600 mM sodium acetate in 100 mM sodium hydroxide. Eluents were degassed and stored under helium atmosphere. The following gradient program was applied for separation: 0–40 min 100% A, 40–55 min linear increase of B from 0 to 100%, 55–70 min 100% A. The injection volume was 25 µL, the flow rate was set to 1.0 mL/min for a total run time of 70 min. For calibration, analytical standards of raffinose, maltose, sucrose, glucose, fructose, sorbitol and mannitol were used in various dilutions, between 0.1 and 30 mg/100 mL. All calibrations were found to be linear in the respective calibration range ($R^2 > 0.99$). Limit of detection (LOD) and limit of quantification (LOQ) were set for a signal to noise ratio of 3 and 10, respectively.

Determination of the total arabinoxylan content was based on the method of Houben et al. [23]. The sample (0.05 ± 0.001 g) was suspended in 1 mL of deionized water and 2 mL of hydrochloric acid (4 M). The homogenized suspensions were incubated for 90 min at 100 °C and homogenized every 10 min. After cooling to room temperature, mixtures were neutralized with 2 mL sodium hydroxide (4 M). Subsequently, 1 mL of Tris buffer (0.2 M, pH = 7.6) and 1 mL of glucose oxidase-catalase solution from Megazyme Int. (Wicklow, Ireland) were added and homogenized. The suspension was incubated for 60 min at 30 °C, centrifuged (10 min, 3500 g, 20 °C) and the supernatant filtered (0.45 µm) into a HPIC vial. Analysis was carried out similarly to the free soluble sugars described above, with the following modifications. The mobile phase consisted of (A) 20 mM sodium hydroxide solution and (B) 600 mM sodium acetate in 100 mM sodium hydroxide. For analysis, the following gradient program was used: 0–30 min 100% A, 30–45 min linear increase of B from 0 to 100%, 45–60 min 100% A. Total run time was 60 min. For calibration, analytical standards of arabinose and xylose were used in various dilutions, between 0.1 and 30 mg/100 mL.

Characterization of process-induced changes in arabinoxylan molar mass was carried out using gel permeation chromatography (GPC). For extraction, 200 mg of ground sample was suspended in 10 mL of sodium nitrate solution (0.1 M), containing 0.02% sodium azide, and incubated for 2.5 h at 90 °C. Subsequently, the mixtures were cooled to 50 °C and after addition of 200 µL lichenase solution (10 U) incubated for 1 h at 50 °C. After addition of 10 µL α-amylase solution (5 mg/mL in 3.6 mM $CaCl_2$) and incubation at 37 °C for 1 h, 50 µL of Carrez I (15% *w*/*v*) and Carrez II (32% *w*/*v*) were added, the mixture was centrifuged and the supernatant filtered (0.45 µm) into a GPC vial. Measurement was carried out using the GPCmax gel permeation chromatography system (Malvern Panalytical, UK).

For separation, a A6000M (300 × 8 mm), Aq GPC/SEC double column, equipped with an AGuard pre-column (50 × 6 mm) was used. The measurement was done isocratic using 0.1 M sodium nitrate solution, containing 0.02% sodium azide, at a flow rate of 1.0 mL/min. The column temperature was held at 30 °C, the run time was 35 min and the injection volume was 100 μL. Discrete pullulan molar mass standards were used for conventional calibration, to determine arabinoxylan molar mass. In vitro protein digestibility (IVPD) and free phenolic compounds were determined as previously reported by Onyango et al. [1].

2.3. Properties of Flours and Doughs

Composite flour was prepared from baker's wheat (WHE) flour (Unga Ltd., Nairobi, Kenya) and native, steamed or malted finger millet (WHE-NFM, WHE-SFM, WHE-MFM) or amaranth (WHE-NAM, WHE-SAM, WHE-MAM) at a ratio of 70:30. The α-amylase activity was measured using K-CERA kit from Megazyme Int. (Wicklow, Ireland). Dough properties were evaluated using a Farinograph-AT and an Extensograph-E (Brabender GmbH & Co. KG., Duisburg, Germany) according to ICC standard methods No. 115/1 and ICC No. 114/1, respectively [20,21].

2.4. Bread Making and Evaluation of Physical and Textural Properties of Breads

Breads were made by the straight dough method, as previously described by Onyango et al. [1] from WHE (control) or composite flours (wheat: non-wheat flour 70:30). The remaining baking ingredients were: sugar (2% flour-weight-basis, fwb, Kibos Sugar & Allied Industries, Kisumu, Kenya), active dry yeast (1% fwb, Angel Yeast Co., Ltd., Beni Suef, Egypt), baker's fat (1% fwb, Bidco Africa Ltd., Nairobi, Kenya) and salt (1% fwb, Kensalt Ltd., Nairobi, Kenya). The farinograph water absorption capacities of the flours were adjusted to reach consistencies of 500 farinograph units (FU). Farinograph water absorption capacity of WHE, WHE-NFM, WHE-SFM and WHE-MFM was 59, 57, 60 and 60%, respectively. Farinograph water absorption capacity of WHE-NAM, WHE-SAM and WHE-MAM was 61, 63 and 62%, respectively. The ingredients were combined and mixed at low speed using a spiral dough hook for 1 min and further kneaded for 5 min at medium speed in a SP22HI planetary mixer (SPAR Food Machinery Mfg. Co. Ltd., Taichung Hsien, Taiwan). After resting for 15 min the dough was divided into 400 g pieces before it was manually rounded and rested for another 15 min. The dough was molded manually, loaded into baking tins (dimensions: L × W × H: 205 × 105 × 70 mm) and proofed for 60 min at 35 °C and 80% relative humidity in a proofing cabinet (National Mfg. Co., Lincoln, NE, USA). After proofing, the tins were placed in a rotary oven (National Mfg. Co., Lincoln, NE, USA) set at 200 °C and baked for 35 min. After de-panning, the loaves were kept in paper bags stored in an incubator at 25 °C for 22 h before further analysis. Bread weight, volume and specific volume were determined as described by Onyango et al. [1]. Briefly, bread was weighed on a Shimadzu analytical balance (Shimadzu Corporation, Kyoto, Japan). Bread volume was determined by displacement of finger millet in a 10 L stainless-steel container. Specific volume was calculated by dividing bread volume with weight. Change in crumb lightness ($\Delta L^* = L^*_{\text{wheat bread}} - L^*_{\text{composite bread}}$), was measured using a Chroma Meter CR-10 (Konica Minolta, Sakai, Japan), in order to determine the impact of the pre-treatments (malting and steaming) of finger millet or amaranth on crumb appearance. Texture Profile Analysis of bread crumb was measured as previously reported by Onyango et al. [1]. Briefly described, 20 mm thick slices of bread were compressed using a 75 mm diameter aluminium cylinder probe (P/75) which was attached to a TA-XT plus Texture Analyser (Stable Micro Systems, Surrey, UK). The operating variables of the probe were calibration height (40 mm), pre-test speed (1 mms^{-1}), test-speed (5 mms^{-1}), post-test speed (5 mms^{-1}), penetration distance (10 mm), trigger force (0.05 N).

2.5. Nutrient Qualities of Breads

Bread was dried at 40 °C and milled using a Bauermeister universal turbo laboratory (UTL) grinder fitted with 500 μm sieve (Bauermeister Maschinenfabrik GmbH, Hamburg-

Altona, Germany). Total starch, digestible starch, protein, IVPD, lipid, dietary fibre, ash, phytate, arabinoxylan, free soluble sugars and total phenol contents were determined as described in Section 2.2.

2.6. Experimental Design and Statistical Data Analysis

All experimental analyses were done in duplicate or triplicate and the results were reported as mean ± standard deviation. The effect of flour type on the properties of flour, dough and bread was evaluated in a single factor experimental design. The data obtained were subjected to one-way analysis of variance. Tukey's Test at a confidence level of 95% was used to evaluate differences in treatment means. The data were analyzed using Minitab 17 statistics software (Minitab Inc., State College, PA, USA).

3. Results and Discussion

3.1. Characterization of Flours

The distribution of free sugars and sugar alcohols in native and modified flours is shown in Table 1. Disaccharides were the major sugars in wheat and native finger millet, whereas disaccharides and trisaccharides were the major sugars in native amaranth. These results agree with those of Dharmaraj and Malleshi [24] who found that glucose, fructose, sucrose and maltose are the main sugars in finger millet; and Becker et al. [25] who reported that sucrose and raffinose are the major sugars in amaranth. The content of free sugars (i.e., monosaccharides, disaccharides and trisaccharides) decreased from 851 to 750 mg/100 g and from 1609 to 1326 mg/100 g in finger millet and amaranth, respectively, after steaming. The loss of free sugars in steamed finger millet is due to leaching during steeping and Maillard reactions during steaming [24]. The content of free sugars increased from 851 to 1311 mg/100 g and from 1609 to 2013 mg/100 g in finger millet and amaranth, respectively, after malting. These changes were attributed to enzymatic hydrolysis of starch into sugars during germination. Starch content declined by 4 and 16% for finger millet and amaranth, respectively, whereas monosaccharide content of the grains increased almost 20 times after malting. The levels of sugar alcohols in all the grains were ≤63 mg/100 g and decreased for finger millet but increased for amaranth after the grains were steamed or malted.

Amaranth is a dicotyledonous plant that is commonly referred to as a pseudocereal because its chemical composition and techno-functionality resemble those of true cereals. However, the starch content of amaranth seeds is lower than that of true cereals, such as wheat and finger millet (Table 1). Amaranth had higher ($p < 0.05$) digestible starch content than wheat or finger millet. Starch granule size is an important factor in determining the rate of starch digestion and, usually, smaller granules are digested faster than larger granules. In this case, the smaller amaranth starch granules (1–2 μm) have higher surface area to volume ratio for enzymatic hydrolysis than the larger finger millet (4–12 μm) and wheat starch (15–35 μm) granules [26].

Finger millet and amaranth had 3 to 5 times more insoluble dietary fibre but 1 to 2 times less soluble dietary fibre than wheat (Table 1). Overall, finger millet and amaranth had 2 to 5 times more total dietary fibre than wheat. The low insoluble dietary fibre content in refined wheat can be attributed to separation of the starchy endosperm from the bran during milling. By contrast, finger millet and amaranth had high insoluble dietary fibre contents, since bran was not separated from the endosperm during milling. Arabinoxylan content declined when finger millet was steamed but increased when it was malted or when amaranth was steamed or malted. The increase in arabinoxylan content in malted grains may be because steeping and germination softened the cell wall tissues resulting in improved extractability [27]. Despite the changes in arabinoxylan contents of the grains after steaming or malting, there was no corresponding change in their average molecular weights (Table 1).

Table 1. Nutrient composition (based on dry weight) and quality of wheat, finger millet and amaranth flour.

Nutrient	Wheat	Finger Millet			Amaranth		
		Native	Steamed	Malted	Native	Steamed	Malted
Monosaccharides (mg/100 g) *	53 ± 1 [g]	77 ± 0 [e]	219 ± 1 [d]	1257 ± 0 [a]	65 ± 0 [f]	282 ± 1 [c]	1030 ± 0 [b]
Disaccharides (mg/100 g) **	710 ± 0 [c]	692 ± 1 [d]	460 ± 0 [f]	54 ± 0 [g]	784 ± 0 [b]	593 ± 1 [e]	817 ± 0 [a]
Trisaccharides (mg/100 g) ***	104 ± 1 [d]	82 ± 1 [e]	71 ± 1 [f]	nd	760 ± 0 [a]	451 ± 0 [b]	226 ± 0 [c]
Sugar alcohols (mg/100 g) ****	12 ± 0 [f]	30 ± 0 [b]	15 ± 0 [d]	7 ± 0 [g]	14 ± 0 [e]	18 ± 0 [c]	63 ± 1 [a]
Total starch (g/100 g)	73 ± 0 [bc]	82 ± 0 [a]	83 ± 1 [a]	79 ± 1 [ab]	69 ± 1 [c]	61 ± 5 [d]	58 ± 0 [d]
Digestible starch (% of total starch)	88 ± 2 [b]	84 ± 1 [b]	86 ± 3 [b]	88 ± 1 [b]	97 ± 1 [a]	97 ± 0 [a]	98 ± 2 [a]
Insoluble dietary fibre (g/100 g)	2.3 ± 0.2 [d]	12 ± 0 [a]	12 ± 0 [ab]	11 ± 0 [ab]	7.6 ± 0.2 [c]	8.5 ± 0.9 [c]	10 ± 2 [b]
Soluble dietary fibre (g/100 g)	1.3 ± 0.3 [a]	0.6 ± 0.2 [b]	0.6 ± 0.5 [b]	0.8 ± 0.3 [b]	0.7 ± 0.3 [b]	1.0 ± 0.1 [ab]	1.0 ± 0.0 [ab]
Total dietary fibre (g/100 g)	3.6 ± 0.3 [c]	13 ± 0 [a]	12 ± 1 [a]	12 ± 0 [a]	8.3 ± 0.4 [b]	9.5 ± 0.9 [b]	11 ± 2 [a]
Arabinoxylan (mg/100 g)	1312 ± 0 [d]	1555 ± 2 [b]	1455 ± 1 [c]	2017 ± 3 [a]	1061 ± 2 [g]	1184 ± 0 [f]	1228 ± 1 [e]
Arabinoxylan molecular weight (kDa)	195 ± 25 [a]	177 ± 16 [a]	189 ± 17 [a]	166 ± 8 [a]	99 ± 4 [b]	139 ± 15 [ab]	93 ± 10 [b]
Total protein (g/100 g)	15 ± 1 [a]	11 ± 0 [bc]	9 ± 0 [c]	9 ± 1 [c]	14 ± 2 [ab]	16 ± 1 [a]	18 ± 2 [a]
In vitro protein digestibility (% of total protein)	80 ± 4 [b]	88 ± 2 [ab]	79 ± 2 [b]	80 ± 1 [b]	87 ± 4 [ab]	92 ± 0 [a]	93 ± 1 [a]
Lipid (g/100 g)	1.8 ± 0.1 [c]	1.3 ± 0.0 [d]	1.6 ± 0.1 [cd]	1.4 ± 0.3 [cd]	8.0 ± 0.1 [ab]	7.6 ± 0.3 [b]	8.3 ± 0.1 [a]
Ash (g/100 g)	0.8 ± 0.0 [c]	3.9 ± 0.0 [a]	3.4 ± 0.5 [ab]	3.1 ± 0.0 [b]	2.9 ± 0.1 [b]	2.8 ± 0.0 [b]	3.2 ± 0.0 [b]
Phytate (mg/100 g)	621 ± 69 [c]	1260 ± 133 [c]	1087 ± 37 [c]	1144 ± 311 [c]	1366 ± 310 [bc]	2062 ± 107 [ab]	2209 ± 176 [a]
Total phenolic content (mg GAE/100 g)	103 ± 5 [c]	162 ± 2 [a]	162 ± 2 [a]	142 ± 6 [b]	39 ± 0 [f]	68 ± 4 [e]	85 ± 0 [d]

* Glucose and fructose; ** sucrose and maltose; *** raffinose; **** sorbitol and mannitol. nd: not detected. Values presented as mean ± standard deviation; $n = 3$. Values in the same row with different superscript letters are significantly different at $p < 0.05$.

The net change in protein content of grains after malting is influenced by the balance between leached water-soluble peptides versus starch breakdown via respiration. Thus, protein content of malted finger millet may have declined because the loss of water-soluble peptides exceeded the degree of starch degradation. In contrast, protein content in malted amaranth increased because starch breakdown exceeded the leaching of water-soluble peptides. Although the contents of water-soluble peptides were not determined, changes in starch contents due to germination vary substantially and are likely to have an impact on the protein contents of the grains. Amaranth lost a greater amount of starch (16%) after germination than finger millet (4%). The IVPD of finger millet and amaranth were between 87 and 88% and did not change ($p > 0.05$) after malting or steaming. These results differ from published literature, which indicate that IVPD of finger millet and amaranth increase after malting or steaming [24,28,29]. The native materials had inherently high IVPD contents, which did not further increase after malting or steaming. Other authors have reported lower IVPD values in native finger millet and amaranth and substantial increases after steaming or germination. Dharmaraj and Malleshi [24] reported that IVPD in finger millet increased from 79 to 91% after steaming, whereas Hejazi and Orsat [29] found that it increased from 74 to 92% after germination. Olawoye and Gbadamosi [28] found that IVPD increased from 36% in native amaranth to 58 and 65% after steaming and germination, respectively.

The lipid, ash, phytate and phenolic acid contents of the grains reflected their different botanical origins and effect of processing (Table 1). Amaranth had higher ($p < 0.05$) lipid content than wheat or finger millet. Finger millet and amaranth had higher ($p < 0.05$) ash and phytate contents than refined wheat. Phytate content of finger millet did not change ($p > 0.05$) whereas that of amaranth increased after steaming or malting. Generally, phytate content decreases after germination [29] due to synthesis or activation of endogenous phytases, which hydrolyse myo-inositol 1,2,3,4,5,6-hexakisphosphate (IP6) into lower inositol phosphates such as IP5, IP4, IP3, IP2, IP1 and myo-inositol. However, phytate content may also increase after malting [30] if the lower forms of phytic acid are co-eluted as total phytic acid during extraction [31]. Phenolic acid contents of native flours followed the order:

amaranth < wheat < finger millet. In finger millet, the phenolic acid content did not change ($p > 0.05$) after steaming but increased ($p < 0.05$) after malting. Malted or steamed amaranth contained higher ($p > 0.05$) phenolic acid content than in the native grain. Phenolic acid content increases in grains after malting due to the action of esterases on phenolic acid esters linked to arabinoxylans and other non-starch polysaccharides [27].

3.2. Properties of Flours and Doughs

The α-amylase activities of the flours and dough properties derived from the farinograms are shown in Table 2. There were no significant differences ($p > 0.05$) in the α-amylase activities of the flours. Especially noteworthy were the low α-amylase activities of flours containing malted finger millet or amaranth. Although germination induces de novo synthesis of α-amylase in grains, the diastatic activity can be regulated or inactivated by heat treatment [19].

Table 2. Enzyme activity of flours and farinogram properties of doughs.

Flour	α-Amylase Activity (CU/g)	WAC (%)	DDT (min)	Stability (min)	DS (FU)	FQN (mm)
WHE	0.6 ± 0.1	59 ± 0.2 ^{e}	1.9 ± 0.2 ^{b}	3.6 ± 0.3 ^{c}	76 ± 4 ^{d}	40 ± 3 ^{d}
WHE-NFM	0.6 ± 0.0	58 ± 0.1 ^{e}	1.8 ± 0.4 ^{b}	5.5 ± 0.1 ^{a}	122 ± 2 ^{c}	55 ± 1 ^{c}
WHE-SFM	0.4 ± 0.2	60 ± 0.0 ^{d}	1.5 ± 0.1 ^{b}	5.2 ± 0.3 ^{ab}	113 ± 7 ^{c}	56 ± 1 ^{c}
WHE-MFM	0.7 ± 0.0	61 ± 0.2 ^{bc}	1.4 ± 0.3 ^{b}	2.5 ± 0.0 ^{d}	168 ± 11 ^{b}	32 ± 1 ^{e}
WHE-NAM	0.5 ± 0.1	61 ± 0.1 ^{c}	3.8 ± 0.4 ^{a}	5.0 ± 0.7 ^{ab}	114 ± 6 ^{c}	70 ± 1 ^{a}
WHE-SAM	0.4 ± 0.0	63 ± 0.3 ^{a}	3.8 ± 0.3 ^{a}	4.1 ± 0.1 ^{bc}	132 ± 8 ^{c}	66 ± 4 ^{ab}
WHE-MAM	0.6 ± 0.2	62 ± 0.1 ^{b}	4.2 ± 0.1 ^{a}	4.2 ± 0.1 ^{bc}	193 ± 1 ^{a}	61 ± 1 ^{bc}

CU/g: ceralpha units/g; WHE: wheat; NFM: native finger millet; SFM: steamed finger millet; MFM: malted finger millet; NAM: native amaranth; SAM: steamed amaranth; MAM: malted amaranth; WAC: water absorption capacity; DDT: dough development time; DS: degree of softening; FQN: farinograph quality number; FU: farinograph units. Values presented as mean ± standard deviation; $n = 3$. Values in the same column followed by the same lower-case letter are not significantly different from each other ($p < 0.05$). Values in the same column not followed by lower-case letter are not significantly different from each other ($p < 0.05$).

The water absorption capacity of wheat is determined by its protein, arabinoxylan and damaged starch contents, hardness and particle size index [32]. This value is enhanced further in composite flours with high protein or dietary fibre contents [5,15], as was noted for amaranth and finger millet. Dietary fibre has huge impact on water absorption capacity of flour because the numerous hydroxyl groups in the molecular structure of non-starch polysaccharides allow for multiple water interactions through hydrogen bonds [6,33]. In addition, the high water absorption capacity of WHE-NAM, WHE-SAM and WHE-MAM doughs could be attributed to the high water binding capacity of amaranth starch granules and albumins [12,15].

The WHE-NAM, WHE-SAM and WHE-MAM had higher dough development times than wheat or WHE-NFM, WHE-SFM and WHE-MFM doughs. Composite doughs, except WHE-MFM, had higher dough stabilities than wheat. However, prolonged mixing of doughs showed that composite doughs had higher ($p < 0.05$) degrees of softening compared to wheat (Table 2). The quantity and quality of gluten proteins determine the mixing behaviour of hydrated wheat and the rheological character of optimally mixed dough. When wheat flour is hydrated and kneaded, discrete masses of gluten protein are transformed into a continuous cohesive viscoelastic network. During kneading, dough resistance increases to an optimal state before it begins to decrease. The changes in resistance to mixing are recorded in the farinograph as dough development time, dough stability and degree of softening. The gluten protein network, formed during kneading, is responsible for retaining carbon dioxide produced during fermentation and in the initial stages of baking, thus determining bread volume and crumb structure [34]. While in wheat doughs gluten is the determining factor for dough development and stability, in composite doughs, dietary fibre [5,6,33] and proteins [11,12] of the non-wheat constituents also play an important role. Dietary fibre increases dough development time, because non-starch polysaccharides require more time to absorb water before dough reaches optimal consistency [5]. With respect to amaranth, the albumin proteins also form intermolecular disulphide bonds with wheat glutenins and produce dough with rheological character similar to glutenin polymers in wheat [11,12]. Despite the positive effects of finger millet and amaranth on the development and stability of composite doughs, prolonged mixing of these doughs eventually destroyed and weakened their gluten networks and increased their degrees of softening. The farinograph quality number was positively correlated with dough development time and stability. The WHE-NAM, WHE-SAM and WHE-MAM doughs had high farinograph quality numbers, which agreed with their long dough development times and high dough stabilities. In contrast, WHE-MFM dough had the lowest farinograph quality number, which was consistent with its short dough development time and low dough stability.

Composite doughs had lower ($p < 0.05$) energies, extensibilities and resistances to extension than wheat dough at all incubation times (Table 3). These findings are similar to those of Koletta et al. [5] and Mlakar et al. [15] and show that composite doughs were more rigid and required less work to stretch compared to wheat. The viscoelastic character of wheat is influenced by the two gluten fractions: gliadin and glutenin. Glutenin polymers form viscoelastic networks that provide strength (resistance to extension) and elasticity to dough, whereas gliadin acts as plasticizer within the glutenin polymer [34]. The low dough strengths of composite doughs can be explained by the high content of dietary fibre in non-wheat flours, which hindered formation of gluten viscoelastic networks. The ratio of maximum resistance to extension/extensibility (MR/E) increased when incubation time was extended from 45 to 90 min (Table 3). However, when incubation time was further extended to 135 min, MR/E of WHE-NFM, WHE-SFM and WHE-MFM decreased by between 21 and 30%. In contrast, MR/E of wheat and WHE-NAM decreased by smaller margins of about 10%. The MR/E of WHE-SAM did not change whereas that of WHE-MAM increased by 17% when incubation time was prolonged to 135 min. The positive effect of amaranth on MR/E in composite doughs was attributed to the interaction of amaranth albumins with glutenin polymers [11,12]. Dough with high MR/E value has high strength relative to extensibility and, up to a certain limit, is expected to give bread with a high volume.

Table 3. Extensogram properties of dough.

Dough	45 min				90 min				135 min			
	Energy (cm^2)	E (mm)	MR (EU)	MR/E	Energy (cm^2)	E (mm)	MR (EU)	MR/E	Energy (cm^2)	E (mm)	MR (EU)	MR/E
WHE	127 ± 11 a	167 ± 10 a	626 ± 62 a	3.9 ± 0.5 a	102 ± 6 a	139 ± 3 a	661 ± 33 a	4.8 ± 0.2 b	70 ± 8 a	122 ± 10 a	523 ± 22 a	4.3 ± 0.3 ab
WHE-NFM	54 ± 6 b	93 ± 1 b	446 ± 43 b	4.8 ± 0.4 a	38 ± 1 b	74 ± 3 c	432 ± 18 b	5.9 ± 0.1 a	16 ± 2 b	68 ± 7 b	189 ± 14 d	2.8 ± 0.1 cd
WHE-SFM	45 ± 0 bc	85 ± 0 b	405 ± 8 b	4.8 ± 0.1 a	35 ± 1 bc	70 ± 1 c	432 ± 17 b	6.2 ± 0.3 a	25 ± 3 b	66 ± 5 b	321 ± 16 b	4.9 ± 0.1 a
WHE-MFM	44 ± 3 bc	88 ± 2 b	383 ± 36 b	4.4 ± 0.6 a	29 ± 6 bc	72 ± 4 c	330 ± 46 cd	4.6 ± 0.4 b	17 ± 5 b	63 ± 7 b	204 ± 52 cd	3.2 ± 0.4 c
WHE-NAM	43 ± 3 bc	89 ± 4 b	379 ± 12 b	4.3 ± 0.0 a	39 ± 1 b	79 ± 5 bc	410 ± 18 bc	5.3 ± 0.5 ab	32 ± 3 b	76 ± 1 b	352 ± 33 b	4.7 ± 0.5 a
WHE-SAM	27 ± 3 c	99 ± 8 b	198 ± 4 c	2.0 ± 0.1 b	22 ± 0 c	89 ± 1 b	183 ± 3 e	2.1 ± 0.1 c	20 ± 1 b	84 ± 2 b	178 ± 4 d	2.1 ± 0.0 d
WHE-MAM	28 ± 1 c	104 ± 0 b	199 ± 9 c	1.9 ± 0.1 b	29 ± 2 bc	88 ± 2 b	252 ± 7 de	2.9 ± 0.0 c	31 ± 2 b	84 ± 3 b	285 ± 6 bc	3.4 ± 0.0 bc

WHE: wheat; NFM: native finger millet; SFM: steamed finger millet; MFM: malted finger millet; NAM: native amaranth; SAM: steamed amaranth; MAM: malted amaranth; E: extensibility; MR: maximum resistance to extension; EU: extensograph units. Values presented as mean ± standard deviation; $n = 3$. Values in the same column followed by the same lower-case letter are not significantly different from each other ($p < 0.05$).

3.3. Physical and Textural Properties of Breads

Substantial differences regarding bread volume and colour, as well as the crumb structure, were visible depending on the type of composite flour used (Figure 1). The weights of breads ranged between 335–344 g and the volumes ranged between 1110–1448 cm^3 (Table 4). The specific volumes of composite breads were lower by between 9–28% compared to wheat bread. Specific volume is an important quality parameter of bread because it is largely associated with the appearance of bread. The distinctive high volume of bread is attributed to gluten, which influences the gas retention properties of fermenting dough [34]. Substitution of wheat with gluten-free flour reduces bread volume due to the combined effects of gluten dilution and disruption of gluten matrix by non-starch polysaccharides [5,6].

Partial dehydration of gluten due to competition with fibre for hydration is responsible for the structural changes of gluten matrix and collapse of the gluten polymeric network [4]. In addition, dietary fibre disrupts formation and physical properties of gluten network through interactions of its reactive components (especially ferulic acid monomers) with gluten proteins [35]. The high water-holding capacity of dietary fibre also reduces the amount of steam generated, which results in decreased loaf volume.

Figure 1. Cut-through sections of breads produced using 100% wheat flour, 70% wheat + 30% native finger millet flour and 70% wheat + 30% amaranth flour.

The WHE-NAM and WHE-MAM breads had higher ($p < 0.05$) specific volumes and lower ($p < 0.05$) crumb firmness than the other composite breads (Table 4). Crumb firmness is inversely related to specific volume and breads with low specific volumes tend to have high crumb firmness because of their compact and closed crumb structure [5,8]. Crumb firmness in composite bread is influenced by the botanical origin of non-wheat flour and degree of wheat substitution [5,7,8]. Dietary fibre is the main cause of high crumb firmness in composite breads, since it strengthens the walls which surround air bubbles in the crumb [6,33]. The low crumb firmness of WHE-NAM and WHE-MAM breads could be attributed to formation of stable disulphide linkages between amaranth albumins and wheat glutenin polymers [11]. Silva-Sánchez et al. [12] found that albumin isolates (1–3% w/w) in a bread recipe improves its volume and crumb texture. However, the low specific volume and high crumb firmness of WHE-SAM bread indicate absence of albumin–gluten interactions in its dough probably because albumins lost their functionality through denaturation during steaming. Steaming decreases, whereas germination increases, the content of albumins in amaranth [36]. Although drying (90 °C) germinated amaranth decreases the amount of water-soluble proteins, the net amount is still higher than in native or steamed amaranth [36] and contributes to low crumb firmness.

The impact of gluten dilution and interference during gluten network formation in composite formulas was evident in the poorer crumb structure of composite breads compared to wheat bread. Composite breads had lower ($p < 0.05$) crumb cohesiveness, resilience and springiness than wheat bread (Table 4). Crumb chewiness (product of crumb firmness, cohesiveness and springiness), which indicates the energy required to chew bread into a state suitable for swallowing, closely imitated crumb firmness rather than cohesiveness or springiness of the breads. Crumb chewiness of WHE-NAM and WHE-MAM breads were not significantly different ($p > 0.05$) to WHE bread. In addition, WHE-NAM and WHE-MAM breads were more cohesive and resilient than WHE-SAM or WHE-NFM, WHE-SFM and WHE-MFM breads. The better crumb texture of WHE-NAM and WHE-MAM breads compared to the other composite breads was attributed to the presence of functionally active albumins in amaranth, as explained before.

Table 4. Physical and textural properties of bread.

Bread	Weight (g)	Volume (cm^3)	Specific Volume (cm^3/g)	Firmness (N)	Cohesiveness **	Resilience **	Springiness (%)	Chewiness (N)	ΔL*
WHE	341 ± 2 ^{ab}	1448 ± 58 ^{a}	4.3 ± 0.2 ^{a}	3.0 ± 0.5 ^{d}	0.74 ± 0.02 ^{a}	0.31 ± 0.02 ^{a}	91 ± 1 ^{a}	2.0 ± 0.3 ^{e}	-
WHE-NFM	335 ± 2 ^{c}	1135 ± 30 ^{d}	3.4 ± 0.1 ^{cd}	7.2 ± 1.0 ^{bc}	0.56 ± 0.02 ^{d}	0.22 ± 0.01 ^{de}	88 ± 1 ^{b}	3.5 ± 0.5 ^{bc}	−20 ± 1 ^{c}
WHE-SFM	340 ± 1 ^{ab}	1135 ± 70 ^{d}	3.3 ± 0.1 ^{cd}	8.8 ± 0.8 ^{b}	0.57 ± 0.04 ^{d}	0.23 ± 0.02 ^{cde}	86 ± 1 ^{bc}	4.3 ± 0.6 ^{b}	−19 ± 1 ^{c}
WHE-MFM	344 ± 1 ^{a}	1070 ± 26 ^{d}	3.1 ± 0.1 ^{d}	6.6 ± 0.5 ^{c}	0.55 ± 0.01 ^{d}	0.22 ± 0.01 ^{e}	86 ± 2 ^{bc}	3.1 ± 0.3 ^{cd}	−21 ± 1 ^{c}
WHE-NAM	339 ± 2 ^{b}	1240 ± 28 ^{c}	3.7 ± 0.1 ^{bc}	4.2 ± 0.4 ^{d}	0.67 ± 0.01 ^{bc}	0.27 ± 0.01 ^{b}	86 ± 1 ^{bc}	2.4 ± 0.2 ^{de}	−8 ± 3 ^{a}
WHE-SAM	344 ± 2 ^{a}	1110 ± 42 ^{d}	3.2 ± 0.2 ^{d}	10.7 ± 1.4 ^{a}	0.63 ± 0.03 ^{c}	0.25 ± 0.01 ^{bcd}	86 ± 1 ^{bc}	5.8 ± 0.6 ^{a}	−10 ± 4 ^{ab}
WHE-MAM	344 ± 2 ^{a}	1350 ± 26 ^{b}	3.9 ± 0.1 ^{b}	2.7 ± 0.2 ^{d}	0.68 ± 0.02 ^{b}	0.26 ± 0.01 ^{bc}	85 ± 1 ^{c}	1.6 ± 0.1 ^{e}	−13 ± 2 ^{b}

WHE: wheat; NFM: native finger millet; SFM: steamed finger millet; MFM: malted finger millet; NAM: native amaranth; SAM: steamed amaranth; MAM: malted amaranth. $\Delta L^* = L^*_{wheat\ bread} - L^*_{composite\ bread}$. ** Dimensionless terms. Values presented as mean ± standard deviation; $n = 3$. Values in the same column followed by the same lower-case letter are not significantly different from each other ($p < 0.05$).

The change in crumb lightness (ΔL*) of composite breads was closely related to the colours of native finger millet and amaranth flours. The lightness index (L*) of wheat flour was 81 ± 3. Finger millet has darker (*t*-test, $p < 0.001$) seed coat pigmentation (L* = 64 ± 3) than amaranth (L* = 73 ± 2). Consequently, WHE-NFM, WHE-SFM and WHE-MFM breads were darker ($p < 0.05$) compared to WHE-NAM, WHE-SAM and WHE-MAM breads (Table 4). Crumb lightness of WHE-MFM or WHE-SFM breads was not significantly different ($p > 0.05$) to WHE-NFM bread. In contrast, WHE-SAM and WHE-MAM breads had darker crumbs than WHE-NAM bread. The darker crumbs of WHE-SAM and WHE-MAM breads may be associated with Maillard and caramelization reactions in the crumb arising from the high contents of free sugars in steamed or malted amaranth. Due to the potential adverse health effects of Maillard reaction products, such as acrylamide [37], the development of WHE-SAM and WHE-MAM breads must be further optimized.

3.4. Nutrient Qualities of Bread

The WHE-NAM, WHE-SAM and WHE-MAM breads contained higher ($p < 0.05$) monosaccharide but lower ($p < 0.05$) disaccharide contents than wheat or WHE-NFM, WHE-SFM and WHE-MFM breads (Table 5). Trisaccharides were not present whereas the contents of sugar alcohols were less than 25 mg/100 g in all breads. The total sugar contents of the breads were cumulative values of the sugars naturally present in the flours (Table 1), sugar used in the breadmaking recipe and sugars derived from diastatic activity on damaged starch. The total content of free sugars (i.e., monosaccharides and disaccharides) increased from 2924 mg/100 g in WHE-NFM to 3160 mg/100 g in WHE-SFM bread. By contrast, it decreased from 3862 mg/100 g in WHE-NAM to 3762 mg/100 g in WHE-SAM bread. The total content of free sugars was higher in WHE-MFM (3666 mg/100 g) and WHE-MAM (4799 mg/100 g) than in WHE-NFM (2924 mg/100 g) and WHE-NAM (3862 mg/100 g), respectively.

There were no significant differences ($p > 0.05$) in the starch and protein contents and digestibilities of the different breads (Table 5). The WHE-NAM, WHE-SAM and WHE-MAM breads had higher ($p < 0.05$) lipid contents than wheat or WHE-NFM, WHE-SFM and WHE-MFM breads due to the higher lipid content of amaranth (Table 1). Composite breads had higher ($p < 0.05$) ash, phytate and phenolic acid contents than wheat bread due to the inherently higher amounts of these compounds in whole-milled finger millet and amaranth (Table 1). Composite breads had higher arabinoxylan and insoluble and total dietary fibre contents but lower soluble dietary fibre contents than wheat bread, which originated from the different dietary fibre composition of amaranth and finger millet compared to wheat. Since regular consumption of dietary fibre, in particular arabinoxylans, is recommended for a healthy diet [38,39], the composite breads had a higher nutritional value than the wheat breads. The WHE-NAM, WHE-SAM and WHE-MAM breads had lower arabinoxylan molecular weights than wheat or WHE-NFM, WHE-SFM and WHE-MFM. Higher molar mass arabinoxylans are generally associated with better nutraceutical properties, due to increased viscosity in the intestine [39], indicating lower nutritional value for amaranth composite breads.

Table 5. Nutrient composition (based on dry weight) and quality of bread.

Nutrient	WHE	WHE-NFM	WHE-SFM	WHE-MFM	WHE-NAM	WHE-SAM	WHE-MAM
Monosaccharides (mg/100 g) *	1047 ± 1^{g}	1347 ± 0^{f}	1532 ± 1^{e}	1715 ± 2^{d}	3275 ± 1^{b}	3253 ± 2^{c}	4085 ± 1^{a}
Disaccharides (mg/100 g) **	2877 ± 2^{a}	1577 ± 0^{d}	1628 ± 1^{c}	1951 ± 1^{b}	587 ± 0^{f}	509 ± 0^{g}	714 ± 1^{e}
Sugar alcohols (mg/100 g) ***	23 ± 0^{b}	25 ± 0^{a}	19 ± 0^{c}	15 ± 0^{e}	11 ± 0^{g}	13 ± 0^{f}	17 ± 0^{d}
Total starch (g/100 g)	78 ± 1	77 ± 1	78 ± 3	78 ± 0	76 ± 0	76 ± 0	76 ± 0
Digestible starch (% of total starch)	96 ± 4	96 ± 3	95 ± 2	95 ± 2	98 ± 2	98 ± 1	98 ± 1
Insoluble dietary fibre (g/100 g)	2.7 ± 0.4^{c}	5.4 ± 0.2^{a}	5.5 ± 0.1^{a}	5.5 ± 0.2^{a}	4.4 ± 0.4^{b}	4.1 ± 0.3^{b}	4.5 ± 0.3^{b}
Soluble dietary fibre (g/100 g)	1.8 ± 0.2^{a}	1.7 ± 0.3^{ab}	1.3 ± 0.1^{b}	1.4 ± 0.2^{b}	1.5 ± 0.2^{ab}	1.6 ± 0.1^{ab}	1.5 ± 0.2^{ab}
Total dietary fibre (g/100 g)	4.5 ± 0.4^{c}	7.1 ± 0.3^{a}	6.8 ± 0.2^{a}	6.9 ± 0.2^{a}	6.0 ± 0.5^{b}	5.7 ± 0.2^{b}	6.0 ± 0.1^{b}
Arabinoxylan (mg/100 g)	1363 ± 0^{g}	1375 ± 0^{f}	1413 ± 1^{d}	1480 ± 1^{b}	1497 ± 0^{a}	1410 ± 0^{e}	1441 ± 1^{c}
Arabinoxylan molecular weight (kDa)	153 ± 5^{a}	120 ± 16^{bc}	134 ± 10^{ab}	119 ± 6^{bc}	91 ± 7^{cd}	90 ± 0^{cd}	85 ± 6^{d}
Total protein (g/100 g)	14 ± 1	12 ± 0	12 ± 0	15 ± 2	15 ± 1	14 ± 2	15 ± 1
In vitro protein digestibility (% of total protein)	91 ± 3	89 ± 1	83 ± 5	87 ± 1	89 ± 2	84 ± 1	86 ± 2
Lipid (g/100 g)	2.1 ± 0.5^{ab}	1.4 ± 0.3^{b}	1.2 ± 0.2^{b}	1.4 ± 0.2^{b}	2.7 ± 0.3^{a}	2.9 ± 0.0^{a}	2.9 ± 0.2^{a}
Ash (g/100 g)	1.6 ± 0.2^{c}	2.5 ± 0.1^{a}	2.4 ± 0.0^{a}	2.2 ± 0.0^{ab}	2.2 ± 0.0^{ab}	2.2 ± 0.0^{ab}	1.9 ± 0.1^{bc}
Phytate (mg/100 g)	170 ± 36^{b}	609 ± 141^{a}	551 ± 7^{a}	598 ± 8^{a}	668 ± 15^{a}	698 ± 16^{a}	669 ± 44^{a}
Total phenolic content (mg GAE/100 g)	59 ± 3^{d}	88 ± 7^{bc}	84 ± 9^{bc}	94 ± 11^{b}	60 ± 3^{d}	74 ± 9^{cd}	122 ± 10^{a}

* Glucose and fructose; ** sucrose and maltose; *** sorbitol and mannitol. WHE: wheat; NFM: native finger millet; SFM: steamed finger millet; MFM: malted finger millet; NAM: native amaranth; SAM: steamed amaranth; MAM: malted amaranth; GAE: gallic acid equivalent. Values presented as mean ± standard deviation; $n = 3$. Values in the same row followed by the same lower-case letter are not significantly different from each other ($p < 0.05$). Values in the same row not followed by a lower-case letter are not significantly different from each other ($p < 0.05$).

4. Conclusions

The impact of native, steamed or malted finger millet and amaranth on dough and bread quality was investigated. While the properties of wheat dough are primarily determined by gluten, in the composite doughs, dietary fibre and protein from finger millet and amaranth were found to have an effect as well. In general, doughs containing finger millet had poorer rheological qualities than doughs containing amaranth. Amongst composite doughs, WHE-NAM and WHE-MAM had the best rheological properties, which translated to breads with high volume and good crumb texture. The suitability of amaranth for making composite bread was attributed to its albumin fraction that forms stable disulphide linkages to wheat glutenin, whereas the poor baking quality of finger millet was attributed to its dietary fibre fraction by hindering the formation of gluten viscoelastic networks. The addition of finger millet or amaranth did not change the starch and protein contents or digestibilities of bread. However, they improved the dietary fibre, ash and phenolic acid contents of bread. This study shows that the type of grain and its modification influences the quality of composite dough and bread. Based on the results, the use of native or malted amaranth appears as a promising approach for the production of high quality breads with the added benefit of significantly higher dietary fibre content than the reference wheat bread. There is a need for further optimization to increase the amount of amaranth that can be added to composite bread without quality deterioration. This could make an increase in bread protein content possible. Furthermore, future studies should determine the acrylamide content when using malted amaranth, to ensure consumer safety. With respect to finger millet, steaming and malting were not suitable to improve its breadmaking potential. Hence, other techniques of flour modification should be explored in future studies to enlarge the range of applications for this crop.

Author Contributions: Conceptualization, C.O. and M.S.; methodology, C.O., S.K.L., K.L., A.H., I.S. and M.S.; formal analysis, C.O. and M.S.; investigation, C.O., S.K.L., K.L., A.H., I.S. and M.S.; resources, C.O., A.H., I.S. and M.S.; data curation, C.O., S.K.L., K.L., A.H., I.S. and M.S.; writing—original draft preparation, C.O.; writing—review and editing, C.O., S.K.L., K.L., A.H., I.S. and M.S.; visualization, C.O., A.H., I.S. and M.S.; supervision, C.O., A.H., I.S. and M.S.; project administration,

C.O. and M.S.; funding acquisition, C.O. and M.S. All authors have read and agreed to the published version of the manuscript.

Funding: This research was funded by the Alexander von Humboldt Foundation (Bonn, Germany) through a Research Group Linkage Fellowship to Calvin Onyango and Marcus Schmidt, grant number 3.4-1128929-KEN-IP. The APC was covered by the Max Rubner-Institut.

Institutional Review Board Statement: Not applicable.

Informed Consent Statement: Not applicable.

Data Availability Statement: Data is contained within the article.

Acknowledgments: The authors would like to thank Lidia Arent, Annika Lange, Regine Hilleckes and Doris Kagerer for their analytical support.

Conflicts of Interest: The authors declare no conflict of interest.

References

1. Onyango, C.; Luvitaa, S.K.; Unbehend, G.; Haase, N. Physico-chemical properties of flour, dough and bread from wheat and hydrothermally-treated finger millet. *J. Cereal Sci.* **2020**, *93*, 102954. [CrossRef]
2. Angioloni, A.; Collar, C. Suitability of Oat, Millet and Sorghum in Breadmaking. *Food Bioprocess Technol.* **2013**, *6*, 1486–1493. [CrossRef]
3. Angioloni, A.; Collar, C. Effects of pressure treatment of hydrated oat, finger millet and sorghum flours on the quality and nutritional properties of composite wheat breads. *J. Cereal Sci.* **2012**, *56*, 713–719. [CrossRef]
4. Zhou, Y.; Dhital, S.; Zhao, C.; Ye, F.; Chen, J.; Zhao, G. Dietary fiber-gluten protein interaction in wheat flour dough: Analysis, consequences and proposed mechanisms. *Food Hydrocoll.* **2020**, *111*, 106203. [CrossRef]
5. Koletta, P.; Irakli, M.; Papageorgiou, M.; Skendi, A. Physicochemical and technological properties of highly enriched wheat breads with wholegrain non wheat flours. *J. Cereal Sci.* **2014**, *60*, 561–568. [CrossRef]
6. Skendi, A.; Biliaderis, C.; Papageorgiou, M.; Izydorczyk, M.S. Effects of two barley β-glucan isolates on wheat flour dough and bread properties. *Food Chem.* **2010**, *119*, 1159–1167. [CrossRef]
7. Bhol, S.; Bosco, S.J.D. Influence of malted finger millet and red kidney bean flour on quality characteristics of developed bread. *LWT Food Sci. Technol.* **2014**, *55*, 294–300. [CrossRef]
8. Sanz-Penella, J.; Wronkowska, M.; Soral-Smietana, M.; Haros, M. Effect of whole amaranth flour on bread properties and nutritive value. *LWT Food Sci. Technol.* **2013**, *50*, 679–685. [CrossRef]
9. Ferrero, C. Hydrocolloids in wheat breadmaking: A concise review. *Food Hydrocoll.* **2017**, *68*, 15–22. [CrossRef]
10. Schoenlechner, R.; Szatmari, M.; Bagdi, A.; Tömösközi, S. Optimisation of bread quality produced from wheat and proso millet (*Panicum miliaceum* L.) by adding emulsifiers, transglutaminase and xylanase. *LWT Food Sci. Technol.* **2013**, *51*, 361–366. [CrossRef]
11. Oszvald, M.; Tamás, C.; Rakszegi, M.; Tömösközi, S.; Békés, F.; Tamás, L. Effects of incorporated amaranth albumins on the functional properties of wheat dough. *J. Sci. Food Agric.* **2009**, *89*, 882–889. [CrossRef]
12. Silva-Sánchez, C.; González-Castañeda, J.; Rodriguez, A.D.L.; De La Rosa, A.B. Functional and Rheological Properties of Amaranth Albumins Extracted From Two Mexican Varieties. *Plant Foods Hum. Nutr.* **2004**, *59*, 169–174. [CrossRef]
13. Guardianelli, L.M.; Salinas, M.V.; Puppo, M.C. Hydration and rheological properties of amaranth-wheat flour dough: Influence of germination of amaranth seeds. *Food Hydrocoll.* **2019**, *97*, 105242. [CrossRef]
14. Mlakar, S.G.; Bavec, M.; Turinek, M.; Bavec, F. Rheological properties of dough made from grain amaranth-cereal composite flours based on wheat and spelt. *Czech J. Food Sci.* **2009**, *27*, 309–319. [CrossRef]
15. Tosi, E.A.; Ré, E.D.; Masciarelli, R.; Sánchez, H.; Osella, C.; de la Torre, M.A. Whole and Defatted Hyperproteic Amaranth Flours Tested as Wheat Flour Supplementation in Mold Breads. *LWT Food Sci. Technol.* **2002**, *35*, 472–475. [CrossRef]
16. Patil, S.S.; Rudra, S.G.; Varghese, E.; Kaur, C. Effect of extruded finger millet (*Eleusine coracan* L.) on textural properties and sensory acceptability of composite bread. *Food Biosci.* **2016**, *14*, 62–69. [CrossRef]
17. Charoenthaikij, P.; Jangchud, K.; Jangchud, A.; Prinyawiwatkul, W.; Tungtrakul, P. Germination conditions affect selected quality of composite wheat-germinated brown rice flour and bread formulations. *J. Food Sci.* **2010**, *75*, S312–S318. [CrossRef]
18. Hugo, L.F.; Rooney, L.W.; Taylor, J.R.N. Fermented Sorghum as a Functional Ingredient in Composite Breads. *Cereal Chem.* **2003**, *80*, 495–499. [CrossRef]
19. Hugo, L.F.; Rooney, L.W.; Taylor, J.R.N. Malted Sorghum as a Functional Ingredient in Composite Bread. *Cereal Chem.* **2000**, *77*, 428–432. [CrossRef]
20. *ICC Standards. No. 114/1*; Method for Using Brabender Extensograph. International Association for Cereal Science and Technology: Vienna, Austria, 2008.
21. *ICC Standards. No. 115/1*; Method for Using Brabender Farinograph. International Association for Cereal Science and Technology: Vienna, Austria, 1992.
22. Schmidt, M.; Sciurba, E. Determination of FODMAP contents of common wheat and rye breads and the effects of processing on the final contents. *Eur. Food Res. Technol.* **2021**, *247*, 395–410. [CrossRef]

23. Houben, R.; De Ruijter, C.; Brunt, K. Determination of the Pentosan Content of Wheat Products by Hydrolysis, Glucose Oxidase Treatment and Analysis by HPAEC/PAD. *J. Cereal Sci.* **1997**, *26*, 37–46. [CrossRef]
24. Dharmaraj, U.; Malleshi, N.G. Changes in carbohydrates, proteins and lipids of finger millet after hydrothermal processing. *LWT Food Sci. Technol.* **2011**, *44*, 1636–1642. [CrossRef]
25. Becker, R.; Wheeler, E.L.; Lorenz, K.; Stafford, A.E.; Grosjean, O.K.; Betschart, A.A.; Saunders, R.M. A Compositional Study of Amaranth Grain. *J. Food Sci.* **1981**, *46*, 1175–1180. [CrossRef]
26. Qi, X.; Tester, R.F. Effect of native starch granule size on susceptibility to amylase hydrolysis. *Starch Staerke* **2016**, *68*, 807–810. [CrossRef]
27. Rao, M.V.S.S.T.S.; Muralikrishna, G. Non-starch polysaccharides and bound phenolic acids from native and malted finger millet (ragi, *E. coracana*, Indaf-15). *Food Chem.* **2001**, *72*, 187–192.
28. Olawoye, B.T.; Gbadamosi, S.O. Effect of different treatments on in vitro protein digestibility, antinutrients, antioxidant prop-erties and mineral composition of *Amaranthus viridis* seed. *Cogent Food Agric.* **2017**, *3*, 1296402. [CrossRef]
29. Hejazi, S.N.; Orsat, V. Malting process optimization for protein digestibility enhancement in finger millet grain. *J. Food Sci. Technol.* **2016**, *53*, 1929–1938. [CrossRef] [PubMed]
30. Udeh, H.O.; Duodu, K.G.; Jideani, A.I.O. Effect of malting period on physicochemical properties, minerals, and phytic acid of finger millet (*Eleusine coracana*) flour varieties. *Food Sci. Nutr.* **2018**, *6*, 1858–1869. [CrossRef]
31. Qvirist, L.; Carlsson, N.G.; Andlid, T. Assessing phytase activity—Methods, definitions and pitfalls. *J. Biol. Meth.* **2015**, *2*, E16. [CrossRef]
32. Sapirstein, H.; Wu, Y.; Koksel, F.; Graf, R. A study of factors influencing the water absorption capacity of Canadian hard red winter wheat flour. *J. Cereal Sci.* **2018**, *81*, 52–59. [CrossRef]
33. Gomez, M.; Ronda, F.; Blanco, C.A.; Caballero, P.A.; Apesteguía, A. Effect of dietary fibre on dough rheology and bread quality. *Eur. Food Res. Technol.* **2003**, *216*, 51–56. [CrossRef]
34. Goesaert, H.; Brijs, K.; Veraverbeke, W.S.; Courtin, C.M.; Gebruers, K.; Delcour, J.A. Wheat flour constituents: How they impact bread quality, and how to impact their functionality. *Trends Food Sci. Technol.* **2005**, *16*, 12–30. [CrossRef]
35. Noort, M.W.; van Haaster, D.; Hemery, Y.; Schols, H.A.; Hamer, R.J. The effect of particle size of wheat bran fractions on bread quality—Evidence for fibre–protein interactions. *J. Cereal Sci.* **2010**, *52*, 59–64. [CrossRef]
36. Gamel, T.H.; Linssen, J.P.; Mesallem, A.S.; Damir, A.A.; Shekib, L.A. Effect of seed treatments on the chemical composition and properties of two amaranth species: Starch and protein. *J. Sci. Food Agric.* **2005**, *85*, 319–327. [CrossRef]
37. Mollakhalili-Meybodi, N.; Khorshidian, N.; Nematollahi, A.; Arab, M. Acrylamide in bread: A review on formation, health risk assessment, and determination by analytical techniques. *Environ. Sci. Pollut. Res.* **2021**, *28*, 15627–15645. [CrossRef]
38. EFSA Panel on Dietetic Products, Nutrition and Allergies. Scientific opinion on dietary reference values for carbohydrates and dietary fibre. *EFSA J.* **2010**, *8*, 1462.
39. Saeed, F.; Pasha, I.; Anjum, F.M.; Sultan, M.T. Arabinoxylans and Arabinogalactans: A Comprehensive Treatise. *Crit. Rev. Food Sci. Nutr.* **2011**, *51*, 467–476. [CrossRef]

foods

Article

Evolutionary Wheat Populations in High-Quality Breadmaking as a Tool to Preserve Agri-Food Biodiversity

Marco Spaggiari [1], Mia Marchini [2], Luca Calani [1], Rossella Dodi [3], Giuseppe Di Pede [1], Margherita Dall'Asta [4], Francesca Scazzina [1], Andrea Barbieri [5], Laura Righetti [1], Silvia Folloni [2,*], Roberto Ranieri [2], Chiara Dall'Asta [1] and Gianni Galaverna [1]

1 Department of Food and Drug, University of Parma, Parco Area delle Scienze 17/A, 43124 Parma, Italy; marco.spaggiari1@studenti.unipr.it (M.S.); luca.calani@unipr.it (L.C.); giuseppe.dipede@unipr.it (G.D.P.); francesca.scazzina@unipr.it (F.S.); laura.righetti@unipr.it (L.R.); chiara.dallasta@unipr.it (C.D.); gianni.galaverna@unipr.it (G.G.)
2 Open Fields s.r.l., Strada Madonna dell'Aiuto 7/A, 43126 Parma, Italy; m.marchini@openfields.it (M.M.); r.ranieri@openfields.it (R.R.)
3 Department of Veterinary Science, University of Parma, Strada del Taglio 10, 43126 Parma, Italy; rossella.dodi@unipr.it
4 Faculty of Agriculture, Food and Environmental Sciences, Catholic University of the Sacred Heart, via Emilia Parmense 84, 29122 Piacenza, Italy; margherita.dallasta@unicatt.it
5 Molino Grassi SpA, via Emilia ovest 347, Fraore, 43126 Parma, Italy; andreabarbieri@molinograssi.it
* Correspondence: s.folloni@openfields.it; Tel.: +39-05211812730

Abstract: Plant biodiversity preservation is one of the most important priorities of today's agriculture. Wheat (*Triticum* spp. L.) is widely cultivated worldwide, mostly under a conventional and monovarietal farming method, leading to progressive biodiversity erosion. On the contrary, the evolutionary population (EP) cultivation technique is characterized by mixing and sowing together as many wheat genotypes as possible to allow the crop to genetically adapt over the years in relation to specific pedoclimatic conditions. The objective of this study was to assess the nutritional, chemical and sensory qualities of three different breads obtained using different organic EP flours, produced following a traditional sourdough process and compared to a commercial wheat cultivar bread. Technological parameters, B-complex vitamins, microelements, dietary fibre and phenolic acids were determined in raw materials and final products. Flours obtained by EPs showed similar characteristics to the commercial wheat cultivar flour. However, significant differences on grain technological quality were found. The breads were comparable with respect to chemical and nutritional qualities. Overall, the sensory panellists rated the tasted breads positively assigning the highest score to those produced with EPs flours (6.75–7.02) as compared to commercial wheat cultivar-produced bread (cv. Bologna, 6.36).

Keywords: evolutionary populations; sourdough bread; consumer perception; wheat (*Triticum aestivum* L.); bread composition

Citation: Spaggiari, M.; Marchini, M.; Calani, L.; Dodi, R.; Di Pede, G.; Dall'Asta, M.; Scazzina, F.; Barbieri, A.; Righetti, L.; Folloni, S.; et al. Evolutionary Wheat Populations in High-Quality Breadmaking as a Tool to Preserve Agri-Food Biodiversity. *Foods* **2022**, *11*, 495. https://doi.org/10.3390/foods11040495

Academic Editor: Marina Carcea

Received: 29 December 2021
Accepted: 5 February 2022
Published: 9 February 2022

1. Introduction

Agriculture, the first actor composing the agri-food system, is currently facing two interconnected crises, such as climate change and biodiversity loss. These challenges are jeopardizing the possibility to provide food manufacturers with high quality raw materials, without affecting price or yield. In conventional agriculture, cereal crops are cultivated repeatedly as monocultures or in rotations that include only two species relying on external inputs such as chemical fertilizers and pesticides [1,2]. On the other hand, ecological principles are followed when considering cereal cultivation in marginal areas, such as mountains, high hills, or organic farming. Among these approaches, the use of a higher inter- and intra-specific diversity and the selection of naturally evolved varieties adapted to the pedoclimatic context over the years [3] are the most efficient ones to ensure cereal yield and quality [4].

On this account, the evolutionary populations (EP) have been introduced with the aim to increase the cultivated biodiversity while ensuring adaptation to the specific pedoclimatic conditions and climate change effect. This concept, introduced more than 60 years ago [5] and now applied by an increasing number of low input farmers [6], relies on the mixing and sowing together of as many genotypes of the same species as possible [7]. At the European Union (EU) level, in 2022 the new organic Regulation came into force describing the rules for certified organic production [8,9]. Regulation EU 218/848 defined new options for reproductive plant material available for organic farmers including evolutionary populations within the organic heterogeneous material (OHM) category. The fact that the seeds of evolutionary populations can now be marketed will most likely increase their availability and their cultivation in the EU.

One of the main concerns regarding EPs-produced-bread is related to the poor technological quality for bakery applications. Indeed, evolutionary breeding has been aimed at improving yield stability under low input agriculture rather than technological properties [10]. However, studies are needed to investigate how EP flour responds to the traditional processing of bread-making. Indeed, bread is recognized as a staple food and a cultural driver, synonymous with symbolic values given its wide and varied preparation methods and recipes. Bread is essentially composed of carbohydrates, like starch, polysaccharides and more complex sugars such as dietary fibres, especially when wholemeal flour is used in dough formulation. Nevertheless, it is a vehicle of other important nutrients belonging to lipids (fatty acids), vitamins (B-group) and bioactive compounds (phenolic compounds). Additionally, the bread formulation method plays an important role on both nutritional and organoleptic characteristics.

Today, sourdough manufacturing is receiving greater attention mainly due to the synergistic effect of specific lactic acid bacteria and yeast strains capable of modifying the whole dough structure and composition, leading to dietary fibre and bioactive solubilization and specific sensory properties [11–14]. Moreover, sourdough processing is perceived by consumers as a traditional technique which could be considered as added value [15] and a useful tool for a potential whole grain exploitation.

In relation to this, food industry drivers and trends are constantly changing. In fact, consumer food choices are shifting to virtuous producers who consider environmental issues and food system sustainability while designing their food products [16]. Consumers are also starting to pay more attention to the sensory characteristics of food, and their inputs are used by food companies to develop new products [17,18]. The new methodologies developed include CATA (check-all-that-apply) questionnaires, which consist of a lists of words and phrases from which respondents must pick all options they deem relevant [19]. Although a novelty in the fields of sensory and consumer science, these kinds of questionnaires were already being used for vast ranges of products, including bread [19–23]. The latter studies have confirmed that CATA questionnaires are a quick, easy, and dependable way to collect information on consumers' sensory perceptions when it comes to food and can provide similar information to the time-worn descriptive evaluations by skilled assessors [24].

Given the above, the aim of this study was to (i) study the suitability of organic wheat flours (Type I) obtained from EPs cultivated during the 2016–2017 growing season in the Emilia-Romagna Apennines, Italy, for a traditional sourdough bread-making process; (ii) to analyse the chemical and nutritional profile of the flours and the obtained breads and finally (iii) to assess the consumers' sensory perception by acceptability and check-all-that-apply (CATA) tests.

2. Materials and Methods

2.1. Chemicals

Acetonitrile, ethyl acetate, formic acid, acetic acid, methanol (>99.9%) were HPLC-grade, hydrochloric acid (HCl, 37.0%), sodium hydroxide (NaOH, >98.0%), caffeic acid (>98%), p-hydroxybenzoic acid (>99%), p-coumaric acid (>98%), sinapic acid (>98%), gallic acid (>98%) and trans-ferulic acid (>99%), *Folin-Ciocalteu's* reagent solution were purchased from Sigma-Aldrich (St. Louis, MO, USA). The cis-ferulic acid was obtained by total conversion of a trans-ferulic acid solution under UV light.

2.2. Plant Materials

Three bread wheat (*T. aestivum* L.) EPs (Bio2, Grossi and ICARDA) and a modern bread wheat variety (Bologna) were cultivated in a farm located in Vogno di Toano (600 m a.s.l), in the Emilia-Romagna Apennines (Italy) under organic farming, over the 2016–2017 growing season. In October 2016 manure was distributed on the fields and harrowing was performed in order to prepare the soil for sowing. Sowing was performed on 31 October 2016 at a sowing rate of 300 seeds/mq. The seedling emergency date was 5 December 2016 and the harvesting date was 5 July 2017. No treatment was performed for pest control.

The initial nucleus of Bio2 and Grossi EPs consisted of material deriving from long-term conservation, crossbreeding and multiplication activities of local heritage varieties by the Azienda Agraria Sperimentale Stuard (Parma, Italy) and from the Claudio Grossi farm (Parma, Italy), respectively. The local heritage varieties were Ardito, Autonomia B, Carosella, Fiorello, Frassineto, Gentilrosso, Mentana, Terminillo, Verna, Virgilio for Bio2 and Ardito, Virgilio, Miracolo, Gentilrosso, Poulard di Ciano for Grossi.

EP ICARDA was assembled in 2009 by Salvatore Ceccarelli and Stefania Grando with the collaboration of the bread wheat breeders of the International Centre for Agriculture Research in Dry Areas (ICARDA, Beirut, Lebanon) and contained F2, F3 and F4 of 1996 crosses. It arrived in Italy in 2010 thanks to the Italian Association for Organic Agriculture (AIAB, Rome, Italy), in the framework of the EU-FP7 Solibam project. For this, it is also known as Solibam bread wheat EP. In this study, four samples of the ICARDA population were collected from different Italian farms and mixed before sowing. The modern bread wheat Bologna, used as a reference, is a variety by Società Italiana Sementi (SIS, San Lazzaro di Savena, Bologna, Italy).

2.3. Cereal Grain Milling and Bread Formulation

2.3.1. Technological Quality Analysis of the Wheat Flours

Test weight and protein content of EPs and Bologna variety were determined using an Infratec 1241 near infrared (NIR) spectrophotometer (FOSS Analytical, Hilleroed, Denmark).

To analyze thousand kernel weight, reading was set at 1000 grains in an optical seed counter (Contador, Pfeuffer, Kitzingen, Germany) and the weight of the grain was measured with a precision balance (SBC 53, Scaltec Instruments, Göttingen, Niedersachsen, Germany).

An aliquot of each wheat grain was milled using a Bona laboratory mill (Labormill, Monza, Italy) and analysed for rheological behaviour following the UNI EN ISO 27971/2008 test method [25] by means of an Alveograph (NG Model, Chopin, Villeneuve-la-Garenne, Cedex France), evaluating the baking strength (W, 10^{-4} J) and the curve configuration ratio (P/L ratio, where P (mm) = dough tenacity; L (mm) = dough extensibility).

2.3.2. Flour Preparation

After appropriate cleaning, the kernels were tempered overnight at room temperature by adding a sufficient amount of water to obtain 16.5% final moisture. The grains were milled into flours using an industrial pilot plant (MLU 202; Bühler, Uzwil, Switzerland) consisting of three breaks (B1 to B3), three reduction (C1 to C3) passages and one laboratory bran duster. Milling fractions from the pilot plant accounted for flour (~65.9% extraction rate, ER), middlings (~10.8% ER) and bran (~17.9% ER). Based on an analysis of the total ash content (American Association of Cereal Chemists, Inc., AACC Method 08-12.01) [26], the flours obtained from all EPs were classified as Type 1 (0.65 < ashes ≤ 0.80 dry basis) while flour from the cv. Bologna was found to be a Type 00 flour (ashes ≤ 0.55 d.b.) in conformity with the Italian standard set out in the Presidential Decree 187/2001 [27]. Therefore, to obtain the same commercial type of flours for all samples, a Type 1 flour was prepared from the Bologna variety by combining 12.27% of middlings (ashes = 2.74% d.b.) with the Type 00 flour obtained (ashes= 0.45% d.b.) according to the equation:

$$(gf * af) + (gm * am) = (gm + gf) * ax \quad (1)$$

where g is the grams of flour (f) or middlings (m), a is the ash content (%, d.b.) of flour (f), middlings (m) and reconstituted flour (x). After reconstitution, cv. Bologna Type 1 flour (FBo) had an 80% ER against the 66.2%, 64.8% and 64.7% of Bio2 EP Type 1 flour (FB), Grossi EP Type 1 flour (FG) and ICARDA EP Type 1 flour (FI), respectively.

2.3.3. Bread Formulation

Four breads (Bio2, ICARDA, Grossi EPs and cv. Bologna Type 1 flours, Figure 1) were produced twice in a baking laboratory by the same professional baker using sourdough manufacturing process. The recipe was: wheat flour (2500 g), sourdough (750 g, prepared by the professional baker), salt (60 g), malt (45 g), extra virgin olive oil (30 mL) and water (~1250 mL). The sourdough starter, commonly used by the same baker in bread-making, was fed twice with organic bread wheat flour Type 0 (Molino Grassi, Parma, Italy) and left to leaven in a prover under controlled conditions (30 °C, 86% relative humidity, RH) for two days. Small adjustments to the bread-making process were made in terms of leavening time, while the dough's workability was improved by the baker's expertise. All breads were prepared by mixing the ingredients in a spiral mixer (SPI 45 F E, Esmach, Vicenza, Italy) for 10 min at low speed and 8 min at high speed. More water was added during the kneading depending on the dough's workability resulting in the following water additions: 480 mL for bread produced using cv. Bologna (BBo), 440 mL for bread produced using ICARDA and Grossi EPs (BI and BG, respectively), 380 mL for bread produced using Bio2 EP (BB). Bulk fermentation was carried out in a prover (BFM 6080, Climother, Bongard Esmach, Italy) under controlled conditions (28 °C, 86% RH) for 90 min. The fermented dough was then divided into 1 kg loaves and placed back into the prover to rest for 15–30 min. Subsequently, the loaves were put into rattan baking molds, proved (28 °C, 86% RH) for 80 min and baked for 60 min at 215 °C in an electric oven (EMT 4/6040, Tagliavini, Parma, Italy). After baking, the loaves were cooled to room temperature, cut into equal slices and immediately used for the sensory and hedonic analysis, or otherwise lyophilized, homogeneously minced under nitrogen, and kept at −20 °C until extraction and analysis.

2.4. *Protein, Lipids, Dietary Fibre Components and Carbohydrates of Breads*

Fat content was determined by Soxhlet (American association Of Analytical Chemistry international, AOAC 922.06 [28]), using diethyl-ether as solvent. FAs profile was determined according to Dall'Asta et al. [29]. The FAs were identified and the relative percentage, calculated using the area under each peak. Results were also reported as saturated (SFA), monounsaturated (MUFA) and polyunsaturated (PUFA) fatty acids in accordance with their unsaturation degree.

Crude nitrogen content was determined following the Kjeldahl method (AOAC 950.36 [28]) using 5.7 as conversion factor. The analysis of high molecular weight insoluble dietary fibre (HMWIDF), high molecular weight soluble dietary fibre (HMWSDF), low molecular weight soluble dietary fibre (LMWSDF) and total dietary fibre (TDF) content in flours and formulated breads was carried out by an external accredited laboratory of food analysis (UNI CEI EN ISO/IEC 17025:2005 [30], Accredia, Lab. n. 0490), using an official enzymatic-gravimetric method (AOAC 2011.25 2013, [28]). Carbohydrates were determined by difference. Lastly, the determination of resistant starch (RS) was undertaken using the AOAC Method 2002.02 [28] for Resistant starch (Megazyme kit, USA). Results were expressed as g/100 g on dry weight basis.

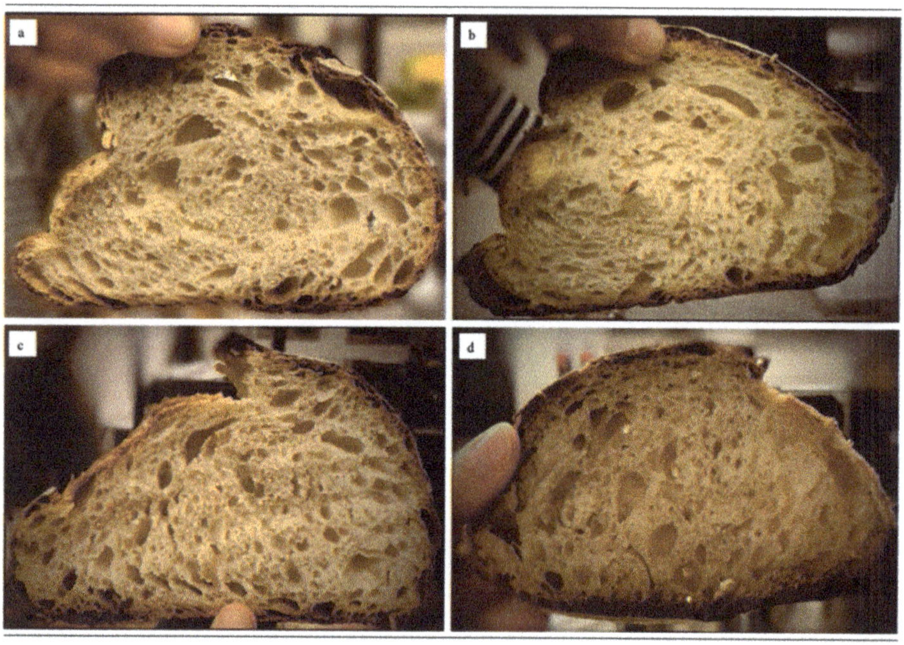

Figure 1. Pictures of the slices of the different breads. (**a**) BB, bread produced using Bio2 EP; (**b**) BI, bread produced using ICARDA EP; (**c**) BG, bread produced using Grossi EP; (**d**) BBo, bread produced using cv. Bologna.

2.5. Determination of Magnesium (Mg), Zinc (Zn), Iron (Fe), Selenium (Se) Content of Flours and Breads

The analyses of Mg, Zn, Fe and Se were carried out by an external accredited laboratory of food analysis (UNI CEI EN ISO/IEC 17025:2005 [30], Accredia, Lab. n. 0490), using an inductively coupled plasma with mass spectrometer (ICP-MS) analytical method [31] (UNI EN 13805:2014). Results were expressed as mg/100 g for Mg, Zn and Fe and μg/100 g for Se on a dry weight basis.

2.6. Sample Extraction for Soluble and Insoluble Phenolic Compounds of Flours and Breads

Soluble and insoluble phenolic compounds were extracted from both flours and bread samples following the protocol proposed by Zaupa and colleagues [32]. The obtained extracts were dissolved in an opportune solvent and volume, used for the Ultra High-Performance Liquid Chromatography coupled to tandem mass spectrometry (UHPLC-MS/MS) analysis and the total phenolic content assay.

2.6.1. Soluble and Insoluble Total Phenolic Content (TPC)

Soluble and insoluble total phenolic content (TPC) of bread samples were analysed by the *Folin–Ciocalteu's* method [33]. A calibration curve using gallic acid as reference compound (100–1000 mg/Kg) was prepared for quantification. Results were reported as mg of gallic acid equivalents (GAE) per Kg on dry weight basis.

2.6.2. Soluble and Insoluble Phenolic Acids Profile Using UHPLC-MS/MS

Phenolic acids (PA) profiling of bread samples was extracted according to Zaupa et al. [32] and analysed using a UHPLC Dionex Ultimate 3000 separation system coupled to a triple quadrupole mass spectrometer (TSQ Vantage; Thermo Fisher Scientific) following the protocol reported by Spaggiari and colleagues [34]. For quantification, two different calibration sets (0.05–5 and 5–100 mg/mL) were prepared using phenolic acids standard reference materials. Results were expressed as mg/Kg on dry weight basis.

2.7. Determination of Thiamine, Nicotinic Acid and Nicotinamide, and Folic Acid Content

For the extraction of the thiamine, nicotinic acid, nicotinamide and folic acid, the method proposed by Leporati et al. [35], was used. Results were expressed as mg/100 g with the only exception of folic acid (μg/100 g). The extracts were analysed using an Accela UPLC 1250 equipped with a linear ion trap MS (LTQ XL, Thermo Fisher Scientific Inc., San Jose, CA, USA) attached to an electrospray ionization probe (H-ESI-II; Thermo Fisher Scientific Inc., San Jose, CA, USA). Separation was performed on an Acquity UPLC HSS T3 (2.1 × 100 mm) column (Waters, Milford, MA, USA). The volume injected was 3 μL, and the oven temperature was set to 40 °C. The elution gradient was performed using CH_3CN (0.1% formic acid) as mobile phase A and H_2O (0.1% formic acid) as mobile phase B, at a flow rate of 0.3 mL/min, starting with 99% B and 1% A for 2 min, then eluent B decreased at 20% and A increased at 80% in 2 min, and maintained for further 2 min. Finally, the initial conditions were restored (total run time = 13 min). Data processing was performed using Xcalibur 2.2 software from Thermo Fisher Scientific Inc., (San Jose, CA, USA). The vitamins analysis was carried out in positive ionization mode, the MS worked with a capillary temperature set to 275 °C, while the source heater temperature was at 200 °C. The sheath gas (nitrogen) flow was 40 unit, while auxiliary and sweep gases (both nitrogen) were equal to 5 and 0 units, respectively. The spray voltage was 3.5 kV. The S-Lens value was 115 V. Vitamins were monitored using an MRM (multiple reaction monitoring) scan mode with the characteristic transitions reported in Table S1.

2.8. Acceptability and Check-All-That-Apply (CATA) Analysis of Formulated Breads

Consumers' sensory and hedonic perception of breads was assessed with an acceptability and CATA test. Breads were produced few hours prior to analysis following the recipe described above. After baking, the loaves were cooled and cut into half-slices of 1 cm thickness with a well-balanced crumb-to-crust ratio, packed separately in paper bags and labelled with a random three-digit code; the samples were simultaneously presented on a plate in randomized order and in blind condition. Water and unsalted crackers were provided as palate cleansers between samples. The panel consisted of 59 untrained consumers (46% male, 54% female, aged between 18 and 70 years old) who were asked to answer a CATA questionnaire consisting of 21 sensory characteristics listed in randomized order across assessors, selecting all the attributes they considered appropriate to describe the breads as well as their personal 'ideal' product. The terms used in the CATA test were the following: pleasant smell, unpleasant smell, smell of yoghurt, pleasant crust colour, unpleasant crust colour, golden crust colour, pale crust colour, soft crust, crunchy crust, pleasant crumb colour, unpleasant crumb colour, soft crumb, hard crumb, pleasant aftertaste, unpleasant aftertaste, salty taste, sweet taste, acid taste, mediocre, good, excellent bread.

After the CATA test, the consumers judged the acceptability of bread samples by rating aroma, taste, crust and crumb consistency, crust and crumb colour, appearance and overall acceptability with a 9-point hedonic scale [1 = dislike extremely, 2 = dislike very much, 3 = dislike, 4 = dislike slightly, 5 = neither like nor dislike, 6 = like slightly, 7 = like, 8 = like very much and 9 = like extremely].

2.9. Statistical Analysis

All analyses were performed at least in triplicate and reported as mean ± standard deviation (S.D. of each parameter are reported in Supplementary Information). To verify significant differences between samples, data obtained from the instrumental analyses and from the acceptability test were statistically analysed by performing one-way analysis of variance (ANOVA) followed by Duncan's post-hoc test at <alpha> = 0.05 using SPSS Software Version 25.0 (SPSS Inc., USA). Data obtained from the CATA test were organized by compiling a contingency table to count how many times each attribute was used to describe each bread. Cochran's Q statistic was performed to evaluate significant differences between products across the attributes. In order to identify relationships between attributes and samples, a sensory map of the products was obtained by performing a correspondence analysis (CA), performed with TIBCO Statistica Version 13.3 (TIBCO Software Inc., USA).

3. Results and Discussion

3.1. Milling and Technological Quality of Wheat

Table 1 shows the grain quality parameters of EPs in comparison to the cv. Bologna.

Table 1. Grain quality parameters of EPs and cv. Bologna.

Wheat	Test Weight (kg/hL)	Thousand Kernel Weight (g)	Protein Content (% d.m.)	Alveograph			
				W (10^{-4} J)	P (mm H_2O)	L (mm)	P/L
Bio2 EP	74 ^{a}	44 ^{b}	16.82 ^{b}	130.5 ^{b}	67.5 ^{d}	134.0 ^{b}	0.5 ^{a}
ICARDA EP	78 ^{a}	45 ^{b}	16.39 ^{b}	152.5 ^{c}	59.0 ^{c}	129.5 ^{b}	0.5 ^{a}
Grossi EP	77 ^{a}	47 ^{c}	16.93 ^{b}	106.5 ^{a}	55.0 ^{b}	108.5 ^{a}	0.5 ^{a}
Bologna	79 ^{a}	32 ^{a}	13.27 ^{a}	288.0 ^{d}	48.5 ^{a}	98.5 ^{a}	0.5 ^{a}

Results are reported as mean (n = 3). Protein content is expressed as g/100 g on dry matter (d.m.). Standard deviation is reported in Table S2. Different letters in the same column indicate significant differences among samples (<alpha> = 0.05). EP, evolutionary wheat population.

The protein content of all EPs grains (mean value ≈16.7%) was significantly (<alpha> = 0.05) higher than that of cv. Bologna (≈13%), although no differences were found among the EPs protein percentages. Protein content of cereal grains is an important parameter which determines their technological use [36], although protein levels have only partly a genetical basis and depend mostly on management practices and the environment [37]. The technological use of proteins is related to gluten proteins, i.e., glutenin and gliadin, located in the endosperm [36]. In general terms, there is a negative relationship between protein concentration and grain yield [37].

Furthermore, the alveographic parameters W and P/L are crucial for the assessment of wheat flours strength and extensibility [38]. The baking industry requires high W values (>$180 \cdot 10^{-4}$ J) combined with a balanced P/L index (0.40–0.50). As expected, significant differences (<alpha> = 0.05) were found between W parameter of EPs and cv. Bologna, which recorded the highest baking strength ($288 \cdot 10^{-4}$ J). Among EPs, ICARDA showed the highest W value ($152.5 \cdot 10^{-4}$ J), followed by BB ($130.5 \cdot 10^{-4}$ J) and BG ($106.5 \cdot 10^{-4}$ J). Besides, the P/L ratio showed a mean value ≈ 0.5 with no significant difference among samples (<alpha> = 0.05). Overall, ICARDA EP showed the most promising quality parameters among EPs for bread-making. Moreover, Bologna flour's rheological parameters confirm its suitability for long-leavening bakery specialties [39].

During milling, to produce the same "Type" of flour (Type 1) according to the Italian legislation (Presidential Decree 187/2001), as defined by the ash level, middlings had to be added exclusively for FBo, indicating, for the Bologna variety, a different milling behaviour and/or an ash distribution particularly concentrated in the aleurone and bran layers, allowing for very high milling yields (i.e., ER at equal concentration of ashes) as already noticed by the Italian milling industry. In detail, the different milling behaviour of EPs compared to FBo can be attributed to a different grain hardness. Cv. Bologna is known—by industrial millers—to contain a small and hard kernel [39], and to have outstanding milling behaviour since the aleurone layer (with high ash content) detaches very well from the endosperm yielding a white flour with low ash content. On the contrary, from what we have observed in our study, milling of EPs caused portions of the aleurone layer to be released into the flour, resulting in higher ash levels.

3.2. Lipid Content and Fatty Acids Profile of Breads

Lipids play an important role on both sensory and technological quality of food products [40]. The crude fat analysed in bread was the highest for BBo and BG followed by BI and BB (Table 2).

Table 2. Nutritional and chemical composition of the bread formulated using the wheat evolutionary population (BB, BI and BG) and bread produced using flour from cv. Bologna wheat (BBo).

	BB	BI	BG	BBo
Energetic value (kJ) *	1005.0	1058.1	1041.1	961.6
Energetic value (kcal) *	240.2	252.9	248.8	229.8
Carbohydrates (g/100 g)	48.3 ^{a}	49.7 ^{a}	47.7 ^{a}	46.2 ^{a}
Total dietary fibre (g/100 g)	4.55 ^{a}	4.22 ^{a}	4.64 ^{a}	5.18 ^{b}
Lipids (g/100 g)	0.83 ^{a}	1.0 ^{b}	1.20 ^{c}	1.22 ^{c}
SFA (%)	31.8 ^{a}	32.2 ^{a}	31.7 ^{a}	31.0 ^{a}
MUFA (%)	42.9 ^{a}	45.2 ^{b}	45.2 ^{b}	42.7 ^{a}
PUFA (%)	25.3 ^{c}	22.6 ^{a}	23.0 ^{b}	26.3 ^{d}
Ω-6/Ω-9	0.53 ^{b}	0.45 ^{a}	0.45 ^{a}	0.55 ^{b}
Proteins (g/100 g)	12.4 ^{a}	11.3 ^{a}	12.1 ^{a}	11.3 ^{a}
Mg (mg/100 g)	24.5 ^{a}	22.1 ^{a}	24.1 ^{a}	31.6 ^{b}
Zn (mg/100 g)	0.85 ^{b}	0.75 ^{a}	0.82 ^{a}	0.82 ^{a}
Fe (mg/100 g)	1.37 ^{c}	0.86 ^{a}	1.09 ^{b}	1.38 ^{c}
Se (μg/100 g)	8.07 ^{a}	8.11 ^{a}	8.95 ^{b}	8.77 ^{b}
Thiamine (mg/100 g)	0.24 ^{b}	0.18 ^{a}	0.20 ^{a}	0.43 ^{c}
Nicotinic acid (mg/100 g)	<LOQ	<LOQ	<LOQ	<LOQ
Folic acid (μg/100 g)	<LOQ	<LOQ	<LOQ	<LOQ
Nicotinamide (mg/100 g)	1.77 ^{b}	1.75 ^{ab}	1.62 ^{a}	2.18 ^{c}

Results are reported as mean (n = 3). Standard deviation is reported in Table S3. Different superscipts letters $^{a–d}$ in the same row indicate significant differences among samples (<alpha> = 0.05). <LOQ Folic acid: 5 μg/100 g; <LOQ Nicotinic acid: 0.01 mg/100 mg, Mg, magnesium; Zn, zinc; Fe, iron; Se, selenium; NAM, nicotinamide; BB, bread produced using BIO2 EP; BI, bread produced using ICARDA EP; BG, bread produced using Grossi EP; BBo, bread produced using cv. Bologna. *: Calories (kJ and kcal) were calculated as sum of nutritive components.

Since the amount of extra virgin olive oil used in the recipe was the same, the differences could be attributed to the lipid content of the wheat grains. Concerning the fatty acids profile, results are reported as Supplementary Material (see Figure S1). Oleic (C18:1), linoleic (C18:2), palmitic (C16:0) and linolenic (C18:3) acids were the most abundant in all breads formulated, in line with previous findings [41]. However, only C18:1 fatty acid was found significantly different between BI and BG, with the latter showing the highest content. In fact, the MUFA and PUFA varied among breads (Table 2), resulting in BG and BI with higher MUFA and BBo with higher PUFA. Endogenous wheat lipids have been studied to demonstrate their influence in breadmaking and showing their ability to stabilize the gas bubbles by aligning at gas-liquid interface during dough maturation [42]. In this context, the differences in both amount and quality of lipid fraction of the EPs, despite its lower content, might be considered a positive source of variation for producing breads. Moreover, the n-6/n-3 ratio is an important nutritional parameter, that shall stay below 1 [43]. All breads herein produced exhibited a healthy lipid index <1.

3.3. Total Dietary Fibre (TDF) and DF Classes of Flours and Breads

Dietary fibres are important components of cereal grains due to their well-documented beneficial properties [44]. The physiological effects are highly dependent on their physical and chemical characteristics (i.e., monomer composition, particle size, etc.) [45]. Regarding the TDF content of the breads herein formulated, no differences were found (Table 2). Overall, the breads might use the nutritional claim "source of fibre" (≥3 g TDF/100 g bread, [46]). Furthermore, a detailed analysis of the different dietary fibre classes of flours (Figure 2A) indicated a significantly higher HMWIDF content of cv. Bologna (<alpha> = 0.05) in respect to FI and FG. The latter could be ascribable to the middlings supplementation to native cv. Bologna flour which increased the final amount of these substances in flour. Concerning breads (Figure 2B) no differences were found among fibre classes. Moreover, the insoluble component slightly, although not significantly, increased after processing, ranging from 0.86 to 2.24 g/100 g in flours and from 1.60 to 2.40 g/100 g in breads. This could be related to the formation of resistant starch occurred during bread-making process (Figure 2C) [47,48]. In fact, the starch is subjected to gelatinization and retrogradation processes inducing physico-chemical modifications of available starch originally present in the flour. The derived component, resistant starch, is a fraction which results resistant to the digestion and contribute to increase the overall fibre fraction in breads. Likewise, lipids and dietary fibres greatly influence the bread dough rheological properties and its textural quality [49].

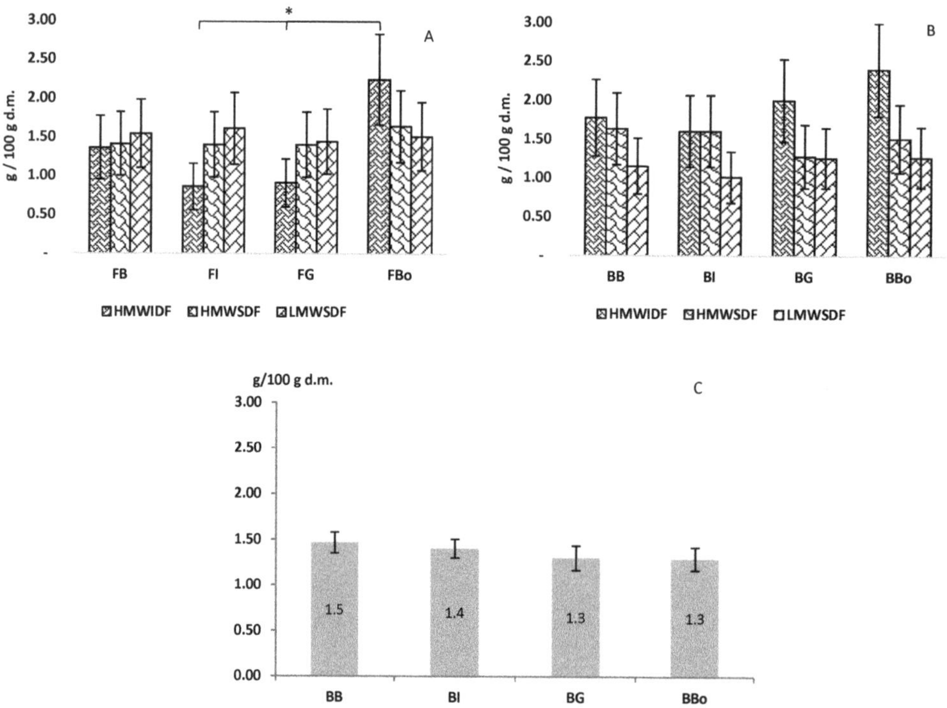

Figure 2. Classes of dietary fibres found in flours (**A**) and breads (**B**), together with resistant starch (**C**) determined in breads. Results are reported as mean ± standard deviation and expressed as g/100 g dry matter. * Indicates a significant difference <alpha> = 0.05. HMWIDF, high molecular weight insoluble dietary fibre; HMWSDF, high molecular weight soluble dietary fibre; LMWSDF, low molecular weight soluble dietary fibre; FB, BIO2 EP Type 1 flour; FI, ICARDA EP Type 1 flour; FG, Grossi EP Type 1 flour; FBo, cv. Bologna Type 1 flour; BB, bread produced using Bio2 EP; BI, bread produced using ICARDA EP; BG, bread produced using Grossi EP; BBo, bread produced using cv. Bologna.

3.4. Selected Micronutrients Content of Flours and Breads

The content of important minerals (Mg, Zn, Fe, and Se) was analysed in flours (Table 3) and breads (Table 2).

The results obtained were in line with reference reported in various international databases [50–52]. Overall, the content of Mg, Zn, and Fe diminished after flour transformation, although Se content increased by around 3 times (as average) in all formulated breads. This reduction phenomenon could be related to some complexation in kneading and cooking phases [53] while the increased Se content was also reported elsewhere [54] probably due to the microorganism metabolism or the cell lysis itself. B-complex vitamins are important nutrients, essential for several human physiological functions. The content of thiamine, nicotinic acid and folic acid, were quantified in flours (Table 3) and then in breads (Table 2). Thiamine content in flours was higher for FBo and FG, in the range of values reported by Mihhalevski et al. [55]. While nicotinic acid was never detected in flours and breads, nicotinamide content increased significantly and among breads BBo totalized the highest content. The latter could be probably due to the fermentation of the sourdough processing [56]. Concerning the stability of B-vitamins during processing, thiamine can resist under the bread-making conditions (pH 4–5, high temperature), similar to nicotinamide [55]. Folic acid, was only found in FB samples, although after processing was detected as <LOQ. A high variability is usually found in group-B vitamin content of wheat grains, possibly due to the difficult analytical procedure and varietal differences [57].

Table 3. Micronutrients content in flours.

	FB	FI	FG	FBo
Mg (mg/100 g) *	29.2 a	26.1 a	28.5 a	44.2 b
Zn (mg/100 g) *	1.13 b	0.97 a	1.08 a	1.17 b
Fe (mg/100 g) *	1.80 c	1.02 a	1.29 b	1.85 c
Se (μg/100 g) **	2.66 a	2.40 a	3.39 b	3.96 b
Thiamine (mg/100 g) *	0.29 b	0.22 a	0.33 bc	0.36 c
Nicotinic acid (mg/100 g) *	<LOQ	<LOQ	<LOQ	<LOQ
Nicotinamide (mg/100 g) *	0.43 a	<LOQ	0.51 ab	0.56 b
Folic acid (μg/100 g) **	21.8 b	<LOQ a	<LOQ a	<LOQ a

Results are expressed as mean (n = 3). Standard deviation is reported in Table S4. Different superscripts letters a–c in the same column indicate significant difference (<alpha> = 0.05). * <LOQ, 0.01 mg/100 g; ** <LOQ, 0.5 μg/100 g. FB, BIO2 EP Type 1 flour; FI, ICARDA EP Type 1 flour; FG, Grossi EP Type 1 flour; FBo, cv. Bologna Type 1 flour.

3.5. Phenolic Compounds from Flours to Breads

Phenolic compounds in cereals are mainly present as simple phenolic acids, which are located in the outermost fraction of the seed (i.e., bran). For this reason, they can occur in soluble and mainly in insoluble form, thus strictly linked to the fibrous material of vegetable cells [58]. The TPC and PA profile of flours and formulated breads were reported in Table 4.

Concerning flour samples, the soluble component was negligible compared to the insoluble fraction. Furthermore, ferulic acid was the most abundant among PAs, as previously reported by other authors [34,58,59]. However, the TPC of bread showed a higher soluble component compared to the insoluble one. There are several potential explanations for this, mostly ascribed to the complex chemical reactions and modification involving metabolic processes and the high temperature during the transformation of flour into dough and bread. The most interesting phenolic acid transformation is ascribed to the action of fermentation which is shown to be crucial for the release of phenolic acids from the matrix, increasing their bioavailability for human digestion [60,61]. However, the thermal treatment applied during baking could be detrimental, degrading the thermolabile phenolic or complexing them in Maillard's reaction-derived compounds lowering their final content in bread, as occurred in this study. Moreover, the formation of peptides which might interfere with the *Folin–Ciocalteu's* assay and Maillard reaction's soluble compounds [62] must be accounted for when interpreting the results of TPC method. In terms of abundance, both TPC and PA content of BBo were the highest among products, because of the middlings addition. However, variability in phenolic acid content of different wheat varieties is well known, with their biosynthesis strongly influenced by environmental stimuli [63]. As with other phenolic compounds, phenolic acids can act as antioxidants. Therefore, considering this property, a higher content of phenolic compounds might be translated to a higher protection against oxidation, hence a more stable product from both sensory and technological viewpoints.

3.6. Check-All-That-Apply (CATA) Analysis of Breads

Sensory analysis was carried out by including breads produced with cv. Bologna flour type 00 (without middlings addition, BBo t00 sample) as additional control. These breads were produced by applying the same processing conditions of other breads. The newly formulated breads were assessed by 59 consumers using CATA test. This method is valuable to understand the consumer perception of a specific food product. Therefore, a list of sensory attributes related to flavour, appearance, taste, texture and smell are evaluated by untrained panellists, which are allowed to select all the attributes better describing the product perception.

A preliminary correspondence analysis (CA) on the CATA dataset including BBo t00, bread produced using cv. Bologna flour type 00 and BBo t1, bread produced using cv. Bologna flour type 1 was performed (87% of the total variance explained, Figure S2). The breads prepared with EPs flours and the control sample BBo t1 were grouped in the centre of the plot, due to the fact that BBo t00 was perceived as a very different sample compared to the others (Figure S2). Data were confirmed by hedonic sensory evaluation data, which showed BBo t00 as the least appreciated sample (overall acceptability: 6.15 ± 1.20).

Since the aim of the work was to produce and characterize breads produced under the same processing conditions, assessing the suitability of EPs for bread-making in comparison with a commercial variety and from flours belonging to the same commercial type according to the Italian legislation (Type 1 flours), we repeated the correspondence analysis including only breads obtained from Type 1 flours. In such a way, the differences between EPs and the BBo t1 control could be better explained.

After executing a Cochran's Q analysis of results, a significant difference (<alpha> = 0.05) in consumer perception for 14 out of 21 attributes among the different samples was found. In fact, assessors detected significant differences between samples for texture attributes (soft crust, crunchy crust, soft crumb), colour descriptors (unpleasant crust colour, pleasant and unpleasant crumb colour), smell (pleasant and unpleasant), taste (salty, acid), aftertaste (pleasant and unpleasant) and overall judgement (mediocre and excellent bread). Biplot shown in Figure 3 represents the visual configuration of the breads and their discriminating attributes in the first two dimensions of the correspondence analysis performed on the CATA dataset (92.9% of the total variance explained).

It can be observed that the ideal concept of bread for the panellists matched the "excellent" descriptor (right quadrant), and the breads prepared using EPs flours (BI, BG, BB) were grouped in the lower quadrants of Figure 3, and all intensely associated with sensory attributes of great impact for consumers. More in detail, BI was perceived by judges as having a "pleasant crumb colour", "crunchy crust", "soft crumb" and "pleasant smell", attributes, which all had significant difference (<alpha> = 0.05) following Cochran's Q test. In addition to previous positive sensory attributes, the judges perceived the presence of an "acid taste" and an "unpleasant aftertaste" for both BG and BB, which are clustered together and therefore closest to the attribute "mediocre bread". Quality parameters such as bread volume, acidic taste and colour are deeply influenced by the sourdough processing due to enzymatic reactions occurring during fermentation [64]. However, the visual sensory characteristics referred to the crust colour ("unpleasant" and "pale") did not have a significant difference. On the other hand, the control sample produced with cv. Bologna was visually located distant from the EPs-bread samples. According to CATA data, the bread was found close to "hard crumb", "unpleasant smell", "soft crumb" and "unpleasant crumb colour" descriptors, which could be related to the different flour preparation method affecting the sensory characteristics of the finished product [40]. Based on the frequency of the attribute selection, consumers described their ideal bread as having a pleasant crust and crumb colour (74% and 61%, respectively), pleasant smell (76%), golden crust (78%), crunchy crust (96%), soft crumb (87%), pleasant aftertaste (69%), salty taste (61%), and being good (31%) and excellent (63%). When comparing bread samples to the ideal product, no bread directly corresponded to the ideal one, but BI was the closest to it.

Table 4. Total phenolic content (TPC) and phenolic acid (PA) profile in their free (soluble) and bound (insoluble) forms.

Sample	TPC		4-HB		p-C		Caff		t-Fer		c-Fer	Sin	
	Free	Bound	Free	Bound	Free	Bound	Free	Bound	Free	Bound		Free	Bound
Flours	mg GAE/Kg d.m.		mg/Kg d. m.										
FB	256.22 ^{a}	895.95 ^{a}	0.07 ^{a}	<LOQ	<LOQ	0.11 ^{a}	0.21 ^{b}	0.25 ^{a}	1.53 ^{b}	2.48 ^{b}	0.59 ^{a}	0.90 ^{b}	1.25 ^{b}
FI	217.70 ^{a}	838.51 ^{a}	0.09 ^{a}	<LOQ	0.07 ^{a}	0.12 ^{a}	0.17 ^{a}	0.25 ^{a}	1.56 ^{b}	2.21 ^{a}	1.10 ^{b}	0.80 ^{a}	0.99 ^{a}
FG	221.76 ^{a}	912.84 ^{a}	<LOQ	<LOQ	0.08 ^{a}	0.12 ^{a}	0.23 ^{b}	0.32 ^{b}	1.33 ^{a}	3.25 ^{c}	1.05 ^{b}	0.96 ^{b}	1.32 ^{b}
FBo	390.49 ^{b}	855.41 ^{a}	<LOQ	<LOQ	<LOQ	0.18 ^{b}	0.37 ^{c}	0.52 ^{c}	1.73 ^{b}	2.66 ^{ab}	0.91 ^{b}	0.82 ^{a}	1.17 ^{b}
Breads													
BB	343.81 ^{a}	217.97 ^{a}	<LOQ	0.51 ^{a}	<LOQ	1.47 ^{b}	<LOQ	0.37 ^{a}	1.32 ^{a}	44.25 ^{a}	21.47 ^{a}	<LOQ	4.07 ^{b}
BI	480.93 ^{c}	182.89 ^{a}	<LOQ	0.45 ^{a}	<LOQ	1.21 ^{a}	<LOQ	0.29 ^{a}	1.86 ^{a}	42.16 ^{a}	15.96 ^{a}	0.34 ^{a}	3.73 ^{a}
BG	414.83 ^{b}	186.81 ^{a}	<LOQ	0.73 ^{b}	0.11 ^{a}	1.79 ^{c}	<LOQ	0.32 ^{a}	2.29 ^{ab}	47.23 ^{a}	26.76 ^{a}	0.38 ^{a}	6.12 ^{c}
BBo	490.29 ^{c}	355.86 ^{b}	0.21 ^{a}	0.94 ^{c}	0.11 ^{a}	2.31 ^{c}	<LOQ	0.63 ^{b}	2.41 ^{b}	73.64 ^{b}	25.52 ^{a}	<LOQ	6.19 ^{c}

Results are expressed as mean (n = 3). Standard deviation is reported in Table S5. Different superscripts letters $^{a–c}$ in the same column indicate significant difference (<alpha> = 0.05). <LOQ: 0.05 mg/kg. GAE, Gallic Acid Equivalents; d.m., dry weight; 4-HB, hydroxybenzoic acid; p-C, para coumaric acid; caff, caffeic acid; t-fer, *trans*-ferulic acid; c-fer, *cis*-ferulic acid; Sin, sinapic acid. FB, BIO2 EP Type 1 flour; FI, ICARDA EP Type 1 flour; FG, Grossi EP Type 1 flour; FBo, cv. Bologna Type 1 flour; BB, bread produced using BIO2 EP; BI, bread produced using ICARDA EP; BG, bread produced using Grossi EP; BBo, bread produced using cv. Bologna.

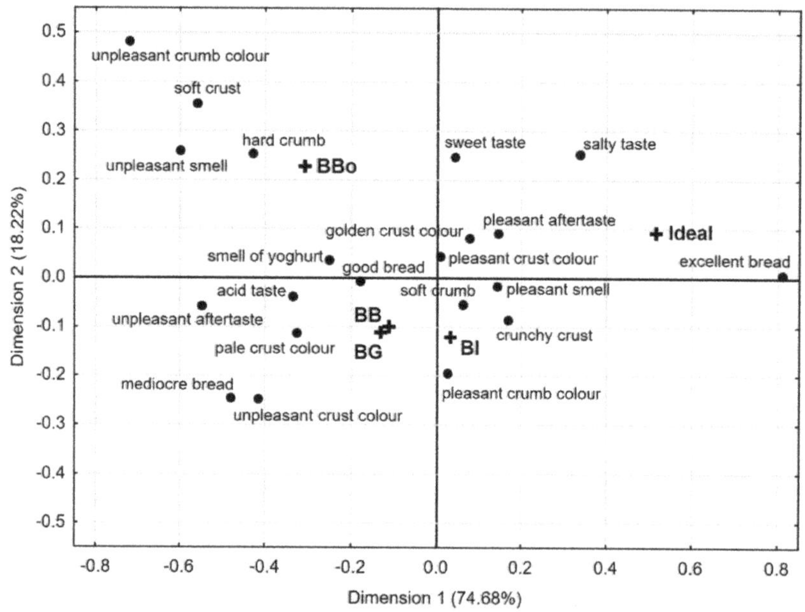

Figure 3. Correspondence analysis of the bread samples and sensory attributes. BB, bread produced using Bio2 EP; BI, bread produced using ICARDA EP; BG, bread produced using Grossi EP; BBo, bread produced using cv. Bologna.

Overall, CATA test provided different sensory profiles descriptive of the bread samples, thus allowing an evaluation of the similarities and differences between breads produced by different types of flours.

The average scores obtained from hedonic sensory evaluation for each attribute of bread samples were reported in Table 5.

Table 5. Sensory scores of breads obtained from acceptability test.

Bread	Texture		Colour		Appearance	Aroma	Taste	Overall Acceptability
	Crust	Crumb	Crust	Crumb				
BI	6.95 ^{b}	7.05 ^{a}	6.81 ^{a}	6.78 ^{ab}	7.05 ^{a}	6.51 ^{a}	6.69 ^{a}	7.02 ^{b}
BB	6.71 ^{b}	6.92 ^{a}	6.78 ^{a}	6.97 ^{b}	7.00 ^{a}	6.46 ^{a}	6.42 ^{a}	6.73 ^{ab}
BG	6.85 ^{b}	6.78 ^{a}	6.88 ^{a}	7.10 ^{b}	7.15 ^{a}	6.27 ^{a}	6.15 ^{a}	6.75 ^{ab}
BBo	6.08 ^{a}	6.41 ^{a}	6.83 ^{a}	6.39 ^{a}	6.59 ^{a}	6.24 ^{a}	6.08 ^{a}	6.36 ^{a}

Results are expressed as mean (n = 59). Standard deviation is reported in Table S6. Different superscripts letters $^{a–c}$ in the same column indicate significant differences among samples (<alpha> = 0.05). BB, bread produced using BIO2 EP; BI, bread produced using ICARDA EP; BG, bread produced using Grossi EP; BBo, bread produced using cv Bologna.

One-way ANOVA revealed significant differences (<alpha> = 0.05) between bread samples for crust texture, crumb colour and overall acceptability. More in detail, the crust texture of the breads made from EPs received significantly higher scores than the ones from the modern cv. Bologna (6.95, 6.85, 6.71 for BI, BG and BB, respectively). BG and BB were the preferred samples in terms of crumb colour (7.10 and 6.97, respectively), while BBo received the lowest score (6.39). In general, although overall acceptance was higher than 6 for all the breads, BI received the highest score (7.02), BG and BB had an intermediate score evaluation (6.75 and 6.73, respectively) and BBo resulted the least appreciated sample (6.36), thus integrating the results obtained with the CATA method.

4. Conclusions

The use of wheat (*Triticum aestivum.* L.) evolutionary populations cultivated in marginal areas under organic farming appeared to provide an environmental-friendly and market-oriented method to produce bread with an overall good nutritional quality (source of fibre) and final consumer perception. Moreover, this agricultural practice enhances the farmer's expertise, allowing them to play a fundamental role in agrobiodiversity preservation. To the best of our knowledge, this is the first study on the overall quality and sensory attributes of novel breads formulated using wheat EPs cultivated in large scale, and finally compared to bread produced using a modern bread wheat variety. Although the technological quality for EP flours, as measured by the processing industry (W, P/L), seemed unsuitable for bread making, the sourdough baking carried out during the present study allowed excellent workability of the EPs doughs and good structure of the loaves with regular alveolation. From a chemical and nutritional perspective, the breads were comparable, despite middlings requiring addition for FBo to produce the same commercial "Type" of flour (Type 1). Considering consumer perception, which is an important parameter to accounted for in new product development, the bread produced using EPs was associated with positive sensory characteristics. Finally, the combination of sensory and chemical analysis permitted a better description of the utilization of wheat EPs for breadmaking. Results herein presented are valuable to pave the way for further studies dedicated to the formulation of new foodstuffs exploiting the EP potential in a strong collaboration with farmers.

5. Study Limitations and Future Perspectives

The quality of wheat is dependent on genotype but also on climatic conditions [32]. Since this study is based on one source (one year of wheat production), the outcomes of the research should be confirmed by analysing flours obtained from more sowing seasons. This is even more true in recent years where climate change is showing its effects. EPs have been shown to guarantee a stable production in a climate change scenario [7] and it would be interesting to evaluate whether they can also guarantee a stable grain technological quality.

Future perspectives should include the characterization of breads from a physicochemical and technological point of view.

Supplementary Materials: The following supporting information can be downloaded at: https://www.mdpi.com/article/10.3390/foods11040495/s1, Figure S1: Fatty acids (FAs) profile of the different breads. Results are reported as cumulative percentage (%) of FAs. BB, bread produced using BIO2 EP; BI, bread produced using ICARDA EP; BG, bread produced using Grossi EP; BBo, bread produced using cv. Bologna; Figure S2: Correspondence analysis of the bread samples and sensory attributes including a Bologna type 00 control bread. BB, bread produced using Bio2 EP; BI, bread produced using ICARDA EP; BG, bread produced using Grossi EP; BBo t00, bread produced using cv. Bologna flour type 00; BBo t1, bread produced using cv. Bologna flour type 1. Table S1: Mass spectrometry characteristics of nicotinamide, nicotinic acid, thiamine, and folic acid. Table S2: Standard deviation (n = 3) of the grain quality parameters of EPs and cv. Bologna. Table S3: Standard deviation (n = 3) of the nutritional and chemical composition of the bread formulated using the wheat evolutionary population (BB, BI and BG) and bread produced using flour from cv. Bologna wheat (BBo). Table S4: Standard deviation (n = 3) of the micronutrients content in flours. Table S5: Standard deviation (n = 3) of the total phenolic content (TPC) and phenolic acid (PA) profile in their free (soluble) and bound (insoluble) forms. Table S6: Standard deviation (n = 59) of the sensory scores of breads obtained from acceptability test.

Author Contributions: M.S.: data discussion, manuscript writing; S.F., M.S., M.M. and C.D.: manuscript editing and revision; S.F., G.G., C.D. and R.R.: conceptualization, supervision; M.S., L.R. and L.C.: chemical data acquisition and elaboration; M.M. and C.D.: sensory analysis design and elaboration; M.S., R.D., G.D.P., M.D. and F.S.: nutritional data acquisition and discussion; A.B.: rheological data acquisition; M.M. and S.F.: flour preparation and rheological data discussion; G.G. and R.R.: project administration and funding acquisition. All authors have read and agreed to the published version of the manuscript.

Funding: This research was part of the project "Competitiveness increase of high hill and mountain farms through cereal biodiversity valorisation under organic farming—Bio2", supported by Regione Emilia-Romagna, Italy, through the Rural Development Programme 2014–2020—Operation Type 16.1.01—Focus Area 2A http://www.bioalquadrato.it/ (accessed on 7 November 2021).

Informed Consent Statement: Informed consent was obtained from all subjects involved in the study.

Data Availability Statement: All data included in this study are available upon request by contacting the corresponding author.

Acknowledgments: All authors are highly grateful to Salvatore Ceccarelli (Consultant freelance) and Cristina Piazza (STUARD demonstration farm, Parma, IT) for the invaluable technical assistance. Authors also thank Eleonora Carini (University of Parma) for useful suggestions in constructing the CATA test.

Conflicts of Interest: The authors declare no conflict of interest.

Ethical Statement: Prior to sensory analysis, volunteer panellists were informed about the aim of the study, its non-commercial objective, its anonymity and the possible use of the results for scientific purposes. The judges were informed about the bread composition. Panellists were bread regular consumers. Subjects suffering from gluten intolerance or allergy were not allowed to participate.

Abbreviations

BB	bread produced using BIO2 EP
BBo	bread produced using cv. Bologna;
BG	bread produced using Grossi EP;
BI	bread produced using ICARDA EP;
CATA	check-all-that-apply analysis;
CA	correspondence analysis;
EP	evolutionary wheat population;
ER	extraction rate;
FA	fatty acids;
FB	BIO2 EP Type 1 flour;
FBo	cv. Bologna Type 1 flour;
FG	Grossi EP Type 1 flour;
FI	ICARDA EP Type 1 flour;
GAE	gallic acid equivalents;
GC-MS	gas chromatography coupled to mass spectrometry;
HMWIDF	high molecular weight insoluble dietary fibre;
HMWSDF	high molecular weight soluble dietary fibre;
ICP-MS	inductively coupled plasma with mass spectrometer;
LMWSDF	low molecular weight soluble dietary fibre;
MUFA	monounsaturated fatty acids;
MRM	multiple reaction monitoring;
NIR	near infrared;
ANOVA	analysis of variance;
PUFA	polyunsaturated fatty acids;
SFA	saturated fatty acids;
TDF	total dietary fibre,
TPC	total phenolic content;
UHPLC-MS/MS	ultra-high-performance liquid chromatography coupled to tandem mass spectrometry;
UPLC-ESI-LTQ/MS	ultra-performance liquid chromatograph electrospray ionization coupled to linear trap quadrupole mass spectrometer.

References

1. Malézieux, E.; Crozat, Y.; Dupraz, C.; Laurans, M.; Makowski, D.; Ozier-Lafontaine, H.; Rapidel, B.; de Tourdonnet, S.; Val-antin-Morison, M. Mixing plant species in cropping systems: Concepts, tools and models: A review. *Agron. Sustain. Dev.* **2009**, *29*, 43–62. [CrossRef]
2. Bowles, T.M.; Mooshammer, M.; Socolar, Y.; Calderón, F.; Cavigelli, M.A.; Culman, S.W.; Deen, W.; Drury, C.F.; Garcia, A.G.Y.; Gaudin, A.C.M.; et al. Long-term evidence shows that crop-rotation diversification increases agricultural resilience to adverse growing conditions in North America. *One Earth* **2020**, *2*, 284–293. [CrossRef]
3. Weiner, J.; Andersen, S.B.; Wille, W.K.M.; Griepentrog, H.W.; Olsen, J.M. Evolutionary Agroecology: The potential for cooperative, high density, weed-suppressing cereals. *Evol. Appl.* **2010**, *3*, 473–479. [CrossRef] [PubMed]
4. Murphy, K.; Lammer, D.; Lyon, S.; Carter, B.; Jones, S.S. Breeding for organic and low-input farming systems: An evolutionary–participatory breeding method for inbred cereal grains. *Renew. Agric. Food Syst.* **2005**, *20*, 48–55. [CrossRef]
5. Suneson, C.A. An Evolutionary Plant Breeding Method 1. *J. Agron.* **1956**, *48*, 188–191. [CrossRef]
6. Ceccarelli, S.; Grando, S. Participatory plant breeding: Who did it, who does it and where? *Exp. Agric.* **2019**, *56*, 1–11. [CrossRef]
7. Ceccarelli, S.; Grando, S.; Maatougui, M.; Michael, M.; Slash, M.; Haghparast, R.; Rahmanian, M.; Taheri, A.; Al-Yassin, A.; Benbelkacem, A.; et al. Plant breeding and climate changes. *J. Agric. Sci.* **2010**, *148*, 627–637. [CrossRef]
8. Regulation (EU) 2018/848 of the European Parliament and of the Council of 30 May 2018 on Organic Production and Labelling of Organic Products and Repealing Council Regulation (EC) No 834/2007. Available online: https://eur-lex.europa.eu/legal-content/en/ALL/?uri=CELEX:32018R0848 (accessed on 7 November 2021).
9. Batur, F.; Bocci, R.; Bartha, B. Marketing Farmers' Varieties in Europe: Encouraging Pathways with Missing Links for the Recognition and Support of Farmer Seed Systems. *Agronomy* **2021**, *11*, 2159. [CrossRef]
10. Migliorini, P.; Spagnolo, S.; Torri, L.; Arnoulet, M.; Lazzerini, G.; Ceccarelli, S. Agronomic and quality characteristics of old, modern and mixture wheat varieties and landraces for organic bread chain in diverse environments of northern Italy. *Eur. J Agron.* **2016**, *79*, 131–141. [CrossRef]
11. Gobbetti, M.; Rizzello, C.G.; Di Cagno, R.; De Angelis, M. How the sourdough may affect the functional features of leavened baked goods. *Food Microbiol.* **2014**, *37*, 30–40. [CrossRef]
12. Poutanen, K.; Flander, L.; Katina, K. Sourdough and cereal fermentation in a nutritional perspective. *Food Microbiol.* **2009**, *26*, 693–699. [CrossRef] [PubMed]
13. Ferri, M.; Serrazanetti, D.I.; Tassoni, A.; Baldissarri, M.; Gianotti, A. Improving the functional and sensorial profile of cereal-based fermented foods by selecting Lactobacillus plantarum strains via a metabolomics approach. *Food Res. Int.* **2016**, *89*, 1095–1105. [CrossRef]
14. Filannino, P.; Bai, Y.; Di Cagno, R.; Gobbetti, M.; Gänzle, M.G. Metabolism of phenolic compounds by Lactobacillus spp. during fermentation of cherry juice and broccoli puree. *Food Microbiol.* **2015**, *46*, 272–279. [CrossRef] [PubMed]
15. Hersleth, M.; Berggren, R.; Westad, F.; Martens, M. Perception of bread: A comparison of consumers and trained assessors. *J. Food Sci.* **2005**, *70*, S95–S101. [CrossRef]
16. Guiné, R.P.F.; Bartkiene, E.; Florença, S.G.; Djekić, I.; Bizjak, M.Č.; Tarcea, M.; Leal, M.; Ferreira, V.; Rumbak, I.; Orfanos, P.; et al. Environmental Issues as Drivers for Food Choice: Study from a Multinational Framework. *Sustainability* **2021**, *13*, 2869. [CrossRef]
17. Valentin, D.; Chollet, S.; Lelièvre, M.; Abdi, H. Quick and dirty but still pretty good: A review of new descriptive methods in food science. *Int. J. Food Sci. Technol.* **2012**, *47*, 1563–1578. [CrossRef]
18. Varela, P.; Ares, G. Sensory profiling, the blurred line between sensory and consumer science. A review of novel methods for product characterization. *Food Res. Int.* **2012**, *48*, 893–908. [CrossRef]
19. Ares, G.; Antúnez, L.; Giménez, A.; Roigard, C.M.; Pineau, B.; Hunter, D.C.; Jaeger, S.R. Further investigations into the reproducibility of check-all-that-apply (CATA) questions for sensory product characterization elicited by consumers. *Food Qual. Prefer.* **2014**, *36*, 111–121. [CrossRef]
20. Nguyen, Q.C.; Wahlgren, M.B.; Almli, V.L.; Varela, P. Understanding the role of dynamic texture perception in consumers' expectations of satiety and satiation. A case study on barley bread. *Food Qual. Prefer.* **2017**, *62*, 218–226. [CrossRef]
21. Cunha, L.M.; Fonseca, S.C.; Lima, R.C.; Loureiro, J.; Pinto, A.S.; Vaz Patto, M.C.; Brites, C. Consumer-driven improvement of maize bread formulations with legume fortification. *Foods* **2019**, *8*, 235. [CrossRef]
22. Boukid, F.; Gentilucci, V.; Vittadini, E.; De Montis, A.; Rosta, R.; Bosi, S.; Dinelli, G.; Carini, E. Rediscovering bread quality of "old" Italian wheat (*Triticum aestivum* L. ssp. aestivum.) through an integrated approach: Physicochemical evaluation and consumers' perception. *LWT* **2020**, *122*, 109043. [CrossRef]
23. Piga, A.; Conte, P.; Fois, S.; Catzeddu, P.; Del Caro, A.; Sanguinetti, A.M.; Fadda, C. Technological, Nutritional and Sensory Properties of an Innovative Gluten-Free Double-Layered Flat Bread Enriched with Amaranth Flour. *Foods* **2021**, *10*, 920. [CrossRef]
24. Ares, G.; Tárrega, A.; Izquierdo, L.; Jaeger, S.R. Investigation of the number of consumers necessary to obtain stable sample and descriptor configurations from check-all-that-apply (CATA) questions. *Food Qual. Prefer.* **2014**, *31*, 135–141. [CrossRef]
25. *SR EN ISO 27971*; Cereals and Cereal Products—Common Wheat (*Triticum aestivum* L.). Determination of Alveograph Properties of Dough at Constant Hydration from Commercial or Test Flours and Test Milling Methodology; International Organization for Standardization: Geneva, Switzerland, 2008.

26. AACC International. *Approved Methods of Analysis*, 11th ed.; Method 08-12.01; Ash in Farina and Semolina; AACC International: St. Paul, MN, USA, 1999. Available online: https://www.cerealsgrains.org/resources/Methods/Pages/08TotalAsh.aspx (accessed on 7 November 2021).
27. Decreto Presidente della Repubblica 187. Regolamento per la Revisione della Normativa sulla Produzione e Commercializzazione di Sfarinati e Paste Alimentari. 2001. Available online: https://www.politicheagricole.it/flex/cm/pages/ServeBLOB.php/L/IT/IDPagina/2772 (accessed on 7 November 2021).
28. AOAC. *Official Methods of Analysis of the Association of Official Analytical Chemists 402*, 16th ed.; Science and Education: Washington, DC, USA, 1995.
29. Dall'Asta, C.; Cirlini, M.; Morini, E.; Rinaldi, M.; Ganino, T.; Chiavaro, E. Effect of chestnut flour supplementation on physico-chemical properties and volatiles in bread making. *LWT* **2013**, *53*, 233–239. [CrossRef]
30. *ISO/IEC 17025:2005*; General Requirements for the Competence of Testing and Calibration Laboratories; 2nd ed.; International Organization for Standardization: Geneva, Switzerland, 2005.
31. *UNI EN 13805:2014*; Foodstuffs—Determination of Trace Elements—Pressure Digestion; European Committee for Standardization: Brussels, Belgium, 2014.
32. Zaupa, M.; Calani, L.; Del Rio, D.; Brighenti, F.; Pellegrini, N. Characterization of total antioxidant capacity and (poly)phenolic compounds of differently pigmented rice varieties and their changes during domestic cooking. *Food Chem.* **2015**, *187*, 338–347. [CrossRef] [PubMed]
33. Singleton, V.L.; Orthofer, R.; Lamuela-Raventós, R.M. Analysis of total phenols and other oxidation substrates and antioxidants by means of folin-ciocalteu reagent. *Methods Enzymol.* **1999**, *299*, 152–178. [CrossRef]
34. Spaggiari, M.; Calani, L.; Folloni, S.; Ranieri, R.; Dall'Asta, C.; Galaverna, G. The impact of processing on the phenolic acids, free betaine and choline in Triticum spp. L. whole grains and milling by-products. *Food Chem.* **2020**, *311*, 125940. [CrossRef]
35. Leporati, A.; Catellani, D.; Suman, M.; Andreoli, R.; Manini, P.; Niessen, W.M.A. Application of a liquid chromatography tandem mass spectrometry method to the analysis of water-soluble vitamins in Italian pasta. *Anal. Chim. Acta* **2005**, *531*, 87–95. [CrossRef]
36. Mefleh, M.; Conte, P.; Fadda, C.; Giunta, F.; Piga, A.; Hassoun, G.; Motzo, R. From ancient to old and modern durum wheat varieties: Interaction among cultivar traits, management, and technological quality. *J. Sci. Food Agric.* **2019**, *99*, 2059–2067. [CrossRef]
37. Oury, F.X.; Berard, P.; Brancourt-Hulmel, M.; Heumez, E.; Pluchard, P.; Rousset, M.; Doussinault, G.; Rolland, B.; Trottet, M.; Giraud, A.; et al. Yield and Grain Protein Concentration in Bread Wheat: A Review and a Study of Multi-Annual Data from a French Breeding Program [Triticum aestivum L.]. *J. Genet. Breed.* **2003**, *57*, 59–68. Available online: https://agris.fao.org/agris-search/search.do?recordID=IT2005601351 (accessed on 7 November 2021).
38. Huen, J.; Börsmann, J.; Matullat, I.; Böhm, L.; Stukenborg, F.; Heitmann, M.; Zannini, E.; Arendt, E.K. Wheat flour quality evaluation from the baker's perspective: Comparative assessment of 18 analytical methods. *Eur. Food Res. Technol.* **2018**, *244*, 535–545. [CrossRef]
39. SIS (Società Italiana Sementi). Available online: http://www.sisonweb.com/images/allProdotti/Bologna%202015.pdf (accessed on 13 November 2021).
40. Heiniö, R.L.; Noort, M.W.J.; Katina, K.; Alam, S.A.; Sozer, N.; de Kock, H.L.; Hersleth, M.; Poutanen, K. Sensory characteristics of wholegrain and bran-rich cereal foods—A review. *Trends Food Sci. Technol.* **2016**, *47*, 25–38. [CrossRef]
41. Tavoletti, S.; Foligni, R.; Mozzon, M.; Pasquini, M. Comparison between fatty acid profiles of old and modern varieties of T. turgidum and T. aestivum: A case study in central Italy. *J. Cereal Sci.* **2018**, *82*, 198–205. [CrossRef]
42. Melis, S.; Delcour, J.A. Impact of wheat endogenous lipids on the quality of fresh bread: Key terms, concepts, and underlying mechanisms. *Compr. Rev. Food Sci. Food Saf.* **2020**, *19*, 3715–3754. [CrossRef]
43. EFSA Panel on Dietetic Products, Nutrition, and Allergies (NDA). Scientific Opinion on Dietary Reference Values for fats, including saturated fatty acids, polyunsaturated fatty acids, monounsaturated fatty acids, trans fatty acids, and cholesterol. *EFSA J.* **2016**, *8*, 1461.
44. Raninen, K.; Lappi, J.; Mykkänen, H.; Poutanen, K. Dietary fiber type reflects physiological functionality: Comparison of grain fiber, inulin, and polydextrose. *Nutr. Rev.* **2011**, *69*, 9–21. [CrossRef]
45. Anderson, J.W.; Baird, P.; Davis, R.H.; Ferreri, S.; Knudtson, M.; Koraym, A.; Waters, V.; Williams, C.L. Health benefits of dietary fiber. *Nutr. Rev.* **2009**, *67*, 188–205. [CrossRef]
46. European Commission. EU Register on Nutrition and Health Claims Made on Foods. 2006, OJEU. Available online: https://ec.europa.eu/food/safety/labelling_nutrition/claims/register/public/?event=register.home (accessed on 7 November 2021).
47. Amaral, O.; Guerreiro, C.S.; Gomes, A.; Cravo, M. Resistant starch production in wheat bread: Effect of ingredients, baking conditions and storage. *Eur. Food Res. Technol.* **2016**, *242*, 1747–1753. [CrossRef]
48. Djurle, S.; Andersson, A.A.M.; Andersson, R. Effects of baking on dietary fibre, with emphasis on β-glucan and resistant starch, in barley breads. *J. Cereal Sci.* **2018**, *79*, 449–455. [CrossRef]
49. Ma, S.; Wang, Z.; Liu, N.; Zhou, P.; Bao, Q.; Wang, X. Effect of wheat bran dietary fibre on the rheological properties of dough during fermentation and Chinese steamed bread quality. *Int. J. Food Sci. Technol.* **2021**, *56*, 1623–1630. [CrossRef]
50. AESAN/BEDCA. Base de Datos Española de Composición de Alimentos. 2018, V 1.0. Available online: https://www.bedca.net/bdpub/ (accessed on 7 November 2021).

51. Gnagnarella, P.; Parpinel, M.; Salvini, S.; Franceschi, S.; Palli, D.; Boyle, P. The update of the Italian Food Composition Database. *J. Food Comp. Anal.* **2004**, *17*, 509–522. [CrossRef]
52. U.S. Department of Agriculture (USDA), A. R. S. USDA National Nutrient Database for Standard Reference, Release 27. 2014, In Database. Available online: https://data.nal.usda.gov/dataset/composition-foods-raw-processed-prepared-usda-national-nutrient-database-standard-reference-release-27 (accessed on 7 November 2021).
53. Martins, Z.E.; Pinto, E.; Almeida, A.A.; Pinho, O.; Ferreira, I.M.P.L.V.O. Fibre fortification of wheat bread: Impact on mineral composition and bioaccessibility. *Food Funct.* **2017**, *8*, 1979–1987. [CrossRef] [PubMed]
54. Hart, D.J.; Fairweather-Tait, S.J.; Broadley, M.R.; Dickinson, S.J.; Foot, I.; Knott, P.; McGrath, S.P.; Mowat, H.; Norman, K.; Scott, P.R.; et al. Selenium concentration and speciation in biofortified flour and bread: Retention of selenium during grain biofortification, processing and production of Se-enriched food. *Food Chem.* **2011**, *126*, 1771–1778. [CrossRef] [PubMed]
55. Mihhalevski, A.; Nisamedtinov, I.; Hälvin, K.; Ošeka, A.; Paalme, T. Stability of B-complex vitamins and dietary fiber during rye sourdough bread production. *J. Cereal Sci.* **2013**, *57*, 30–38. [CrossRef]
56. Gobbetti, M.; De Angelis, M.; Di Cagno, R.; Calasso, M.; Archetti, G.; Rizzello, C.G. Novel insights on the functional/nutritional features of the sourdough fermentation. *Int. J. Food Microbiol.* **2019**, *302*, 103–113. [CrossRef]
57. Batifoulier, F.; Verny, M.A.; Chanliaud, E.; Rémésy, C.; Demigné, C. Variability of B vitamin concentrations in wheat grain, milling fractions and bread products. *Eur. J. Agron.* **2006**, *25*, 163–169. [CrossRef]
58. Brandolini, A.; Castoldi, P.; Plizzari, L.; Hidalgo, A. Phenolic acids composition, total polyphenols content and antioxidant activity of Triticum monococcum, Triticum turgidum and Triticum aestivum: A two-years evaluation. *J. Cereal Sci.* **2013**, *58*, 123–131. [CrossRef]
59. Abdel-Aal, E.S.M.; Rabalski, I. Effect of baking on free and bound phenolic acids in wholegrain bakery products. *J. Cereal Sci.* **2013**, *57*, 312–318. [CrossRef]
60. Anson, N.M.; Selinheimo, E.; Havenaar, R.; Aura, A.-M.; Mattila, I.; Lehtinen, P.; Bast, A.; Poutanen, K.; Haenen, G. Bioprocessing of wheat bran improves in vitro bioaccessibility and colonic metabolism of phenolic compounds. *J. Agric. Food Chem.* **2009**, *57*, 6148–6155. [CrossRef]
61. Tian, W.; Chen, G.; Tilley, M.; Li, Y. Changes in phenolic profiles and antioxidant activities during the whole wheat bread-making process. *Food Chem.* **2021**, *345*, 128851. [CrossRef]
62. Michalska, A.; Amigo-Benavent, M.; Zielinski, H.; del Castillo, M.D. Effect of bread making on formation of Maillard reaction products contributing to the overall antioxidant activity of rye bread. *J. Cereal Sci.* **2008**, *48*, 123–132. [CrossRef]
63. Fares, C.; Menga, V.; Codianni, P.; Russo, M.; Perrone, D.; Suriano, S.; Savino, M.; Rascio, A. Phenolic acids variability and grain quality of organically and conventionally fertilised old wheats under a warm climate. *J. Sci. Food Agric.* **2019**, *99*, 4615–4623. [CrossRef] [PubMed]
64. Katina, K.; Heiniö, R.-L.; Autio, K.; Poutanen, K. Optimization of sourdough process for improved sensory profile and texture of wheat bread. *LWT-Food Sci. Technol.* **2006**, *39*, 1189–1202. [CrossRef]

foods

MDPI

Review

The Role of Ancient Grains in Alleviating Hunger and Malnutrition

Mahsa Majzoobi [1,*], Shima Jafarzadeh [2], Shahla Teimouri [1], Mehran Ghasemlou [1], Milad Hadidi [3] and Charles S. Brennan [1]

1 Biosciences and Food Technology, RMIT University, Bundoora West Campus, Plenty Road, Melbourne, VIC 3083, Australia; shahla.teimouri2@rmit.edu.au (S.T.); mehran.ghasemlou2@rmit.edu.au (M.G.); charles.brennan@rmit.edu.au (C.S.B.)
2 School of Civil and Mechanical Engineering, Curtin University, Bentley, WA 6102, Australia; s.jafarzadehkhosravi@ecu.edu.au
3 Department of Organic Chemistry, Faculty of Chemical Sciences and Technologies, University of Castilla-La Mancha, 13001 Ciudad Real, Spain; milad.hadidi@gmail.com
* Correspondence: mahsa.majzoobi@rmit.edu.au

Abstract: Meeting the United Nation's sustainable development goals for zero hunger becomes increasingly challenging with respect to climate change and political and economic challenges. An effective strategy to alleviate hunger and its severe implications is to produce affordable, nutrient-dense, and sustainable food products. Ancient grains were long-forgotten due to the dominance of modern grains, but recently, they have been rediscovered as highly nutritious, healthy and resilient grains for solving the nutrition demand and food supply chain problems. This review article aims to critically examine the progress in this emerging field and discusses the potential roles of ancient grains in the fight against hunger. We provide a comparative analysis of different ancient grains with their modern varieties in terms of their physicochemical properties, nutritional profiles, health benefits and sustainability. A future perspective is then introduced to highlight the existing challenges of using ancient grains to help eradicate world hunger. This review is expected to guide decision-makers across different disciplines, such as food, nutrition and agronomy, and policymakers in taking sustainable actions against malnutrition and hunger.

Keywords: sustainable grains; combating hunger; malnutrition; ancient cereals

Citation: Majzoobi, M.; Jafarzadeh, S.; Teimouri, S.; Ghasemlou, M.; Hadidi, M.; Brennan, C.S. The Role of Ancient Grains in Alleviating Hunger and Malnutrition. *Foods* **2023**, *12*, 2213. https://doi.org/10.3390/foods12112213

Academic Editors: Laura Gazza and Francesca Nocente

Received: 29 April 2023
Revised: 27 May 2023
Accepted: 29 May 2023
Published: 31 May 2023

1. Introduction

Hunger is a major problem in developing countries, and it is mostly related to food shortages/famine caused by various factors, including environmental stresses, geo–economic and political issues. However, in developed countries where food is abundant, hidden hunger or malnutrition caused by an imbalanced intake of nutrients is often observed. Despite the fact that one of the Sustainable Development Goals (SDG, Goal 2) of the UN is to eradicate hunger by 2030, the incidences of hunger and food insecurity are increasing. Recent reports by the UN show that the number of people affected by hunger has increased rapidly over the last five years and has reached about 828 million people in 2021, with a prediction that it will affect 670 million people in 2030. In 2021, nearly 2.3 billion people (mostly women and children) were severely or moderately food insecure, and about 3.1 billion people could not afford a healthy diet [1]. With the increasing incidents of climate shocks, geopolitical issues and disruption of the food supply chain, achieving the UN goal of zero hunger has become more critical and also more challenging [2].

Among different food sources, cereals have great roles in tackling hunger since they are the main staple food around the world and have the greatest shares in providing energy and other vital nutrients for humans [3]. Thus, one of the strategies to achieve zero hunger is to maintain the genetic diversity of the grains and produce nutrient-dense grains with improved health benefits that are highly resistant to environmental stresses and diseases and also can be readily processed into quality foods (Goal 2: Zero Hunger—United Nations Sustainable Development).

In terms of genetic background, cereals are dived into "modern" and "ancient" cereals. Unlike modern grains, ancient grains are under-utilised crops that have not been selected by breeding programs [4]. Until now, many aspects of ancient grains have been discovered, including their nutrient and health benefits, physicochemical properties, food applications and their contribution to food sustainability and diversity [5–8]. Thus, it is critical to find more applications for ancient cereals, especially to address global food challenges.

The main aim of this review article is to discuss the opportunities and challenges of ancient cereals as versatile crops to address the UN SDG of zero hunger as well as the global issue of malnutrition. This review paper has collected previous knowledge published on all types of ancient cereals in terms of physicochemical properties, nutritional profile and food industry applications.

This collective information can be of interest to researchers, grain breeders, producers, food manufacturers, climate advocates and policymakers to obtain a better understanding of how ancient grains can diversify our foods, especially as a solution for global hunger. It can also assist the food industry in making informed decisions and include more ancient grains in food products to produce healthier and more sustainable foods.

2. Ancient Cereals

Ancient cereals are those species of grains that have not been subjected to any selection or breeding by humans and have maintained specific genetic properties from their wild ancestors, such as ear height, low harvest index, brittle rachis and brittle individual variation [4]. Ancient grains include varieties of wheat (Spelt, Khorasan wheat or Kamut, Einkorn and Emmer); green wheat, barley; wild rice, oats; sorghum; millets, and pseudo-cereals of teff, amaranth; buckwheat and quinoa. In some references, freekeh and bulgur have been considered ancient grains even though they are made from ordinary wheat [5].

Many ancient grains are ancestors of modern grains. For example, the crossing between a diploid species of chamois (*Aegilops tauschii* Coss.) and Emmer (ancient wheat) resulted in Spelt, which was mutated over several generations to convert into common wheat [6].

At the dawn of civilisation, ancient cereals used to provide a vital food source in the human diet. However, over the centuries, the selection of domesticated species with higher production yields and improved techno-functional properties has led to a dramatic decline in the production of other grains and the dominance of only a few grains—known as leading cereals—including wheat, rice, corn and barley [7]. This has generated significant food security concerns, especially with increasing the adverse impacts of climate change and supply chain disruptions due to the global pandemic and geopolitical and socioeconomic issues [8]. However, in recent years, ancient grains are regaining worldwide attention for a variety of reasons. The production of ancient grains is regarded as being environmentally friendly, generating low carbon footprints as they require less irrigation, pesticides and fertilisers compared to many normal grains. Ancient grains are also suitable for climate-smart agriculture since they can tolerate harsh growing conditions [9]. In addition, ancient grains are recognised as rich sources of nutrients and bioactive compounds with numerous health benefits [4]. Therefore, they are a key player in developing sustainable food systems and are well-positioned to tackle food insecurity caused by the ongoing climate change.

3. Ancient Grains vs. Modern Grains

The comparison between ancient and modern grains, especially in terms of composition and nutritional value, is still controversial and needs further accurate research. This is mostly because of the lack of comprehensive studies, as the full impacts of plant genetics (g), environmental factors € and their interactions (g $\times$ e) on the physicochemical properties of the grains have not been fully considered and determined in many studies, which hinders the accuracy of the findings [10]. However, from some previous studies that factored in the variables affecting the physicochemical properties of the grains, it is obvious that ancient grains have lower yields than modern grains, which is one of their main limitations. Nevertheless, increasing the yield of the modern grains diminishes their protein contents and other valuable nutrients that can negatively affect the health benefits and technological properties of the grains, such as quality of bread making [6]. Ancient grains are more tolerant to biotic and abiotic stresses [8] and often contain more protein, dietary fibre, bioactive compounds and antioxidant activity and show improved health benefits (see Tables 1 and 2).

Table 1. Chemical composition of ancient grains (%, dry basis).

Ancient Grains	Carbohydrate	Starch	Dietary Fibre	Protein	Lipid	Ash	References
Spelt wheat	68–72	52–65	10.7–13.9	14.6–15.7	1.7–1.9	1.7–1.9	[6,7]
Emmer wheat	63.5–68.5	52–65	7.2–12.0	14–16	1.8–2.8	2.1–2.3	[6]
Einkorn wheat	60–64	58–68	9.3–12.8	13.5–15.4	2.0–2.8	2.6–2.2	[6]
Barley	64–75%	59.1–61.6	12.8–17.2	11.7–13.6	1.4–3.9	1.5–4.5	[11]
Oat	75–80	54.9–63.6	8.5–13	10.0–15.0	3.0–8.0	1.7–1.9	[12]
Millet	65–80.6	62–70	1.52–4.65	6.2–14.5	1.2–8.2	0.73–3.3	[13]
Wild rice	71–84	56–79	1.15–1.93	10–15.5	0.7–1.23	1.1–2.0	[14]
Green wheat	73–80	45–68	12.0–19.0	11.0–15.0	1.32–2.7	0.8–2.0	[15]
Sorghum	57–83	55–79	1.0–7.4	7–15	2–3	0.68–4.2	[16,17]
Amaranth	63.8–65.2%	65–75%	6.7–11.4%	12.5–13.5%	5.7–7.2%	1.5–2.8%	[18,19]
Quinoa	65	58.1–64.2	16.5	12.8	3.9	2.4	[20]
Teff	67	-	12.1	13	5	2.2	[21]
Chia	3.4	-	21.1–33.3-	18.9	31.2	2.9	[22]
Buckwheat	65	54.5–57.4	13.8	15.1	2.9	1.9	[19,23]

Table 2. Major micronutrients, antioxidants and health benefits of the ancient grains.

Ancient Grains	Vitamins	Minerals	Main Antioxidants	Health Benefits	Ref.
Spelt	Vit. B1: 0.14–0.17 mg/100 g	Zn: 47 mg/kg Fe: 50 mg/kg P: 4.7 g/kg	Ferulic acids: 223–502 μg/g	Modulating postprandial glycemia and insulin level	[10]
Emmer	Vit. B1: 0.42 mg/100 g	Zn: 54 mg/kg Fe: 49 mg/kg P: 5.1 g/kg	Ferulic acids: 323–711 μg/g	Reducing total cholesterol, LDL cholesterol and blood glucose	[24]
Einkorn	Vit. B2: 0.45 mg/100 g	Zn: 36–84 mg/kg Fe: 32–85 mg/ kg Mn: 26–92 g/kg P: 5.2 g/kg Cu: 4.1–10 mg/kg	Ferulic acids: 207–442 μg/g	Enhancing blood carotenoid level, antioxidant activities that reduce cardiovascular disease and hypoallergenic effects	[6,25]
Barley	Vit. B1: 0.35 mg/100 g; Vit. B2: 0.091 mg/100 g Vit. E: 0.85–3.15 mg/100 g	Zn: 6–245 mg/kg Fe: 26–334 mg/kg P: 3320–5020 mg/kg	Ferulic acid: 4.5–102 mg/100 g	Reducing blood cholesterol levels and increasing insulin response in diabetics, lowering blood glucose levels, weight control, gut regulation, preventing colon cancer	[26]
Oats	Vit. B1: 50 mg/kg; Vit. B2: 1.4 mg/kg	Zn: 39 mg/kg Fe: 38 mg/kg P: 3.7 g/kg	Ferulic acids: 24–40.8 μg/100 g	Reducing the serum cholesterol, excellent antioxidant and anti-inflammatory activities, improving gut health and reducing risks of cardiovascular diseases	[27]

Table 2. *Cont.*

Ancient Grains	Vitamins	Minerals	Main Antioxidants	Health Benefits	Ref.
Millet	Vit. C: 0.04 mg/100 g Vit. A: 0.015 mg/100 g Vit. B1: 0.15–0.52 mg/100 g Vit. B2: 0.09–0.28 mg/100 g Vit. B3: 1.1–4.5 mg/100 g	Ca: 23–350 mg/100 g Fe: 1.18–53.39 mg/100 g P: 255–509 mg/100 g Zn: 0.73–4.2 mg/100 g Mg: 78–201 mg/100 g	TPC: 36–445 mg/100 g TFC: 51–202 mg/100 g Ferulic acid: 3.3–36.6 mg/100 g	Antioxidative and antiproliferative activities; therapeutic intervention in type 2 diabetes; alleviation of cardiovascular diseases, liver injury and cancer; lowering blood pressure.	[28]
Wild rice	Vit. B1: 0.30–0.63 mg/100 g Vit. B2: 0.07–0.2 mg/100 g Vit. E: 0.2–4.8 mg/100 g	Ca: 21–24 mg/100 g Fe: 1.60–3.17 mg/100 g Mg: 106–120 mg/100 g Mn: 0.93–1.45 mg/100 g P: 236–384 mg/100 g K: 145–244 mg/100 g Na: 1.34–5.86 mg/100 g Zn: 1.25–2.83 mg/100 g	TPC: 16.98–58.8 mg/100 g Ferulic acid: 24.1–35.5 mg/100 g Sinapic acid: 5.5–9.6 mg/100 g p-coumaric acid: 1.1–4.3 mg/100 g	Alleviation of insulin resistance and lipotoxicity; atherosclerosis prevention; anti-inflammatory, anti-hypertensive and immunomodulatory effects; antiobesity; antianaphylactic actions; prevention and treatment of cardiovascular disease; cholesterol-lowering and anti-atherogenic effects	[14,29]
Green wheat	Vit. B: 1.80 mg/100 g Vit. B2: 0.19 mg/100 g Vit. B3: 1.30 mg/100 g Vit. C: 4.5 mg/100 g Vit. E: 0.2–0.6 mg/100 g	Na: 4–12.5 mg/100 g Ca: 32–63 mg/100 g K: 369–451 mg/100 g Mg: 160–202 mg/100 g P:412 mg/100 g Cu: 0.49 mg/100 g	Ferulic acid: 1444 mg/100 g	Preventive and treatment effects on chronic degenerative diseases caused by oxidative stress; reducing the risk factors for obesity, diabetes, cardiovascular diseases and cancer; antianemia effects	[14,29,30]
Sorghum	Vit E: 1.95 mg/100 g α-tochopherol: 0.122–0.525 mg/100 g Vit A (β-carotene): 0.054–0.134 mg/100 g Thiamine: 0.08 mg/100 g Riboflavin: 0.21 mg/100 g Pyridoxine: 0.17 mg/100 g	Ca: 665.6 mg/100 g Fe: 168.8 mg/100 g K: 26,940 mg/100 g Mn: 141.2 mg/100 g Na: 292.5 mg/100 g P: 32,727 mg/100 g Zn: 432.8 mg/100 g Mg: 12,010 mg/100 g	TPC: 109–1040 mg/100 g TFC: 11–61 mg/100 g Ferulic acid: 2.40–86.8 mg/100 g caffeic acid: 1.43–8.17 mg/100 g p-coumaric acid: 0.68–8.17 mg/100 g	Reducing the risk of cardiovascular disease, cancer, diabetes, dyslipidaemia and coeliac disease; antiallergic properties	[16,31–40]
Amaranth	Vit. B3: 64.4 mg/100 g Vit. E: 1.54 mg/100 g Vit. C: 64.4 mg/100 g	Fe: 7.61 mg/100 g Zn: 287 mg/100 g Mg: 248 mg/100 g Mn: 3.3 mg/100 g P: 508 mg/100 g Cal: 159 mg/100 g	Protocatechuic *p*-Hydroxybenzoic *p*-coumaric Ferulic acid	Anti-radical Antioxidant Anti-inflammatory Anti-diabetic Anti-cancer Improving gut health	[23,41]
Quinoa	Vit. B3: 0.01–8 mg/100 g Vit. E: 24.7 mg/100 g Vit. C: 4–49.3 mg/100 g Folate: 0.2 mg/100 g	Fe: 5.5 mg/100 g Zn: 1.8 mg/100 g Mg: 206 mg/100 g Cal: 32.9 mg/100 g	Gallic acid Caffeic acid Ferulic acid p-coumaric p-Hydroxybenzoic acid Vanillic acid	Antioxidant activity Anti-obesity Antimicrobial Skin protection Anti-inflammatory Anti-diabetic Preventing cardiovascular disease and childhood malnutrition Improving gut health	[23,41]
Teff	Vit. B1: 0.3 mg/100 g Vit. B3: 3.3 mg/100 g Vit. E: 0.08 mg/100 g Vit. C: 88 mg/100 g	Fe: 7.63 mg/100 g Zn: 3.63 mg/100 g Mg: 184 mg/100 g P: 427 mg/100 g K: 427 mg/100 g Cal: 180 mg/100 g	Catechin Ferulic acid Rosmarinic acid *p*-coumaric acid	Anti-radical Antioxidant Anti-inflammatory	[42]
Chia	Vit. B2: 0.17 mg/100 g Vit. B3: 8.83 mg/100 g Vit. B1: 0.62 mg/100 g Vit. E: 8.1 mg/100 g Vit. C: 1.6 mg/100 g	Ca: 455 mg/100 g P: 585 mg/100 g K: 585 mg/100 g MG: 340 mg/100 g Fe: 8.54 mg/100 g Zn: 3.7 mg/100 g	Caffeic acid Chlorogenic acid Quercetin Kaempferol	Anti-hypertensive Antioxidant activity Anticholesterolemic Anthropometrics Hypoglycemic	[22,43]
Buckwheat	Vit. B3: 2.1–18 mg/100 g Vit. E: 9.5–16.4 mg/100 g	Fe: 4.7 mg/100 g Zn: 1.0 mg/100 g Mg: 203 mg/100 g Ca: 60.9 mg/100 g	Rutin Ferulic acid caffeic acid gallic acid *p*-Coumaric	Anti-inflammatory Anti-hypertensive Antioxidant activity Anti-obesity Antidiabetic activity Anti-cancer Improving gut health	[41,44]

Comparing ancient wheat and modern wheat for their potential to elicit coeliac disease has found similar immunoreactivity of both cultivars and, hence, the breeding of modern wheat is not responsible for the prevalence of coeliac disease [45,46].

Preliminary in vivo and in vitro studies indicated that the consumption of different ancient grains could be better tolerated by non-coeliac wheat-sensitive individuals and those who suffer from irritable bowel syndrome. However, children aged 3–13 years old with wheat sensitivity seem to show similar reactions to both ancient and modern wheat cultivars.

A few individuals only sensitised to alpha-amylase/trypsin inhibitor showed no reaction to Einkorn since the corresponding gene is missing in this grain [47]. For wheat grains, it has been reported that the starch digestibility of bread made with ancient wheat and modern wheat is not related to the release year of the cultivar and indicated it is doubtful that the wheat breeding program has affected starch digestibility [48].

Ancient wheat and barley are considered gluten-containing grains and are unsafe for coeliac patients. Although ancient wheat has higher gluten than modern wheat, their gliadins are in the form of more digestible and less toxic but still unsafe for coeliac patients [18,49].

4. Physicochemical, Nutritional Profile and Health Benefits of the Ancient Grains

4.1. Wheat

Archaeological evidence shows that wheat most likely appeared first in Lebanon, Syria, Turkey, Egypt and Ethiopia. The domestication of wheat is likely to have begun around 10,000 years ago in the Fertile Crescent, and since then, wheat has been regarded as the most cultivated crop in the world [25]. The most common ancient wheat species include Einkorn (*Triticum monococcum*), Emmer (*Triticum dicoccum*), Khorasan (*Triticum turgidum* ssp. *turanicum*) and Spelt (*Triticum spelta*). Wheat grains have lengths mainly between 5 and 9 mm and shapes that may vary from spherical to flattened. The 1000-kernel weight of Spelt is ~44 g, which is much higher than that of Einkorn (~28 g) [50]. As shown in Table 1, Einkorn and Emmer wheat are typically composed of 53–72% carbohydrates (mainly starch), 12.5–12.7% protein, 10.6–12.5% dietary fibre, 2.1% lipids and 1–3% minerals. The main interest in the worldwide adaptation of ancient wheat species could be related to their high protein contents and production yield and their high tolerance to many biotic and abiotic stresses. The high-yielding modern wheat produced by breeding programs often have lower protein content than ancient grains. Higher protein contents (~18%) in Einkorn wheat than other cultivars of Emmer (~15%) and Spelt (~13%) have been reported [6]. Ancient wheat species contain slightly lower carbohydrate contents than modern wheat. Within the ancient wheat group, Spelt and Einkorn have the lowest carbohydrate contents (~67–69%). The starch content of ancient wheat species is often lower than modern cultivars, and its composition varies greatly from modern wheat. For instance, Einkorn has lower resistant starch content (25.6 g/kg) than modern wheat (30–88 g/kg), whereas Spelt, Emmer and Einkorn contain 30–32% rapidly digestible starch, 26–59% slowly digestible starch and 2.3–2.4% resistant starch [51]. Einkorn showed a higher content of lipids compared to common wheat. Modern wheat varieties may have a rich content of mineral and dietary fibre compared to Einkorn and Emmer wheat. Ancient wheat species also contain fewer anti-nutrients than common wheat. The phytic acid contents of the Einkorn and Emmer wheat were between 1594 and 1863 mg/100 g [52].

A comparison between old and modern wheat cultivars showed higher health-relevant benefits of old cultivars. It has been indicated that the consumption of bakery products made with Khorasan wheat can enhance the immune functions in patients with severe symptoms and sleep disorders [6].

4.2. Green Wheat (Freekeh)

Premature green wheat, or freekeh, is an ancient whole grain with a history spanning thousands of years. Green wheat is produced from wheat harvested early, at the end of the milky stage, when culms and spikes are green. Grain shape, plumpness and greenness determine the quality of freekeh. Green wheat has a high initial moisture content that varies from 40–45% (wet basis), but during the drying process, it loses about 40% of its weight [30,53,54]. Depending on moisture content, kernel length, width and thickness differ from 6.24 to 6.66 mm, 3.65 to 4.22 mm and 3.43 to 3.85 mm, respectively. In addition, the mass of 1000 seeds varies from 15 to 51 g at different maturation stages [55]. To produce green wheat, often, immature durum wheat (*Triticum durum*) and, sometimes, immature bread wheat (*Triticum aeisvum*) are used. The *Zenit* and *Diyarbakır* spp. durum wheat is favoured for this purpose [30,56].

Green wheat is used as a raw material in the production of many foods and healthy drinks. Roasted green wheat, which is commonly known as freekah (also known as frekeh or frikah), has been a popular staple food in Middle Eastern, North African, and Chinese cuisines for centuries. Roasting improves the flavour of the grains; however, it causes huge losses to their nutritional quality [30].

Green wheat contains 73–80% carbohydrates, 11–15% protein and 12–19% dietary fibre (Table 1). The starch content of green wheat is 45% and 68%, and its resistant starch content is about 8.0 to 10%. Due to its higher resistant starch and dietary fibre content and lower GI (52–54) compared to wheat, green wheat is more suitable for people with diabetes and for weight control.

Green wheat has a significantly greater proportion of essential amino acids, particularly lysine, methionine and threonine, and has better protein digestibility than normal wheat. Its total fatty-acid content varies from 1.32 to 2.7%, which is higher than that of yellow wheat. Palmitic acid is the dominant saturated fatty acid, and linoleic acid is the dominant unsaturated fatty acid [56].

The total mineral content in green wheat is higher than that in mature yellow wheat. Green wheat is a rich source of bioactive compounds. The total phenolic content, flavonoid content and antioxidant properties of green wheat are about twice that of wheat. Nevertheless, green wheat contains antinutrient compounds, such as phytate (660–700 mg/100 g), which is formed during the maturation of the seeds [30,56]. The freekeh grains harvested at earlier stages have the lowest phytic acid and phytate contents, which are nutritionally quite desirable [55]. The food applications of freekeh are limited to some traditional and homemade foods; however, due to increased knowledge about the nutritional and health benefits of green wheat, an increase in the global consumption of green wheat is expected. A few studies have shown the applications of green wheat in the formulation of healthy foods. For example, it has been found that the inclusion of green-wheat flour in the preparation of noodles can enhance the quality of the noodles and reduce their predicted GI [30].

4.3. Barley

Barley is a highly nutritious and adaptable ancient grain crop with growing cultivation all over the world. It is globally cultivated as the fourth most popular cereal in terms of production after wheat, rice and corn. Barley may have originated in Southeast Asia, including China, Tibet and Nepal [57]. There is limited information on the domestication of barley grains. A study reported the genome sequences of ancient barley grains excavated at Yoram Cave in the Judean Desert in Israel [58]. This report suggested that barley grains cultivated in the present day closely resemble those of old cultivars, although there is evidence for gene flow between the two populations. Barley grains are generally larger than wheat, with a 1000-kernel weight of about 40–45 g, and appear with a bright, light-yellow colour. Typical barley cultivars have distinct two-layered cells with adherent hulls departed at harvest maturity. However, hull-less varieties of barley have a low prevalence but are cultivated from certain seeds [59]. Today, more than 70% of barley grains are used for animal feed, about 20% are used for malting and brewing industries, and only a very small fraction is directly used in the human diet [57].

The chemical composition and nutritional profile of barley are given in Tables 1 and 2, respectively. Generally, barley contains protein (10–17%), carbohydrates (~65–68%), lipids (2–4%), dietary fibres (18–22%), β-glucan (4–9%), minerals (1.5–2.5%) and vitamins (~2%). It contains ~14–20% rapidly digestible starch, ~20–25% slowly digestible starch and about

2.2% resistant starch that would help regulate the rate of glucose release in barley-containing foods in the human body. Barley kernel contains several bioactive compounds, including β-glucans, lignans, phytosterols and polyphenols. The relatively high β-glucan content present in barley helps to lower serum cholesterol levels and control blood glucose and insulin resistance. Barley is also a good potential source of a range of vitamins, including B1 (0.35 mg/100 g), B2 (0.091 mg/100 g) and E (0.85–3.15 mg/100 g). More recently, research has focused on the nutritional profiles of germinated barley grains as a food ingredient that could be rich in antioxidant compounds useful in functional food applications [60].

4.4. *Barley*

Barley is a highly nutritious and adaptable ancient grain crop with growing cultivation all over the world. It is globally cultivated as the fourth most popular cereal in terms of production after wheat, rice, and corn. Barley may have been originated from South-Eastern Asia including China, Tibet and Nepal [55]. There is limited information on domestication of barley grains. A study reported the genome sequences of ancient barley grains excavated at Yoram Cave in the Judean Desert in Israel [56]. This report suggested that barley grains cultivated in present-day closely resemble those of old cultivars, although there is evidence for gene flow between the two populations. Barley grains are generally larger than wheat with a 1000 kernel weight of about 40–45 g and appear with a bright, light-yellow colour. Typical barley cultivars have distinct two-layered cell with adherent hulls departed at harvest maturity. However, hull-less varieties of barley have a low prevalence but are cultivated from certain seeds [57]. Today, more than 70% of barley grains are used for animal feed; about 20% are used for malting and brewing industries; and only a very small fraction is directly used in human diet [55].

The chemical composition and nutritional profile of barley are given in Tables 1 and 2, respectively. Generally, barley contains protein (10–17%), carbohydrates (~65–68%), lipids (2–4%), dietary fibres (18–22%), β-glucan (4–9%), minerals (1.5–2.5%), and vitamins (~2%). It contains ~14–20% rapidly digestible starch, ~20–25% slowly digestible starch and about 2.2% resistant starch that would help regulate rate of glucose release barley containing foods in human body. Barley kernel contains several bioactive compounds including β-glucans, lignans, phytosterols and polyphenols. The relatively high β-glucan content present in barley, helps to lower serum cholesterol levels, control blood glucose and insulin resistance. Barley is also a good potential source for a range of vitamins including B1 (0.35 mg/100 g), B2 (0.091 mg/100 g), and E (0.85–3.15 mg/100 g). More recently research has focussed on the nutritional profiles of germinated barley grains as a food ingredient which could be rich in antioxidant compounds useful in functional food applications [58].

4.5. *Oats*

Oat (*Avena* L., *Poaceae* family) is a valuable cereal crop in many countries with a primary usage for animal feed, but due to its health benefits, its food applications are growing rapidly. However, the world production of oat for human food is still lower than other grains due to the lower yield and high cost of production and transport (due to the low density of oat grains) [30]. Oats have a 1000-kernel weight of about 34–35 g and have been grown from ancient times in many parts of the world, particularly in Northern and Eastern Europe [61].

As shown in Table 1, oats contain carbohydrates (75–80%), protein (10–15%), lipids (3–8%) and β-glucan (4%). In contrast to other cereals, a distinguished feature of oat grains is their high protein content and distinct and balanced amino acid composition. The amino acid composition of oat grains is superior to that of other cereals because its major storage protein is globulin, with higher concentrations of essential amino acids such as lysine than other cereals [62]. Oats are rich in carbohydrates, including ~60% starch with about 15% rapidly digestible starch, 8–9% slowly digestible starch and 76% resistant starch [63].

As shown in Table 2, oat is a highly nutritious crop and a rich source of soluble dietary fibre (β-glucan), functional and bioactive compounds, fatty acids (e.g., linoleic and oleic acids) and minerals, especially calcium, iron and zinc. These bioactive ingredients have been shown to enhance the antioxidant content of foods such as crackers or biscuits compared to wheat flour, thus indicating a potential use of oat flour as a nutritional enhancer for the food industry. The main nutritional implications and health benefits of oats in human diets are attributed to the presence of a significant amount of β-glucan that reduces blood cholesterol and glucose [63]. Phytic acids (270–290 mg/100 g) and tannins (38–46 mg/100 g) are the main antinutrients in oat [27].

4.6. Sorghum

Sorghum is a drought-tolerant cereal belonging to the *Poaceae* grass family and originating in the northeast quadrant of Africa. It is the world's fifth most important cereal after wheat, rice, maize and barley, with over 58.7 million tons of total production in 2020. The United States is the most significant producer of this crop, followed by Nigeria, Ethiopia, India, Mexico and China [31,32]. Sorghum is a very genetically diverse crop, with over 24 diverse species identified to date. Notable among these is *S. bicolor*, known for its food use and considered one of the most important species in modern commercial breeding programs. *S. bicolor* originated from its wild progenitor *Sorghum bicolor* L. Moench subsp. *Verticilliflorum*. *Sorghum bicolor* (L.) Moench is categorised into five major races: *bicolor* (the primitive type), *guinea*, *caudatum*, *kafir* and *durra* with various physical and biochemical properties [27]. Sorghum varieties have been classified based on different characteristics. However, based on the end-use applications, sorghum is classified into five groups, including sweet sorghum (syrup and biofuel), grain (biofuel, human food and animal feed), fibre, forage/fodder (animal feed) and broomcorn (broom-making) [32].

Sorghum has small seeds with pigmented pericarp, and the most commercially available varieties are black, white and red [16,33]. White sorghum is used for food products, while red sorghum is utilised primarily in the alcohol distillation industry [34]. Sorghum grains are ovoid with one end more pointed; the grain diameter ranges between 4 and 8 mm, and the mean weight of 1000 grains varies from 20 to 60 g. As shown in Table 1, starch is the main component of sorghum (about 70%); however, sorghum grains show the highest content of resistant starch (4–21%) and lowest starch digestibility (~19–37% rapidly digestible starch) and glycemic index among cereal crops [35].

The major protein fractions in sorghum are prolamins (kafirins), followed by glutelins; however, it has a low content of essential amino acids such as lysine, methionine and isoleucine [36].

The lipid in sorghum grains is made up of saturated fats and a high concentration of unsaturated fatty acids. Sorghum, especially red sorghum, is a rich source of various phytochemicals, mainly phenolic acid (mostly ferulic acid), flavonoids and tannins, with substantial health-promoting effects (Table 2).

Sorghum grains, especially pigmented grains, have limited applications as human foods due to the presence of condensed tannins contributing to bitter taste, phytates, cyanogenic glycosides and trypsin inhibitors, which are considered the major antinutritional factors. However, varying food-processing methods such as sprouting, cooking, fermentation, steaming and flaking can reduce the antioxidants in sorghum [36]. In addition, low-tannin sorghum varieties have been identified and bred that have been used as an alternative for corn to feed animals [37]. It is also possible to reduce the tannin content of sorghum using food-processing methods such as milling followed by soaking in 0.3% Na_2CO_3 solution for 8 h [38]. Novel applications of sorghum include the production of plant-based protein, healthy foods and gluten-free products, and ethanol and biofuel production has emerged [39]. The digestibility of sorghum starch has been shown to vary dependent upon variety and may therefore be a useful flour-based ingredient for the optimisation of the glycaemic index of starch-based foods [40].

4.7. Millet

Millets are small-seeded species of cereal crops belonging to the family *Poaceae*, which originated in the arid and semi-arid regions of Asia and Africa. It has a short growing season and is resistant to pests and diseases. Millet has five genera: Panicum, Setaria, Echinochloa, Pennisetum and Paspalum [57]. The most important cultivated varieties of millets are foxtail millet (*Setaria italica*), pearl millet (*Pennisetum glaucum*), proso millet (*Panicum miliaceum*), barnyard millet (*Echinochola crusgalli*), finger millet (*Eleusine coracana*), brown top millet (*Panicum ramosum*), kodo millet (*Paspalum scrobiculatum*) and teff millet (*Eragrostis tef*). Millet is the sixth most high-yielding grain in the world, with a total annual production of 30.4 million tons, but is still considered an underutilised grain [31,57]. Millet seeds have small and round shapes with different colours. The seed size varies between 3 and 4 mm, the 1000-kernel weight of millet varieties is about 2.5–3.0 g and the bulk density and true density are about 0.67–0.55 gmL^{-1} and 1.36–1.79 gmL^{-1}, respectively [57,64]. As shown in Table 1, the main constituent of millet is its starch (62 to 70%), and some reports indicated that millet contains about 4–5% resistant starch, 6–7% slowly digestible starch and ~10–11% rapidly digestible starch (RDS) [65]. The second major component of millet is protein. The amino acid profile of pearl millet is better than that of sorghum and maize, and is comparable to that of wheat, barley and rice, and lysine is the first limited amino acid in millet cultivars [66]. Among millets, finger millet is relatively better balanced in essential amino acids because it contains more lysine, threonine and valine. The crude fat content in finger millet has been reported in the range of 1.54 to 3.77%. Linolenic acid and oleic acid are the two dominant fatty acids in the millet varieties [67].

Among millets, finger millet is the richest source of calcium and iron, with levels higher than those of sorghum, barley, maize and wheat. Millet grains are rich in several phytochemicals, particularly phenolic compounds. Finger millet has been shown to have the highest phenolic content and antioxidant activities compared to proso and foxtail millets [67]. Millets also have antinutrients, such as phytic acid (296–620 mg/100 g), tannins (31–343 mg/100 g) and trypsin inhibitors, which may reduce the bioavailability of minerals [28]. Millets are often subjected to different processing methods such as dehulling, decortication, soaking, germination, malting, milling, cooking, roasting, popping, radiation and fermentation to improve the nutritional and sensory properties of millets for developing new food (Xiu et al., 2022). Millet has some food applications, including the production of gluten-free foods, bakery products and porridge [28,68].

4.8. Wild Rice

Wild rice, known as a health-promoting grain, is the seed of an aquatic plant belonging to the genus Zizania, family *Poaceae* [29]. Wild rice (*Zizania* spp.) originated from North America over 10,000 years ago and then dispersed into East Asia and other parts of the world [69]. It consists of four species: *Zizania palustris* L., *Zizania aquatica* L., *Zizania texana* H. and *Zizania latifolia* G [14].

The seeds of wild rice have long and narrow cylindrical shapes approximately 4.7 to 9.2 mm long and 1.6–2.8 mm wide. The grain colour of these wild rice varies from light red–brown to dark brown with a 1000-kernel weight of 23–37 g [69]. As shown in Tables 1 and 2, wild rice is rich in minerals, vitamins, starch, dietary fibre, protein and antioxidant phytochemicals, and is low in fat. Wild rice contains about 56–79% starch as the main constituent. Wild rice starch has shorter chains of amylose and longer chains of amylopectin, which causes a slower in vitro digestion rate compared to that of domesticated rice. It contains about 60% rapidly digestible starch, ~4% slowly digestible starch and ~5% resistant starch [14,29]. The resistant starch content of the wild rice is about 10.8%, which is significantly higher than white rice (~1.4%) and red rice (~0.95%). It also contains about 6.8% dietary fibre content, which is considerably higher than that of red rice (~2.6%) and white rice (~0.42%) [70].

Protein (10–15.5%) is the second main constituent of wild rice, which is much higher in content and efficiency ratio than that in white rice (~10%) and red rice (~11%). The essential amino-acid profile of wild rice is generally better and more balanced than that of other grains. Threonine and lysine are the limiting amino acids in all varieties of wild rice [14,69].

As a whole grain, wild rice is a rich source of phenolic compounds and flavonoids, and this level of antioxidant phenolic compounds is 10–15 times higher than that of white rice. Ferulic acid is the predominant phenolic acid, followed by sinapic acid and p-coumaric acid. Other phytochemical constituents of wild rice are flavonoid glycosides and flavan-3-ols. In addition to phenolic compounds, anthocyanins and carotenoids such as lutein were found in wild rice, thus providing a more complete profile of the antioxidants in wild rice [14,69,70]. Traditionally, wild rice has been exploited to treat a variety of ailments in Chinese medicinal practice [29]. Several health benefits of wild rice are listed in Table 2.

4.9. *Amaranth*

Amaranth (*Amaranthus* spp.), a pseudocereal and a member of the *Amaranthaceae* family, is a less explored species with an excellent nutritional profile for human consumption. Amaranth has a diverse range of 60 species but has three common species (*Amaranth hypochodriacus, Amaranth cruentus* and *Amaranth caudatus*) domesticated for their seeds [71]. China is the largest producer of amaranth in the world, followed by the United States, Canada and Argentina. Owing to its high nutritional quality, such as balanced content of essential amino acids and unsaturated fatty acids, as well as being gluten-free, amaranth is gaining importance among consumers, food producers and the scientific community [72]. Amaranth protein contains a high amount of lysine, which is a limited amino acid in almost all cereals and other pseudocereal grains [73]. Its protein is also abundant in cysteine and methionine, two essential amino acids that contain sulphur. The *Amaranthus* species is recognised as a source of important vitamins, such as vitamin C, carotene, folate and B_6, among cereals and vegetables (see Table 2). Aside from its nutritional value, amaranth grain includes several bioactive compounds with potential health benefits. The total phenolic content in amaranth grains ranges from 21.2 to 57.0 mg gallic acid/100 g dry weight, mainly containing ferulic acid followed by quercetin and isorhamnetin. Phytate (0.09%) and saponins (4.96 mg/100 g) are the main antinutrients in amaranth [23,74].

4.10. *Quinoa*

Quinoa (*Chenopodium quinoa* Willd.) is a pseudocereal commonly known as the "golden grain" and has long been considered a source of nourishment and sustenance for Andean indigenous societies. Quinoa grain is mainly cultivated in the South American Andes region; however, over the past decades, it has been introduced in North America, Europe, Africa and Australia. Quinoa production has continuously expanded over the last few decades, and by 2013, the international year of quinoa, quinoa production and consumption had increased dramatically [23,74].

Quinoa flour is used to make a variety of toasted and baked goods, including bread, cookies, biscuits, noodles, pasta and pancakes. In addition, quinoa grains can be fermented to produce alcoholic beverages such as beer owing to its high starch level. Owing to its high nutritional quality and adaptability, quinoa is traditionally used in livestock feeding. Quinoa grains contain no gluten. Additionally, it has a high amount of nutrient ingredients such as proteins, dietary fibres, vitamins, fatty acids and minerals (see Tables 1 and 2 for chemical composition and nutritional profile). The protein content of quinoa grains varied from 12.8 to 16.7%, which is higher than those of corn, rice and barley. The two main storage proteins in quinoa grain are albumins (35%) and globulins (37%). Quinoa proteins are recognised as high-quality proteins due to their great amount and well-balanced composition of essential amino acids. Quinoa protein contains a high concentration of lysine (2.4–7.8 g/100 g protein), methionine (0.3–9.1 g/100 g protein) and threonine (2.1–8.9 g/100 g protein), which are the limiting amino acids in ancient cereals such as maize and wheat [23,74,75].

Similar to other grains, starch is the most important carbohydrate component (32–69% of total carbohydrates). Its total dietary fibre content (7.0–16.5%) is comparable to modern cereals such as wheat. In addition to having a high protein content and good bioavailability, quinoa also has an intriguing lipid content (3.9–7.4%) that is higher than that of wheat and rice, making it a viable oil seed alternative source. The vitamin content, such as for vitamin C, E and folic acid, are greater than those of most other grains, and there is great potential to use quinoa as a functional food ingredient in mainstay food-processing applications. Quinoa has several health benefits in high-risk groups such as children and the elderly, as well as having prebiotic and probiotic effects [41]. However, it also contains phytate, saponin, tannins and protease inhibitor as the main antinutrients [18].

4.11. *Teff*

Teff (*Eragrostis tef*) is a nutritious, gluten-free pseudocereal grain that is native to Ethiopia and Eritrea. It is a staple food in these countries and is often used to make traditional dishes such as injera (a sour fermented pancake-like flat bread). Teff is a rich source of protein (12–15%) and fibre (6–8%) [21]. Teff contains a high level of lysine, which is an essential amino acid that is important for growth and tissue repair. Teff is a good source of minerals, including iron and calcium, which are beneficial for individuals with anaemia or osteoporosis. Teff is also a good source of resistant starch, which can help improve digestion and blood sugar control [18,21].

Teff also contains a variety of phytochemicals and antioxidants, including phenolic acids and flavonoids, which have been shown to have anti-inflammatory and anti-cancer properties and can reduce the risk of chronic diseases [42].

Phytic acid, tannins and protease inhibitors are the main antinutritional factors in teff [21]. To minimise the negative effects of these compounds, traditional methods of processing, such as fermentation, soaking and germination, can be used to reduce the levels of anti-nutritional compounds in teff. Teff can be ground into flour and used to make a variety of baked goods, including bread, pancakes and cakes. It can also be cooked and eaten as a porridge or added to salads and stews. Phytate, tannins, oxalates and saponins are the main antinutrients in teff [21,76].

4.12. *Chia*

Chia (*Salvia hispanica*) is a pseudocereal native to Mexico and Central America. It is a member of the mint family (*Lamiaceae*) and is closely related to other species such as sage and oregano. The chia seeds are small and oval in shape, measuring about 1–2 mm in diameter. They are black, brown or white in colour and have a glossy surface. The chia plant is drought-tolerant, making it suitable for dryland farming [43,77,78]. Chia seeds are an excellent source of dietary fibre (~34%), lipids (~33%) and protein (~18%). The protein content in chia seeds is composed of essential amino acids, such as lysine and arginine, and non-essential amino acids, such as alanine and aspartic acid. The chia seed lipid is rich in polyunsaturated acids with beneficial health impacts and, recently, has been extracted and characterised for food applications. Chia seeds are great sources of bioactive compounds such as omega-3 fatty acids (60–64%) and are a good source of minerals. Phytate and trypsin inhibitors are the major antinutrients in chia seeds [22,43,77,78].

4.13. *Buckwheat*

Buckwheat (*Fagopyrum esculentum*) is a pseudocereal that belongs to the family *Polygonaceae*. It is small and dark-coloured, typically brown or black, and is often used as a grain-like food source. Buckwheat is a hardy plant that can grow in a variety of soil types and climates, it is tolerant to frost and can be grown as a cover crop or as a green manure crop [44,74]. The seed of the buckwheat plant is a good source of carbohydrates (~65%), mainly in the form of complex carbohydrates, such as starch and dietary fibre. Additionally, it has a significant amount of protein (14–16%) of high quality, as it includes all essential amino acids, including lysine and arginine, which are often not present in other plant-based protein sources. Buckwheat is also rich in vitamins, such as B and E, and minerals (see Table 2). Some studies have revealed that the buckwheat seed contains a small amount of phytate, trypsin inhibitors and lectins, which can reduce the digestibility of proteins and cause allergic reactions in some individuals. The high levels of flavonoids present in buckwheat, particularly rutin, have been found to have antioxidant and anti-inflammatory properties, and they also have prebiotic and probiotic benefits [74].

5. Current Food Applications of Ancient Grains

Figure 1 provides a summary of some traditional and emerging food-processing techniques of ancient grains. Traditionally, ancient grains have been processed using minimal food-processing techniques to convert them into edible forms with improved organoleptic properties, such as homemade bakery products, porridge, soups, fermented products and ready-to-eat seasoned grains. The common processing methods used for this purpose are de-braning, soaking, roasting, milling, steaming, sprouting, popping and flaking to produce ready-to-eat salted grains and fermented products [22,27,79]. However, with increasing knowledge about the nutritional quality and health benefits of ancient grains, they have been in the spotlight in the production of emerging foods, such as healthy foods, plant proteins, high-fibre foods, low GI foods and allergy-free products, using modern food-processing techniques and often marketed at premium prices. Examples of these modern techniques are extrusion, microwave, ohmic heating, ultrasound, 3D printing and high-pressure processing [11,12,44]. Sprouting/germination and high-pressure processing have been used to reduce the antinutrients and improve the organoleptic properties of the ancient grains, and high-pressure processed ancient grains with reduced antinutrients and improved organoleptic properties have been successfully produced and used in the production of various foods such as pasta and bread [13,15,80]. There is also a growing interest in isolating different functional components from ancient grains, such as starch, protein, bran and fibre, oil and bioactive compounds, which can then be used in the production of healthy foods, nutraceuticals and pharmaceuticals [17,19,20,38].

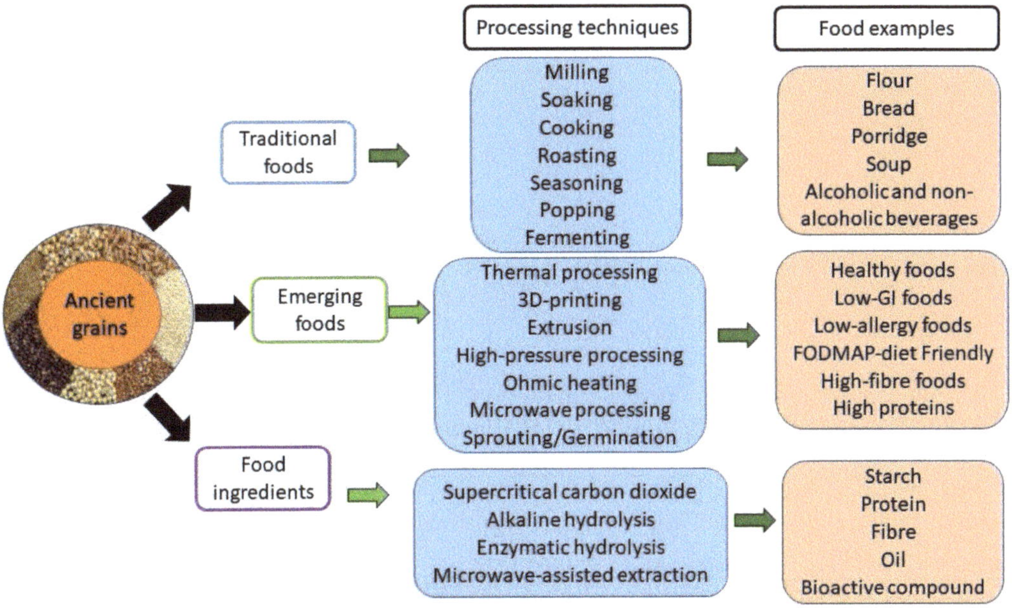

Figure 1. Traditional and emerging processing techniques to convert ancient grains into various products.

6. How Can Ancient Grains Prevent Hunger and Malnutrition?

Ancient grains can have a great contribution in mitigating food hunger and malnutrition for several reasons, as discussed below (summarised in Figure 2).

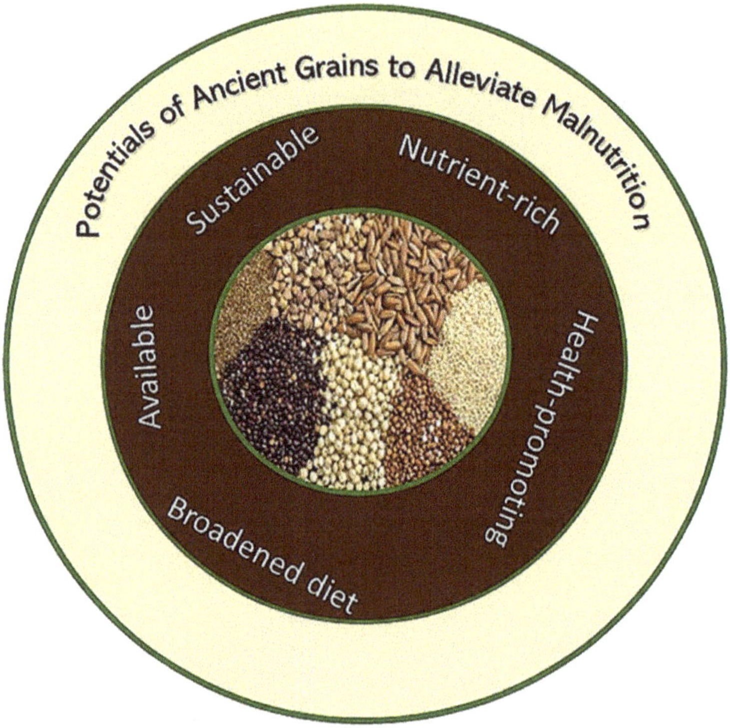

Figure 2. A spectrum of ancient grains illustrating the prospects of ancient grains to fight world hunger and malnutrition.

6.1. Ancient Grains as Highly Resilient Crops

Drought, extreme temperatures, water shortage, nutrient-poor soils and uncontrolled plant diseases and pests are the main factors threatening modern grains, causing food shortages and famine, especially in developing countries with a high prevalence of hunger. Unlike modern cereals, ancient grains have a diverse genetic ability to withstand many biotic and abiotic stresses [8]. This feature is highly valuable in supporting food security and establishing resilient agriculture in a wide range of climates [8].

6.2. Ancient Grains as Nutrient-Dense and Health-Promoting Foods

Ancient grains are natural and economical sources of nutrients and bioactive compounds that can provide a sufficient amount of carbohydrates, high-quality proteins, essential amino acids, dietary fibres, minerals, vitamins and bioactive compounds to supply energy and nutrients for healthy body functions and to combat hunger and malnutrition [11,25]. Many ancient grains such as sorghum, amaranth and chia seeds are rich sources of protein and lysine which is the lacking amino acid in modern grains. Thus, they can be an excellent source of plant-based protein, which is in high demand, especially in developing countries, due to the high cost of animal products that results in protein deficiency. Ancient grains are also great sources of vitamins (vitamins B1, B3, B6, folate and vitamin E) and minerals, especially Fe, Zn and Ca, and can be used to address minerals and vitamin deficiency caused by hunger and malnutrition. However, due to the presence of some antinutrients, developing pre-treatment technologies are required to increase the digestibility of proteins and the bioavailability of the minerals and vitamins [11,18].

Some tested ancient grains such as oat, teff, and sorghum naturally contain high levels of resistant starch with low digestible starch and hence are considered low GI foods. Resistant starch, which is not digestible in the body, acts as a dietary fibre with numerous health benefits, including appetite reduction and reducing the risk of obesity, improving postprandial glucose and insulin responses and also acting as a prebiotic compound for improving gut microbiome in the human body [18].

Ancient grains have shown positive effects to address many health issues related to malnutrition and hunger, such as cardiovascular diseases, diabetes type 2, cancer, weight control, IBS (irritable bowel syndrome) and digestion. It has also been reported that the consumption of ancient grains could improve both gastrointestinal symptoms (e.g., IBS) and inflammatory profiles in different groups [12,49,81].

6.3. *Ancient Grains to Diversify Food Sources*

Unprecedented environmental, climate and political problems threaten food security by disrupting the food supply chain hence supply and production diversification is of great importance. It is also well known that a diverse diet (i.e., consisting of a larger number of food sources, e.g., a number of cereals and pseudocereals) can provide a wide range of nutrients required for human health and hence planning a diverse diet is an important strategic approach for tackling hunger and malnutrition. Currently, only a few modern grains, including wheat, rice and corn, are the major grain contributors (sources) to human nutrition. However, a food system based on only modern grains is not sustainable due to their high susceptibility to biotic and abiotic stresses. In addition, the selection of high-yielding cultivars reduces their nutritional quality. The inclusion of ancient cereals in our diet can therefore diversify food sources, support food security and enrich the nutritional quality of the foods [5].

6.4. *Ancient Grains for Special Diet Foods*

People who require a special diet, such as those suffering from a digestive disorder, metabolic syndrome, food allergy and intolerance, are more at risk of malnutrition. Most ancient grains can be used as healthy and highly nutritious gluten-free alternatives to modern grains such as wheat, rice and corn [18,34]. Ancient grains cause fewer allergic reactions and are also more tolerable than normal grains for FODMAP diet foods [49].

Some ancient grains are rich sources of resistant and slowly digestible starch, which can be used for the production of low GI and low-calorie foods suitable for weight control and diabetes [13,15]. They can be used as a source of plant protein required in meat-free diets and also in countries where access to other protein sources is limited. Some ancient cereals have been added to produce low-fat foods. For instance, the hydrophilic properties of chia seeds enable them to be substituted for eggs and fat in food recipes [22].

6.5. *Ancient Grains to Support Small-Scale Farmers*

Economic crisis and poverty are directly related to food shortage and hunger. Small-scale farmers are highly vulnerable to job insecurity due to the high cost of modern agriculture. Growing ancient grains in developing countries can create jobs for small-scale farmers and support their income which facilitates access to better nutrition with minimal inputs such as water, land and fertiliser. This can also increase access to locally grown, highly nutritious and affordable food sources and reduce the need for importing grains from other countries [8].

7. Major Shortcomings of the Ancient Grains in to Fight against Hunger

Despite many advantages and health benefits of ancient grains, they have remained under-utilised due to their limitations, including low production yields and hence reduced availability compared to modern grains; lack of knowledge and technology of pre- and post-harvest processing; the presence of some anti-nutritional factors such as phytic acids, tannins and lectins (some causing bitter taste); and limited knowledge on their food processing, consumer perceptions, sensory studies and marketing. Since ancient grains have been neglected for many years, limited knowledge is available about their germplasms, different varieties, production, functionality and value-addition [5,18].

8. Concluding Remarks

For fighting hunger, relying only on high-yielding modern grains is highly unreliable and can lead to catastrophic outcomes because the existing major crops are highly prone to adverse climate changes and low-input environments and are not nutritionally balanced. Despite having low yields, ancient grains have excellent nutritional profiles and health benefits and are highly resistant to various biotic and abiotic stresses. Thus, growing a balanced combination of both modern and ancient grains is required to obtain more sustainable, diversified and nutritious foods to tackle hunger and malnutrition. Nevertheless, ancient grains are still highly under-utilised, and further research is necessary to turn these valuable grains into a real opportunity to tackle global hunger.

A research priority is to improve the production yields of ancient grains to increase their mass production and economic return, e.g., by selecting and breeding different cultivars and their best production performance conditions. It is also necessary to find feasible, industry-friendly and environmentally safe strategies to eliminate antinutrients, which have negative effects on the nutritional quality, health benefits and sensory properties of ancient grains.

With the fast-pacing food industry, there is an urgent need to use novel technologies to create functional food ingredients that replace existing ingredients in small- and large-scale food production settings. Moreover, underpinning the effects of modern food-processing techniques on the physicochemical, quality, nutritional properties, stability and sensory attributes of ancient grains is of prime importance.

Further research is required to develop new, affordable and healthy foods from ancient grains for special diet requirements.

It is also necessary to identify ancient grains that are naturally low in allergens and antinutrients, such as phytate and tannins, to improve the bioavailability of the nutrients.

Author Contributions: Conceptualization (M.M. & C.S.B.); Collecting literature information and data (M.M., S.J., S.T., M.G., M.H.); Preparation of first and final drafts (M.M.); Preparation of the Graphical Abstract, Figures, Tables and References (M.M.). All authors have read and agreed to the published version of the manuscript.

Funding: This research received no external funding.

Data Availability Statement: The data presented in this study are available on request from the corresponding author.

Conflicts of Interest: The authors declared that they have no conflict of interest.

References

1. Chen, X.; Shuai, C.; Wu, Y. Global food stability and its socio-economic determinants towards sustainable development goal 2 (Zero Hunger). In *Sustainable Development*; Wiley: Hoboken, NJ, USA, 2022.
2. Bangar, S.P.; Sandhu, K.S.; Trif, M.; Manjunatha, V.; Lorenzo, J.M. Germinated Barley Cultivars: Effect on physicochemical and bioactive properties. *Food Anal. Methods* **2022**, *15*, 2505–2512. [CrossRef]
3. Nani, M.; Krishnaswamy, K. Physical and functional properties of ancient grains and flours and their potential contribution to sustainable food processing. *Int. J. Food Prop.* **2021**, *24*, 1529–1547. [CrossRef]
4. Longin, C.F.H.; Würschum, T. Back to the future; Tapping into ancient grains for food diversity. *Trends Plant Sci.* **2016**, *21*, 731–737. [CrossRef] [PubMed]
5. Biel, W.; Jaroszewska, A.; Stankowski, S.; Sobolewska, M.; Kępińska-Pacelik, J. Comparison of yield, chemical composition and farinograph properties of common and ancient wheat grains. *Eur. Food Res. Technol.* **2021**, *247*, 1525–1538. [CrossRef]
6. Bordoni, A.; Danesi, F.; Di Nunzio, M.; Taccari, A.; Valli, V. Ancient wheat and health: A legend or the reality? A review on KAMUT khorasan wheat. *Int. J. Food Sci. Nutr.* **2017**, *68*, 278–286. [CrossRef]

7. Cheng, A. Review: Shaping a sustainable food future by rediscovering long-forgotten ancient grains. *Plant Sci.* **2018**, *269*, 136–142. [CrossRef]
8. Sharma, S.; Sahni, P. Germination behaviour, techno-functional characteristics, antinutrients, antioxidant activity and mineral profile of lucerne as influenced by germination regimes. *J. Food Meas. Charact.* **2021**, *15*, 1796–1809. [CrossRef]
9. Shewry, P.R. Do ancient types of wheat have health benefits compared with modern bread wheat? *J. Cereal Sci.* **2018**, *79*, 469–476. [CrossRef]
10. Dieterich, W.; Schuster, C.; Gundel, P.; Scherf, K.A.; Pronin, D.; Geisslitz, S.; Börner, A.; Neurath, M.F.; Zopf, Y. Proteins from modern and ancient wheat cultivars: Impact on immune cells of healthy individuals and patients with NCGS. *Nutrients* **2022**, *14*, 4257. [CrossRef]
11. Pronin, D.; Börner, A.; Scherf, K.A. Old and modern wheat (*Triticum aestivum* L.) cultivars and their potential to elicit celiac disease. *Food Chem.* **2021**, *339*, 127952. [CrossRef]
12. Sievers, S.; Rohrbach, A.; Beyer, K. Wheat-induced food allergy in childhood: Ancient grains seem no way out. *Eur. J. Nutr.* **2020**, *59*, 2693–2707. [CrossRef] [PubMed]
13. Simsek, S.; Budak, B.; Schwebach, C.S.; Ovando-Martínez, M. Starch digestibility properties of bread from hard red spring wheat cultivars released in the last 100 years. *Cereal Chem.* **2020**, *97*, 138–148. [CrossRef]
14. Martínez-Villaluenga, C.; Peñas, E.; Hernández-Ledesma, B. Pseudocereal grains: Nutritional value, health benefits and current applications for the development of gluten-free foods. *Food Chem. Toxicol.* **2020**, *137*, 111178. [CrossRef] [PubMed]
15. Seidita, A.; Mansueto, P.; Giuliano, A.; Chiavetta, M.; Mandreucci, F.; Soresi, M.; Pistone, M.; Compagnoni, S.; Castellucci, D.; Bisso, G.; et al. Potential tolerability of ancient grains in non-celiac wheat sensitivity patients: A preliminary evaluation. *Front. Med.* **2022**, *9*, 995019. [CrossRef] [PubMed]
16. Arzani, A.; Ashraf, M. Cultivated ancient wheats (*Triticum* spp.): A potential source of health-beneficial food products. *Compr. Rev. Food Sci. Food Saf.* **2017**, *16*, 477–488. [CrossRef] [PubMed]
17. Kulathunga, J.; Reuhs, B.L.; Simsek, S. A review: Novel trends in hulled wheat processing for value addition. *Trends Food Sci. Technol.* **2020**, *106*, 232–241. [CrossRef]
18. Shewry, P.R.; Hey, S. Do "ancient" wheat species differ from modern bread wheat in their contents of bioactive components? *J. Cereal Sci.* **2015**, *65*, 236–243. [CrossRef]
19. Kulathunga, J.; Simsek, S. Dietary fiber variation in ancient and modern wheat species: Einkorn, emmer, spelt and hard red spring wheat. *J. Cereal Sci.* **2022**, *104*, 103420. [CrossRef]
20. Al-Mahasneh, M.A.; Rababah, T.M.; Bani-Amer, M.M.; Al-Omari, N.M.; Mahasneh, M.K. Fuzzy and conventional modeling of open sun drying kinetics for roasted green wheat. *Int. J. Food Prop.* **2013**, *16*, 70–80. [CrossRef]
21. Al-Mahasneh, M.; Amer, M.B.; Rababah, T. Modelling moisture sorption isotherms in roasted green wheat using least square regression and neural-fuzzy techniques. *Food Bioprod. Process.* **2012**, *90*, 165–170. [CrossRef]
22. Zhang, K.; Zhao, D.; Song, J.; Guo, D.; Xiao, Y.; Shen, R. Effects of green wheat flour on textural properties, digestive and flavor characteristics of the noodles. *J. Food Process. Preserv.* **2021**, *45*, e15199. [CrossRef]
23. Özboy, Ö.; Özkaya, B.; Özkaya, H.; Köksel, H. Effects of wheat maturation stage and cooking method on dietary fiber and phytic acid contents of firik, a wheat-based local food. *Food/Nahr.* **2001**, *45*, 347–349. [CrossRef]
24. Zhang, K.; Zhang, Y.; Xu, N.; Yang, X.; Zhang, G.; Zhang, Y.; Liu, Q. Study of the protein, antioxidant activity, and starch during in vitro simulated digestion of green wheat and wheat cooked flours. *Int. J. Food Prop.* **2020**, *23*, 722–735. [CrossRef]
25. Delcour, J.A.; Hoseney, C.P. *Principles of Cereal Science and Technology*, 3rd ed.; AACC International: Eagan, MN, USA, 2010.
26. Smith, O.; Clapham, A.; Rose, P.; Liu, Y.; Wang, J.; Allaby, R.G. A complete ancient RNA genome: Identification, reconstruction and evolutionary history of archaeological Barley Stripe Mosaic Virus. *Sci. Rep.* **2014**, *4*, 4003. [CrossRef] [PubMed]
27. Taketa, S.; Amano, S.; Tsujino, Y.; Sato, T.; Saisho, D.; Kakeda, K.; Nomura, M.; Suzuki, T.; Matsumoto, T.; Sato, K.; et al. Barley grain with adhering hulls is controlled by an ERF family transcription factor gene regulating a lipid biosynthesis pathway. *Proc. Natl. Acad. Sci. USA* **2008**, *105*, 4062–4067. [CrossRef]
28. Ge, X.; Jing, L.; Su, C.; Zhang, B.; Zhang, Q.; Li, W. The profile, content and antioxidant activity of anthocyanin in germinated naked barley grains with infrared and hot air drying. *Int. J. Food Sci. Technol.* **2021**, *56*, 3834–3844. [CrossRef]
29. Kaukovirta-Norja, A.; Lehtinen, P. Traditional and Modern Oat-Based Foods. In *Technology of Functional Cereal Products*; Elsevier: Amsterdam, The Netherlands, 2008; pp. 215–232.
30. Sangwan, S.; Singh, R.; Tomar, S.K. Nutritional and functional properties of oats: An update. *J. Innov. Biol.* **2014**, *1*, 3–14.
31. Ferguson, J.J.; Stojanovski, E.; MacDonald-Wicks, L.; Garg, M.L. High molecular weight oat β-glucan enhances lipid-lowering effects of phytosterols. A randomised controlled trial. *Clin. Nutr.* **2020**, *39*, 80–89. [CrossRef]
32. Bhardwaj, R.D.; Kapoor, R.; Grewal, S.K. Biochemical characterization of oat (*Avena sativa* L.) genotypes with high nutritional potential. *LWT Food Sci. Technol.* **2019**, *110*, 32–39.
33. FAOSTAT. Available online: https://www.fao.org/faostat/en/#home (accessed on 29 May 2023).
34. Khoddami, A.; Messina, V.; Vadabalija Venkata, K.; Farahnaky, A.; Blanchard, C.L.; Roberts, T.H. Sorghum in foods: Functionality and potential in innovative products. *Crit. Rev. Food Sci. Nutr.* **2023**, *63*, 1170–1186. [CrossRef]
35. Rad, S.V.; Valadabadi, S.A.R.; Pouryousef, M.; Saifzadeh, S.; Zakrin, H.R.; Mastinu, A. Quantitative and qualitative evaluation of Sorghum bicolor L. under intercropping with legumes and different weed control methods. *Horticulturae* **2020**, *6*, 78. [CrossRef]

36. Rao, S.; Santhakumar, A.B.; Chinkwo, K.A.; Wu, G.; Johnson, S.K.; Blanchard, C.L. Characterization of phenolic compounds and antioxidant activity in sorghum grains. *J. Cereal Sci.* **2018**, *84*, 103–111. [CrossRef]
37. Punia, H.; Tokas, J.; Malik, A.; Sangwan, S. Characterization of phenolic compounds and antioxidant activity in sorghum [*Sorghum bicolor* (L.) Moench] grains. *Cereal Res. Commun.* **2021**, *49*, 343–353. [CrossRef]
38. Palacios, C.E.; Nagai, A.; Torres, P.; Rodrigues, J.A.; Salatino, A. Contents of tannins of cultivars of sorghum cultivated in Brazil, as determined by four quantification methods. *Food Chem.* **2021**, *337*, 127970. [CrossRef]
39. Mohapatra, D.; Patel, A.S.; Kar, A.; Deshpande, S.S.; Tripathi, M.K. Effect of different processing conditions on proximate composition, anti-oxidants, anti-nutrients and amino acid profile of grain sorghum. *Food Chem.* **2019**, *271*, 129–135. [CrossRef]
40. Pan, L.; An, D.; Zhu, W. Low-tannin sorghum grain could be used as an alternative to corn in diet for nursery pigs. *J. Anim. Physiol. Anim. Nutr.* **2021**, *105*, 890–897. [CrossRef]
41. Haliza, W.; Widowati, S. The characteristic of different formula of low tannin sorghum instant porridge. *IOP Conf. Ser. Earth Environ. Sci.* **2021**, *653*, 012124. [CrossRef]
42. Palavecino, P.M.; Curti, M.I.; Bustos, M.C.; Penci, M.C.; Ribotta, P.D. Sorghum pasta and noodles: Technological and nutritional aspects. *Plant Foods Hum. Nutr.* **2020**, *75*, 326–336. [CrossRef]
43. Gao, F.; Li, X.; Li, X.; Liu, Z.; Zou, X.; Wang, L.; Zhang, H. Physicochemical properties and correlation analysis of retrograded starch from different varieties of sorghum. *Int. J. Food Sci. Technol.* **2022**, *57*, 6678–6689. [CrossRef]
44. Li, W.; Wen, L.; Chen, Z.; Zhang, Z.; Pang, X.; Deng, Z.; Liu, T.; Guo, Y. Study on metabolic variation in whole grains of four proso millet varieties reveals metabolites important for antioxidant properties and quality traits. *Food Chem.* **2021**, *357*, 129791. [CrossRef]
45. Suma, P.F.; Urooj, A. Isolation and characterization of starch from pearl millet (*Pennisetum typhoidium*) flours. *Int. J. Food Prop.* **2015**, *18*, 2675–2687. [CrossRef]
46. Gull, A.; Prasad, K.; Kumar, P. Physico-chemical, functional and antioxidant properties of millet flours. *J. Agric. Eng. Food Technol.* **2015**, *2*, 73–75.
47. Slama, A.; Cherif, A.; Sakouhi, F.; Boukhchina, S.; Radhouane, L. Fatty acids, phytochemical composition and antioxidant potential of pearl millet oil. *J. Consum. Prot. Food Saf.* **2020**, *15*, 145–151. [CrossRef]
48. Chauhan, E.; Sarita, S. Effects of processing (germination and popping) on the nutritional and anti-nutritional properties of finger millet (*Eleusine Coracana*). *Curr. Res. Nutr. Food Sci. J.* **2018**, *6*, 566–572. [CrossRef]
49. Dey, S.; Saxena, A.; Kumar, Y.; Maity, T.; Tarafdar, A. Understanding the antinutritional factors and bioactive compounds of kodo millet (*Paspalum scrobiculatum*) and little millet (*Panicum sumatrense*). *J. Food Qual.* **2022**, *2022*, 1578448. [CrossRef]
50. Chu, M.-J.; Liu, X.-M.; Yan, N.; Wang, F.-Z.; Du, Y.-M.; Zhang, Z.-F. Partial purification, identification, and quantitation of antioxidants from wild rice (*Zizania latifolia*). *Molecules* **2018**, *23*, 2782. [CrossRef]
51. Qiu, Y.; Liu, Q.; Beta, T. Antioxidant activity of commercial wild rice and identification of flavonoid compounds in active fractions. *J. Agric. Food Chem.* **2009**, *57*, 7543–7551. [CrossRef]
52. Melini, V.; Acquistucci, R. Health-promoting compounds in pigmented Thai and wild rice. *Foods* **2017**, *6*, 9. [CrossRef]
53. Hou, X.-D.; Yan, N.; Du, Y.-M.; Liang, H.; Zhang, Z.-F.; Yuan, X.-L. Consumption of wild rice (zizania latifolia) prevents metabolic associated fatty liver disease through the modulation of the gut microbiota in mice model. *Int. J. Mol. Sci.* **2020**, *21*, 5375. [CrossRef]
54. Mir, N.A.; Riar, C.S.; Singh, S. Nutritional constituents of pseudo cereals and their potential use in food systems: A review. *Trends Food Sci. Technol.* **2018**, *75*, 170–180. [CrossRef]
55. Coelho, L.M.; Silva, P.M.; Martins, J.T.; Pinheiro, A.C.; Vicente, A.A. Emerging opportunities in exploring the nutritional/functional value of amaranth. *Food Funct.* **2018**, *9*, 5499–5512. [CrossRef] [PubMed]
56. Aderibigbe, O.R.; Ezekiel, O.O.; Owolade, S.O.; Korese, J.K.; Sturm, B.; Hensel, O. Exploring the potentials of underutilized grain amaranth (*Amaranthus* spp.) along the value chain for food and nutrition security: A review. *Crit. Rev. Food Sci. Nutr.* **2022**, *62*, 656–669. [CrossRef] [PubMed]
57. Alvarez-Jubete, L.; Wijngaard, H.; Arendt, E.K.; Gallagher, E. Polyphenol composition and in vitro antioxidant activity of amaranth, quinoa buckwheat and wheat as affected by sprouting and baking. *Food Chem.* **2010**, *119*, 770–778. [CrossRef]
58. Graziano, S.; Agrimonti, C.; Marmiroli, N.; Gullì, M. Utilisation and limitations of pseudocereals (quinoa, amaranth, and buckwheat) in food production: A review. *Trends Food Sci. Technol.* **2022**, *125*, 154–165. [CrossRef]
59. Filho, A.M.M.; Pirozi, M.R.; Borges, J.T.D.S.; Pinheiro Sant'Ana, H.M.; Chaves, J.B.P.; Coimbra, J.S.D.R. Quinoa: Nutritional, functional, and antinutritional aspects. *Crit. Rev. Food Sci. Nutr.* **2017**, *57*, 1618–1630. [CrossRef]
60. Ugural, A.; Akyol, A. Can pseudocereals modulate microbiota by functioning as probiotics or prebiotics? *Crit. Rev. Food Sci. Nutr.* **2022**, *62*, 1725–1739. [CrossRef]
61. Satheesh, N.; Fanta, S.W. Review on structural, nutritional and anti-nutritional composition of teff (*Eragrostis tef*) in comparison with quinoa (*Chenopodium quinoa* Willd.). *Cogent Food Agric.* **2018**, *4*, 1546942. [CrossRef]
62. Barretto, R.; Buenavista, R.M.; Rivera, J.L.; Wang, S.; Prasad, P.V.V.; Siliveru, K. Teff (*Eragrostis tef*) processing, utilization and future opportunities: A review. *Int. J. Food Sci. Technol.* **2021**, *56*, 3125–3137. [CrossRef]
63. Gebremariam, M.M.; Zarnkow, M.; Becker, T. Teff (*Eragrostis tef*) as a raw material for malting, brewing and manufacturing of gluten-free foods and beverages: A review. *J. Food Sci. Technol.* **2014**, *51*, 2881–2895. [CrossRef]

64. Ferreira, D.M.; Nunes, M.A.; Santo, L.E.; Machado, S.; Costa, A.S.G.; Alvarez-Orti, M.; Pardo, J.E.; Oliveira, M.; Alves, R.C. Characterization of chia seeds, cold-pressed oil, and defatted cake: An ancient grain for modern food production. *Molecules* **2023**, *28*, 723. [CrossRef]
65. Gómez-Velázquez, H.D.J.; Aparicio-Fernández, X.; Mora, O.; González Davalos, M.L.; de los Ríos, E.A.; Reynoso-Camacho, R. Chia seeds and chemical-elicited sprouts supplementation ameliorates insulin resistance, dyslipidemia, and hepatic steatosis in obese rats. *J. Food Biochem.* **2022**, *46*, e14136. [CrossRef] [PubMed]
66. Salgado, V.d.S.C.N.; Zago, L.; Antunes, A.E.C.; Miyahira, R.F. Chia (*Salvia hispanica* L.) seed germination: A brief review. *Plant Foods Hum. Nutr.* **2022**, *77*, 485–494. [CrossRef] [PubMed]
67. Knez Hrnčič, M.; Ivanovski, M.; Cör, D.; Knez, Ž. Chia Seeds (*Salvia hispanica* L.): An overview-ohytochemical orofile, isolation methods, and application. *Molecules* **2019**, *25*, 11. [CrossRef] [PubMed]
68. Ahmed, D.A.; Khalid, N.; Ahmad, A.; Abbasi, N.; Msz, L.; Randhawa, M. Phytochemicals and biofunctional properties of buckwheat: A review. *J. Agric. Sci.* **2013**, *152*, 349–369. [CrossRef]
69. Borisjuk, L.; Rolletschek, H.; Radchuk, V. Advances in the understanding of barley plant physiology: Factors determining grain development, composition, and chemistry. In *Achieving Sustainable Cultivation of Barley*; Routledge: Oxford, UK, 2020; pp. 53–96.
70. Zhang, K.; Dong, R.; Hu, X.; Ren, C.; Li, Y. Oat-based foods: Chemical constituents, glycemic index, and the effect of processing. *Foods* **2021**, *10*, 1304. [CrossRef]
71. Tumwine, G.; Atukwase, A.; Tumuhimbise, G.A.; Tucungwirwe, F.; Linnemann, A. Production of nutrient-enhanced millet-based composite flour using skimmed milk powder and vegetables. *Food Sci. Nutr.* **2019**, *7*, 22–34. [CrossRef]
72. Zhang, K.; Wen, Q.; Wang, Y.; Li, T.; Nie, B.; Zhang, Y. Study on the in vitro digestion process of green wheat protein: Structure characterization and product analysis. *Food Sci. Nutr.* **2022**, *10*, 3462–3474. [CrossRef]
73. Rocchetti, G.; Giuberti, G.; Busconi, M.; Marocco, A.; Trevisan, M.; Lucini, L. Pigmented sorghum polyphenols as potential inhibitors of starch digestibility: An in vitro study combining starch digestion and untargeted metabolomics. *Food Chem.* **2020**, *312*, 126077. [CrossRef]
74. Shumoy, H.; Raes, K. Tef: The rising ancient cereal: What do we know about its nutritional and health benefits? *Plant Foods Hum. Nutr.* **2017**, *72*, 335–344. [CrossRef]
75. Abugoch James, L.E. Chapter 1 Quinoa (*Chenopodium quinoa* Willd.): Composition, Chemistry, Nutritional, and Functional Properties. In *Advances in Food and Nutrition Research*; Academic Press: Cambridge, MA, USA, 2009; pp. 1–31.
76. Dinu, M.; Whittaker, A.; Pagliai, G.; Benedettelli, S.; Sofi, F. Ancient wheat species and human health: Biochemical and clinical implications. *J. Nutr. Biochem.* **2018**, *52*, 1–9. [CrossRef]
77. Tekin, M.; Cengiz, M.F.; Abbasov, M.; Aksoy, A.; Canci, H.; Akar, T. Comparison of some mineral nutrients and vitamins in advanced hulled wheat lines. *Cereal Chem.* **2018**, *95*, 436–444. [CrossRef]
78. Singkhornart, S.; Ryu, G.H. Effect of soaking time and steeping temperature on biochemical properties and γ-aminobutyric acid (GABA) content of germinated wheat and barley. *J. Food Sci. Nutr.* **2011**, *16*, 67–73. [CrossRef]
79. Collar, C.; Jiménez, T.; Conte, P.; Fadda, C. Impact of ancient cereals, pseudocereals and legumes on starch hydrolysis and antiradical activity of technologically viable blended breads. *Carbohydr. Polym.* **2014**, *113*, 149–158. [CrossRef] [PubMed]
80. Kaur, K.D.; Jha, A.; Sabikhi, L.; Singh, A. Significance of coarse cereals in health and nutrition: A review. *J. Food Sci. Technol.* **2014**, *51*, 1429–1441. [CrossRef]
81. Punia Bangar, S.; Sharma, N.; Singh, A.; Phimolsiripol, Y.; Brennan, C.S. *Glycaemic* response of pseudocereal-based gluten-free food products: A review. *Int. J. Food Sci. Technol.* **2022**, *57*, 4936–4944. [CrossRef]

foods

MDPI

Review

Modern Processing of Indian Millets: A Perspective on Changes in Nutritional Properties

N. A. Nanje Gowda [1,*], Kaliramesh Siliveru [2,*], P. V. Vara Prasad [3], Yogita Bhatt [1], B. P. Netravati [1] and Chennappa Gurikar [1]

[1] Department of Food Technology, Faculty of Life and Allied Health Sciences, Ramaiah University of Applied Sciences, Bangalore 560054, India; yogitabhatt.ft.ls@msruas.ac.in (Y.B.); netrapalled@gmail.com (B.P.N.); chennappa.ft.ls@msruas.ac.in (C.G.)
[2] Department of Grain Science and Industry, Kansas State University, Manhattan, KS 66506, USA
[3] Department of Agronomy, Kansas State University, Manhattan, KS 66506, USA; vara@ksu.edu
* Correspondence: nanjegowdana@gmail.com (N.A.N.G.); kaliramesh@k-state.edu (K.S.); Tel.: +91-9964477567 (N.A.N.G.); +1-(630)-210-2462 (K.S.)

Abstract: Globally, billions of people are experiencing food insecurity and malnutrition. The United Nations has set a global target to end hunger by 2030, but we are far from reaching it. Over the decade, climate change, population growth and economic slowdown have impacted food security. Many countries are facing the challenge of both undernutrition and over nutrition. Thus, there is a need to transform the food system to achieve food and nutrition security. One of the ways to reach closer to our goal is to provide an affordable healthy and nutritious diet to all. Millets, the nutri-cereals, have the potential to play a crucial role in the fight against food insecurity and malnutrition. Nutri-cereals are an abundant source of essential macro- and micronutrients, carbohydrates, protein, dietary fiber, lipids, and phytochemicals. The nutrient content and digestibility of millets are significantly influenced by the processing techniques. This review article highlights the nutritional characteristics and processing of Indian millets, viz. foxtail, kodo, proso, little, and pearl millets. It also envisages the effect of traditional and modern processing techniques on millet's nutritional properties. An extensive literature review was conducted using the research and review articles related to processing techniques of millets such as fermentation, germination, dehulling, extrusion, cooking, puffing, popping, malting, milling, etc. Germination and fermentation showed a positive improvement in the overall nutritional characteristics of millets, whereas excessive dehulling, polishing, and milling resulted in reduction of the dietary fiber and micronutrients. Understanding the changes happening in the nutrient value of millets due to processing can help the food industry, researchers, and consumers select a suitable processing technique to optimize the nutrient value, increase the bioavailability of nutrients, and help combat food and nutrition security.

Keywords: millets; processing; nutrients; dietary fiber; pearl; foxtail

Citation: Gowda, N.A.N.; Siliveru, K.; Prasad, P.V.V.; Bhatt, Y.; Netravati, B.P.; Gurikar, C. Modern Processing of Indian Millets: A Perspective on Changes in Nutritional Properties. *Foods* **2022**, *11*, 499. https://doi.org/10.3390/foods11040499

Academic Editors: Laura Gazza and Francesca Nocente

Received: 9 January 2022
Accepted: 5 February 2022
Published: 9 February 2022

1. Introduction

Millets are termed as "yesterday's coarse grains and today's nutri-cereals." Millets are considered to be "future crops" as they are resistant to most of the pests and diseases and adapt well to the harsh environment of the arid and semi-arid regions of Asia and Africa [1]. Millets are small-seeded grains, the most common and important for food being sorghum (*Sorghum bicolor* L.), pearl millet (*Pennisetum glaucum*), finger millet (*Eleusine carocana*), teff (*Eragrostis tef*), proso millet (*Panicum miliaceum*), kodo millet (*Paspalum scrobiculatum*), foxtail millet (*Setaria italica*), little millet (*Panicum sumatrense*) and fonio (*Digitaris exilis*) [1]. After decades of negligence, nutri-cereals are making a strong comeback in the Indian cereal's production segment. India dominates the global production of millets with a total share of about 40.62% and an estimated production of about 10.91 million tonnes during 2018–2019 [2]. Although India ranks first in nutri-rich millet production and second in rice and pulses across the globe, it also—unfortunately—ranks second in child malnutrition incidences. India is home to more than one-third of the world's malnourished children [3]. By contrast, the country has also become a hub for diabetic and overweight populace, putting the country under a double burden of malnutrition [4]. The majority of millets are three to five times more nutritious than most cereals (rice, *Oryza sativa*; wheat, *Triticum aestivum*; maize, *Zea mays*) in terms of vitamins, fiber, proteins, and minerals (calcium and iron) and are gluten-free; hence, they are known as "superfoods" [2]. The nutri-rich millets are the viable solution to reduce the rising incidences of malnutrition and metabolic disorders and can enhance the nutrition and food security of the country.

Millets are a highly nutritious crop and contain considerable amounts of vitamins and minerals. Millets are a good source of energy, dietary fiber, slowly digestible starch, and resistant starch, and thus provide sustained release of glucose and thereby satiety [5,6]. Compared to cereals, millets are a good source of protein- and sulphur-containing amino acids (methionine and cysteine) and have a better fatty acid profile [5,7]. However, millets contain a limited amount of lysine and tryptophan, which varies with the cultivar. Millets are rich in vitamin E and vitamin B and in minerals such as calcium, phosphorus, magnesium, manganese, potassium, and iron [1,8]. The abundant nutrients of millets provide multiple benefits such as reducing the incidence of cancer [9,10], obesity and diabetes [11], cardiovascular diseases [12,13], gastrointestinal problems [14], migraine, and asthma [1,15]. Consumption of millets helps manage hyperglycemia due to their lente carbohydrate and high dietary fiber content, thus making millets a perfect food for the diabetic populace [3,15]. Therefore, millets play an important role in the modern diet as a potential source of essential nutrients, especially in underdeveloped and developing countries [16]. Although millets have a diversified and high food value, their consumption, especially by the Indian populace, has not reached a significant level due to various factors, depicted in Figure 1. Recently, these grains have been slowly fueling the start-up revolution to improve nutri-rich food availability and create employment.

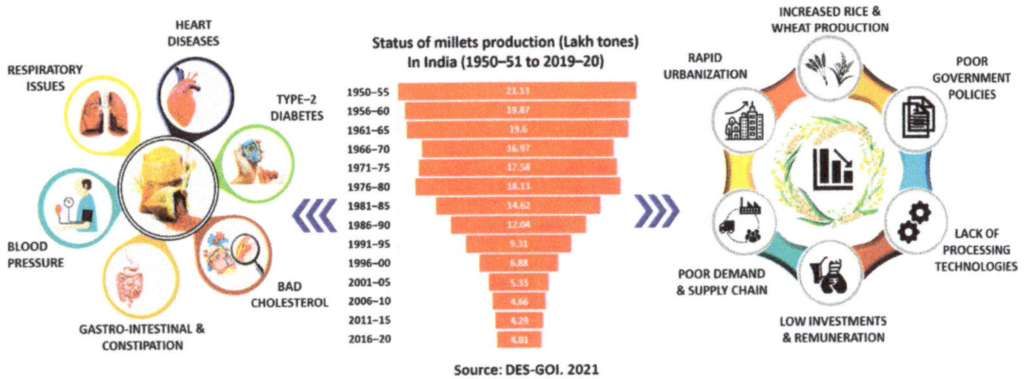

Figure 1. Millets: health benefits, production, and challenges in India. Data taken from various issues [17].

Millets are usually processed before consumption to remove the inedible portions, extend the shelf life, and improve nutritional and sensory properties. Primary processing techniques such as dehulling, soaking, germination, roasting, drying, polishing and milling (size reduction) are followed to make millets fit for consumption. At the same time, modern or secondary processing methods such as fermenting, parboiling, cooking, puffing, popping, malting, baking, flaking, extrusion, etc., are used to develop millet-based value-added processed food products [8]. Although these processing techniques aim to enhance the digestibility and nutrient bioavailability, a significant amount of nutrients are lost during subsequent processing [18]. This review article aims to provide an overview of the effect of processing techniques on the nutritional properties of important Indian millets, viz. pearl millet, proso millet, kodo millet, foxtail millet, and little millet.

2. Methodology

Review was conducted based on the methodology reported earlier with slight modification [19]. The current topic was selected based on a literature survey to identify the gap between the available literature resources pertaining to the effect of processing treatment on specific nutrient components of millet with respect to the Indian scenario. The objective of the review was to evaluate the millet processing treatments in order to identify the appropriate processing treatment for maximum retention of nutrients. The review includes peer-reviewed research articles published in the English language after the year 2016. The articles exclusive to dehulling, fermenting, germination, parboiling, cooking, puffing, popping, malting, and extrusion millet processing were included. The literature review was carried out using databases such as PubMed and Google Scholar as search engines. The common search terms used were millets processing, millet nutrition, dehulling, nutri-cereals processing, value addition to millets, fermenting, germination, parboiling, cooking, puffing, popping, malting, extrusion of millets, etc.

3. Nutritional Characteristic of Selected Indian Millets

3.1. Nutritional Profile of Millets

The nutritional content of food is an important factor in the maintenance of a human body's metabolism and wellness. The nutritional content is critical for developing and maximizing the human genetic potential. Millet's nutrition is comparable to major staple cereals (rice, wheat, and maize), since they are an abundant source of carbohydrates, protein, dietary fiber, micronutrients, vitamins and phytochemicals. Millets provide energy ranging from 320–370 kcal per 100 g of consumption (Table 1). Millets have a larger proportion of non-starchy polysaccharides and dietary fiber compared to staple cereals and comprise 65–75% carbohydrates. Millets with high dietary fiber provide multiple health benefits such as improving gastrointestinal health, blood lipid profile, and blood glucose clearance. Millets with minimal gluten and low glycemic index are healthy options for celiac disorder and diabetes [20]. Millets are also rich in health-promoting phytochemicals such as phytosterols, polyphenols, phytocyanins, lignins, and phyto-oestrogens. These phytochemicals act as antioxidants, immunological modulators, and detoxifying agents, preventing age-related degenerative illnesses such as cardiovascular diseases, type-2 diabetes, and cancer [1]. A study [21] reported that millets contain about 50 different phenolic groups and their derivatives with potent antioxidant capacity, such as flavones, flavanols, flavononols, and ferulic acid. A significant amount of phenolic components, which are important antioxidants in millets, are found in bounded form in proso and finger millet and in free form in pearl millet [22]. Another study [23] reported that proso millet comprises various phytochemicals such as syringic acid, chlorogenic acid, ferulic acid, caffeic acid, and p-coumaric. It has also been reported that almost 65% of the phenolics are present in the bound fraction. The presence of these phytochemicals and important antioxidants indicates the potential benefits of millets to human health. A detailed summary of the nutritional profile of selected Indian millets is discussed below and highlighted in Table 1.

- Proso millet has a higher nutritional value when compared with staple cereals as it contains a higher concentration of minerals and dietary fiber (Table 1). Proso millet is a rich source of vitamins and minerals such as iron (Fe), calcium (Ca), potassium (K), phosphorus (P), zinc (Zn), magnesium (Mg), vitamin B-complex, niacin, and folic acid. Proso millet contains essential amino acids in significantly higher quantities, except for lysine, the limiting amino acid. However, proso millet has an almost 51% higher essential amino acid index than wheat [24]. Moreover, the products prepared from proso millet exhibit a lower glycemic response than staple cereal-based products. A review reported that products prepared from proso millet show a significantly lower glycemic index (GI) compared to wheat- and maize-based products [25].

- Pearl millet shows an energy value comparable to the staple cereals. Pearl millet contains a lesser amount of carbohydrates than the staple cereals, and it mainly contains high amylose starch (20–22%), and the insoluble dietary fiber fraction helps in exhibiting a lower glycemic response. Pearl millet protein is gluten-free and contains a higher prolamin fraction, making it suitable for people with gluten sensitivity. The amino acid score in pearl millet is good; however, it is poor source of lysine, threonine, tryptophan, and other sulphur-containing amino acids [23,26]. Pearl millet is high in omega-3 fatty acids and also important nutritional fatty acids such as alpha-linolenic acid, eicosapentaenoic acid, and docosahexaenoic acid. It also contains other micronutrients such as Fe, Zn, copper (Cu), K, Mg, P, manganese (Mn), and B-vitamins [23].
- Kodo millet provides an energy value similar to the other millets and staple cereals. However, with the exception of finger millet, the protein content of kodo millet is lower than that of other selected millets and it provides gluten-free protein (Table 1). Kodo millets contains high amounts of vitamins and minerals, especially B-complex vitamins, B6, niacin and folic acid, Fe, Ca, Mg, K, and Zn. Kodo millet is very easy to digest and thus can be beneficial for infant and geriatric product formulation.
- Foxtail millet has a greater nutritional value compared to major cereals such as wheat and rice due to its copious dietary fiber content, resistant starch, vitamins, minerals, and essential amino acids, except for lysine and methionine, but it is richer than most cereals. Among the selected millets, foxtail millet contains the highest protein (Table 1). Foxtail millet also contains a high amount of stearic and linoleic acids, which helps in maintaining a good lipid profile.
- Finger millet has the highest carbohydrate content among the selected millets. However, carbohydrates consist primarily of slowly digestible starch, dietary fiber, and resistant starch and thus offer a low glycemic index compared to most common cereals such as rice and wheat [27]. Finger millet contains around 7% protein (Table 1), which is less than that of other millets, but it has a good amino acid score and contains more threonine, lysine, and valine than other millets. Subsequently, micronutrients such as Ca, Fe, Mg, K, and Zn, as well as B-vitamins, especially niacin, B6, and folic acid, are abundantly available.
- The nutritional value of little millet is comparable to other cereal and millet crops. It contains around 8.7% protein and balanced amino acids, and it is a rich source of sulphur-containing amino acids (cysteine and methionine) and lysine, which is lacking in most cereals [28]. It is generally considered to induce a lower glycemic response due to the presence of abundant dietary fiber, resistant starch, and slowly digestible starch [29]. It is also a good source of micronutrients such as Fe, P, and niacin. Recently, many value-added products have been prepared using little millet to capitalize on the health benefits of little millet.

Table 1. Nutritional profile of millets in comparison with cereals (per 100 g).

Grains	Energy (kcal)	Protein (g)	Carbohydrate (g)	Starch (g)	Fat(g)	Dietary Fiber (g)	Minerals (g)	Ca (mg)	P (mg)
Sorghum	334	10.4	67.6	59	1.9	10.2	1.6	27	222
Pearl millet	363	11.6	61.7	55	5	11.4	2.3	27	296
Finger millet	320	7.3	66.8	62	1.3	11.1	2.7	364	283
Proso millet	341	12.5	70.0	-	1.1	-	1.9	14	206
Foxtail millet	331	12.3	60.0	-	4.3	-	3.3	31	290
Kodo millet	353	8.3	66.1	64	1.4	6.3	2.6	15	188
Little millet	329	8.7	65.5	56	5.3	6.3	1.7	17	220

Table 1. *Cont.*

Grains	Energy (kcal)	Protein (g)	Carbohydrate (g)	Starch (g)	Fat(g)	Dietary Fiber (g)	Minerals (g)	Ca (mg)	P (mg)
Barnyard millet	307	11.6	65.5	-	5.8	-	4.7	14	121
Maize	334	11.5	64.7	59	3.6	12.2	1.5	8.9	348
Wheat	321	11.8	64.7	56	1.5	11.2	1.5	39	306
Rice	353	6.8	74.8	71	0.5	4.4	0.6	10	160

Source: Indian Food Composition Tables and nutritive value of Indian foods [30,31].

3.2. *Antinutrient Profile of Millets*

Antinutrients are phytochemical compounds that plants produce naturally for their defense. These antinutritional factors hinder nutrient absorption, leading to reduced nutrient bioavailability and utilization [32]. When consumed uncooked, products containing antinutrients and chemical compounds may be detrimental or even pose health issues in humans, such as micronutrient malnutrition, nutritional deficiency, and bloating. Plant-based foods mainly contain antinutrients such as tannins, phytates, oxalates, trypsin, and chymotrypsin inhibitors [33]. One of the disadvantages of millets is a higher concentration of antinutritional factors compared to wheat and rice. Finger millet contains polyphenols, tannins (0.61%), phytates (0.48%), trypsin inhibitors, and oxalates, which may interfere with the bioavailability of micronutrients and protein digestibility. The goitrogenic compounds in pearl millet are derivatives of phenolic flavonoids, such as C-glycosyl flavones, and their metabolites are responsible for the development of off-odors in the flour during storage [34]. Antinutritional factors due to metal chelation and enzyme inhibition capacity decrease nutrients bioavailability, mainly of minerals and proteins. However, in recent years, antinutritional factors such as polyphenolic compounds have been reported as nutraceuticals for their contribution to antioxidant properties [1]. Most secondary metabolites that function as antinutrients may cause extremely detrimental biological reactions, while others are actively used in nutrition and pharmacologically active drugs. The need of eliminating antinutrients is fulfilled by pretreatment or processing techniques of food grains, such as debranning, soaking, germination, fermentation, and autoclaving. These methods add value to food by enhancing the bioavailability of a few cations such as Ca, Fe, and Zn and also the proteins absorption [8].

4. Mechanical Processing for Millets

Because global food security is at risk, effective utilization of available millet crops to develop an affordable, palatable, and nutrient-rich product is the need of the hour. Millet grains must be processed to remove inedible portions and convert them into cooked and edible form. Therefore, processing is a crucial task, as it increases the bioavailability of nutrients and organoleptic properties and decreases antinutrients [1]. Processing involves multiple techniques such as dehusking/decortication, milling, soaking, germination, fermentation, malting, cooking, and roasting. These operations cause changes in physicochemical attributes that alter the nutrition, function, and physical characteristics of food [15]. Processing may be of two types, namely, primary and secondary processing. Processes such as cleaning, washing (soaking/germination), dehulling, milling (into flour and semolina), and refining to remove the undesired seed coat and antinutritional factors are termed as primary processing, while secondary processing involves converting primary processed raw materials into "ready-to-cook" (RTC) or "ready-to-eat" (RTE) products by flaking, popping, extrusion, and baking [1]. The traditional processing technologies include debranning, milling, roasting, soaking, steaming germination, popping, flaking, ready-to-eat salted grains, and fermented products [35,36]. These processing techniques aim to convert grains into edible forms, with an extended shelf life, improved texture, specific flavor, taste, as well as improved nutritional quality and digestibility [37]. Millet consumption and utilization can be increased by processing them into various by-products, which also reduces the phytate and tannin levels, increases the minerals and amino acids bioavailability, and improves starch and protein digestibility [38]. Processing imparts specific morphological, anatomical, or modulated changes in these bioactive compounds present in whole grains. The processing methods may have positive as well as negative impacts on the nutrient and antinutrient profile. Various research studies on millet processing have shown positive results on the effective usage of millets in a variety of traditional and convenience health foods. Significant levels of phytates, tannins, phenols, and trypsin inhibitors decrease nutrient bioavailability and quality, limiting maximum utilization of nutritional potential in millets [1]. Certain millets contain higher concentrations of unsaturated fatty acids; hence rancidity and off-flavors occur in millet flour during storage due to lipolysis followed by oxidation of "de-esterified fatty acids" [32]. Thus, understanding the influence of processing on nutritional properties is extremely important for effective utilization of millets. It also assists in choosing an appropriate processing technique for millets to maximize nutrient availability, improve palatability, and increase shelf life. The changes in nutritional composition and digestibility with respect to different mechanical processing methods are discussed (Table 2) and summarized (Figure 2).

	Energy	Carbohydrate	Protein	Minerals	Dietary fiber	Fat	Vitamins	Antioxidants
Dehulling	↓	↑	↓	↓	↓	↓	↓	—
Milling/Sieving	—	—	↓	↓	↓	↓	↓	—
Soaking	—	↓	—	↓↑	—	↓	—	↓
Germinating	↑	↓↑	↑	↑	↑	↓↑	↑	↑
Malting	—	—	—	—	↑	↓	—	—
Fermenting	—	↑	↑	↑	↑	↓	↑	—
Roasting	↓	—	↓	↓↑	↓↑	↓↑	—	—
Extrusion	↓	↓	↓	—	↓	—	—	—
Cooking	↓	↓	↓↑	—	↑	↓	—	—
Puffing/ Popping	—	—	↑	↓↑	↓	↓	—	—

Note: (↑):increases, (↓):decreases, (↓↑):decreases or increases, (—): data not available (Reference source: above manuscript)

Figure 2. Inference on nutritional properties changes during different processing methods.

Table 2. Changes in millets nutritional properties with respect to processing methods.

Processing Methods	Millets	Experimental Condition	Inference/Study Outcome	References
Germination	Foxtail	Germinated for 46.5 h (optimized)	Increased protein content (13.75 g/100 g) as compared to raw seeds (10.60 g/100 g). Increased dietary fiber by 5.2%. Elevated the levels of minerals such as Fe, Mg, Ca, and Na. Free, bound, and total phenolics and flavonoids content is increased. Decreased fat content from 3.86 to 2.78 g/100 g.	[39,40]
		Germination at room temp with tap water	Increased protein (by 29.72%) total dietary fiber (58.02%) and total phenolic content (77.42%). Increased level of DPPH radical scavenging was observed.	[20,35]
	Kodo	38.75 °C for 36 h	Elevation in mineral content. Protein and dietary fiber content increased. Total carbohydrates reduced.	[41]
	Pearl Var; Kalukombu (K) and Maharashtra Rabi Bajra (MRB)	Sprouting at room temperature for 72 h	Protein content reduced in MRB variety, while K variety had no significant effect. Fat and ash content reduced. Iron and calcium content significantly increased after germination.	[42]
	Proso	Sprouting for 96 h	Protein and minerals become more biologically accessible.	[43]
Malting	Pearl Var; Ex-Borno	Steeping at 25 °C for 24 h, Germinated at different time intervals, kilned (hot-air oven) at 55 °C for 18 h	Protein content increased from 7.52% (control) to 9.19% (96 h) malted millet flour. Crude fiber increased with an increasing malting period (i.e., 0.77% for control to 1.38% for 96 h malted sample). Decrease in carbohydrate content due to starch hydrolyzed into simple sugars by enzymes such as α- and β-amylase. Fat level was found to be lowest for 96 h of malted samples, which affects energy values of millet flour, but ensures increased shelf life. Kilning and steeping process decreases the level of amino acids (tyrosine, isoleucine, methionine, glycine, cysteine and glutamic acid).	[44]
	Pearl	Alkaline steeping of malted flour (2% Ca (OH_2) and (2% ash solution))	Both the steeping methods increase the protein level of flour samples. Lime steeped millet flour had increased fiber content as compared to ash steeped and control flours. Lime steeping lowered the levels of crude lipid in millet flour. Ca, Mg, and K levels increased while phosphorus and zinc levels decreased as steeping duration progressed.	[45]

Table 2. *Cont.*

Processing Methods	Millets	Experimental Condition	Inference/Study Outcome	References
Soaking	Pearl	Soaking for 24 h	Protein content increased due to the mobilization of stored nitrogen of grains. Fat content and crude fiber increases with sprouting The utilization of energy sources results in reduced carbohydrates.Sprouting reduced minerals (Co, Cr, Mn, Cu, Zn, Fe, Na, and K) due to leaching, but Ca content increased due to degradation of phytic acid.	[46]
	Foxtail Var; white	High-pressure soaking (600 MPa, 60 °C and 120 min)	Protein level decreased from 13.65% (native) to 13.11% (treated sample) due to the formation of protein–starch complex.	[40]
Fermentation	Pearl Var; Sosart 1	Pure cultures of Lactobacillus plantarum	Increase in protein content after 96 h fermentation from 8.7% in unfermented sample to 20.54% in starter culture fermented sample and 20.21% in naturally fermented sample. Lipid content decreased from 10.34 to 0.34 (starter culture sample) and 0.74 (naturally fermented). Carbohydrates decreased with a parallel increase in soluble sugar.	[47]
	Foxtail	Fermentation followed by heat moisture treatment	Increased crude protein content. Decreased the total carbohydrate level. Enhanced the nutritional quality of starch.	[20]
		Fermentation using *L. paracasei* Fn032 strain	Crude protein content increased by 20.51% in the fermented sample. Total carbohydrate decreased to 74.02%.	[48]
Cooking/ Boiling/ Roasting	Pearl	Roasting (150 °C for 5 min)	Increased the percentage bio-accessibility of total polyphenols from 73.2% in native grains to 78.1% in roasted samples. Bio-accessible flavonoid content increased.	[49,50]
		Pressure cooking (15 psi in triple distilled water for 15 to 20 min)	Total polyphenol content decreased by 29%.	
		Blanching 98 °C for 10–20 s	Lowered the percentage of free fatty acids, acid value and fat acidity.	
		Microwave heating	Reduced bio-accessibility of phenolic content.	
	Foxtail	Soaking followed by cooking	Maximum decrease in protein, Fe, and Zn. Increased the bioavailability of soluble Zn and ionizable Fe.	[20]

Table 2. *Cont.*

Processing Methods	Millets	Experimental Condition	Inference/Study Outcome	References
	Kodo	Boiling at 95–100 °C for 25 min	Increased porosity and water absorption capacity. Reduced starch yield.	[38]
		Pressure cooking at 9.8×10^4 Pa for 20 min	High level of resistant starch observed. Enhanced oil absorption capacity.	
		Puffing 230 °C for 3 min	Increased carbohydrate content from 68.35% to 74.38%. Increased protein content from 7.92% to 8.12%. Decreased crude fiber and fat content. Calcium level reduced from 27 to 18 mg/100 g.	[51]
	Proso	Pan and microwave cooking	Increased level of DPPH and FRAP radical scavenging activity. Increased carbohydrate content but decreased fat content. Protein content increased in pan cooking but decreased in microwave cooking.	[35,52]
	Little	Pan and microwave cooking	Carbohydrate content increased, while fat content decreased. Protein content increased in microwave cooking but decreased in pan cooking.	[52]

5. Effect of Processing on Nutritional Properties of Millets

5.1. Proteins

Millets are a rich source of proteins and are widely consumed by vegans. They are regarded as an excellent plant protein with negligible amounts of saturated fats compared to animal proteins. The presence of antinutrients inhibits protein digestibility; hence, reducing the antinutrients level is important. Simple techniques such as dehulling, milling, soaking, and heating decrease the antinutrient levels and increase the in vitro protein digestibility. The impact of various processing methods on the protein digestibility of foxtail millets has been studied [20]. The alkaline cooking, fermentation, germination (40 h at 25 °C), and popping of foxtail millet resulted in improved protein quality. In another study, pan-frying showed increased protein content in proso millet by 9.5% [18]. The puffing or popping of kodo millet increased the protein concentration from 7.92 to 8.12% [53]. The separation of starch granules from the protein matrix during thermal treatment, as well as the destruction of antinutritional components such as trypsin inhibitors and phytate acid, resulted in enhanced protein digestibility as a result of heat treatment or high pressure.

Protein digestibility in cereals, millets, and legumes has been shown to improve throughout the germination and fermentation processes. The germination of foxtail millet resulted in an increment in the protein concentration due to the synthesis of new amino acids [39]. Similar results for the increase of protein during germination of two cultivars of pearl millet, namely Gadarif (11.4% to 13.2%) and Gazeera (14.4% to 16.3%) were observed [54]. A study [55] showed that following germination, the protein concentration of pearl millet increased from 14% to 26%, whereas another study [43] reported the increased protein in proso millet after sprouting for 96 h. A research study on the impact of fermenting pearl millet flour with pure cultures revealed enhanced protein efficiency ratios, true and apparent protein digestibility, and utilizable protein values [55]. In another study, the combined effect of germination, fermentation (12 h and 24 h, respectively) and dry heating of pearl millets resulted in improved "in vitro protein digestibility" (IVPD), indicating that fermentation enhances protein digestibility [54]. The natural fermentation of pearl millet may significantly enhance the protein content [47]. During fermentation, antinutritional factors such as phytate gets degraded and the insoluble protein get converted to soluble protein due to the synthesis of proteolytic enzymes by microflora [56]. The simple technique of soaking pearl millet for 24 h resulted in increased protein due to the mobilization of stored nitrogen [46]. Similarly the malting of pearl millet (24 h soaking, followed by 18 h germination) significantly enhanced the protein [43]. These reports suggest that the soaking, malting germination, and fermentation processes lead to an increment in the total protein and improved protein digestibility, and thus can be used as an effective processing treatment in the development of protein-rich foods. Because these processes do not necessitate sophisticated equipment, they can be employed at the domestic level as well, assisting in the fight against protein–energy malnutrition, which is primarily a concern in underdeveloped nations.

Decortication removes about 12% to 30% of the outer husk, bran, and germ portion of grains, limiting the significant loss of proteins and amino acids such as histidine, lysine, and arginine. According to a study [49], dehulling of pearl millet up to 17.5% had a significant impact on the nutritional contents, increasing protein and digestibility. However, dehulling beyond this point, a substantial decrease in protein occurred. In another study [57] on the milling of pearl millet, bran-rich milled grains showed the highest percentage of IVPD. Similar improvements in millet's IVPD were reported by other authors [53]. Since most of the polyphenolic compounds and antinutrients which precipitate proteins and reduce protein digestibility are present in the hull of millets, the decortication process substantially eliminates them and result in improved protein digestibility.

5.2. Carbohydrates

Carbohydrates of the millets range around 60–75%, with foxtail millet containing the minimum carbohydrate and little millet containing the maximum carbohydrate (Table 1).

Starch is the principal carbohydrate of the millets like other cereals. The amount of available carbohydrates in food grains is affected by various domestic processing and cooking methods such as soaking, sprouting, pressure cooking, autoclaving, and so on [1]. The carbohydrate content of foxtail millet increased significantly, by 1.29% [58]. By contrast, the carbohydrates of pearl millet flour increased non-significantly during the first 24 and 48 h of germination but decreased significantly after 72 h [45]. The increase in carbohydrates during the germination of foxtail millet is associated with the decrease in moisture, ash, crude protein, and fat, because the carbohydrate levels depend on these attributes of the grains [58]. The effect of fermentation and germination on the carbohydrates of pearl millet revealed that germination greatly increases the total soluble sugar concentration, as well as the reducing and non-reducing sugar concentration. When homogenized and autoclaved, the germinated slurry substantially increased the soluble sugars and decreased starch [49,59]. The main reason for reduced starch could be due to the starch hydrolysis during the germination and autoclaving process, resulting in a higher concentration of soluble sugars. In a similar study, fermented pearl millet grains also showed lower levels of starch and higher levels of soluble carbohydrates than native pearl millet grain [60]. Another study revealed a significant rise in the total amount of sugars in proso millet during germination, which could be attributed to starch breakdown [61]. These results indicate that the germination and fermentation processes improve the carbohydrate digestibility by breaking down the complex starch into simple soluble sugars. This shows the importance of germination and fermentation in the development of energy-dense, easily digestible food products such as infant formula. A study [62] reported the effect of decortication and hydrothermal processing on finger millet. They observed that decortication significantly increased the total carbohydrates by around 16%. The reduction in carbohydrates due to decortication is apparent due to the removal of the seed coat. However, no change in total carbohydrates due to hydrothermal treatment was reported, but a slight change in amylose fraction was noted. Furthermore, due to leaching during steeping and the Maillard process during steaming, the sugar concentration reduced from 1.085 to 0.71 g/100 g after hydrothermal processing. These results indicate that carbohydrates behave differently with different processing techniques. An extensive study [32] on the starch digestibility of pearl and proso millet revealed that parboiling significantly reduced the total starch by 5–10% due to starch leaching out during soaking and boiling process. They also observed that parboiled proso and pearl millet had a reduced readily digestible starch fraction (18.2–19.1% to 17.4–18.3%) and thus a lower glycemic index by 1.6–3.9%. These results suggest that parboiling can significantly reduce starch digestibility and therefore can be utilized to formulate products for metabolic diseases such as diabetics and obesity.

5.3. Dietary Fiber

The millet bran fraction is a major and abundant source of dietary fiber, which is characterized as complex polysaccharides that are not readily available. Therefore, removal of the bran fraction during decortication/dehulling results in substantial reduction in fiber component. It was reported that dehulling of about 12% to 30% to remove the kernel is suitable for millet grains as it does not result in significant loss of fiber. However, dehulling of grains beyond 30% results in the substantial loss of dietary fiber [37]. Since most of the millets are consumed in their decorticated form, it is very important to control the extent of dehulling so as to maximize the fiber content. A study [20] on the impact of milling on the fiber components of foxtail millet revealed that the insoluble dietary fiber content of lignin, cellulose, and hemicellulose in the milled fraction was lower than that of whole millet flour, while in foxtail millets the fiber content increases significantly with increasing germination time [39]. This is perhaps due to a change in the structure of the seeds' cell wall polysaccharides, which may affect the tissue histology and disrupt protein carbohydrate interactions. In addition, the results of cell wall biosynthesis leads to increased production of dietary fiber. A study of solid-state fermentation (SSF) on pearl millet with *Rhizopus oligosporus* and *Yarrowia lipolytica* [63] increased the soluble dietary fiber by 176%. Another study revealed that, fermenting the dietary fiber from foxtail millet bran with *Bacillus natto* enhanced the soluble dietary fiber (DF) content by 10.9% and increased the ratio of soluble DF to insoluble DF by 16.8% [64]. Following fermentation, cellulose and hemicellulose breakdown resulted in more porous structure polysaccharides, which explains the changes in DF. Similarly, malting pearl millet for 24 h boosted the fiber level from 0.77% to 0.87% [44]. A study [65] on maize and finger millet-based extruded product showed that the non-starchy polysaccharides reduced from 2.5 g/100 g for raw blend to 1.5 g/100 g for unfermented-extruded blend. The values were further reduced to 0.9 for fermented blends and 1.4 g/100 g for blends treated with lactic or citric acid (different molarities) prior to extrusion. It was also observed that high extrusion temperatures and severe mechanical shear disrupt glycosidic networks and weak bonds between polysaccharide chains of dietary fiber polysaccharides, resulting in a reduction in total NSP. Similarly, the thermal processing of biscuits prepared from pearl millet flour resulted in a change in crude fiber content from 1.26% to 1.75% [63]. Roasting of pearl millet grains at different times and temperatures reduced crude fiber content. Other thermal processes such as puffing and popping on millets resulted a decline in crude fiber by 1.71% and from 18.9 to 15.8 g/100 g, respectively [66]. This could be mainly attributed to the fact that the outer grain layer has the majority of the fiber that is exposed to thermal degradation. To summarize, the reports suggest that dehulling and milling (debranning) operations reduce dietary fiber, while high temperature extrusion processes lead to thermal degradation of dietary fiber. Dietary fiber, particularly that accumulated in the outer bran layer, plays a vital role in reducing type 2 diabetes and constipation. For a healthy millet diet, it is important to discourage millers from polishing millets and to advise consumers to prefer whole millets (unpolished) and their by-products.

5.4. Minerals

Millets are an abundant source of minerals such as K, Mg, Fe, Ca, and Zn, along with vitamins that are mainly accumulated in the aleurone, germ, and pericarp [1]. Soaking millet grains prior to cooking helps to reduce antinutrients while also improving mineral bioavailability. Millet grains soaked in water were shown to have reduced Zn and Fe content, which might be attributed to minerals leaching into the soaking water [67]. Soaking millet grains boosts the "in vitro solubility" of minerals such as Fe and Zn by 2–23%. Soaking the millet grains in hot water (45 to 65 °C) with a pH of 5–6 resulted in a significant increase in bioavailability and a decrease in phytic acid [68]. The mineral content in pearl millet flour was affected by germination and fermentation [49]. Germination of foxtail millet improved and modified the nutrient profile by increasing the mineral compounds availability [20,49]. Germination increased the availability of minerals by the catabolism process of antinutrients such as saponins and polyphenols, which inhibit the mineral bioavailability [39]. A similar increase in the mineral concentration in germinated foxtail millet was reported [69]. Germination also activate phytase-specific phosphatases enzyme called phytases, which hydrolyze phytate into inositol and orthophosphate and release minerals. Therefore, increased levels of minerals such as Mg (101.16 to 107.16 mg/kg), sodium (Na) (63.34 to 69.45 mg/kg), Ca (17.43 to 25.62 mg/kg), and Fe (16.01 to 54.23 mg/kg) were reported for foxtail millet [39]. The mineral content of kodo millet increased from 232.82 to 251.73 mg/100 g after 36 h of germination at 38.75 °C [41]. According to [70], fermentation improved the availability of Ca by 20%, Fe by 27%, and P and Zn by 26%. Bleaching pearl millet for 90 s increased Fe availability from 2.19 to 3.29 mg/100 g in vitro [49].

The decorticated millet grains decreased the total mineral content: Ca by 40%, Fe by 50%, and Zn by 12%; however, it increased the bio-accessibility of the minerals Ca (15 g/100 g), Fe (26 g/100 g), and Zn (24 g/100 g) [53]. The decortication process reduces the antinutrients, which inhibit mineral bioavailability by creating complexes. The antinutrient level reduction leads to an improvement in the bioavailability of minerals [53]. Another study discovered that the whole grain flour of foxtail millet after milling was mineral-rich, while the polished grain flour showed reduced mineral content but with a higher protein content [20]. Semi-polished pearl millet has been shown to significantly reduce ash content (1.5% to 1.3%), which represents the noncombustible portion of minerals. The decrease in the ash content was associated with removal of bran. Minerals such as Ca and P, along with antinutrients, are accumulated in the bran fraction of pearl millet [70]. However, semi-refining reduces the phytate content, which results in improved in vitro bio-accessibility of Fe and Ca. Milling and sieving of finger millet caused a reduction in some minerals such as Fe (6.52 to 3.29 mg), Zn (2.50 to 1.98 mg), and Ca (404.3 to 294.8 mg) [71].

The total Fe content of roasted pearl millet grains increased by 274 percent, which was due to leaching from the roasting iron-pan into millet samples during the high-temperature roasting process [72]. Similar studies on finger millet roasting increased the minerals such as Ca (337.31 to 341.24 mg/100 g) and Fe (3.45 to 3.91 mg/100 g) [73]. Foxtail millets processed through solid-state fermentation (SSF) were rich in important minerals and amino acids [63]. The mineral content was enhanced when fermented foxtail millet flour was incorporated with a single strain of *L. acidophilus* [20]. Studies also indicate that pure culture fermented products increase the bioavailability of minerals [53].

The dark gray color of pearl millet grains restricts their usage in food preparation. This drawback can be overcome by treating millet grains with organic acids (fumaric, acetic, and tartaric acid) or natural acidic materials (tamarind). Various researchers have studied the effect of acid treatment. A study on acid treatment, which includes soaking the grains in 0.2 N HCl solution for 24 h, subsequent washing, blanching (98 °C for 30 s), and sun-drying (2 days), significantly improved the P, Ca, and Fe extractability [74]. This increase in HCl extractability was accompanied by an increase in mineral bioavailability. When compared to native grains, pearl millet treated with acid for 18 h significantly improved the in vitro Fe bio-accessibility. The Fe concentration decreased because of the leaching of minerals naturally accumulated in the pericarp portion during processing [49,53]. The millet-based composite flour incorporated with skimmed-milk powder and vegetables showed a substantial increase in Zn (2.1–4.2 mg/100 g), Ca (143.6–667.8 mg/100 g) and Cu (0.5–0.9 mg/100 g), but no significant changes in Fe (3.4–3.6 mg/100 g) and Mg (4.3–4.4 mg/100 g) [75]. The report suggests that the majority of minerals are accumulated in the germ and bran layer which will be lost during dehulling and sieving operations. However, the process of germination and fermentation was found to increase the mineral content to some extent which could be exploited to develop value-added products.

5.5. Vitamins

Millets when polished/debranned contain a lower nutritional value since the bran and germ components of refined millet flour are eliminated, resulting in a loss of vitamins. Millets are considered superior to wheat, sorghum, and maize in terms of vitamin content and other nutrients that include fats, proteins, and minerals (Table 1). Vitamins along with minerals are naturally accumulated in the aleurone, germ, and pericarp.

Millet grains are high in vitamins such as riboflavin, thiamine, niacin, and folic acid [76]. It has been noted that the germination and fermentation processes in pearl millet affect the vitamin content of the grains. Improved vitamin levels (thiamin) after the fermentation process were reported [49]. Little millet decortication resulted in a 67% reduction in vitamin E [77]. The milling affects the bran portion of the millet grains, which reduces vitamins that are mainly accumulated in the outer bran layer of grains. Milling pearl millet grains resulted in a considerable decrease in vitamin B and a modest reduction in vitamin E, but milling and sieving of finger millet flour tends to decrease vitamins such as thiamine (0.552 to 0.342 mg/100 g) and riboflavin (0.243 to 0.196 mg/100 g) [71]. The germination of finger millet showed increased vitamin C content, from 0.04 to 0.06 mg/100 g [66]. Similarly, increased levels of vitamins (thiamine, niacin) after germination and probiotic fermentation were reported [49,55]. The elevation of some vitamins levels, especially thiamine, niacin, and riboflavin, was observed during finger millet fermentation [78]. Biscuits prepared by replacing refined wheat flour with 45% of foxtail millet flour resulted in an increased value of vitamin content such as niacin (1.41%) and thiamin (0.1836%), except riboflavin (0.09%) [79]. The nutritional and storage characteristics of nutritious millet food of the West African region were studied. It was found that vitamin B2 concentration was likely reduced by 31.4%, 34.3%, and 45.7% after the processing of grain to a meal, flour, and fura, respectively [55]. The studies on milling or dehulling suggest that the vitamins are lost during these processing operations as the majority of vitamins are accumulated in the outer layer of millets. The availability of important vitamins can be improved by germinating the millets and developing by-products from germinated millets.

5.6. Fats

Fats are necessary for calorie supply, brain development, and the absorption and transport of vitamins A, D, E, and K in the body. The germination time has an impact on fat content. For instance, the raw and optimized flour of germinated foxtail millet had 4.4% and 3.6% fat, respectively which was substantially lower than the non-germinated sample. This is due to the fact that the fat is used as an energy source throughout the germination process, which leads to the reduction after germination [39]. A study to investigate the effect of high-pressure soaking on the nutritional characteristics of foxtail millet revealed that the fat content is reduced by 27.98% [40]. This was attributable to the enzymatic activity that creates free and soluble nutrients throughout the germinated phase in foxtail millets. Similarly, another study reported that malting of pearl millet for 24 h resulted in a reduction in fat by 6.34 to 5.55% [44]. During germination the increased enzyme and fat consumption as an energy source might explain the reduction in fat content. According to a study on the influence of different cooking techniques on the characteristic changes of foxtail millet [18], the fat content was highest in the roasted sample (3.2 g), followed by the raw (2.9 g), pressure cooked (2.8 g), germinated (2.6 g), and boiled sample (1.9 g). The effect of pearl millet fermentation on crude fat, reduced its value from 2.25 to 1.70% [63]. Another study on fermentation of pearl millet reported an increase in crude fat content from 1.83 to 3.71% [37,49]. Germination of foxtail millet was found to reduce the fat content, which is related to lipid hydrolysis and fatty acid oxidation that occurs during germination [55]. The foxtail millet grains were germinated at 30 °C and little millet at 35 °C for 24 h after overnight steeping, then tray dried at 60 °C for 6 h and milled for further analysis. The fat content reduced by 17.84% in foxtail millet and increased in little millet by 25.95% [58]. This was due to the changes in energy values since the fat content includes approximately double the energy values of protein and carbohydrate.

Thermal processing of biscuits made from pearl millet flour resulted in a percentage change in crude fat content from 2.25 to 18.77% [63]. Another study focused on thermal processing such as pan cooking and microwave heating on proso millet results showed a decreased level of fat content from 3.24 to 2.3 g/100 g (pan cooking) and from 3.24 to 3.05 g/100 g (microwave cooking), while for little millet, fat content decreased from 1.91 to 1.56 g/100 g (pan cooking) and from 1.91 to 1.79 g/100 g (microwave cooking) [52]. Similarly, roasting decreased the crude fat content by 0.71%, puffing and popping decreased fat content by 0.06% and 1.3–0.63 g/100 g, respectively [66]. The study on the popping of foxtail millet reported having lower value of crude fat content than raw millet [55]. Bleaching of pearl millet for 90 s resulted in a greater drop in free fatty acids level from 44.56 to 20.59 mg/100 g [49].

The use of roller mills for the production of low-fat pearl millet grits was investigated, and it was observed that decortication, tempering, and milling using finer corrugated rollers offered an average output of 61% grits (from whole grains) and 1.2% fat content [49]. By contrast, another study stated that decortication of pearl millet had no significant changes in fat content. It was also observed that when moisture content and milling time increase, the fat, ash, and fiber content reduces [55]. Development of composite millet flour had a higher rate of oil and water absorption capacity than that of millet flour [75]. The oil absorption capacity (OAC) and water absorption capacity (WAC) of the composite flour of different millets increased from 59.2% to 77.9% and from 117% to 225%, respectively. The OAC refers to flour protein's capacity to physically bind fat through capillary attraction, which is essential since fats function as flavor retainers and improve the mouthfeel of foods. The studies provide sufficient evidence on degradation or denaturation of fat at high temperature processing (cooking and popping) as well as reduction in fat content during milling, malting and fermentation processes. The simple processing techniques such as soaking, germination and malting could be the ideal option for manufacturers to develop low-fat food products from millets. The high temperature processing would damage the fat quality and might reduce the taste and flavor of the processed foods.

6. Conclusions

Millets have an energy value similar to staple cereals. Additionally, they provide more significant health benefits due to their high fiber, minerals, vitamins, macro- and micronutrients, and phytochemicals and can help combat chronic disorders. Making millets part of a regular diet can provide an affordable, complete, and healthy meal. It was observed that during germination and fermentation of millets, the dietary fiber, mineral, and vitamin content of most millets improved. Simple processing techniques such as soaking, germination/malting, and fermentation can help tackle the problem of protein–energy malnutrition by improving protein digestibility and the bioavailability of the minerals. However, it was observed that decortication, dehulling, milling, extrusion resulted in a reduction of total proteins, total dietary fiber, and micronutrients. Thus, care should be taken during the decortication of millets, as excessive dehulling can result in lower fiber content and loss of micronutrients due to the loss of nutrient-rich bran and germ portion.

Looking into the variability of the impact of processing on the nutritional characteristics of millets, there is still a need to focus on optimizing the processing techniques for minor millets to make them more acceptable without compromising the health benefits. Moreover, to combat food insecurity and malnutrition, awareness needs to be created at both commercial and household levels regarding the impact of processing methods on the nutritional properties of millets and the health benefits of millets.

Author Contributions: Conceptualization, supervisor lead, writing—original draft preparation, writing—review and editing, N.A.N.G.; conceptualization, writing—review and editing, K.S.; writing—review and editing, P.V.V.P.; writing—original draft preparation, writing—review and editing, Y.B.; writing—original draft preparation, writing—review and editing, B.P.N.; writing—original draft preparation, writing—review and editing, C.G. All authors have read and agreed to the published version of the manuscript.

Funding: This research received no external funding.

Institutional Review Board Statement: Not applicable.

Informed Consent Statement: Not applicable.

Data Availability Statement: Not applicable.

Acknowledgments: This paper is contribution number 22-178-J from the Kansas State University Agricultural Experiment Station.

Conflicts of Interest: The authors declare no conflict of interest.

References

1. Rao, D.B.; Malleshi, N.G.; Annor, G.A.; Patil, J.V. Nutritional and health benefits of millets. In *Millets Value Chain for Nutritional Security: A Replicable Success Model from India*; Indian Institute of Millets Research (IIMR): Hyderabad, India, 2017; p. 112.
2. Ashoka, P.; Gangaiah, B.; Sunitha, N. Millets-foods of twenty first century. *Int. J. Curr. Microbiol. Appl. Sci.* **2020**, *9*, 2404–2410. [CrossRef]
3. Nainwal, K. Conservation of minor millets for sustaining agricultural biodiversity and nutritional security. *J. Pharmacogn. Phytochem.* **2018**, *SP1*, 1576–1580.
4. Dutta, M.; Selvamani, Y.; Singh, P.; Prashad, L. The double burden of malnutrition among adults in India: Evidence from the national family health survey-4 (2015-16). *Epidemiol. Health* **2019**, *41*, 11. [CrossRef]
5. Nithiyanantham, S.; Kalaiselvi, P.; Mahomoodally, M.F.; Zengin, G.; Abirami, A.; Srinivasan, G. Nutritional and functional roles of millets—A review. *J. Food Biochem.* **2019**, *43*, 1–10. [CrossRef]

6. Annor, G.A.; Tyl, C.; Marcone, M.; Ragaee, S.; Marti, A. Why do millets have slower starch and protein digestibility than other cereals? *Trends Food Sci. Technol.* **2017**, *66*, 73–83. [CrossRef]
7. Anitha, S.; Govindaraj, M.; Kane-Potaka, J. Balanced amino acid and higher micronutrients in millets complements legumes for improved human dietary nutrition. *Cereal Chem.* **2020**, *97*, 74–84. [CrossRef]
8. Birania, S.; Rohilla, P.; Kumar, R.; Kumar, N. Post harvest processing of millets: A review on value added products. *Int. J. Chem. Stud.* **2020**, *8*, 1824–1829. [CrossRef]
9. Ramadoss, D.P.; Sivalingam, N. Vanillin extracted from Proso and Barnyard millets induce apoptotic cell death in HT-29 human colon cancer cell line. *Nutr. Cancer* **2020**, *72*, 1422–1437. [CrossRef]
10. Yang, R.; Shan, S.; Zhang, C.; Shi, J.; Li, H.; Li, Z. Inhibitory Effects of Bound Polyphenol from Foxtail Millet Bran on Colitis-Associated Carcinogenesis by the Restoration of Gut Microbiota in a Mice Model. *ACS Appl. Mater. Interfaces* **2020**, *68*, 3506–3517. [CrossRef]
11. Vedamanickam, R.; Anandan, P.; Bupesh, G.; Vasanth, S. Study of millet and non-millet diet on diabetics and associated metabolic syndrome. *Biomedicine* **2020**, *40*, 55–58. [CrossRef]
12. Hegde, P.S.; Rajasekaran, N.S.; Chandra, T.S. Effects of the antioxidant properties of millet species on oxidative stress and glycemic status in alloxan-induced rats. *Nutr. Res.* **2005**, *25*, 1109–1120. [CrossRef]
13. Ren, X.; Yin, R.; Hou, D.; Xue, Y.; Zhang, M.; Diao, X.; Zhang, Y.; Wu, J.; Hu, J.; Hu, X.; et al. The glucose-lowering effect of foxtail millet in subjects with impaired glucose tolerance: A self-controlled clinical trial. *Nutrients* **2018**, *10*, 1509. [CrossRef] [PubMed]
14. Chen, Y.; Xu, J.; Ren, Q. The Effect of Millet Porridge on the Gastrointestinal Function in Mice. *J. Food Nutr. Res.* **2018**, *6*, 152–157. [CrossRef]
15. Gowda, N.N.; Taj, F.; Subramanya, S.; Ranganna, B. Development a table top centrifugal dehuller for small millets. *AMA Agric. Mech. Asia Africa Latin Am.* **2020**, *51*, 72–78.
16. Anbukkani, P.; Balaji, S.J.; Nithyashree, M.L. Production and consumption of minor millets in India-a structural break analysis. *Ann. Agric. Res. New Ser.* **2017**, *38*, 1–8.
17. DES-GOI. Agricultural Statistics at a Glance 2020. In *(Various Issues). Directorate of Economics and Statistics*; Ministry of Agriculture, Government of India: New Delhi, India, 2020.
18. Nazni, S.; Devi, S. Effect of processing on the characteristics changes in barnyard and foxtail millet. *J. Food Process. Technol.* **2016**, *7*, 1–9.
19. Guiné, R.P.F.; Barroca, M.J.; Coldea, T.E.; Bartkiene, E.; Anjos, O. Apple fermented products: An overview of technology, properties and health effects. *Processes* **2021**, *9*, 223. [CrossRef]
20. Sharma, N.; Niranjan, K. Foxtail millet: Properties, processing, health benefits, and uses. *Food Rev. Int.* **2018**, *34*, 329–363. [CrossRef]
21. Azad, M.O.K.; Jeong, D.I.; Adnan, M.; Salitxay, T.; Heo, J.W.; Naznin, M.T.; Lim, J.D.; Cho, D.H.; Park, B.J.; Park, C.H. Effect of different processing methods on the accumulation of the phenolic compounds and antioxidant profile of broomcorn millet (*Panicum Miliaceum* L.) Flour. *Foods* **2019**, *8*, 230. [CrossRef]
22. Chandrasekara, A.; Shahidi, F. Content of insoluble bound phenolics in millets and their contribution to antioxidant capacity. *J. Agric. Food Chem.* **2010**, *58*, 6706–6714. [CrossRef]
23. Zhang, L.; Liu, R.; Niu, W. Phytochemical and antiproliferative activity of proso millet. *PLoS ONE* **2014**, *9*, e104058. [CrossRef] [PubMed]
24. Kalinova, J.; Moudry, J. Content and quality of protein in proso millet (*Panicum miliaceum* L.) varieties. *Plant Foods. Hum. Nutr.* **2006**, *61*, 45–49. [CrossRef] [PubMed]
25. Das, S.; Khound, R.; Santra, M.; Santra, D.K. Beyond bird feed: Proso millet for human health and environment. *Agriculture* **2019**, *9*, 64. [CrossRef]
26. Nambiar, V.S.; Dhaduk, J.J.; Sareen, N.; Shahu, T.; Desai, R. Potential functional implications of pearl millet (*Pennisetum glaucum*) in health and disease. *J. Appl. Pharm. Sci.* **2011**, *1*, 62–67.
27. Gull, A.; Jan, R.; Nayik, G.A.; Prasad, K.; Kumar, P. Significance of finger millet in nutrition, health and value added products: A Review. *J. Environ. Sci. Comput. Sci. Eng. Technol. Sect. C Eng. Technol.* **2014**, *3*, 1601–1608.
28. Neeharika, B.; Suneetha, W.J.; Kumari, B.A.; Tejashree, M. Organoleptic properties of ready to reconstitute little millet smoothie with fruit juices. *Int. J. Environ. Clim. Chang.* **2020**, 78–82. [CrossRef]
29. Patil, K.B.; Chimmad, B.V.; Itagi, S. Glycemic index and quality evaluation of little millet (*Panicum miliare*) flakes with enhanced shelf life. *J. Food. Sci. Technol.* **2015**, *52*, 6078–6082. [CrossRef]
30. NIN. *Indian Food Compostion Tables*; IIMR (Ministry of Health and Family Welfare, GoI): Hyderabad, India, 2017.
31. IIMR. *Nutritional and Health Benefits of Millets*; Indian Institute of Millets Research: Hyderabad, India; ICAR: New Delhi, India, 2017.
32. Bora, P.; Ragaee, S.; Marcone, M. Characterisation of several types of millets as functional food ingredients. *Int. J. Food Sci. Nutr.* **2019**, *70*, 714–724. [CrossRef]
33. Popova, A.; Mihaylova, D. Antinutrients in plant-based foods: A Review. *Open Biotechnol. J.* **2019**, *13*, 68–76. [CrossRef]
34. Taylor, J.R.N.; Emmambux, M.N. Gluten-free foods and beverages from millets. In *Gluten-Free Cereal Products and Beverages*; Academic Press: Cambridge, MA, USA, 2008; pp. 119–148.

35. Pradeep, P.M.; Sreerama, Y.N. Impact of processing on the phenolic profiles of small millets: Evaluation of their antioxidant and enzyme inhibitory properties associated with hyperglycemia. *Food Chem.* **2015**, *169*, 455–463. [CrossRef]
36. Rathore, T.; Singh, R.; Kamble, D.B.; Upadhyay, A.; Thangalakshmi, S. Review on finger millet: Processing and value addition. *Pharma Innov. J.* **2019**, *8*, 283–291.
37. Yousaf, L.; Hou, D.; Liaqat, H.; Shen, Q. Millet: A review of its nutritional and functional changes during processing. *Food Res. Int.* **2021**, *142*, 110197. [CrossRef]
38. Deshpande, S.S.; Mohapatra, D.; Tripathi, M.K.; Sadvatha, R.H. Kodo millet-nutritional value and utilization in Indian foods. *J. Grain Process. Storage* **2015**, *2*, 16–23.
39. Sharma, S.; Saxena, D.C.; Riar, C.S. Antioxidant activity, total phenolics, flavonoids and antinutritional characteristics of germinated foxtail millet (*Setaria italica*). *Cogent Food Agric.* **2015**, *1*, 1081728. [CrossRef]
40. Sharma, N.; Goyal, S.K.; Alam, T.; Fatma, S.; Chaoruangrit, A.; Niranjan, K. Effect of high pressure soaking on water absorption, gelatinization, and biochemical properties of germinated and non-germinated foxtail millet grains. *J. Cereal Sci.* **2018**, *83*, 162–170. [CrossRef]
41. Sharma, S.; Saxena, D.C.; Riar, C.S. Using combined optimization, GC–MS and analytical technique to analyze the germination effect on phenolics, dietary fibers, minerals and gaba contents of kodo millet (*Paspalum scrobiculatum*). *Food Chem.* **2017**, *233*, 20–28. [CrossRef] [PubMed]
42. Suma, P.F.; Urooj, A. Nutrients, Antinutrients & bioaccessible mineral content (in vitro) of pearl millet as influenced by milling. *J. Food. Sci. Technol.* **2014**, *51*, 756–761.
43. Morah, F.N.I.; Etukudo, U.P. Effect of sprouting on nutritional value of panicium miliaceum (Proso Millet). *Edorium. J. Nutr. Diet* **2017**, *4*, 1–4.
44. Obadina, A.O.; Arogbokun, C.A.; Soares, A.O.; de Carvalho, C.W.P.; Barboza, H.T.; Adekoya, I.O. Changes in nutritional and physico-chemical properties of pearl millet (*Pennisetum glaucum*) ex-borno variety flour as a result of malting. *J. Food. Sci. Technol.* **2017**, *54*, 4442–4451. [CrossRef] [PubMed]
45. Bello, F.A. Effect of alkaline steeping on the nutritional, antinutritional and functional properties of malted millet (*Pennisetum glaucum*) flour. *Int. J. Innov. Food Nutr. Sustain. Agric.* **2017**, *5*, 17–23.
46. Iyabo, O.O.; Ibiyinka, O.; Abimbola Deola, O. Comparative study of nutritional, functional and antinutritional properties of white sorghum bicolor (Sorghum) and pennisetum glaucum (Pearl Millet). *Int. J. Eng. Technol. Man. Res.* **2018**, *5*, 151–158. [CrossRef]
47. Chinenye, O.E.; Ayodeji, O.A.; Baba, A.J. Effect of fermentation (Natural and Starter) on the physicochemical, anti-nutritional and proximate composition of pearl millet used for flour production. *Am. J. Biosci. Bioeng.* **2017**, *5*, 12–16.
48. Amadou, I.; Gounga, M.E.; Shi, Y.H.; Le, G.W. Fermentation and heat-moisture treatment induced changes on the physicochemical properties of foxtail millet (Setaria Italica) flour. *Food Bioprod. Process* **2014**, *92*, 38–45. [CrossRef]
49. Rani, S.; Singh, R.; Sehrawat, R.; Kaur, B.P.; Upadhyay, A. Pearl millet processing: A Review. *Nutr. Food. Sci.* **2018**, 30–44. [CrossRef]
50. Hithamani, G.; Srinivasan, K. Effect of domestic processing on the polyphenol content and bioaccessibility in finger millet (Eleusine Coracana) and pearl millet (*Pennisetum glaucum*). *Food Chem.* **2014**, *164*, 55–62. [CrossRef] [PubMed]
51. Patel, A.; Vishwa Vidyalaya, K.; Pradesh, M.; Parihar, P.; Ketki Dhumketi, I.; Anamika Patel, C.; Dhumketi, K. Nutritional evaluation of kodo millet and puffed kodo. *Int. J. Chem. Stud.* **2018**, *6*, 1639–1642.
52. Kumar, S.R.; Sadiq, M.B.; Anal, A.K. Comparative study of physicochemical and functional properties of pan and microwave cooked underutilized millets (Proso and Little). *LWT* **2020**, *128*, 109465. [CrossRef]
53. Jaybhaye, R.V.; Pardeshi, I.L.; Vengaiah, P.C.; Srivastav, P.P. Processing and technology for millet based food products: A review nutrient composition of millets. *J. Ready Eat Food* **2014**, *1*, 32–48.
54. Hassan, A.B.; Mohamed Ahmed, I.A.; Osman, N.M.; Eltayeb, M.M.; Osman, G.A.; Babiker, E.E. Effect of processing treatments followed by fermentation on protein content and digestibility of pearl millet (*Pennisetum typhoideum*) cultivars. *Pak. J. Nutr.* **2006**, *5*, 86–89.
55. Saleh, A.S.M.; Zhang, Q.; Chen, J.; Shen, Q. Millet Grains: Nutritional quality, processing, and potential health benefits. *Compr. Rev. Food Sci. Food Saf.* **2013**, *12*, 281–295. [CrossRef]
56. Rani, M.; Amane, D.; Ananthanarayan, L. Impact of partial replacement of rice with other selected cereals on idli batter fermentation and idli characteristics. *J. Food Sci. Technol.* **2019**, *56*, 1192–1201. [CrossRef] [PubMed]
57. Pushparaj, F.S.; Urooj, A. Influence of processing on dietary fiber, tannin and in vitro protein digestibility of pearl millet. *Food Nutr. Sci.* **2011**, *2*, 895–900.
58. Kulla, S.; Hymavathi, T.V.; Kumari, B.A.; Reddy, R.G.; Rani, C.V.D. Impact of germination on the nutritional, antioxidant and antinutrient characteristics of selected minor millet flours. *Ann. Phytomed. Int. J.* **2021**, *10*, 178–184. [CrossRef]
59. Pawase, P.A.; Shingote, A.; Chavan, U.D. Studies on evaluation and determination of physical and functional properties of millets. (Ragi and Pearl Millet). *Asian J. Dairy Food. Res.* **2019**, *38*, 203–212. [CrossRef]
60. Khetarpaul, N.; Chauhan, B.M. Effect of Germination and fermentation on in vitro starch and protein digestibility of pearl millet. *J. Food. Sci.* **1990**, *55*, 883–884. [CrossRef]
61. Balasubramanian, S.; Sharma, R.; Kaur, J.; Bhardwaj, N. Characterization of modified pearl millet (*Pennisetum typhoides*) starch. *J. Food. Sci. Technol.* **2014**, *51*, 294–300. [CrossRef]

62. Dharmaraj, U.; Malleshi, N.G. Changes in carbohydrates, proteins and lipids of finger millet after hydrothermal processing. *LWT—Food Sci. Technol.* **2011**, *44*, 1636–1642. [CrossRef]
63. Kaur, P.; Purewal, S.S.; Sandhu, K.S.; Kaur, M.; Salar, R.K. Millets: A cereal grain with potent antioxidants and health benefits. *J. Food. Meas. Charact.* **2019**, 793–806. [CrossRef]
64. Chu, J.; Zhao, H.; Lu, Z.; Lu, F.; Bie, X.; Zhang, C. Improved physicochemical and functional properties of dietary fiber from millet bran fermented by Bacillus Natto. *Food Chem.* **2019**, *294*, 79–86. [CrossRef]
65. Onyango, C.; Noetzold, H.; Bley, T.; Henle, T. Proximate composition and digestibility of fermented and extruded uji from maize-finger millet blend. *LWT—Food. Sci. Technol.* **2004**, *37*, 827–832. [CrossRef]
66. Chauhan, E.S. Effects of processing (germination and popping) on the nutritional and anti-nutritional properties of finger millet (*Eleusine coracana*). *Curr. Res. Nutr. Food. Sci.* **2018**, *6*, 566–572. [CrossRef]
67. Bindra, D.; Manju, D. Formulation and evaluation of foods from composite flour blends of sorghum, pearl millet and whole wheat for suitability in diabetic diet. *Int. J. Home Sci.* **2019**, *5*, 220–229.
68. Ertop, M.; Bektaş, M. Enhancement of bioavailable micronutrients and reduction of antinutrients in foods with some processes. *Food Health* **2018**, *4*, 159–165. [CrossRef]
69. Coulibaly, A.; Chen, J. Evolution of energetic compounds, antioxidant capacity, some vitamins and minerals, phytase and amylase activity during the germination of foxtail millet. *Am. J. Food Technol.* **2011**, *6*, 40–51. [CrossRef]
70. Pushparaj, F.S.; Urooj, A. Impact of household processing methods on the nutritional characteristics of pearl millet (Pennisetum typhoideum): A Review. *MOJ Food Process. Technol.* **2017**, *4*, 28–32.
71. Oghbaei, M.; Prakash, J. Effect of primary processing of cereals and legumes on its nutritional quality: A Comprehensive Review. *Cogent Food. Agric.* **2016**, *2*, 1136015. [CrossRef]
72. Obadina, A.; Ishola, I.; Adekoya, O.; Soares, A.; de Carvalho, C.W.; Barboza, H. Nutritional and physico-chemical properties of flour from native and roasted whole grain pearl millet (*Pennisetum glaucum* [L.] R. Br.). *J. Cereal Sci.* **2016**, *70*, 247–252. [CrossRef]
73. Singh, N.; David, J.; Thompkinson, D.K.; Seelam, B.; Rajput, H.; Morya, S. Effect of roasting on functional and phytochemical constituents of finger millet (*Eleusine coracana* L.). *The Pharma Innov. J.* **2018**, *7*, 414–418.
74. Arora, P.; Sehgal, S.; Kawatra, A. Content and HCl-extractability of minerals as affected by acid treatment of pearl millet. *Food Chem.* **2003**, *80*, 141–144. [CrossRef]
75. Tumwine, G.; Atukwase, A.; Tumuhimbise, G.A.; Tucungwirwe, F.; Linnemann, A. Production of nutrient-enhanced millet-based composite flour using skimmed milk powder and vegetables. *Food Sci. Nutr.* **2019**, *7*, 22–34. [CrossRef] [PubMed]
76. Shahidi, F.; Chandrasekara, A. Processing of millet grains and effects on non-nutrient antioxidant compounds. In *Processing and Impact on Active Components in Food*; Academic Press: Cambridge, MA, USA, 2015; pp. 345–352.
77. Kamatar, M.Y.; Kundgol, N.G.; Math, K.K. Impact of decortication on chemical composition, antioxidant content and antioxidant activity of little millet landraces. *Int. J. Eng. Res. Technol.* **2013**, *2*, 1705–1720.
78. Konapur, A.; Gavaravarapur, S.R.M.; Gupta, S.; Nair, K.M. Millets in meeting nutrition security: Issues and way forward for India. *Indian J. Nutr. Diet.* **2014**, *51*, 306–321.
79. Anju, T.; Sarita, S. Suitability of foxtail millet (Setaria Italica) and barnyard millet (Echinochloa Frumentacea) for development of low glycemic index biscuits. *Malays. J. Nutri.* **2010**, *16*, 361–368.

MDPI
St. Alban-Anlage 66
4052 Basel
Switzerland
www.mdpi.com

Foods Editorial Office
E-mail: foods@mdpi.com
www.mdpi.com/journal/foods

www.ingramcontent.com/pod-product-compliance
Lightning Source LLC
Chambersburg PA
CBHW061606210926
51850CB00009B/2230
9783725805075